INTRODUCTION TO
MACHINE LEARNING WITH APPLICATIONS IN INFORMATION SECURITY

Chapman & Hall/CRC
Machine Learning & Pattern Recognition Series

SERIES EDITORS

Ralf Herbrich
Amazon Development Center
Berlin, Germany

Thore Graepel
Microsoft Research Ltd.
Cambridge, UK

AIMS AND SCOPE

This series reflects the latest advances and applications in machine learning and pattern recognition through the publication of a broad range of reference works, textbooks, and handbooks. The inclusion of concrete examples, applications, and methods is highly encouraged. The scope of the series includes, but is not limited to, titles in the areas of machine learning, pattern recognition, computational intelligence, robotics, computational/statistical learning theory, natural language processing, computer vision, game AI, game theory, neural networks, computational neuroscience, and other relevant topics, such as machine learning applied to bioinformatics or cognitive science, which might be proposed by potential contributors.

PUBLISHED TITLES

BAYESIAN PROGRAMMING
Pierre Bessière, Emmanuel Mazer, Juan-Manuel Ahuactzin, and Kamel Mekhnacha

UTILITY-BASED LEARNING FROM DATA
Craig Friedman and Sven Sandow

HANDBOOK OF NATURAL LANGUAGE PROCESSING, SECOND EDITION
Nitin Indurkhya and Fred J. Damerau

COST-SENSITIVE MACHINE LEARNING
Balaji Krishnapuram, Shipeng Yu, and Bharat Rao

COMPUTATIONAL TRUST MODELS AND MACHINE LEARNING
Xin Liu, Anwitaman Datta, and Ee-Peng Lim

MULTILINEAR SUBSPACE LEARNING: DIMENSIONALITY REDUCTION OF
MULTIDIMENSIONAL DATA
Haiping Lu, Konstantinos N. Plataniotis, and Anastasios N. Venetsanopoulos

MACHINE LEARNING: An Algorithmic Perspective, Second Edition
Stephen Marsland

SPARSE MODELING: THEORY, ALGORITHMS, AND APPLICATIONS
Irina Rish and Genady Ya. Grabarnik

A FIRST COURSE IN MACHINE LEARNING, SECOND EDITION
Simon Rogers and Mark Girolami

INTRODUCTION TO MACHINE LEARNING WITH APPLICATIONS IN
INFORMATION SECURITY
Mark Stamp

Chapman & Hall/CRC
Machine Learning & Pattern Recognition Series

INTRODUCTION TO

MACHINE LEARNING WITH APPLICATIONS IN INFORMATION SECURITY

Mark Stamp

San Jose State University
California

CRC Press
Taylor & Francis Group
Boca Raton   London   New York

CRC Press is an imprint of the
Taylor & Francis Group, an **informa** business
A CHAPMAN & HALL BOOK

CRC Press
Taylor & Francis Group
6000 Broken Sound Parkway NW, Suite 300
Boca Raton, FL 33487-2742

© 2018 by Taylor & Francis Group, LLC
CRC Press is an imprint of Taylor & Francis Group, an Informa business

No claim to original U.S. Government works

Printed on acid-free paper

International Standard Book Number-13: 978-1-138-62678-2 (Hardback)

Visit the Taylor & Francis Web site at
http://www.taylorandfrancis.com

and the CRC Press Web site at
http://www.crcpress.com

Printed and bound in the United States of America by
Edwards Brothers Malloy on sustainably sourced paper

To Melody, Austin, and Miles.

Contents

Preface

For the past several years, I've been teaching a class on "Topics in Information Security." Each time I taught this course, I'd sneak in a few more machine learning topics. For the past couple of years, the class has been turned on its head, with machine learning being the focus, and information security only making its appearance in the applications. Unable to find a suitable textbook, I wrote a manuscript, which slowly evolved into this book.

In my machine learning class, we spend about two weeks on each of the major topics in this book (HMM, PHMM, PCA, SVM, and clustering). For each of these topics, about one week is devoted to the technical details in Part I, and another lecture or two is spent on the corresponding applications in Part II. The material in Part I is not easy—by including relevant applications, the material is reinforced, and the pace is more reasonable.

I also spend a week covering the data analysis topics in Chapter 8 and several of the mini topics in Chapter 7 are covered, based on time constraints and student interest.[1]

Machine learning is an ideal subject for substantive projects. In topics classes, I always require projects, which are usually completed by pairs of students, although individual projects are allowed. At least one week is allocated to student presentations of their project results.

A suggested syllabus is given in Table 1. This syllabus should leave time for tests, project presentations, and selected special topics. Note that the applications material in Part II is intermixed with the material in Part I. Also note that the data analysis chapter is covered early, since it's relevant to all of the applications in Part II.

---

[1]Who am I kidding? Topics are selected based on *my* interests, not student interest.

Table 1: Suggested syllabus

Chapter	Hours	Coverage
1. Introduction	1	All
2. Hidden Markov Models	3	All
9. HMM Applications	2	All
8. Data Analysis	3	All
3. Profile Hidden Markov Models	3	All
10. PHMM Applications	2	All
4. Principal Component Analysis	3	All
11. PCA Applications	2	All
5. Support Vector Machines	3	All
12. SVM Applications	3	All
6. Clustering	3	All
13. Clustering Applications	2	All
7. Mini-topics	6	LDA and selected topics
Total	36	

My machine learning class is taught at the beginning graduate level. For an undergraduate class, it might be advisable to slow the pace slightly. Regardless of the level, labs would likely be helpful. However, it's important to treat labs as supplemental to—as opposed to a substitute for—lectures.

Learning challenging technical material requires studying it multiple times in multiple different ways, and I'd say that the magic number is three. It's no accident that students who read the book, attend the lectures, and conscientiously work on homework problems learn this material well. If you are trying to learn this subject on your own, the author has posted his lecture videos online, and these might serve as a (very poor) substitute for live lectures.[2] I'm also a big believer in learning by programming—the more code that you write, the better you will learn machine learning.

Mark Stamp
Los Gatos, California
April, 2017

---

[2]In my experience, in-person lectures are infinitely more valuable than any recorded or online format. Something happens in live classes that will never be fully duplicated in any dead (or even semi-dead) format.

About the Author

My work experience includes more than seven years at the National Security Agency (NSA), which was followed by two years at a small Silicon Valley startup company. Since 2002, I have been a card-carrying member of the Computer Science faculty at San Jose State University (SJSU).

My love affair with machine learning began during the early 1990s, when I was working at the NSA. In my current job at SJSU, I've supervised vast numbers of master's student projects, most of which involve some combination of information security and machine learning. In recent years, students have become even more eager to work on machine learning projects, which I would like to ascribe to the quality of the book that you have before you and my magnetic personality, but instead, it's almost certainly a reflection of trends in the job market.

I do have a life outside of work.[3] Recently, kayak fishing and sailing my Hobie kayak in the Monterey Bay have occupied most of my free time. I also ride my mountain bike through the local hills and forests whenever possible. In case you are a masochist, a more complete autobiography can be found at

http://www.sjsu.edu/people/mark.stamp/

If you have any comments or questions about this book (or anything else) you can contact me via email at mark.stamp@sjsu.edu. And if you happen to be local, don't hesitate to stop by my office to chat.

---

[3]Of course, here I am assuming that what I do for a living could reasonably be classified as work. My wife (among others) has been known to dispute that assumption.

Acknowledgments

The first draft of this book was written while I was on sabbatical during the spring 2014 semester. I first taught most of this material in the fall semester of 2014, then again in fall 2015, and yet again in fall 2016. After the third iteration, I was finally satisfied that the manuscript had the potential to be book-worthy.

All of the students in these three classes deserve credit for helping to improve the book to the point where it can now be displayed in public without excessive fear of ridicule. Here, I'd like to single out the following students for their contributions to the applications in Part II.

Topic	Students
HMM	Sujan Venkatachalam, Rohit Vobbilisetty
PHMM	Lin Huang, Swapna Vemparala
PCA	Ranjith Jidigam, Sayali Deshpande, Annapurna Annadatha
SVM	Tanuvir Singh, Annapurna Annadatha
Clustering	Chinmayee Annachhatre, Swathi Pai, Usha Narra

Extra special thanks go to Annapurna Annadatha and Fabio Di Troia. In addition to her major contributions to two of the applications chapters, Annapurna helped to improve the end-of-chapter exercises. Fabio assisted with most of my recent students' projects and he is a co-author on almost all of my recent papers. I also want to thank Eric Filiol, who suggested broadening the range of applications. This was excellent advice that greatly improved the book.

Finally, I want to thank Randi Cohen and Veronica Rodriguez at the Taylor & Francis Group. Without their help, encouragement, and patience, this book would never have been published.

A textbook is like a large software project, in that it must contain bugs. All errors in this book are solely the responsibility of your humble scribe. Please send me any errors that you find, and I will keep an updated errata list on the textbook website.

Chapter 1

Introduction

I took a speed reading course and read War and Peace *in twenty minutes.*
It involves Russia.
— Woody Allen

1.1 What Is Machine Learning?

For our purposes, we'll view machine learning as a form of statistical discrimination, where the "machine" does the heavy lifting. That is, the computer "learns" important information, saving us humans from the hard work of trying to extract useful information from seemingly inscrutable data.

For the applications considered in this book, we typically train a model, then use the resulting model to score samples. If the score is sufficiently high, we classify the sample as being of the same type as was used to train the model. And thanks to the miracle of machine learning, we don't have to work too hard to perform such classification. Since the model parameters are (more-or-less) automatically extracted from training data, machine learning algorithms are sometimes said to be *data driven*.

Machine learning techniques can be successfully applied to a wide range of important problems, including speech recognition, natural language processing, bioinformatics, stock market analysis, information security, and the homework problems in this book. Additional useful applications of machine learning seem to be found on a daily basis—the set of potential applications is virtually unlimited.

It's possible to treat any machine learning algorithm as a black box and, in fact, this is a major selling points of the field. Many successful machine learners simply feed data into their favorite machine learning black box, which, surprisingly often, spits out useful results. While such an approach can work, the primary goal of this book is to provide the reader with a deeper understanding of what is actually happening inside those mysterious machine learning black boxes.

Why should anyone care about the inner workings of machine learning algorithms when a simple black box approach can—and often does—suffice? If you are like your curious author, you hate black boxes, and you want to know how and why things work as they do. But there are also practical reasons for exploring the inner sanctum of machine learning. As with any technical field, the cookbook approach to machine learning is inherently limited. When applying machine learning to new and novel problems, it is often essential to have an understanding of what is actually happening "under the covers." In addition to being the most interesting cases, such applications are also likely to be the most lucrative.

By way of analogy, consider a medical doctor (MD) in comparison to a nurse practitioner (NP).[1] It is often claimed that an NP can do about 80% to 90% of the work that an MD typically does. And the NP requires less training, so when possible, it is cheaper to have NPs treat people. But, for challenging or unusual or non-standard cases, the higher level of training of an MD may be essential. So, the MD deals with the most challenging and interesting cases, and earns significantly more for doing so. The aim of this book is to enable the reader to earn the equivalent of an MD in machine learning.

The bottom line is that the reader who masters the material in this book will be well positioned to apply machine learning techniques to challenging and cutting-edge applications. Most such applications would likely be beyond the reach of anyone with a mere black box level of understanding.

1.2   About This Book

The focus of this book is on providing a reasonable level of detail for a reasonably wide variety of machine learning algorithms, while constantly reinforcing the material with realistic applications. But, what constitutes a reasonable level of detail? I'm glad you asked.

While the goal here is for the reader to obtain a deep understanding of the inner workings of the algorithms, there are limits.[2] This is not a math book, so we don't prove theorems or otherwise dwell on mathematical theory. Although much of the underlying math is elegant and interesting, we don't spend any more time on the math than is absolutely necessary. And, we'll

---

[1] A physician assistant (PA) is another medical professional that is roughly comparable to a nurse practitioner.

[2] However, these limits are definitely not of the kind that one typically finds in a calculus book.

sometimes skip a few details, and on occasion, we might even be a little bit sloppy with respect to mathematical niceties. The goal here is to present topics at a fairly intuitive level, with (hopefully) just enough detail to clarify the underlying concepts, but not so much detail as to become overwhelming and bog down the presentation.[3]

In this book, the following machine learning topics are covered in chapter-length detail.

Topic	Where
Hidden Markov Models (HMM)	Chapter 2
Profile Hidden Markov Models (PHMM)	Chapter 3
Principal Component Analysis (PCA)	Chapter 4
Support Vector Machines (SVM)	Chapter 5
Clustering (K-Means and EM)	Chapter 6

Several additional topics are discussed in a more abbreviated (section-length) format. These mini-topics include the following.

Topic	Where
k-Nearest Neighbors (k-NN)	Section 7.2
Neural Networks	Section 7.3
Boosting and AdaBoost	Section 7.4
Random Forest	Section 7.5
Linear Discriminant Analysis (LDA)	Section 7.6
Vector Quantization (VQ)	Section 7.7
Naïve Bayes	Section 7.8
Regression Analysis	Section 7.9
Conditional Random Fields (CRF)	Section 7.10

Data analysis is critically important when evaluating machine learning applications, yet this topic is often relegated to an afterthought. But that's not the case here, as we have an entire chapter devoted to data analysis and related issues.

To access the textbook website, point your browser to

```
http://www.cs.sjsu.edu/~stamp/ML/
```

where you'll find links to PowerPoint slides, lecture videos, and other relevant material. An updated errata list is also available. And for the reader's benefit, all of the figures in this book are available in electronic form, and in color.

---

[3]Admittedly, this is a delicate balance, and your unbalanced author is sure that he didn't always achieve an ideal compromise. But you can rest assured that it was not for lack of trying.

In addition, extensive malware and image spam datasets can be found on the textbook website. These or similar datasets were used in many of the applications discussed in Part II of this book.

1.3   Necessary Background

Given the title of this weighty tome, it should be no surprise that most of the examples are drawn from the field of information security. For a solid introduction to information security, your humble author is partial to the book [137]. Many of the machine learning applications in this book are specifically focused on malware. For a thorough—and thoroughly enjoyable—introduction to malware, Aycock's book [12] is the clear choice. However, enough background is provided so that no outside resources should be necessary to understand the applications considered here.

Many of the exercises in this book require some programming, and basic computing concepts are assumed in a few of the application sections. But anyone with a modest amount of programming experience should have no trouble with this aspect of the book.

Most machine learning techniques do ultimately rest on some fancy math. For example, hidden Markov models (HMM) build on a foundation of discrete probability, principal component analysis (PCA) is based on sophisticated linear algebra, Lagrange multipliers (and calculus) are used to show how and why a support vector machine (SVM) really works, and statistical concepts abound. We'll review the necessary linear algebra, and generally cover relevant math and statistics topics as needed. However, we do assume some knowledge of differential calculus—specifically, finding the maximum and minimum of "nice" functions.

1.4   A Few Too Many Notes

Note that the applications presented in this book are largely drawn from your author's industrious students' research projects. Note also that the applications considered here were selected because they illustrate various machine learning techniques in relatively straightforward scenarios. In particular, it is important to note that applications were *not* selected because they necessarily represent the greatest academic research in the history of academic research. It's a noteworthy (and unfortunate) fact of life that the primary function of much academic research is to impress the researcher's (few) friends with his or her extreme cleverness, while eschewing practicality, utility, and clarity. In contrast, the applications presented here are supposed to help demystify machine learning techniques.

Part I

Tools of the Trade

Chapter 2

A Revealing Introduction to Hidden Markov Models

The cause is hidden. The effect is visible to all.
— Ovid

2.1 Introduction and Background

Not surprisingly, a hidden Markov model (HMM) includes a Markov process that is "hidden," in the sense that we cannot directly observe the state of the process. But we do have access to a series of observations that are probabilistically related to the underlying Markov model.

While the formulation of HMMs might initially seem somewhat contrived, there exist a virtually unlimited number of problems where the technique can be applied. Best of all, there are efficient algorithms, making HMMs extremely practical. Another very nice property of an HMM is that structure within the data can often be deduced from the model itself.

In this chapter, we first consider a simple example to motivate the HMM formulation. Then we dive into a detailed discussion of the HMM algorithms. Realistic applications—mostly from the information security domain—can be found in Chapter 9.

This is one of the most detailed chapters in the book. A reason for going into so much depth is that once we have a solid understanding of this particular machine learning technique, we can then compare and contrast it to the other techniques that we'll consider. In addition, HMMs are relatively easy to understand—although the notation can seem intimidating, once you have the intuition, the process is actually fairly straightforward.[1]

---

[1]To be more accurate, your dictatorial author wants to start with HMMs, and that's all that really matters.

The bottom line is that this chapter is the linchpin for much of the remainder of the book. Consequently, if you learn the material in this chapter well, it will pay large dividends in most subsequent chapters. On the other hand, if you fail to fully grasp the details of HMMs, then much of the remaining material will almost certainly be more difficult than is necessary.

HMMs are based on discrete probability. In particular, we'll need some basic facts about conditional probability, so in the remainder of this section, we provide a quick overview of this crucial topic.

The notation "|" denotes "given" information, so that $P(B \mid A)$ is read as "the probability of B, given A." For any two events A and B, we have

$$P(A \text{ and } B) = P(A) P(B \mid A). \tag{2.1}$$

For example, suppose that we draw two cards without replacement from a standard 52-card deck. Let $A = \{1^{\text{st}} \text{ card is ace}\}$ and $B = \{2^{\text{nd}} \text{ card is ace}\}$. Then

$$P(A \text{ and } B) = P(A) P(B \mid A) = 4/52 \cdot 3/51 = 1/221.$$

In this example, $P(B)$ depends on what happens in the first event A, so we say that A and B are *dependent* events. On the other hand, suppose we flip a fair coin twice. Then the probability that the second flip comes up heads is $1/2$, regardless of the outcome of the first coin flip, so these events are *independent*. For dependent events, the "given" information is relevant when determining the sample space. Consequently, in such cases we can view the information to the right of the "given" sign as defining the space over which probabilities will be computed.

We can rewrite equation (2.1) as

$$P(B \mid A) = \frac{P(A \text{ and } B)}{P(A)}.$$

This expression can be viewed as the definition of conditional probability. For an important application of conditional probability, see the discussion of naïve Bayes in Section 7.8 of Chapter 7.

We'll often use the shorthand "A, B" for the joint probability which, in reality is the same as "A and B." Also, in discrete probability, "A and B" is equivalent to the intersection of the sets A and B and sometimes we'll want to emphasize this set intersection. Consequently, throughout this section

$$P(A \text{ and } B) = P(A, B) = P(A \cap B).$$

Finally, matrix notation is used frequently in this chapter. A review of matrices and basic linear algebra can be found in Section 4.2.1 of Chapter 4, although no linear algebra is required in this chapter.

2.2 A Simple Example

Suppose we want to determine the average annual temperature at a particular location on earth over a series of years. To make it more interesting, suppose the years we are focused on lie in the distant past, before thermometers were invented. Since we can't go back in time, we instead look for indirect evidence of the temperature.

To simplify the problem, we only consider "hot" and "cold" for the average annual temperature. Suppose that modern evidence indicates that the probability of a hot year followed by another hot year is 0.7 and the probability that a cold year is followed by another cold year is 0.6. We'll assume that these probabilities also held in the distant past. This information can be summarized as

$$
\begin{array}{cc}
 & \begin{array}{cc} H & C \end{array} \\
\begin{array}{c} H \\ C \end{array} & \left(\begin{array}{cc} 0.7 & 0.3 \\ 0.4 & 0.6 \end{array} \right)
\end{array}
\tag{2.2}
$$

where H is "hot" and C is "cold."

Next, suppose that current research indicates a correlation between the size of tree growth rings and temperature. For simplicity, we only consider three different tree ring sizes, small, medium, and large, denoted S, M, and L, respectively. Furthermore, suppose that based on currently available evidence, the probabilistic relationship between annual temperature and tree ring sizes is given by

$$
\begin{array}{ccc}
 & \begin{array}{ccc} S & M & L \end{array} \\
\begin{array}{c} H \\ C \end{array} & \left(\begin{array}{ccc} 0.1 & 0.4 & 0.5 \\ 0.7 & 0.2 & 0.1 \end{array} \right)
\end{array}.
\tag{2.3}
$$

For this system, we'll say that the *state* is the average annual temperature, either H or C. The transition from one state to the next is a *Markov process*,[2] since the next state depends only on the current state and the fixed probabilities in (2.2). However, the actual states are "hidden" since we can't directly observe the temperature in the past.

Although we can't observe the state (temperature) in the past, we can observe the size of tree rings. From (2.3), tree rings provide us with probabilistic information regarding the temperature. Since the underlying states are hidden, this type of system is known as a *hidden Markov model* (HMM). Our goal is to make effective and efficient use of the observable information, so as to gain insight into various aspects of the Markov process.

---

[2]A Markov process where the current state only depends on the previous state is said to be of order one. In a Markov process of order n, the current state depends on the n consecutive preceding states. In any case, the "memory" is finite—much like your absent-minded author's memory, which seems to become more and more finite all the time. Let's see, now where was I?

For this HMM example, the state transition matrix is

$$A = \begin{pmatrix} 0.7 & 0.3 \\ 0.4 & 0.6 \end{pmatrix}, \tag{2.4}$$

which comes from (2.2), and the observation matrix is

$$B = \begin{pmatrix} 0.1 & 0.4 & 0.5 \\ 0.7 & 0.2 & 0.1 \end{pmatrix}, \tag{2.5}$$

which comes from (2.3). For this example, suppose that the initial state distribution, denoted by π, is

$$\pi = \begin{pmatrix} 0.6 & 0.4 \end{pmatrix}, \tag{2.6}$$

that is, the chance that we start in the H state is 0.6 and the chance that we start in the C state is 0.4. The matrices π, A, and B are *row stochastic*, which is just a fancy way of saying that each row satisfies the requirements of a discrete probability distribution (i.e., each element is between 0 and 1, and the elements of each row sum to 1).

Now, suppose that we consider a particular four-year period of interest from the distant past. For this particular four-year period, we observe the series of tree ring sizes S, M, S, L. Letting 0 represent S, 1 represent M, and 2 represent L, this observation sequence is denoted as

$$\mathcal{O} = \begin{pmatrix} 0, 1, 0, 2 \end{pmatrix}. \tag{2.7}$$

We might want to determine the most likely state sequence of the Markov process given the observations (2.7). That is, we might want to know the most likely average annual temperatures over this four-year period of interest. This is not quite as clear-cut as it seems, since there are different possible interpretations of "most likely." On the one hand, we could define "most likely" as the state sequence with the highest probability from among all possible state sequences of length four. Dynamic programming (DP) can be used to efficiently solve this problem. On the other hand, we might reasonably define "most likely" as the state sequence that maximizes the expected number of correct states. An HMM can be used to find the most likely hidden state sequence in this latter sense.

It's important to realize that the DP and HMM solutions to this problem are not necessarily the same. For example, the DP solution must, by definition, include valid state transitions, while this is not the case for the HMM. And even if all state transitions are valid, the HMM solution can still differ from the DP solution, as we'll illustrate in an example below.

Before going into more detail, we need to deal with the most challenging aspect of HMMs—the notation. Once we have the notation, we'll discuss the three fundamental problems that HMMs enable us to solve, and we'll give detailed algorithms for the efficient solution of each. We also consider critical computational issues that must be addressed when writing any HMM computer program. Rabiner [113] is a standard reference for further introductory information on HMMs.

2.3 Notation

The notation used in an HMM is summarized in Table 2.1. Note that the observations are assumed to come from the set $\{0, 1, \ldots, M - 1\}$, which simplifies the notation with no loss of generality. That is, we simply associate each of the M distinct observations with one of the elements $0, 1, \ldots, M - 1$, so that $\mathcal{O}_i \in V = \{0, 1, \ldots, M - 1\}$ for $i = 0, 1, \ldots, T - 1$.

Table 2.1: HMM notation

Notation	Explanation
T	Length of the observation sequence
N	Number of states in the model
M	Number of observation symbols
Q	Distinct states of the Markov process, $q_0, q_1, \ldots, q_{N-1}$
V	Possible observations, assumed to be $0, 1, \ldots, M - 1$
A	State transition probabilities
B	Observation probability matrix
π	Initial state distribution
$\mathcal{O}$	Observation sequence, $\mathcal{O}_0, \mathcal{O}_1, \ldots, \mathcal{O}_{T-1}$

A generic hidden Markov model is illustrated in Figure 2.1, where the X_i represent the hidden states and all other notation is as in Table 2.1. The state of the Markov process, which we can view as being hidden behind a "curtain" (the dashed line in Figure 2.1), is determined by the current state and the A matrix. We are only able to observe the observations $\mathcal{O}_i$, which are related to the (hidden) states of the Markov process by the matrix B.

For the temperature example in the previous section, the observations sequence is given in (2.7), and we have $T = 4$, $N = 2$, $M = 3$, $Q = \{H, C\}$, and $V = \{0, 1, 2\}$. Note that we let $0, 1, 2$ represent small, medium, and large tree rings, respectively. For this example, the matrices A, B, and π are given by (2.4), (2.5), and (2.6), respectively.

In general, the matrix $A = \{a_{ij}\}$ is $N \times N$ with

$$a_{ij} = P(\text{state } q_j \text{ at } t + 1 \,|\, \text{state } q_i \text{ at } t).$$

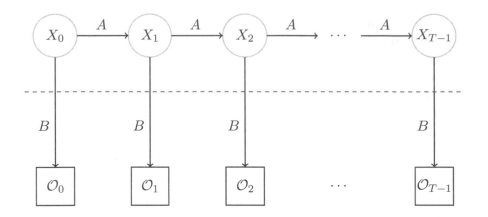

Figure 2.1: Hidden Markov model

The matrix A is always row stochastic. Also, the probabilities a_{ij} are independent of t, so that the A matrix does not change. The matrix $B = \{b_j(k)\}$ is of size $N \times M$, with

$$b_j(k) = P(\text{observation } k \text{ at } t \,|\, \text{state } q_j \text{ at } t).$$

As with the A matrix, B is row stochastic, and the probabilities $b_j(k)$ are independent of t. The somewhat unusual notation $b_j(k)$ is convenient when specifying the HMM algorithms.

An HMM is defined by A, B, and π (and, implicitly, by the dimensions N and M). Thus, we'll denote an HMM as $\lambda = (A, B, \pi)$.

Suppose that we are given an observation sequence of length four, which is denoted as

$$\mathcal{O} = (\mathcal{O}_0, \mathcal{O}_1, \mathcal{O}_2, \mathcal{O}_3).$$

The corresponding (hidden) state sequence is

$$X = (X_0, X_1, X_2, X_3).$$

We'll let π_{X_0} denote the probability of starting in state X_0, and $b_{X_0}(\mathcal{O}_0)$ denotes the probability of initially observing $\mathcal{O}_0$, while a_{X_0,X_1} is the probability of transiting from state X_0 to state X_1. Continuing, we see that the probability of a given state sequence X of length four is

$$P(X, \mathcal{O}) = \pi_{X_0} b_{X_0}(\mathcal{O}_0) a_{X_0,X_1} b_{X_1}(\mathcal{O}_1) a_{X_1,X_2} b_{X_2}(\mathcal{O}_2) a_{X_2,X_3} b_{X_3}(\mathcal{O}_3). \quad (2.8)$$

Note that in this expression, the X_i represent indices in the A and B matrices, not the names of the corresponding states.[3]

---

[3] Your kindly author regrets this abuse of notation.

Consider again the temperature example in Section 2.2, where the observation sequence is $\mathcal{O} = (0, 1, 0, 2)$. Using (2.8) we can compute, say,

$$P(HHCC) = 0.6(0.1)(0.7)(0.4)(0.3)(0.7)(0.6)(0.1) = 0.000212.$$

Similarly, we can directly compute the probability of each possible state sequence of length four, for the given observation sequence in (2.7). We have listed these results in Table 2.2, where the probabilities in the last column have been normalized so that they sum to 1.

Table 2.2: State sequence probabilities

State	Probability	Normalized probability
$HHHH$	0.000412	0.042787
$HHHC$	0.000035	0.003635
$HHCH$	0.000706	0.073320
$HHCC$	0.000212	0.022017
$HCHH$	0.000050	0.005193
$HCHC$	0.000004	0.000415
$HCCH$	0.000302	0.031364
$HCCC$	0.000091	0.009451
$CHHH$	0.001098	0.114031
$CHHC$	0.000094	0.009762
$CHCH$	0.001882	0.195451
$CHCC$	0.000564	0.058573
$CCHH$	0.000470	0.048811
$CCHC$	0.000040	0.004154
$CCCH$	0.002822	0.293073
$CCCC$	0.000847	0.087963

To find the optimal state sequence in the dynamic programming (DP) sense, we simply choose the sequence with the highest probability, which in this example is $CCCH$. To find the optimal state sequence in the HMM sense, we choose the most probable symbol at each position. To this end we sum the probabilities in Table 2.2 that have an H in the first position. Doing so, we find the (normalized) probability of H in the first position is 0.18817 and the probability of C in the first position is 0.81183. Therefore, the first element of the optimal sequence (in the HMM sense) is C. Repeating this for each element of the sequence, we obtain the probabilities in Table 2.3.

From Table 2.3, we find that the optimal sequence—in the HMM sense—is $CHCH$. Note that in this example, the optimal DP sequence differs from the optimal HMM sequence.

Table 2.3: HMM probabilities

	Position in state sequence			
	0	1	2	3
$P(H)$	0.188182	0.519576	0.228788	0.804029
$P(C)$	0.811818	0.480424	0.771212	0.195971

2.4   The Three Problems

There are three fundamental problems that we can solve using HMMs. Here, we briefly describe each of these problems, then in the next section we discuss efficient algorithms for their solution.

2.4.1   HMM Problem 1

Given the model $\lambda = (A, B, \pi)$ and a sequence of observations $\mathcal{O}$, determine $P(\mathcal{O} \,|\, \lambda)$. That is, we want to compute a score for the observed sequence $\mathcal{O}$ with respect to the given model λ.

2.4.2   HMM Problem 2

Given $\lambda = (A, B, \pi)$ and an observation sequence $\mathcal{O}$, find an optimal state sequence for the underlying Markov process. In other words, we want to uncover the hidden part of the hidden Markov model. This is the problem that was discussed in some detail above.

2.4.3   HMM Problem 3

Given an observation sequence $\mathcal{O}$ and the parameter N, determine a model of the form $\lambda = (A, B, \pi)$ that maximizes the probability of $\mathcal{O}$. This can be viewed as training a model to best fit the observed data. We'll solve this problem using a discrete hill climb on the parameter space represented by A, B, and π. Note that the dimension M is determined from the training sequence $\mathcal{O}$.

2.4.4   Discussion

Consider, for example, the problem of speech recognition—which happens to be one of the earliest and best-known applications of HMMs. We can use the solution to HMM Problem 3 to train an HMM λ to, for example, recognize the spoken word "yes." Then, given an unknown spoken word, we can use the solution to HMM Problem 1 to score this word against this model λ and determine the likelihood that the word is "yes." In this case, we don't need to solve HMM Problem 2, but it is possible that such a solution—which uncovers the hidden states—might provide additional insight into the underlying speech model.

2.5 The Three Solutions

2.5.1 Solution to HMM Problem 1

Let $\lambda = (A, B, \pi)$ be a given HMM and let $\mathcal{O} = (\mathcal{O}_0, \mathcal{O}_1, \ldots, \mathcal{O}_{T-1})$ be a series of observations. We want to find $P(\mathcal{O} \mid \lambda)$.

Let $X = (X_0, X_1, \ldots, X_{T-1})$ be a state sequence. Then by the definition of B we have

$$P(\mathcal{O} \mid X, \lambda) = b_{X_0}(\mathcal{O}_0) b_{X_1}(\mathcal{O}_1) \cdots b_{X_{T-1}}(\mathcal{O}_{T-1})$$

and by the definition of π and A it follows that

$$P(X \mid \lambda) = \pi_{X_0} a_{X_0, X_1} a_{X_1, X_2} \cdots a_{X_{T-2}, X_{T-1}}.$$

Since

$$P(\mathcal{O}, X \mid \lambda) = \frac{P(\mathcal{O} \cap X \cap \lambda)}{P(\lambda)}$$

and

$$P(\mathcal{O} \mid X, \lambda) P(X \mid \lambda) = \frac{P(\mathcal{O} \cap X \cap \lambda)}{P(X \cap \lambda)} \cdot \frac{P(X \cap \lambda)}{P(\lambda)} = \frac{P(\mathcal{O} \cap X \cap \lambda)}{P(\lambda)}$$

we have

$$P(\mathcal{O}, X \mid \lambda) = P(\mathcal{O} \mid X, \lambda) P(X \mid \lambda).$$

Summing over all possible state sequences yields

$$
\begin{aligned}
P(\mathcal{O} \mid \lambda) &= \sum_X P(\mathcal{O}, X \mid \lambda) \\
&= \sum_X P(\mathcal{O} \mid X, \lambda) P(X \mid \lambda) \qquad (2.9) \\
&= \sum_X \pi_{X_0} b_{X_0}(\mathcal{O}_0) a_{X_0, X_1} b_{X_1}(\mathcal{O}_1) \cdots a_{X_{T-2}, X_{T-1}} b_{X_{T-1}}(\mathcal{O}_{T-1}).
\end{aligned}
$$

The direct computation in (2.9) is generally infeasible, since the number of multiplications is about $2TN^T$, where T is typically large and $N \geq 2$. One of the major strengths of HMMs is that there exists an efficient algorithm to achieve this same result.

To determine $P(\mathcal{O} \mid \lambda)$ in an efficient manner, we can use the following approach. For $t = 0, 1, \ldots, T - 1$ and $i = 0, 1, \ldots, N - 1$, define

$$\alpha_t(i) = P(\mathcal{O}_0, \mathcal{O}_1, \ldots, \mathcal{O}_t, X_t = q_i \mid \lambda). \qquad (2.10)$$

Then $\alpha_t(i)$ is the probability of the partial observation sequence up to time t, where the underlying Markov process is in state q_i at time t.

The crucial insight is that the $\alpha_t(i)$ can be computed recursively—and efficiently. This recursive approach is known as the *forward algorithm*, or α-pass, and is given in Algorithm 2.1.

Algorithm 2.1 Forward algorithm

1: **Given:**
   Model $\lambda = (A, B, \pi)$
   Observations $\mathcal{O} = (\mathcal{O}_0, \mathcal{O}_1, \ldots, \mathcal{O}_{T-1})$
2: **for** $i = 0, 1, \ldots, N - 1$ **do**
3:     $\alpha_0(i) = \pi_i b_i(\mathcal{O}_0)$
4: **end for**
5: **for** $t = 1, 2, \ldots, T - 1$ **do**
6:     **for** $i = 0, 1, \ldots, N - 1$ **do**
7:
$$\alpha_t(i) = \left(\sum_{j=0}^{N-1} \alpha_{t-1}(j) a_{ji} \right) b_i(\mathcal{O}_t)$$
8:     **end for**
9: **end for**

The forward algorithm only requires about $N^2 T$ multiplications. This is in stark contrast to the naïve approach, which has a work factor of more than $2TN^T$. Since T is typically large and N is relatively small, the forward algorithm is highly efficient.

It follows from the definition in (2.10) that

$$P(\mathcal{O} \mid \lambda) = \sum_{i=0}^{N-1} \alpha_{T-1}(i).$$

Hence, the forward algorithm gives us an efficient way to compute a score for a given sequence $\mathcal{O}$, relative to a given model λ.

2.5.2   Solution to HMM Problem 2

Given the model $\lambda = (A, B, \pi)$ and a sequence of observations $\mathcal{O}$, our goal here is to find the most likely state sequence. As mentioned above, there are different possible interpretations of "most likely"—for an HMM, we maximize the expected number of correct states. In contrast, a dynamic program finds the highest-scoring overall path. As we have seen, these solutions are not necessarily the same.

First, we define

$$\beta_t(i) = P(\mathcal{O}_{t+1}, \mathcal{O}_{t+2}, \ldots, \mathcal{O}_{T-1} \,|\, X_t = q_i, \lambda)$$

for $t = 0, 1, \ldots, T-1$, and $i = 0, 1, \ldots, N-1$. The $\beta_t(i)$ can be computed recursively (and efficiently) using the *backward algorithm*, or β-*pass*, which is given here in Algorithm 2.2. This is analogous to the α-pass discussed above, except that we start at the end and work back toward the beginning.

Algorithm 2.2 Backward algorithm

1: **Given:**
   Model $\lambda = (A, B, \pi)$
   Observations $\mathcal{O} = (\mathcal{O}_0, \mathcal{O}_1, \ldots, \mathcal{O}_{T-1})$
2: **for** $i = 0, 1, \ldots, N-1$ **do**
3:     $\beta_{T-1}(i) = 1$
4: **end for**
5: **for** $t = T-2, T-3, \ldots, 0$ **do**
6:     **for** $i = 0, 1, \ldots, N-1$ **do**
7:         $\displaystyle \beta_t(i) = \sum_{j=0}^{N-1} a_{ij} b_j(\mathcal{O}_{t+1}) \beta_{t+1}(j)$
8:     **end for**
9: **end for**

Now, for $t = 0, 1, \ldots, T-1$ and $i = 0, 1, \ldots, N-1$, define

$$\gamma_t(i) = P(X_t = q_i \,|\, \mathcal{O}, \lambda).$$

Since $\alpha_t(i)$ measures the relevant probability up to time t and $\beta_t(i)$ measures the relevant probability after time t, we have

$$\gamma_t(i) = \frac{\alpha_t(i)\beta_t(i)}{P(\mathcal{O}\,|\,\lambda)}.$$

Recall that the denominator $P(\mathcal{O}\,|\,\lambda)$ is obtained by summing $\alpha_{T-1}(i)$ over i. From the definition of $\gamma_t(i)$ it follows that the most likely state at time t is the state q_i for which $\gamma_t(i)$ is maximum, where the maximum is taken over the index i. Then the most likely state at time t is given by

$$\widetilde{X}_t = \max_i \gamma_t(i).$$

2.5.3   Solution to HMM Problem 3

Here we want to adjust the model parameters to best fit the given observations. The sizes of the matrices (N and M) are known, while the elements of A, B, and π are to be determined, subject to row stochastic conditions. The fact that we can efficiently re-estimate the model itself is perhaps the more impressive aspect of HMMs.

For $t = 0, 1, \ldots, T-2$ and $i, j \in \{0, 1, \ldots, N-1\}$, define the "di-gammas" as

$$\gamma_t(i, j) = P(X_t = q_i, X_{t+1} = q_j \mid \mathcal{O}, \lambda).$$

Then $\gamma_t(i, j)$ is the probability of being in state q_i at time t and transiting to state q_j at time $t+1$. The di-gammas can be written in terms of α, β, A, and B as

$$\gamma_t(i, j) = \frac{\alpha_t(i) a_{ij} b_j(\mathcal{O}_{t+1}) \beta_{t+1}(j)}{P(\mathcal{O} \mid \lambda)}.$$

For $t = 0, 1, \ldots, T-2$, we see that $\gamma_t(i)$ and $\gamma_t(i, j)$ are related by

$$\gamma_t(i) = \sum_{j=0}^{N-1} \gamma_t(i, j).$$

Once the $\gamma_t(i, j)$ have been computed, the model $\lambda = (A, B, \pi)$ is re-estimated using Algorithm 2.3. The HMM training algorithm is known as Baum-Welch re-estimation, and is named after Leonard E. Baum and Lloyd R. Welch, who developed the technique in the late 1960s while working at the Center for Communications Research (CCR),[4] which is part of the Institute for Defense Analyses (IDA), located in Princeton, New Jersey.

The numerator of the re-estimated a_{ij} in Algorithm 2.3 can be seen to give the expected number of transitions from state q_i to state q_j, while the denominator is the expected number of transitions from q_i to any state.[5] Hence, the ratio is the probability of transiting from state q_i to state q_j, which is the desired value of a_{ij}.

The numerator of the re-estimated $b_j(k)$ in Algorithm 2.3 is the expected number of times the model is in state q_j with observation k, while the denominator is the expected number of times the model is in state q_j. Therefore, the ratio is the probability of observing symbol k, given that the model is in state q_j, and this is the desired value for $b_j(k)$.

Re-estimation is an iterative process. First, we initialize $\lambda = (A, B, \pi)$ with a reasonable guess, or, if no reasonable guess is available, we choose

---

[4]Not to be confused with Creedence Clearwater Revival [153].

[5]When re-estimating the A matrix, we are dealing with expectations. However, it might make things clearer to think in terms of frequency counts. For frequency counts, it would be easy to compute the probability of transitioning from state i to state j. That is, we would simply count the number of transitions from state i to state j, and divide this count by the total number of times we could be in state i. This is the intuition behind the re-estimation formula for the A matrix, and a similar statement holds when re-estimating the B matrix. In other words, don't let all of the fancy notation obscure the relatively simple ideas that are at the core of the re-estimation process.

Algorithm 2.3 Baum-Welch re-estimation

1: **Given:**
$\gamma_t(i)$, for $t = 0, 1, \ldots, T - 1$ and $i = 0, 1, \ldots, N - 1$
$\gamma_t(i, j)$, for $t = 0, 1, \ldots, T - 2$ and $i, j \in \{0, 1, \ldots, N - 1\}$
2: **for** $i = 0, 1, \ldots, N - 1$ **do**
3:    $\pi_i = \gamma_0(i)$
4: **end for**
5: **for** $i = 0, 1, \ldots, N - 1$ **do**
6:    **for** $j = 0, 1, \ldots, N - 1$ **do**
7:       $a_{ij} = \sum_{t=0}^{T-2} \gamma_t(i, j) \bigg/ \sum_{t=0}^{T-2} \gamma_t(i)$
8:    **end for**
9: **end for**
10: **for** $j = 0, 1, \ldots, N - 1$ **do**
11:    **for** $k = 0, 1, \ldots, M - 1$ **do**
12:       $b_j(k) = \sum_{\substack{t \in \{0,1,\ldots,T-1\} \\ \mathcal{O}_t = k}} \gamma_t(j) \bigg/ \sum_{t=0}^{T-1} \gamma_t(j)$
13:    **end for**
14: **end for**

---

random values such that $\pi_i \approx 1/N$ and $a_{ij} \approx 1/N$ and $b_j(k) \approx 1/M$. It's critical that A, B, and π be randomized, since exactly uniform values will result in a local maximum from which the model cannot climb. And, as always, π, A and B must be row stochastic.

The complete solution to HMM Problem 3 can be summarized as follows.

1. Initialize, $\lambda = (A, B, \pi)$.

2. Compute $\alpha_t(i)$, $\beta_t(i)$, $\gamma_t(i, j)$ and $\gamma_t(i)$.

3. Re-estimate the model $\lambda = (A, B, \pi)$ using Algorithm 2.3.

4. If $P(\mathcal{O} \,|\, \lambda)$ increases, goto 2.

In practice, we would want to stop when $P(\mathcal{O} \,|\, \lambda)$ does not increase by some predetermined threshold, say, ε. We could also (or alternatively) set a maximum number of iterations. In any case, it's important to verify that the model has converged, which can usually be determined by perusing the B matrix.[6]

---

[6]While it might seem obvious to stop iterating when the change in $P(\mathcal{O} \,|\, \lambda)$ is small, this requires some care in practice. Typically, the change in $P(\mathcal{O} \,|\, \lambda)$ is very small over

2.6   Dynamic Programming

Before completing our discussion of the elementary aspects of HMMs, we make a brief detour to show the close relationship between dynamic programming (DP) and HMMs. The executive summary is that a DP can be viewed as an α-pass where "sum" is replaced by "max." More precisely, for π, A, and B as above, the dynamic programming algorithm, which is also known as the Viterbi algorithm, is given in Algorithm 2.4.

Algorithm 2.4 Dynamic programming

1: **Given:**
        Model $\lambda = (A, B, \pi)$
        Observations $\mathcal{O} = (\mathcal{O}_0, \mathcal{O}_1, \ldots, \mathcal{O}_{T-1})$
2: **for** $i = 0, 1, \ldots, N-1$ **do**
3:      $\delta_0(i) = \pi_i b_i(\mathcal{O}_0)$
4: **end for**
5: **for** $t = 1, 2, \ldots, T-1$ **do**
6:      **for** $i = 0, 1, \ldots, N-1$ **do**
7:          $\delta_t(i) = \displaystyle\max_{j \in \{0,1,\ldots,N-1\}} \left(\delta_{t-1}(j) a_{ji} b_i(\mathcal{O}_t) \right)$
8:      **end for**
9: **end for**

At each successive t, a dynamic program determines the probability of the best path ending at each of the states $i = 0, 1, \ldots, N-1$. Consequently, the probability of the best overall path is

$$\max_{j \in \{0,1,\ldots,N-1\}} \delta_{T-1}(j). \qquad (2.11)$$

It is important to realize that (2.11) only gives the optimal probability, not the corresponding path. By keeping track of each preceding state, the DP procedure given here can be augmented so that we can recover the optimal path by tracing back from the highest-scoring final state.

Consider again the example in Section 2.2. The initial probabilities are

$$P(H) = \pi_0 b_0(0) = 0.6(0.1) = 0.06 \text{ and } P(C) = \pi_1 b_1(0) = 0.4(0.7) = 0.28.$$

The probabilities of the paths of length two are given by

$$P(HH) = 0.06(0.7)(0.4) = 0.0168$$

---

the first several iterations. The model then goes through a period of rapid improvement—at which point the model has converged—after which the the change in $P(\mathcal{O} \mid \lambda)$ is again small. Consequently, if we simply set a threshold, the re-estimation process might stop immediately, or it might continue indefinitely. Perhaps the optimal approach is to combine a threshold with a minimum number of iterations—the pseudo-code in Section 2.8 uses this approach.

$$P(HC) = 0.06(0.3)(0.2) = 0.0036$$
$$P(CH) = 0.28(0.4)(0.4) = 0.0448$$
$$P(CC) = 0.28(0.6)(0.2) = 0.0336$$

and hence the best (most probable) path of length two ending with H is CH while the best path of length two ending with C is CC. Continuing, we construct the diagram in Figure 2.2 one level or stage at a time, where each arrow points to the next element in the optimal path ending at a given state. Note that at each stage, the dynamic programming algorithm only needs to maintain the highest-scoring path ending at each state—not a list of all possible paths. This is the key to the efficiency of the algorithm.

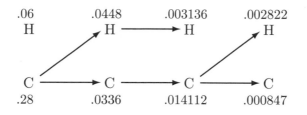

Figure 2.2: Dynamic programming

In Figure 2.2, the maximum final probability is 0.002822, which occurs at the final state H. We can use the arrows to trace back from H to find that the optimal path is $CCCH$. Note that this agrees with the brute force calculation in Table 2.2.

Underflow is a concern with a dynamic programming problem of this form—since we compute products of probabilities, the result will tend to 0. Fortunately, underflow is easily avoided by simply taking logarithms. An underflow-resistant version of DP is given in Algorithm 2.5.

Algorithm 2.5 Dynamic programming without underflow

1: **Given:**
    Model $\lambda = (A, B, \pi)$
    Observations $\mathcal{O} = (\mathcal{O}_0, \mathcal{O}_1, \ldots, \mathcal{O}_{T-1})$
2: **for** $i = 0, 1, \ldots, N - 1$ **do**
3:     $\widehat{\delta}_0(i) = \log(\pi_i b_i(\mathcal{O}_0))$
4: **end for**
5: **for** $t = 1, 2, \ldots, T - 1$ **do**
6:     **for** $i = 0, 1, \ldots, N - 1$ **do**
7:         $\widehat{\delta}_t(i) = \max_{j \in \{0,1,\ldots,N-1\}} \left(\widehat{\delta}_{t-1}(j) + \log(a_{ji}) + \log(b_i(\mathcal{O}_t)) \right)$
8:     **end for**
9: **end for**

Not surprisingly, for the underflow-resistant version in Algorithm 2.5, the optimal score is given by

$$\max_{j \in \{0,1,\ldots,N-1\}} \widehat{\delta}_{T-1}(j).$$

Again, additional bookkeeping is required to determine the optimal path.

2.7 Scaling

The three HMM solutions in Section 2.5 all require computations involving products of probabilities. It's very easy to see, for example, that $\alpha_t(i)$ tends to 0 exponentially as T increases. Therefore, any attempt to implement the HMM algorithms as given in Section 2.5 will inevitably result in underflow. The solution to this underflow problem is to scale the numbers. However, care must be taken to ensure that the algorithms remain valid.

First, consider the computation of $\alpha_t(i)$. The basic recurrence is

$$\alpha_t(i) = \sum_{j=0}^{N-1} \alpha_{t-1}(j) a_{ji} b_i(\mathcal{O}_t).$$

It seems sensible to normalize each $\alpha_t(i)$ by dividing by

$$\sum_{j=0}^{N-1} \alpha_t(j).$$

Following this approach, we compute scaling factors c_t and the scaled $\alpha_t(i)$, which we denote as $\widehat{\alpha}_t(i)$, as in Algorithm 2.6.

To verify Algorithm 2.6 we first note that $\widehat{\alpha}_0(i) = c_0 \alpha_0(i)$. Now suppose that for some t, we have

$$\widehat{\alpha}_t(i) = c_0 c_1 \cdots c_t \alpha_t(i). \tag{2.12}$$

Then

$$
\begin{aligned}
\widehat{\alpha}_{t+1}(i) &= c_{t+1} \widetilde{\alpha}_{t+1}(i) \\
&= c_{t+1} \sum_{j=0}^{N-1} \widehat{\alpha}_t(j) a_{ji} b_i(\mathcal{O}_{t+1}) \\
&= c_0 c_1 \cdots c_t c_{t+1} \sum_{j=0}^{N-1} \alpha_t(j) a_{ji} b_i(\mathcal{O}_{t+1}) \\
&= c_0 c_1 \cdots c_{t+1} \alpha_{t+1}(i)
\end{aligned}
$$

and hence (2.12) holds, by induction, for all t.

Algorithm 2.6 Scaling factors

1: **Given:**
$\quad\quad \alpha_t(i)$, for $t = 0, 1, \ldots, T-1$ and $i = 0, 1, \ldots, N-1$
2: **for** $i = 0, 1, \ldots, N-1$ **do**
3: $\quad\quad \widetilde{\alpha}_0(i) = \alpha_0(i)$
4: **end for**
5: $c_0 = 1/\sum\limits_{j=0}^{N-1} \widetilde{\alpha}_0(j)$
6: **for** $i = 0, 1, \ldots, N-1$ **do**
7: $\quad\quad \widehat{\alpha}_0(i) = c_0 \widetilde{\alpha}_0(i)$
8: **end for**
9: **for** $t = 1, 2, \ldots, T-1$ **do**
10: $\quad\quad$ **for** $i = 0, 1, \ldots, N-1$ **do**
11: $\quad\quad\quad \widetilde{\alpha}_t(i) = \sum\limits_{j=0}^{N-1} \widehat{\alpha}_{t-1}(j) a_{ji} b_i(\mathcal{O}_t)$
12: $\quad\quad$ **end for**
13: $\quad\quad c_t = 1 \bigg/ \sum\limits_{j=0}^{N-1} \widetilde{\alpha}_t(j)$
14: $\quad\quad$ **for** $i = 0, 1, \ldots, N-1$ **do**
15: $\quad\quad\quad \widehat{\alpha}_t(i) = c_t \widetilde{\alpha}_t(i)$
16: $\quad\quad$ **end for**
17: **end for**

From (2.12) and the definitions of $\widetilde{\alpha}$ and $\widehat{\alpha}$ it follows that

$$\widehat{\alpha}_t(i) = \alpha_t(i) \bigg/ \sum_{j=0}^{N-1} \alpha_t(j). \tag{2.13}$$

From equation (2.13) we see that for all t and i, the desired scaled value of $\alpha_t(i)$ is indeed given by $\widehat{\alpha}_t(i)$.

From (2.13) it follows that

$$\sum_{j=0}^{N-1} \widehat{\alpha}_{T-1}(j) = 1.$$

Also, from (2.12) we have

$$\sum_{j=0}^{N-1} \widehat{\alpha}_{T-1}(j) = c_0 c_1 \cdots c_{T-1} \sum_{j=0}^{N-1} \alpha_{T-1}(j)$$

$$= c_0 c_1 \cdots c_{T-1} P(\mathcal{O} \,|\, \lambda).$$

Combining these results gives us

$$P(\mathcal{O} \,|\, \lambda) = 1 \Big/ \prod_{j=0}^{T-1} c_j.$$

It follows that we can compute the log of $P(\mathcal{O} \,|\, \lambda)$ directly from the scaling factors c_t as

$$\log\big(P(\mathcal{O} \,|\, \lambda)\big) = -\sum_{j=0}^{T-1} \log c_j. \tag{2.14}$$

It is fairly easy to show that the same scale factors c_t can be used in the backward algorithm by simply computing $\widehat{\beta}_t(i) = c_t \beta_t(i)$. We then determine $\gamma_t(i,j)$ and $\gamma_t(i)$ using the same formulae as in Section 2.5, but with $\widehat{\alpha}_t(i)$ and $\widehat{\beta}_t(i)$ in place of $\alpha_t(i)$ and $\beta_t(i)$, respectively. The resulting gammas and di-gammas are then used to re-estimate π, A, and B.

By writing the original re-estimation formulae (as given in lines 3, 7, and 12 of Algorithm 2.3) directly in terms of $\alpha_t(i)$ and $\beta_t(i)$, it is a straightforward exercise to show that the re-estimated π and A and B are exact when $\widehat{\alpha}_t(i)$ and $\widehat{\beta}_t(i)$ are used in place of $\alpha_t(i)$ and $\beta_t(i)$. Furthermore, $P(\mathcal{O} \,|\, \lambda)$ isn't required in the re-estimation formulae, since in each case it cancels in the numerator and denominator. Therefore, (2.14) determines a score for the model, which can be used, for example, to decide whether the model is improving sufficiently to continue to the next iteration of the training algorithm.

2.8   All Together Now

Here, we give complete pseudo-code for solving HMM Problem 3, including scaling. This pseudo-code also provides virtually everything needed to solve HMM Problems 1 and 2.

1. Given

   Observation sequence $\mathcal{O} = (\mathcal{O}_0, \mathcal{O}_1, \ldots, \mathcal{O}_{T-1})$.

2. Initialize

   (a) Select N and determine M from $\mathcal{O}$. Recall that the model is denoted $\lambda = (A, B, \pi)$, where $A = \{a_{ij}\}$ is $N \times N$, $B = \{b_j(k)\}$ is $N \times M$, and $\pi = \{\pi_i\}$ is $1 \times N$.

   (b) Initialize the three matrices A, B, and π. You can use knowledge of the problem when generating initial values, but if no such information is available (as is often the case), let $\pi_i \approx 1/N$ and let $a_{ij} \approx 1/N$ and $b_j(k) \approx 1/M$. Always be sure that your initial values satisfy the row stochastic conditions (i.e., the elements of each row sum to 1, and each element is between 0 and 1). Also, make sure that the elements of each row are *not* exactly uniform.

(c) Initialize each of the following.

minIters = minimum number of re-estimation iterations
ε = threshold representing negligible improvement in model
iters = 0
oldLogProb = $-\infty$

3. Forward algorithm or α-pass

```
// compute α₀(i)
c₀ = 0
for i = 0 to N − 1
    α₀(i) = πᵢbᵢ(𝒪₀)
    c₀ = c₀ + α₀(i)
next i
// scale the α₀(i)
c₀ = 1/c₀
for i = 0 to N − 1
    α₀(i) = c₀α₀(i)
next i
// compute αₜ(i)
for t = 1 to T − 1
    cₜ = 0
    for i = 0 to N − 1
        αₜ(i) = 0
        for j = 0 to N − 1
            αₜ(i) = αₜ(i) + αₜ₋₁(j)aⱼᵢ
        next j
        αₜ(i) = αₜ(i)bᵢ(𝒪ₜ)
        cₜ = cₜ + αₜ(i)
    next i
    // scale αₜ(i)
    cₜ = 1/cₜ
    for i = 0 to N − 1
        αₜ(i) = cₜαₜ(i)
    next i
next t
```

4. Backward algorithm or β-pass

> // Let $\beta_{T-1}(i) = 1$ scaled by c_{T-1}
> for $i = 0$ to $N - 1$
> $\beta_{T-1}(i) = c_{T-1}$
> next i
> // β-pass
> for $t = T - 2$ to 0 by -1
>   for $i = 0$ to $N - 1$
> $\beta_t(i) = 0$
>   for $j = 0$ to $N - 1$
> $\beta_t(i) = \beta_t(i) + a_{ij} b_j(\mathcal{O}_{t+1}) \beta_{t+1}(j)$
>   next j
>   // scale $\beta_t(i)$ with same scale factor as $\alpha_t(i)$
> $\beta_t(i) = c_t \beta_t(i)$
>   next i
> next t

5. Compute the gammas and di-gammas

> for $t = 0$ to $T - 2$
>   denom $= 0$
>   for $i = 0$ to $N - 1$
>   for $j = 0$ to $N - 1$
>   denom $=$ denom $+ \alpha_t(i) a_{ij} b_j(\mathcal{O}_{t+1}) \beta_{t+1}(j)$
>   next j
>   next i
>   for $i = 0$ to $N - 1$
> $\gamma_t(i) = 0$
>   for $j = 0$ to $N - 1$
> $\gamma_t(i,j) = \big(\alpha_t(i) a_{ij} b_j(\mathcal{O}_{t+1}) \beta_{t+1}(j)\big)/$denom
> $\gamma_t(i) = \gamma_t(i) + \gamma_t(i,j)$
>   next j
>   next i
> next t
> // Special case for $\gamma_{T-1}(i)$
> denom $= 0$
> for $i = 0$ to $N - 1$
>   denom $=$ denom $+ \alpha_{T-1}(i)$
> next i
> for $i = 0$ to $N - 1$
> $\gamma_{T-1}(i) = \alpha_{T-1}(i)/$denom
> next i

6. Re-estimate the model $\lambda = (A, B, \pi)$

```
// re-estimate π
for i = 0 to N − 1
    πᵢ = γ₀(i)
next i
// re-estimate A
for i = 0 to N − 1
    for j = 0 to N − 1
        numer = 0
        denom = 0
        for t = 0 to T − 2
            numer = numer + γₜ(i, j)
            denom = denom + γₜ(i)
        next t
        aᵢⱼ = numer/denom
    next j
next i
// re-estimate B
for i = 0 to N − 1
    for j = 0 to M − 1
        numer = 0
        denom = 0
        for t = 0 to T − 1
            if(𝒪ₜ == j) then
                numer = numer + γₜ(i)
            end if
            denom = denom + γₜ(i)
        next t
        bᵢ(j) = numer/denom
    next j
next i
```

7. Compute $\log\big(P(\mathcal{O}\,|\,\lambda)\big)$

```
logProb = 0
for i = 0 to T − 1
    logProb = logProb + log(cᵢ)
next i
logProb = −logProb
```

8. To iterate or not to iterate, that is the question.

```
iters = iters + 1
δ = |logProb − oldLogProb|
if(iters < minIters or δ > ε) then
    oldLogProb = logProb
    goto 3.
else
    return λ = (A, B, π)
end if
```

2.9   The Bottom Line

Hidden Markov models are powerful, efficient, and extremely useful in practice. Virtually no assumptions need to be made, yet the HMM process can extract significant statistical information from data. Thanks to efficient training and scoring algorithms, HMMs are practical, and they have proven useful in a wide range of applications. Even in cases where the underlying assumption of a (hidden) Markov process is questionable, HMMs are often applied with success. In Chapter 9 we consider selected applications of HMMs. Most of these applications are in the field of information security.

In subsequent chapters, we often compare and contrast other machine learning techniques to HMMs. Consequently, a clear understanding of the material in this chapter is crucial before proceeding with the remainder of the book. The homework problem should help the dedicated reader to clarify any remaining issues. And the applications in Chapter 9 are highly recommended, with the English text example in Section 9.2 being especially highly recommended.

2.10   Problems

> *When faced with a problem you do not understand,*
> *do any part of it you do understand, then look at it again.*
> — Robert Heinlein

1. Suppose that we train an HMM and obtain the model $\lambda = (A, B, \pi)$ where

$$A = \begin{pmatrix} 0.7 & 0.3 \\ 0.4 & 0.6 \end{pmatrix}, \quad B = \begin{pmatrix} 0.1 & 0.4 & 0.5 \\ 0.7 & 0.2 & 0.1 \end{pmatrix}, \quad \pi = \begin{pmatrix} 0.0 & 1.0 \end{pmatrix}.$$

Furthermore, suppose the hidden states correspond to H and C, respectively, while the observations are S, M, and L, which are mapped to 0, 1, and 2, respectively. In this problem, we consider the observation sequence $\mathcal{O} = (\mathcal{O}_0, \mathcal{O}_1, \mathcal{O}_2) = (M, S, L) = (1, 0, 2)$.

a) Directly compute $P(\mathcal{O} \mid \lambda)$. That is, compute

$$P(\mathcal{O} \mid \lambda) = \sum_X P(\mathcal{O}, X \mid \lambda)$$

using the probabilities in $\lambda = (A, B, \pi)$ for each of the following cases, based on the given observation sequence $\mathcal{O}$.

$P(\mathcal{O}, X = HHH) = \underline{} \cdot \underline{} \cdot \underline{} \cdot \underline{} \cdot \underline{} \cdot \underline{} = \underline{}$

$P(\mathcal{O}, X = HHC) = \underline{} \cdot \underline{} \cdot \underline{} \cdot \underline{} \cdot \underline{} \cdot \underline{} = \underline{}$

$P(\mathcal{O}, X = HCH) = \underline{} \cdot \underline{} \cdot \underline{} \cdot \underline{} \cdot \underline{} \cdot \underline{} = \underline{}$

$P(\mathcal{O}, X = HCC) = \underline{} \cdot \underline{} \cdot \underline{} \cdot \underline{} \cdot \underline{} \cdot \underline{} = \underline{}$

$P(\mathcal{O}, X = CHH) = \underline{} \cdot \underline{} \cdot \underline{} \cdot \underline{} \cdot \underline{} \cdot \underline{} = \underline{}$

$P(\mathcal{O}, X = CHC) = \underline{} \cdot \underline{} \cdot \underline{} \cdot \underline{} \cdot \underline{} \cdot \underline{} = \underline{}$

$P(\mathcal{O}, X = CCH) = \underline{1.0} \cdot \underline{0.2} \cdot \underline{0.6} \cdot \underline{0.7} \cdot \underline{0.4} \cdot \underline{0.5} = \underline{}$

$P(\mathcal{O}, X = CCC) = \underline{} \cdot \underline{} \cdot \underline{} \cdot \underline{} \cdot \underline{} \cdot \underline{} = \underline{}$

The desired probability is the sum of these eight probabilities.

b) Compute $P(\mathcal{O} \mid \lambda)$ using the α pass. That is, compute

$\alpha_0(0) = \underline{} \cdot \underline{} = \underline{}$

$\alpha_0(1) = \underline{1.0} \cdot \underline{0.2} = \underline{}$

$\alpha_1(0) = (\underline{} \cdot \underline{} + \underline{} \cdot \underline{}) \cdot \underline{} = \underline{}$

$\alpha_1(1) = (\underline{} \cdot \underline{} + \underline{} \cdot \underline{}) \cdot \underline{} = \underline{}$

$\alpha_2(0) = (\underline{} \cdot \underline{} + \underline{} \cdot \underline{}) \cdot \underline{} = \underline{}$

$\alpha_2(1) = (\underline{} \cdot \underline{} + \underline{} \cdot \underline{}) \cdot \underline{} = \underline{}$

where we initialize

$$\alpha_0(i) = \pi_i b_i(\mathcal{O}_0), \text{ for } i = 0, 1, \ldots, N - 1$$

and the recurrence is

$$\alpha_t(i) = \left(\sum_{j=0}^{N-1} \alpha_{t-1}(j) a_{ji} \right) b_i(\mathcal{O}_t)$$

for $t = 1, 2, \ldots, T-1$ and $i = 0, 1, \ldots, N-1$. The desired probability is given by

$$P(\mathcal{O} \mid \lambda) = \sum_{i=0}^{N-1} \alpha_{T-1}(i).$$

c) In terms of N and T, and counting only multiplications, what is the work factor for the method in part a)? What is the work factor for the method in part b)?

2. For this problem, use the same model λ and observation sequence $\mathcal{O}$ given in Problem 1.

   a) Determine the best hidden state sequence (X_0, X_1, X_2) in the dynamic programming sense.

   b) Determine the best hidden state sequence (X_0, X_1, X_2) in the HMM sense.

3. Summing the numbers in the "probability" column of Table 2.2, we find $P(\mathcal{O} \mid \lambda) = 0.009629$ for $\mathcal{O} = (0, 1, 0, 2)$.

   a) By a similar direct calculation, compute $P(\mathcal{O} \mid \lambda)$ for each observation sequence of the form $\mathcal{O} = (\mathcal{O}_0, \mathcal{O}_1, \mathcal{O}_2, \mathcal{O}_3)$, where $\mathcal{O}_i \in \{0, 1, 2\}$. Verify that $\sum P(\mathcal{O} \mid \lambda) = 1$, where the sum is over the observation sequences of length four. Note that you will need to use the probabilities for A, B, and π given in equations (2.4), (2.5), and (2.6) in Section 2.2, respectively.

   b) Use the forward algorithm to compute $P(\mathcal{O} \mid \lambda)$ for the same observation sequences and model as in part a). Verify that you obtain the same results as in part a).

4. From equation (2.9) and the definition of $\alpha_t(i)$ in equation (2.10), it follows that

$$\alpha_t(i) = \sum_X \pi_{X_0} b_{X_0}(\mathcal{O}_0) a_{X_0, X_1} b_{X_1}(\mathcal{O}_1) \cdots a_{X_{t-2}, X_{t-1}} b_{X_{t-1}}(\mathcal{O}_{t-1}) a_{X_{t-1}, i} b_i(\mathcal{O}_t)$$

where $X = (X_0, X_1, \ldots, X_{t-1})$. Use this expression for $\alpha_t(i)$ to directly verify the forward algorithm recurrence

$$\alpha_t(i) = \left(\sum_{j=0}^{N-1} \alpha_{t-1}(j) a_{ji} \right) b_i(\mathcal{O}_t).$$

5. As discussed in this chapter, the forward algorithm is used solve HMM Problem 1, while the forward algorithm and backward algorithm together are used to compute the gammas, which are then used to solve HMM Problem 2.

   a) Explain how you can solve HMM Problem 1 using the backward algorithm instead of the forward algorithm.

b) Using the model $\lambda = (A, B, \pi)$ and the observation sequence $\mathcal{O}$ in Problem 1, compute $P(\mathcal{O}|\lambda)$ using the backward algorithm, and verify that you obtain the same result as when using the forward algorithm.

6. This problem deals with the Baum-Welch re-estimation algorithm.

a) Write the re-estimation formulae, as given in lines 3, 7, and 12 of Algorithm 2.3, directly in terms of the $\alpha_t(i)$ and $\beta_t(i)$.

b) Using the re-estimation formulae obtained in part a), substitute the scaled values $\widehat{\alpha}_t(i)$ and $\widehat{\beta}_t(i)$ for $\alpha_t(i)$ and $\beta_t(i)$, respectively, and show that the resulting re-estimation formulae are exact.

7. Instead of using c_t to scale the $\beta_t(i)$, we can scale each $\beta_t(i)$ by

$$d_t = 1 \Big/ \sum_{j=0}^{N-1} \widetilde{\beta}_t(j)$$

where the definition of $\widetilde{\beta}_t(i)$ is analogous to that of $\widetilde{\alpha}_t(i)$ as given in Algorithm 2.6.

a) Using the scaling factors c_t and d_t show that the Baum-Welch re-estimation formulae in Algorithm 2.3 are exact with $\widehat{\alpha}$ and $\widehat{\beta}$ in place of α and β.

b) Write $\log\big(P(\mathcal{O}|\lambda)\big)$ in terms of c_t and d_t.

8. When training, the elements of λ can be initialized to approximately uniform. That is, we let $\pi_i \approx 1/N$ and $a_{ij} \approx 1/N$ and $b_j(k) \approx 1/M$, subject to the row stochastic conditions. In Section 2.5.3, it is stated that it is a bad idea to initialize the values to exactly uniform, since the HMM would be stuck at a local maximum and hence it could not climb to an improved solution. Suppose that $\pi_i = 1/N$ and $a_{ij} = 1/N$ and $b_j(k) = 1/M$. Verify that the re-estimation process leaves all of these values unchanged.

9. In this problem, we consider generalizations of the HMM formulation discussed in this chapter.

a) Consider an HMM where the state transition matrix is time dependent. Then for each t, there is an $N \times N$ row-stochastic $A_t = \{a_{ij}^t\}$ that is used in place of A in the HMM computations. For such an HMM, provide pseudo-code to solve HMM Problem 1.

b) Consider an HMM of order two, that is, an HMM where the underlying Markov process is of order two. Then the state at time t depends on the states at time $t - 1$ and $t - 2$. For such an HMM, provide pseudo-code to solve HMM Problem 1.

10. Write an HMM program for the English text problem in Section 9.2 of Chapter 9. Test your program on each of the following cases.

   a) There are $N = 2$ hidden states. Explain your results.

   b) There are $N = 3$ hidden states. Explain your results.

   c) There are $N = 4$ hidden states. Explain your results.

   d) There are $N = 26$ hidden states. Explain your results.

11. In this problem, you will use an HMM to break a simple substitution ciphertext message. For each HMM, train using 200 iterations of the Baum-Welch re-estimation algorithm.

   a) Obtain an English plaintext message of 50,000 plaintext characters, where the characters consist only of lower case a through z (i.e., remove all punctuation, special characters, and spaces, and convert all upper case to lower case). Encrypt this plaintext using a randomly generated shift of the alphabet. Remember the key.

   b) Train an HMM with $N = 2$ and $M = 26$ on your ciphetext from part a). From the final B matrix, determine the ciphertext letters that correspond to consonants and vowels.

   c) Generate a digraph frequency matrix A for English text, where a_{ij} is the count of the number of times that letter i is followed by letter j. Here, we assume that a is letter 0, b is letter 1, c is letter 2, and so on. This matrix must be based on 1,000,000 characters where, as above, only the 26 letters of the alphabet are used. Next, add five to each element in your 26×26 matrix A. Finally, normalize your matrix A by dividing each element by its row sum. The resulting matrix A will be row stochastic, and it will not contain any 0 probabilities.

   d) Train an HMM with $N = M = 26$, using the first 1000 characters of ciphertext you generated in part a), where the A matrix is initialized with your A matrix from part c). Also, in your HMM, do not re-estimate A. Use the final B matrix to determine a putative key and give the fraction of putative key elements that match the actual key (as a decimal, to four places). For example, if 22 of the 26 key positions are correct, then your answer would be $22/26 = 0.8462$.

12. Write an HMM program to solve the problem discussed in Section 9.2, replacing English text with the following.

   a) French text.

   b) Russian text.

   c) Chinese text.

13. Perform an HMM analysis similar to that discussed in Section 9.2, replacing English with "Hamptonese," the mysterious writing system developed by James Hampton. For information on Hamptonese, see

    http://www.cs.sjsu.edu/faculty/stamp/Hampton/hampton.html

14. Since HMM training is a hill climb, we are only assured of reaching a local maximum. And, as with any hill climb, the specific local maximum that we find will depend on our choice of initial values. Therefore, by training a hidden Markov model multiple times with different initial values, we would expect to obtain better results than when training only once.

    In the paper [16], the authors use an expectation maximization (EM) approach with multiple random restarts as a means of attacking homophonic substitution ciphers. An analogous HMM-based technique is analyzed in the report [158], where the effectiveness of multiple random restarts on simple substitution cryptanalysis is explored in detail. Multiple random restarts are especially helpful in the most challenging cases, that is, when little data (i.e., ciphertext) is available. However, the tradeoff is that the work factor can be high, since the number of restarts required may be very large (millions of random restarts are required in some cases).

    a) Obtain an English plaintext message consisting of 1000 plaintext characters, consisting only of lower case a through z (i.e., remove all punctuation, special characters, and spaces, and convert all upper case letters to lower case). Encrypt this plaintext using a randomly selected shift of the alphabet. Remember the key. Also generate a digraph frequency matrix A, as discussed in part c) of Problem 11.

    b) Train n HMMs, for each of $n = 1$, $n = 10$, $n = 100$, and $n = 1000$, following the same process as in Problem 11, part d), but using the $T = 1000$ observations generated in part a) of this problem. For a given n select the best result based on the model scores and give the fraction of the putative key that is correct, calculated as in Problem 11, part d).

    c) Repeat part b), but only use the first $T = 400$ observations.

    d) Repeat part c), but only use the first $T = 300$ observations.

15. The Zodiac Killer murdered at least five people in the San Francisco Bay Area in the late 1960s and early 1970s. Although police had a prime suspect, no arrest was ever made and the murders remain officially unsolved. The killer sent several messages to the police and to local newspapers, taunting police for their failure to catch him. One of these

messages contained a homophonic substitution consisting of 408 strange symbols.[7] Not surprisingly, this cipher is known as the Zodiac 408. Within days of its release, the Zodiac 408 was broken by Donald and Bettye Harden, who were schoolteachers from Salinas, California. The Zodiac 408 ciphertext is given below on the left, while the corresponding plaintext appears on the right.

```
I L I K E K I L L I N G P E O P L
E B E C A U S E I T I S S O M U C
H F U N I T I S M O R E F U N T H
A N K I L L I N G W I L D G A M E
I N T H E F O R R E S T B E C A U
S E M A N I S T H E M O S T D A N
G E R O U E A N A M A L O F A L L
T O K I L L S O M E T H I N G G I
V E S M E T H E M O S T T H R I L
L I N G E X P E R E N C E I T I S
E V E N B E T T E R T H A N G E T
T I N G Y O U R R O C K S O F F W
I T H A G I R L T H E B E S T P A
R T O F I T I S T H A E W H E N I
D I E I W I L L B E R E B O R N I
N P A R A D I C E A N D A L L T H
E I H A V E K I L L E D W I L L B
E C O M E M Y S L A V E S I W I L
L N O T G I V E Y O U M Y N A M E
B E C A U S E Y O U W I L L T R Y
T O S L O I D O W N O R A T O P M
Y C O L L E C T I O G O F S L A V
E S F O R M Y A F T E R L I F E E
B E O R I E T E M E T H H P I T I
```

Note the (apparently intentional) misspellings in the plaintext, including "FORREST", "ANAMAL", and so on. Also, the final 18 characters (underlined in the plaintext above) appear to be random filler.

a) Solve the Zodiac 408 cipher using the HMM approach discussed in Section 9.4. Initialize the A matrix as in part c) of Problem 11, and do not re-estimate A. Use 1000 random restarts of the HMM, and 200 iterations of Baum-Welch re-estimation in each case. Give your answer as the percentage of characters of the actual plaintext that are recovered correctly.

b) Repeat part a), but use 10,000 random restarts.

c) Repeat part b), but use 100,000 random restarts.

d) Repeat part c), but use 1,000,000 random restarts.

---

[7]The Zodiac 408 ciphertext was actually sent in three parts to local newspapers. Here, we give the complete message, where the three parts have been combined into one. Also, a homophonic substitution is like a simple substitution, except that the mapping is many-to-one, that is, multiple ciphertext symbols can map to one plaintext symbol.

e) Repeat part a), except also re-estimate the A matrix.

f) Repeat part b), except also re-estimate the A matrix.

g) Repeat part c), except also re-estimate the A matrix.

h) Repeat part d), except also re-estimate the A matrix.

16. In addition to the Zodiac 408 cipher, the Zodiac Killer (see Problem 15) released a similar-looking cipher with 340 symbols. This cipher is known as the Zodiac 340 and remains unsolved to this day.[8] The ciphertext is given below.

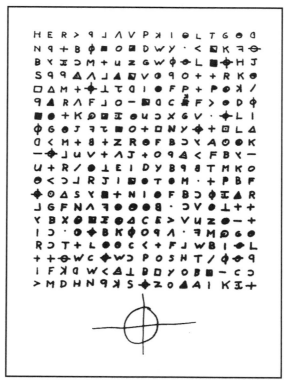

a) Repeat Problem 15, parts a) through d), using the Zodiac 340 in place of the Zodiac 408. Since the plaintext is unknown, in each case, simply print the decryption obtained from your highest scoring model.

b) Repeat part a) of this problem, except use parts e) through h) of Problem 15.

---

[8]It is possible that the Zodiac 340 is not a cipher at all, but instead just a random collection of symbols designed to frustrate would-be cryptanalysts. If that's the case, your easily frustrated author can confirm that the "cipher" has been wildly successful.

Chapter 3

A Full Frontal View of Profile Hidden Markov Models

The sciences do not try to explain,
they hardly even try to interpret,
they mainly make models.
— John von Neumann

3.1 Introduction

Here, we introduce the concept of a profile hidden Markov model (PHMM). The material in this chapter builds directly on Chapter 2 and we'll assume that the reader has a good understanding of HMMs.

Recall that the key reason that HMMs are so popular and useful is that there are efficient algorithms to solve each of the three problems that arise—training, scoring, and uncovering the hidden states. But, there are significant restrictions inherent in the HMM formulation, which limit the usefulness of HMMs in some important applications.

Perhaps the most significant limitation of an HMM is the Markov assumption, that is, the current state depends only on the previous state. The time-invariant nature of an HMM is a closely related issue.[1] These limitations make the HMM algorithms fast and efficient, but they prevent us from making use of positional information within observation sequences. For some types of problems, such information is critically important.

---

[1] According to your self-referential author's comments in Chapter 2, we can consider higher order Markov processes, in which case the current state can depend on n consecutive previous states. But, the machinery becomes unwieldy, even for relatively small n. And, even if we consider higher order Markov processes, we still treat all positions in the sequence the same, as this only changes how far back in history we look.

A PHMM can be viewed as a series of HMMs where, in effect, we define a new B matrix at each offset in the training data. Recall from Chapter 2 that for an HMM, the B matrix contains probability distributions that relate the observations to the hidden states. Furthermore, in an HMM, the B matrix represents the average behavior over the training sequence. By having multiple B matrices, in a PHMM we can make explicit use of positional information contained in training sequences. But, before we can determine such B matrices, we must first align multiple training sequences. In contrast, for an HMM there is no need to align training sequences, since the position within a sequence—relative to other training sequences—is irrelevant. Consequently, for an HMM we can (and do) simply append the training data into one long observation super-sequence. But, when training a PHMM, alignment of multiple observation sequences is at the very heart of the technique.

Another potential issue with HMMs is that we do not explicitly account for insertions or deletions that might occur relative to the training sequence. Generally, this is not a problem with HMMs, since the technique is statistical in nature, and the average behavior will not be significantly affected by a few insertions or deletions. However, if we do want to account for positional information—as in a PHMM—then we'll need to deal explicitly with the possibility of insertions and deletions, since a single insertion or deletion could cause two otherwise similar sequences to align badly. Again, with a standard hidden Markov model, extraneous elements (i.e., insertions) or "missing" elements (i.e., deletions) within a sequence are ignored when training and scoring, since a small number of such elements will have a negligible impact on the resulting model.

Aligning the observation sequences is the most challenging part of training a profile hidden Markov model. Although there are many ways to align multiple sequences, doing so efficiently and in a reasonably stable manner is certainly challenging. But, once we have aligned the sequences, computing the matrices that define the actual PHMM is trivial. In this sense, the PHMM training process is virtually the opposite of that used in an HMM. When training an HMM, we simply append observation sequence, which can be viewed as a trivial "alignment," but when determining the matrices that define the HMM, clever algorithms (forward algorithm, backwards algorithm, and Baum-Welch re-estimation) are used. In contrast, when training a PHMM, we use clever algorithms to align the training sequences, but once this has been done, constructing the PHMM matrices is easy.

In this chapter, we first provide an overview of PHMMs. Then we consider a few simple examples to illustrate important aspects of the technique. In particular, we focus on sequence alignment, since that is the most challenging aspect of training a PHMM. In Chapter 10, we consider realistic applications of PHMMs to problems in information security, including malware detection and masquerade detection.

3.2   Overview and Notation

To train a PHMM, we must first construct a multiple sequence alignment (MSA) from a set of training sequences. As the name suggests, an MSA consists of an alignment of several different (training) sequences. Finding an optimal simultaneous alignment of multiple sequences is computationally infeasible, so instead we'll first determine pairwise alignments and then combine the pairwise alignments into an MSA.

When aligning sequences in a PHMM, we allow gaps to be introduced, which enables us to align more symbols. However, the more gaps that are present, the easier it is for a sequence to match during the scoring phase, and hence the less specific—and the less informative—is the resulting model. Therefore, we want to penalize gaps. In addition, certain matches might be better than other types of matches, and a near miss should be penalized less than a bad miss. To account for such cases, we employ a substitution matrix, which is discussed in more detail below. But, before we turn our attention to the detail of pairwise alignment and MSA construction, we discuss PHMM notation, which differs significantly from the notation used for HMMs.

For the remainder of this section, we'll only consider PHMM state transitions, which correspond to the elements of the A matrix in an HMM. For now, we do not deal with emission[2] probabilities, which correspond to the B matrix in an HMM. Before we can sensibly discuss emissions, we need to fully develop the ideas behind pairwise alignments and multiple sequence alignments—topics that we'll cover in Sections 3.3 and 3.4, respectively.

In a PHMM, we'll distinguish between three types of states, namely, match, insert, and delete states. A *match state* is essentially equivalent to a state in a standard HMM, while insert and delete states arise from allowing insertions and deletions when aligning sequences. This will all be made more precise below, but first let's consider the simplest case, where every state in the MSA is a match state. Then the state transitions are entirely straightforward—in Figure 3.1, we illustrate a PHMM that has $N = 4$ match states, and no insert or delete states. Again, the diagram in Figure 3.1 only deals with state transitions, and does not include any information about emissions. Also, for notational convenience, we'll sometimes refer to the begin state as M_0 and the end state as M_{N+1}.

Figure 3.1: PHMM without gaps

---

[2]PHMM emissions are the same as HMM observations.

In most real-world applications, we need to insert gaps into an MSA when aligning sequences. If we have too many gaps, then the emissions probabilities are unreliable. We refer to such an unreliable position as an *insert state*. Note that an insert state can follow a match state (or the begin state) and that multiple insertions can occur before we transition to the next match state. When including both match and insert states, we can model PHMM state transitions as illustrated in Figure 3.2.

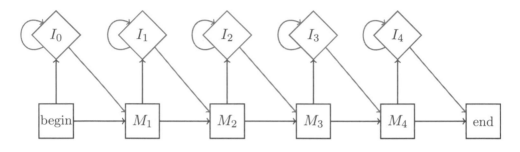

Figure 3.2: PHMM with insertions

Note that in the pure-match PHMM in Figure 3.1, we always transition from match state M_i to match state M_{i+1}. However, when insert states are also included, as in Figure 3.2, we now have the possibility of multiple transitions from each state, and hence the transitions themselves are probabilistic. This is a major modification, as compared to an HMM.

A *delete state* is a state where no emission occurs. We model each deletion as skipping a match state, and hence consecutive deletions correspond to skipping consecutive match states.[3] In addition, after a deletion (or series of deletions), we must transition to an emission state and, consequently, only a match (or insert) state can follow a delete state.

In Figure 3.3, we illustrate a PHMM that includes both match and delete states. As with a PHMM that includes insertions, this simplified PHMM allows for different types of state transitions.

Generically, a PHMM includes match, insert, and delete states, as illustrated in Figure 3.4. This illustration is essentially the PHMM equivalent of the hidden states (and transitions) in an HMM. The rather complicated illustration in Figure 3.4 only accounts for the state transitions in the PHMM, and does not include any information about emissions. In comparison to the generic HMM illustrated in Figure 2.1 of Chapter 2, the PHMM illustration in Figure 3.4 only deals with the hidden part of the model. That is, Figure 3.4 only deals with the structure of the A matrix in a PHMM.

---

[3]Actually, a deletion can skip a match or insert state, or some combination thereof. However, we'll keep things simple at this point, and only consider the interaction between match and delete states.

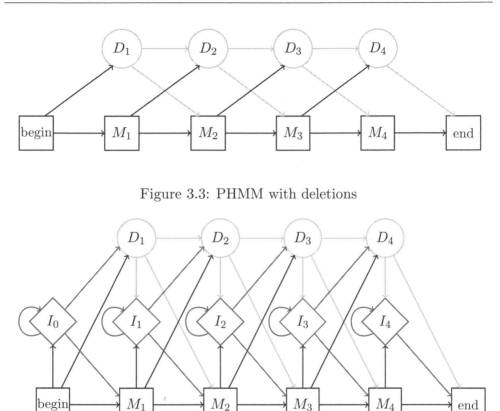

Figure 3.3: PHMM with deletions

Figure 3.4: Profile hidden Markov model

The standard notation for a PHMM [47] is summarized in Table 3.1. Note that the A matrix includes all of the transitions that are illustrated in Figure 3.4. That is, in addition to transitions of the type $a_{M_i M_{i+1}}$, we have match-to-delete transitions $a_{M_i D_{i+1}}$, insert-to-match transitions $a_{I_i M_i}$, delete-to-insert transitions $a_{D_i I_{i+1}}$, and so on.

It may be instructive to compare the PHMM notation in Table 3.1 to the standard HMM notation, which is given in Table 2.1 in Chapter 2. In an HMM, we refer to observed symbols, while a PHMM has emitted symbols. In a PHMM (as with an HMM), we associate the emitted (observed) symbols with integers. There are many other similarities and a few notable differences that should become clear in the discussion below.

Next, we turn our attention to generating pairwise alignments. Then we consider the process of constructing a multiple sequence alignment (MSA) from a collection of pairwise alignments, and we show how to generate the PHMM matrices from an MSA. Finally, we consider PHMM scoring, which is slightly more complex than scoring with an HMM, due primarily to the greater complexity in the state transitions.

Table 3.1: PHMM notation

Notation	Explanation
X	Emitted symbols, $X_1, X_2, \ldots, X_m$, where $m \leq N + 1$
N	Number of states
M	Match states, $M_1, M_2, \ldots, M_N$
I	Insert states, $I_0, I_1, \ldots, I_N$
D	Delete states, $D_1, D_2, \ldots, D_N$
π	Initial state distribution
A	State transition probability matrix
$a_{M_i M_{i+1}}$	Transition probability from M_i to M_{i+1}
E	Emission probability matrix
$\varepsilon_{M_i}(k)$	Emission probability of symbol k at state M_i
λ	The PHMM, $\lambda = (A, E, \pi)$

3.3 Pairwise Alignment

To train a PHMM, we need an MSA, which we'll construct from a collection of pairwise alignments. Consequently, we'll first consider a method to align a pair of sequences from a given training set.

Ideally, we would like to globally align a pair of sequences, that is, we want an alignment that accounts for as many elements as possible. However, we also want to minimize the number of gaps that are inserted, since gaps tend to weaken the resulting alignment by making it more generic. By using a local alignment strategy instead of a global approach, we can often significantly reduce the number of gaps. The tradeoff is that a local alignment may not utilize all of the information available in the sequences.

To simplify the local alignment problem, we'll illustrate such an alignment where only the initial and ending parts of the sequences can remain unaligned. For example, suppose that we want to align the sequences

CBCBJILIIJEJE and GCBJIIIJJEG.

In Table 3.2 we give a global alignment of these sequences, and we illustrate a local alignment where the initial and final parts of the sequences are not aligned. Note that we use "-" to represent an inserted gap, while "*" is an omitted symbol (i.e., omitted from consideration in the local alignment), and "|" indicates that the corresponding elements are aligned.

For the global alignment in Table 3.2, we are able to align nine out of fifteen of the positions (i.e., 60%), while for the local alignment, eight of the ten positions under consideration are correctly aligned (80%). Consequently, the model resulting from this local alignment is likely to be more faithful to

Table 3.2: Global vs local alignment

Unaligned sequences	`CBCBJILIIJEJE` `GCBJIIIJJEG`

Global alignment	`-CBCBJILIIJEJE-`
	`   I   III III II`
	`GC--BJI-IIJ-JEG`

Local alignment	`***CBJILII-JE**`
	`   IIII II II`
	`***CBJI-IIJJE**`

the training data—and, in a sense, stronger—as compared to the model we obtain from the global alignment. Therefore, in practice we'll most likely want to consider local alignments. However, to simplify the presentation, in the remainder of this chapter, we only consider global alignments.

To construct a pairwise alignment, it's standard practice to use dynamic programming. For dynamic programming (see Section 2.6 of Chapter 2), we must have meaningful scores when comparing elements. In the context of sequence alignment, we'll specify an $n \times n$ substitution matrix S, where n is the number of distinct symbols.

For example, consider the problem of masquerade detection [61], where we want to detect an attacker who has gained access to a legitimate user's account. Such an attacker might try to evade detection by masquerading as the legitimate user. That is, the attacker might attempt to behave in almost the same manner as the legitimate user, so as to avoid triggering any warning based on unusual activity. Suppose that in a simplified masquerade detection system, we monitor the four operations in Table 3.3.

Table 3.3: Masquerade detection example

Notation	Explanation
E	Send email
G	Play games
C	C programming
J	Java programming

In a masquerade detection system, we'll collect information from an active user and compare the user's behavior to the expected behavior of the currently logged-in user. If the behavior differs significantly, then we flag the user as a possible intruder. To employ a PHMM in such a detection system, we would first need to collect sequences representing typical usage patterns for the user whose behavior we want to model. Training the PHMM would include constructing an MSA from the resulting sequences. To construct such an MSA, we first construct pairwise alignments using dynamic programming, and such a dynamic program relies on a substitution matrix S.

For the operations given in Table 3.3, it would seem reasonable to consider C programming and Java programming as more similar than, say, game playing and programming. Under these (and similar) assumptions, a plausible substitution matrix S might be

$$
\begin{array}{c|cccc}
  & E & G & C & J \\
\hline
E & 9 & -4 & 2 & 2 \\
G & -4 & 9 & -5 & -5 \\
C & 2 & -5 & 10 & 7 \\
J & 2 & -5 & 7 & 10 \\
\end{array}
\tag{3.1}
$$

The substitution matrix in (3.1) penalizes a transition from email to game playing (or vice versa), for example, but not a transition from C programming to Java programming.

In an application such as DNA sequencing, the substitution matrix S could be based on well-established biological principles. However, in many applications, a useful substitution matrix can be difficult to ascertain. For example, the problem of masquerade detection based on UNIX commands has been widely studied [61]. For this problem, the matrix S specifies relationships between UNIX commands—information that may not be easily quantified.

As mentioned previously, we allow gaps to be inserted when aligning sequences, but gaps tend to weaken the resulting model. Consequently, in addition to a substitution matrix S, we also define a gap penalty function. Two generic types of gap penalties functions are often used. The simplest of these is a *linear gap penalty* of the form

$$
g(x) = ax \tag{3.2}
$$

where x is the length of the gap. A linear function implies that the penalty for each gap inserted is the same. In contrast, an *affine gap penalty* is of the form

$$
g(x) = a + b(x - 1). \tag{3.3}
$$

In the affine case, a is the cost to open a gap, while b is the cost of extending an existing gap one more position. An affine gap penalty function could be used, for example, to penalize the opening of a gap more severely than the continuation of an existing gap. Of course, if we choose $a = b$ in equation (3.3) then we obtain the linear gap penalty function in equation (3.2).

A substitution matrix S and a gap penalty function g together determine the tradeoff between inserting gaps into an alignment, as opposed to allowing a misalignment between symbols. An example of a pairwise alignment that includes both gaps and misalignments appears in Table 3.4.

Table 3.4: Example of a pairwise alignment [9]

Unaligned sequences
AABNBAFCDBAAEAABCEDAEQCDABABBAF4NBBMBTYBAAAAABBCD
AABBAFCDBAAEAOACEDAEQAABCDBALF4BBASBAAAAFBABCCD

Alignment with gaps
AABNBAFCDBAAEA-ABCEDAEQCD-ABABBA-F4NBBMBTY--BAAAA--ABB-CD
AAB-BAFCDBAAEAOA-CEDAEQ--AABCDBALF4-BB----ASBAAAAFBAB-CCD

Given a pair of sequences, a substitution matrix S, and a gap penalty function, we can align the sequences via dynamic programming. We'll use the notation in Table 3.5 when describing the dynamic program used for pairwise alignment.

Table 3.5: PHMM pairwise alignment

Notation	Explanation
X	First sequence to align, $(X_1, X_2, \ldots, X_n)$
Y	Second sequence to align, $(Y_1, Y_2, \ldots, Y_m)$
$Z_{i\ldots j}$	Subsequence $Z_i, Z_{i+1}, \ldots, Z_j$ of sequence Z
$s(p, q)$	Score (or penalty) when substituting symbol p for q
$g(n)$	Cost of extending gap of length $n - 1$
F, G	Matrices of size $n + 1 \times m + 1$
$F(i, j)$	Optimal score for aligning $X_{1\ldots i}$ with $Y_{1\ldots j}$
$G(i, j)$	Number of gaps used to generate $F(i, j)$

The dynamic program is initialized with

$$G(i, 0) = F(i, 0) = 0$$
$$G(0, j) = j$$
$$F(0, j) = \sum_{n=1}^{j} g(n).$$

Note that $F(0, j)$ is the cost (or penalty) associated with aligning j gaps.

The dynamic program recursion is given by

$$F(i,j) = \max \begin{cases} F(i-1,j-1) + s(X_i, Y_j) & \text{case 1} \\ F(i-1,j) + g(G(i-1,j)) & \text{case 2} \\ F(i,j-1) + g(G(i,j-1)) & \text{case 3} \end{cases} \qquad (3.4)$$

where the function $G(i,j)$ is defined by

$$G(i,j) = \begin{cases} 0 & \text{if case 1 holds} \\ G(i-1,j) + 1 & \text{if case 2 holds} \\ G(i,j-1) + 1 & \text{if case 3 holds} \end{cases}$$

where we say that case i "holds," provided that it's the case that yields the max in (3.4). This dynamic program will determine the optimal alignment, in the sense of the highest scoring overall path,[4] relative to the specified substitution matrix S and gap penalty function g.

3.4   Multiple Sequence Alignment

We can use the dynamic programming method discussed above to construct a pairwise alignment for any two training sequences. Now we'll address the problem of constructing an MSA from a collection of pairwise alignments.

For efficiency, we'll use a *progressive alignment* strategy to construct the MSA. That is, we'll start with one pair of aligned sequences and merge it with another aligned pair, and merge that result with another, and so on. At each step in this process, we include one more sequence into the MSA, until all training sequences have been included. The advantage of a progressive approach is that it's far more efficient than aligning multiple sequences simultaneously. However, one significant disadvantage of progressive alignment is that it is likely to be unstable, in the sense that the order in which the pairwise alignments are considered can have a major impact on the resulting MSA. Of particular concern is that the order can affect the number of gaps that are inserted into the MSA, and we generally want to minimize gaps.

Many different progressive alignment strategies are possible. Here, we discuss an approach based on the Feng-Doolittle algorithm [51].

To construct an MSA, we proceed as follows, where we assume that we are given a set of n training sequences, a substitution matrix S, and a gap penalty function g.

1. Compute pairwise alignments for all $\binom{n}{2}$ pairs of sequences in the training set using dynamic programming, as described in Section 3.3. For

---

[4]Alternatively, we could use an HMM to construct pairwise alignments. Recall from Chapter 2 that an HMM maximizes the expected number of correct states, as opposed to finding the highest-scoring overall path.

each pairwise alignment, we retain the score from the dynamic program that was used to generate the alignment—the higher the score, the better the alignment.

2. Select a set of $n - 1$ pairwise alignments that includes all n sequences from the original training set, and maximizes the sum of the pairwise alignment scores.

3. Use Prim's algorithm [111] to generate a minimum spanning tree for these $n - 1$ pairwise alignments, based on their pairwise alignment scores.

4. Add pairwise alignments to the MSA based on the spanning tree (from highest score to lowest score), inserting gaps as needed.

The gap penalty function g that was used for pairwise alignment is also used during the MSA construction.

For example, suppose we have ten training sequences that yield the pairwise alignment scores in Table 3.6. That is, element (i, j) in Table 3.6 is the score obtained from the dynamic program when aligning training sequence i with training sequence j.

Table 3.6: Example of pairwise alignment scores

	1	2	3	4	5	6	7	8	9	10
1	—	85	63	74	70	84	61	57	62	70
2	85	—	79	73	66	59	94	61	59	51
3	63	79	—	75	68	60	55	85	52	65
4	74	73	75	—	105	54	60	78	59	53
5	70	66	68	105	—	40	61	79	58	39
6	84	59	60	54	40	—	68	45	75	78
7	61	94	55	60	61	68	—	64	72	42
8	57	61	85	78	79	45	64	—	50	70
9	62	59	52	59	58	75	72	50	—	81
10	70	51	65	53	39	78	42	70	81	—

We then select a set of nine of these pairs so that each of the ten sequences is included at least once, while maximizing the sum of the corresponding scores. Based on the scores in Table 3.6, we find that the set

$$\{(4,5), (2,7), (1,2), (3,8), (1,6), (9,10), (2,3), (5,8), (6,10)\}$$

satisfies the criteria—all sequences are included and the sum of the pairwise alignment scores is maximized. The minimum spanning tree corresponding to these pairwise alignments is given in Figure 3.5, where the nodes are labeled with the training sequence number, and the edges are labeled with pairwise alignment scores.

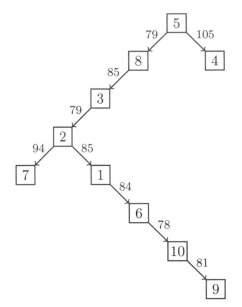

Figure 3.5: Minimum spanning tree

At this point, we have constructed a minimum spanning tree that includes every sequence in the training set. This spanning tree will now be used to generate the MSA which, in turn, will enable us to easily determine the PHMM.

To generate an MSA from a minimum spanning tree we start with the pairwise alignment at the root. Then we traverse the tree, adding the specified new sequence into the alignment at each step. For the example in Figure 3.5, we consider the pairwise alignments in the order

$$(5,4), (5,8), (8,3), (3,2), (2,7), (2,1), (1,6), (6,10), (10,9).$$

With the exception of the initial pair, one new sequence is added to the MSA at each step.

One step in the MSA construction is illustrated in Table 3.7. At this particular step, we have already included sequences 5, 4, 8, and 3, based on the pairwise alignments

$$(5,4), \quad (5,8), \quad \text{and} \quad (8,3)$$

and we are in the process of adding sequence 2, based on the pairwise alignment $(3,2)$. At the intermediate steps, we use the notation "+" to represent gaps that are inserted to align the new sequence with the existing MSA. This is in contrast to the symbol "−", which we reserve for gaps in the pairwise alignments. The final MSA appears in Table 3.8, where all gaps are again indicated using the symbol "−". Be sure to note that gaps have proliferated as we have included more sequences into the progressive alignment. For additional details on this specific MSA, see the paper [9].

Table 3.7: Snapshots of MSA construction

Sequence	MSA at intermediate step
	Alignment
5	`CDABBAFCDB1AAEAA+CEDA+EQ+CDABABABALF4LBBAFBSBAAAAA`
4	`2AABBAFCDABA+EAABCEDCDEQFCDABA+APALF4+BBA++SBAAAAA`
8	`++AABA+CDB+AAEAA+CEDCDEQ+CDABPBA+ABF4+BBAFBSBMAAAA`
3	`A+ABBAFCDABA+EAA+CEDCDEQA++ABFBAN++F4+BBAFBTYBAAAA`

Sequence	Next pairwise alignment
	Alignment
2	`A-ABNBAFCD-BAAEAABCEDA-EQ-CDABAB--BAF4NBBM-BTYBAAAA`
3	`A+AB-BAFCDABA+EAA+CEDCDEQA++ABFBAN++F4+BBAFBTYBAAAA`

Sequence	MSA after including sequence 2
	Alignment
5	`CDAB+BAFCDB1AAEAA+CEDA+EQ+CDABABABALF4LBBAFBSBAAAAA`
4	`2AAB+BAFCDABA+EAABCEDCDEQFCDABA+APALF4+BBA++SBAAAAA`
8	`++AA+BA+CDB+AAEAA+CEDCDEQ+CDABPBA+ABF4+BBAFBSBMAAAA`
3	`A+AB+BAFCDABA+EAA+CEDCDEQA++ABFBAN++F4+BBAFBTYBAAAA`
2	`A+ABNBAFCD+BAAEAABCEDA+EQ+CDABAB++BAF4NBBM+BTYBAAAA`

Table 3.8: Final MSA

Sequence	Alignment
1	`A-AB-BAFCD-B-AAEAOACEDA-EQ---A-ABCDBALF4-BBASB---AAAAFB`
2	`A-ABNBAFCD-B-AAEAABCEDA-EQ-CDABAB--BA-F4NBBM-BTYBAAAA--`
3	`A-AB-BAFCDAB-A-EAA-CEDCDEQA--ABFBAN---F4-BBAFBTYBAAAA--`
4	`2AAB-BAFCDAB-A-EAABCEDCDEQFCDABA-APAL-F4-BBA--SBAAAAA--`
5	`CDAB-BAFCDB1-AAEAA-CEDA-EQ-CDABABABAL-F4LBBAFBSBAAAAA--`
6	`CDABAAA----B-A-EA-ACEDCDEQ---A-ABCD-A-F4-BBASB---AAAAFB`
7	`CDAB--A-CDAB-A-EAA-CEDA-EQ-CDABCDCDAA-F4MBB--ATYBAAAA--`
8	`--AA-BA-CDB--AAEAA-CEDCDEQ-CDABPBA-AB-F4-BBAFBSBMAAAA--`
9	`CDAB--RBAFABPAAEA-ACEDCDEQAABCDAFAL---F4NBBASB---AAAAMB`
10	`A-ABAA-----B-AAEA-ACEDCDEQAABAFA------F4BNBASB---AAAAFB`

3.5   PHMM from MSA

A PHMM is determined directly from an MSA. In fact, the probabilities in
the model $\lambda = (A, E, \pi)$ are easily determined from the MSA. The process of
generating a PHMM from an MSA is entirely straightforward, since the probabilities are based only on counts of elements that appear in the MSA. First,
we consider the emission probability matrix E, then we turn our attention to
the state transition matrix A.

Recall that the PHMM includes match, insert, and delete states. We
define a *conservative column* of the MSA as one for which half or less of the
elements are gaps. Conservative columns correspond to match states of the
model. On the other hand, if the majority of elements in a column are gaps,
the column represents an insert state. The role of delete states will become
clear later.

Consider the simple MSA example in Table 3.9. In this example, we
see that columns 1, 2, and 6 are conservative, and hence correspond to
match states. On the other hand, columns 3, 4, and 5 are not conservative. From the PHMM state diagram in Figure 3.4 it's clear that consecutive
non-conservative columns correspond to a single insert state, as illustrated in
Table 3.9.

Table 3.9: MSA example

M_1	M_2		I_2		M_3
E	C	-	-	-	-
E	C	-	E	-	G
-	C	G	E	J	G
E	G	-	-	J	G
E	G	-	-	-	G
1	2	3	4	5	6

Emissions occur at match and insert states. The probabilities in the
emission matrix E are determined from the MSA based on the symbol counts
in each state. Referring to the MSA in Table 3.9, for column 1 we have

$$\varepsilon_{M_1}(\text{E}) = 4/4, \;\; \varepsilon_{M_1}(\text{G}) = 0/4, \;\; \varepsilon_{M_1}(\text{C}) = 0/4, \;\; \varepsilon_{M_1}(\text{J}) = 0/4 \qquad (3.5)$$

since all four of the (non-gap) symbols that appear are E.

Any model that includes probabilities of zero is prone to overfit the training data, since nearby sequences are completely eliminated from consideration. Several standard methods are available to remove zero probabilities.

Here, we employ the *add-one rule*, [47] which consists of adding one to each numerator, and so as to maintain probabilities, also adding the total number of symbols to each denominator. Since there are four distinct symbols in our example, applying the add-one rule to the probabilities in equation (3.5) yields

$$\varepsilon_{M_1}(E) = (4{+}1)/(4{+}4) = 5/8, \ \varepsilon_{M_1}(G) = 1/8, \ \varepsilon_{M_1}(C) = 1/8, \ \varepsilon_{M_1}(J) = 1/8.$$

For the insert state I_2, the natural probabilities are

$$\varepsilon_{I_2}(E) = 2/5, \ \varepsilon_{I_2}(G) = 1/5, \ \varepsilon_{I_2}(C) = 0/5, \ \varepsilon_{I_2}(J) = 2/5,$$

which come from the ratios of the emitted symbols in the dashed box in Table 3.9. Using the add-one rule, the insert state probabilities become

$$\varepsilon_{I_2}(E) = 3/9, \ \varepsilon_{I_2}(G) = 2/9, \ \varepsilon_{I_2}(C) = 1/9, \ \varepsilon_{I_2}(J) = 3/9.$$

All emission probabilities for the example in Table 3.9, are given Table 3.10, where we have used the add-one rule. Note that for any state where we have no information (e.g., I_1 in this example), we specify a uniform distribution.

Table 3.10: Emission probabilities for the MSA in Table 3.9

—	$\varepsilon_{I_0}(E) = 1/4$
—	$\varepsilon_{I_0}(G) = 1/4$
—	$\varepsilon_{I_0}(C) = 1/4$
—	$\varepsilon_{I_0}(J) = 1/4$
$\varepsilon_{M_1}(E) = 5/8$	$\varepsilon_{I_1}(E) = 1/4$
$\varepsilon_{M_1}(G) = 1/8$	$\varepsilon_{I_1}(G) = 1/4$
$\varepsilon_{M_1}(C) = 1/8$	$\varepsilon_{I_1}(C) = 1/4$
$\varepsilon_{M_1}(J) = 1/8$	$\varepsilon_{I_1}(J) = 1/4$
$\varepsilon_{M_2}(E) = 1/9$	$\varepsilon_{I_2}(E) = 3/9$
$\varepsilon_{M_2}(G) = 3/9$	$\varepsilon_{I_2}(G) = 2/9$
$\varepsilon_{M_2}(C) = 4/9$	$\varepsilon_{I_2}(C) = 1/9$
$\varepsilon_{M_2}(J) = 1/9$	$\varepsilon_{I_2}(J) = 3/9$
$\varepsilon_{M_3}(E) = 1/8$	$\varepsilon_{I_3}(E) = 1/4$
$\varepsilon_{M_3}(G) = 5/8$	$\varepsilon_{I_3}(G) = 1/4$
$\varepsilon_{M_3}(C) = 1/8$	$\varepsilon_{I_3}(C) = 1/4$
$\varepsilon_{M_3}(J) = 1/8$	$\varepsilon_{I_3}(J) = 1/4$

We note in passing that there is an inherent tradeoff between the length of the training sequences and the number of such sequences. On the one hand, many relatively short sequences will tend to result in a larger number of gaps in the MSA. On the other hand, if we have only a few relatively long sequences, then each state in the PHMM will have too few symbols to generate reliable emission probabilities. The ideal balance between the number and length of training sequences is sure to be problem-specific; see the example in Section 10.3 of Chapter 10 for a realistic case where this issue is addressed.

Next, we consider state transition probabilities, that is, we show how to derive the A matrix from an MSA. Again, we illustrate the process using the simple MSA in Table 3.9.

Intuitively, the probabilities should be given by

$$a_{mn} = \frac{\text{number of transitions from state } m \text{ to state } n}{\text{total number of transitions from state } m \text{ to any state}}.$$

And, as with the emission probabilities, we'll use the add-one rule when calculating state transition probabilities.

Consider the MSA in Table 3.9, and let B denote the begin state. We have

$$a_{BM_1} = 4/5 \tag{3.6}$$

since four of the five elements in column 1 are matches. Similarly,

$$a_{BD_1} = 1/5 \text{ and } a_{BI_0} = 0/5 \tag{3.7}$$

since one element in column 1 represents delete state D_1 and insert state I_0 is empty.

Again, to avoid zero probabilities, we'll apply the add-one rule. However, instead of adding one for each symbol, we add one for each possible transition, namely, match, insert, and delete. Thus, using the add-one rule, equations (3.6) and (3.7) yield

$$a_{BM_1} = (4+1)/(5+3) = 5/8, \ a_{BD_1} = 2/8, \text{ and } a_{BI_0} = 1/8.$$

As with the emission probabilities, in cases where there is no data, we set the transition probabilities to uniform. In the current example, we have no transitions from I_1, and consequently we set

$$a_{I_1 M_2} = a_{I_1 I_1} = a_{I_1 D_2} = 1/3.$$

Next, consider the delete state D_1, which corresponds to the "–" that appears in column 1 of Table 3.9. We see that the transition from D_1 is to a match state in column 2. Consequently, without the add-one rule, we have

$$a_{D_1 M_2} = 1/1 = 1, \ a_{D_1 I_1} = 0/1 = 0, \text{ and } a_{D_1 D_2} = 0/1 = 0$$

and applying the add-one rule gives us

$$a_{D_1 M_2} = (1+1)/(1+3) = 2/4, \ a_{D_1 I_1} = 1/4, \text{ and } a_{D_1 D_2} = 1/4.$$

Now consider match state M_2. In the bottom row, no letter appears in the boxed region of the MSA in Table 3.9 and, consequently, for this row, we transition directly from M_2 to M_3. Similarly, in the top row, we transition from M_2 to D_3. However, the three middle rows all transition from M_2 to I_2. Therefore, the natural probabilities are

$$a_{M_2 M_3} = 1/5, \ a_{M_2 D_3} = 1/5, \text{ and } a_{M_2 I_2} = 3/5.$$

Applying the add-one rule, we obtain

$$a_{M_2 M_3} = 2/8, \ a_{M_2 D_3} = 2/8, \text{ and } a_{M_2 I_2} = 4/8.$$

Finally, we calculate transition probabilities for I_2. Note that there are five symbols in I_2, and of these, three transition to M_3, specifically, the E in the second row, the J in the third row, and the J in the fourth row. Both of the remaining symbols (G and E in the third row) transition to symbols in I_2. Therefore,

$$a_{I_2 M_3} = 3/5 \text{ and } a_{I_2 I_2} = 2/5$$

and applying the add-one rule yields

$$a_{I_2 M_3} = 4/8, \ a_{I_2 I_2} = 3/8, \text{ and } a_{I_2 D_3} = 1/8.$$

The complete set of transition probabilities for the MSA in Table 3.9 appears in Table 3.11, where the add-one rule has been applied.

Table 3.11: Transition probabilities for the MSA in Table 3.9

$a_{BM_1} = 5/8$	$a_{I_0 M_1} = 1/3$	—
$a_{BI_0} = 1/8$	$a_{I_0 I_0} = 1/3$	—
$a_{BD_1} = 2/8$	$a_{I_0 D_1} = 1/3$	—
$a_{M_1 M_2} = 5/7$	$a_{I_1 M_2} = 1/3$	$a_{D_1 M_2} = 2/4$
$a_{M_1 I_1} = 1/7$	$a_{I_1 I_1} = 1/3$	$a_{D_1 I_1} = 1/4$
$a_{M_1 D_2} = 1/7$	$a_{I_1 D_2} = 1/3$	$a_{D_1 D_2} = 1/4$
$a_{M_2 M_3} = 2/8$	$a_{I_2 M_3} = 4/8$	$a_{D_2 M_3} = 1/3$
$a_{M_2 I_2} = 4/8$	$a_{I_2 I_2} = 3/8$	$a_{D_2 I_2} = 1/3$
$a_{M_2 D_3} = 2/8$	$a_{I_2 D_3} = 1/8$	$a_{D_2 D_3} = 1/3$
$a_{M_3 E} = 5/6$	$a_{I_3 E} = 1/2$	$a_{D_3 E} = 2/3$
$a_{M_3 I_3} = 1/6$	$a_{I_3 I_3} = 1/2$	$a_{D_3 I_3} = 1/3$

To conclude this section, we summarize the process used to train a PHMM. Here, we assume that we are given a set of training sequences and that a substitution matrix S and gap penalty function g have been defined.

1. Construct pairwise alignments for the training sequences using S and g. Typically, dynamic programming is used in this step.

2. From the pairwise alignments, construct an MSA. In the example above, we used a spanning tree and a progressive alignment strategy. For efficiency, progressive alignment is generally employed.

3. Use the resulting MSA to determine the PHMM. The probabilities that constitute $\lambda = (A, E, \pi)$ are determined directly from the MSA. To avoid zero probabilities, use some form of pseudo-counts, such as the add-one rule.

3.6 Scoring

Having constructed a PHMM from an MSA, we can use the resulting model to score a given sequence. The score will tell us how well the sequence matches the training set—a relatively high score indicates a good match while a relatively low score indicates a poor match. We can then determine a threshold for classification of unknown samples. Recall that for an HMM, we score using the forward algorithm. A similar—although somewhat more complex—algorithm is used to compute scores with a PHMM.

Suppose we are given a PHMM specified by $\lambda = (A, E, \pi)$ and an emission sequence X. Our goal is to compute $P(X \mid \lambda)$, that is, we want to score the given sequence to determine how well it matches the given PHMM. Note that this corresponds to HMM Problem 1 (see Sections 2.4 and 2.5 of Chapter 2), which we solved using the forward algorithm.

Before presenting the PHMM version of the forward algorithm, we show that the probability of an emission sequence $P(X \mid \lambda)$ can be calculated in a straightforward, but computationally inefficient manner. Analogous to an HMM, the brute-force approach to calculating $P(X \mid \lambda)$ consists of summing the probabilities of all possible paths that can emit the sequence X. Since a PHMM includes match, insert, and delete states, determining the possible paths is significantly more complex than for an HMM.

Recall that a symbol is only emitted when a PHMM is in an insert or match state. Consider, for example, a sequence $X = (X_1, X_2)$ emitted by a PHMM for which $N = 2$. Such a PHMM has thirteen possible paths that can generate X, specifically, the thirteen paths listed in Table 3.12. Figure 3.6 provides an illustration of the paths in Table 3.12, where we have denoted the begin state as M_0, and the end state as $M_{N+1} = M_3$.

Calculating probabilities directly for each possible path in a PHMM results in an exponential work factor. Fortunately, we can efficiently compute $P(X \mid \lambda)$ using a version of the forward algorithm. Again, the PHMM

Table 3.12: Possible paths for PHMM with $N = 2$

	I_0	I_1	I_2	M_1	M_2
1	X_1, X_2	—	—	—	—
2	X_1	X_2	—	—	—
3	X_1	—	X_2	—	—
4	X_1	—	—	X_2	—
5	X_1	—	—	—	X_2
6	—	X_1, X_2	—	—	—
7	—	X_1	X_2	—	—
8	—	X_1	—	—	X_2
9	—	—	X_1, X_2	—	—
10	—	X_2	—	X_1	—
11	—	—	X_2	X_1	—
12	—	—	—	X_1	X_2
13	—	—	X_2	—	X_1

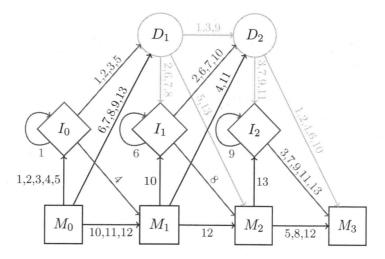

Figure 3.6: PHMM with $N = 2$ illustrating paths in Table 3.12

version of the forward algorithn is very much analogous to the forward algorithm in an HMM. However, the PHMM forward algorithm is more complicated, due to the presence of insert and delete states.

As with an HMM, the PHMM forward algorithm recursively determines
the score of a given sequence with respect to a given model. This enables us
to compute the desired score in an efficient manner. And, as with the HMM
forward algorithm, the key to this efficiency is the re-use of (partial) scores.

The PHMM forward algorithm recursive relations [47] are given by

$$F_j^M(i) = \log\left(\frac{\varepsilon_{M_j}(X_i)}{q_{X_i}}\right) + \log\Big(a_{M_{j-1}M_j}\exp\big(F_{j-1}^M(i-1)\big)$$
$$+ a_{I_{j-1}M_j}\exp\big(F_{j-1}^I(i-1)\big)$$
$$+ a_{D_{j-1}M_j}\exp\big(F_{j-1}^D(i-1)\big)\Big)$$

$$F_j^I(i) = \log\left(\frac{\varepsilon_{I_j}(X_i)}{q_{X_i}}\right) + \log\Big(a_{M_jI_j}\exp\big(F_j^M(i-1)\big)$$
$$+ a_{I_jI_j}\exp\big(F_j^I(i-1)\big)$$
$$+ a_{D_jI_j}\exp\big(F_j^D(i-1)\big)\Big)$$

$$F_j^D(i) = \log\Big(a_{M_{j-1}D_j}\exp\big(F_{j-1}^M(i)\big)$$
$$+ a_{I_{j-1}D_j}\exp\big(F_{j-1}^I(i)\big)$$
$$+ a_{D_{j-1}D_j}\exp\big(F_{j-1}^D(i)\big)\Big)$$

where X_i is the ith symbol in the sequence X and the base case for the recursion is $F_0^M(0) = 0$. Here, q_{X_i} is the distribution of the symbol X_i in the "random model," that is, the symbol distribution for a randomly-selected sequence. Also, $F_j^M(i)$ denotes the score for the subsequence $X_1, \ldots, X_i$ up to state j. Note that due to insertions and deletions, the indices i and j need not coincide, which is one major difference as compared to an HMM. Finally, in this recursion, some insert and delete terms are not defined, such as $F_0^I(0)$ and $F_0^D(0)$. These undefined terms are simply ignored when computing scores.

From the recurrence relations above, we see that the $F_j^M(i)$ depends on $F_{j-1}^M(i-1)$, $F_{j-1}^I(i-1)$, and $F_{j-1}^D(i-1)$, along with the respective transition probabilities, and similar statements hold for $F_j^I(i)$ and $F_j^D(i)$. Also, emission probabilities are used when calculating $F_j^M(i)$ and $F_j^I(i)$, but not for $F_j^D(i)$, since delete states are not emission states. The state M_0 and the state M_{N+1} are the begin and end states, respectively. As with delete states, the begin and end states do not emit symbols.

To further clarify the forward algorithm in the PHMM context, suppose that we want to score a sequence $X = (X_1, X_2, \ldots, X_L)$ of length L using a PHMM with N match states. Let $M_1, M_2, \ldots, M_N$ denote the match states, with states $B = M_0$ and $E = M_{N+1}$ being the begin and end states, respectively. The scoring process can then be summarized as follows.

1. Calculate $F_N^M(L)$, $F_N^I(L)$, and $F_N^D(L)$.

2. In the recursive process used to calculate $F_N^M(L)$, many other intermediate values are computed, including $F_{N-1}^M(L-1)$, $F_N^I(L-1)$, and so on. These values are saved for later use. After $F_N^D(L)$ has been calculated, most intermediate values are known, which makes subsequent scoring passes highly efficient.

3. During the scoring calculation, some terms, such as $F_0^I(0)$ and $F_0^M(2)$ are not defined. Whenever an undefined term is encountered, exclude it from the calculation.

4. The terms $F_N^M(L)$, $F_N^I(L)$, and $F_N^D(L)$ give the scores of the sequence X up to state N, ending in a match, insert, or delete state, respectively. The product of these scores with their respective end transition probabilities yields the final score, that is,

$$\texttt{score} = \log\Big(a_{M_N E}\exp\big(F_N^M(L)\big)$$
$$+ \, a_{I_N E}\exp\big(F_N^I(L)\big) \tag{3.8}$$
$$+ \, a_{D_N E}\exp\big(F_N^D(L)\big)\Big)$$

We have thus computed a log-odds score for the sequence X.

Figure 3.7 illustrates the PHMM version of the forward algorithm. The final step in the scoring calculation is illustrated in Figure 3.8.

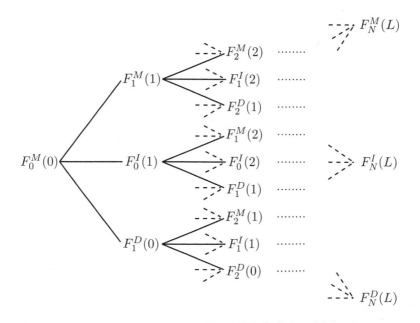

Figure 3.7: Forward algorithm recursion

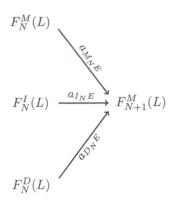

Figure 3.8: Final score

As it's described above, the PHMM score depends on the length of the scored sequence and, therefore, such scores cannot be directly compared for sequence of different length. To eliminate the length-dependence, we can simply divide the final score by the sequence length and thereby obtain a per-symbol score. Using this approach, we can compare scores obtained on sequences of any length.

The time complexity for the PHMM scoring algorithm is $O(NT)$, where N is the number of match states and T is the length of the scored sequence. This level of complexity makes the algorithm competitive with many other scoring techniques.

3.7   The Bottom Line

A PHMM can be viewed as a generalization of an HMM, in the sense that additional state transitions (i.e., insert and delete) are considered, and positional information is explicitly taken into account. To deal with positional information, in effect we define a distinct emission probability matrix—in HMM nomenclature, the B matrix—at each position in the sequence. In contrast, the B matrix for an HMM is fixed, which implies that it represents the average behavior over all positions in the training sequence. The PHMM emission and state transition probabilities are obtained from a multiple sequence alignment (MSA). Generating the MSA is the most challenging part of training a PHMM.

PHMMs should be considered in cases where the position of an element within a sequence is critical. Such problems occur, for example, when analyzing sequences that arise in biological applications. In contrast, for applications where positional information is not significant, a standard HMM is simpler and will likely yield stronger results.

In this chapter, we illustrated the PHMM process using a much-simplified example from intrusion detection, specifically, from the realm of masquerade detection. This particular problem is explored in much more detail in Chapter 10, where additional PHMM examples from the field of information security are also discussed.

3.8   Problems

1. PHMM notation appears in Table 3.1 and the corresponding notation for an HMM is given in Table 2.1 of Chapter 2. In Section 3.2 we noted that one notational difference between HMMs and PHMMs is that observations in an HMM are known as emissions in a PHMM. One similarity is that for both HMMs and PHMMs, we associate the observations with positive integers. List two additional similarities and two additional differences between HMMs and PHMMs with respect to the notation.

2. The match states of a PHMM are analogous to the states in an HMM.

    a) Suppose that we allow only match states in a PHMM. Then the PHMM state transitions correspond to those in Figure 3.2. If N is the number of match states, how many elements does the PHMM state transition matrix A contain?

    b) Suppose that we only allow match and insert states in a PHMM. Then the PHMM state transitions correspond to Figure 3.2. If N is the number of match states, how many elements does the PHMM state transition matrix A contain?

    c) Suppose that we only allow match and delete states in a PHMM. Then the PHMM state transitions correspond to Figure 3.3. If N is the number of match states, how many elements does the PHMM state transition matrix A contain?

    d) Suppose that we allow match, insert, and delete states in a PHMM. Then the PHMM state transitions correspond to Figure 3.4. If N is the number of match states, how many elements does the PHMM state transition matrix A contain?

3. Consider the MSA in Table 3.8. For each of the 55 columns in this MSA, specify whether the column corresponds to a match or insert state. For each match and insert state, determine the emission probabilities, using the add-one rule.

4. Let S be the substitution matrix in equation (3.1) and define a linear gap penalty function as $g(x) = -3x$. Construct a table of pairwise (global)

alignment scores, analogous to Table 3.6, for the four sequences

EJG, GEECG, CGJEE, and JJGECCG.

Use the dynamic program recursion in equation (3.4).

5. A *dot-matrix plot* can be used to visually identify local alignments between sequences $X = (X_1, X_2, \ldots, X_n)$ and $Y = (Y_1, Y_2, \ldots, Y_m)$. To construct such a plot, we first write the sequence X horizontally and the sequence Y vertically, with Y positioned to the left and above the X sequence. Then we put a dot at the intersection of each position where $X_i = Y_j$. Matching subsequences will appear as line segments parallel to the main diagonal.[5] Based on the following sequences, construct dot-matrix plots for the indicated pairs and discuss the results.

number	sequence
1	CDABBAFCDBAAEAACEDAEQCDABABABALFLBBAFBSBAAAAA
2	AABBAFCDABAEAABCEDCDEQFCDABAAPALFBBASBAAAAA
3	AABACDBAAEAACEDCDEQCDABPBAABFBBAFBSBMAAAA

a) Sequences 1 and 2.

b) Sequences 1 and 3.

c) Sequences 2 and 3.

6. Consider the pairwise alignment scores in Table 3.6.

a) Show that the set

$$\{(4, 5), (2, 7), (1, 2), (3, 8), (1, 6), (9, 10), (2, 3), (5, 8), (6, 10)\}$$

is optimal, in the sense that it is a minimal set containing all 10 sequences, which maximizes the sum of the pairwise alignment scores.

b) Implement Prim's algorithm and use your implementation to verify that the tree given in Figure 3.5 is a minimum spanning tree. List any other minimum spanning trees that you can find.

7. In Section 3.4, we discussed a progressive alignment strategy for constructing an MSA. An iterative strategy could be used instead of—or in conjunction with—a progressive approach. In this problem, we consider a hill climb for constructing an MSA.

We'll generate our initial ordering using the same process outlined in Section 3.4. That is, we use pairwise alignment scores to select $n - 1$

---

[5] We could shade the points based on the scoring matrix, and thereby also obtain information on near misses. But for this problem, we'll keep it simple.

pairwise alignments that include all n sequences from the training set, and which maximizes the sum of the corresponding alignment scores. Then we use Prim's algorithm to generate a minimum spanning tree for these $n-1$ pairwise alignments, and we add pairwise alignments to the MSA based on this spanning tree. For the example in Figure 3.5, the sequences were ordered as $(5, 4, 8, 3, 2, 7, 1, 6, 10, 9)$ and this ordering was used to generate the MSA. For our hill climb, we compute a score for this MSA. Then we swap a pair of elements in the permutation (i.e., the ordering of the sequences), generate a new MSA, and compute its score. If the score has improved, we retain the swap. We continue this process, only retaining those swaps that improve the MSA score.

When swapping elements of the permutation, we first swap all adjacent pairs, then swap pairs at distance two, then pairs at distance three, and so on. Furthermore, each time the MSA score improves, we start over from the beginning of this swapping schedule. The hill climb is done when we have made $\binom{n}{2}$ consecutive swaps without the score improving. This hill climb strategy is essentially the same as that used in Jakobsen's algorithm, which is described in detail in Section 9.4.1 of Chapter 9.

a) In this hill climb algorithm, we need to compute a score for each MSA constructed. How can we compute a reasonable score for an MSA?

b) Comment on the advantages and disadvantages of this hill climb, as compared to the progressive alignment strategy in Section 3.4.

8. Determine the PHMM corresponding to the MSA in Table 3.8. Use the add-one rule when computing probabilities.

9. Verify all of the probabilities in Tables 3.10 and 3.11. Show your work.

10. Using the forward algorithm as given in Section 3.6, score the following sequences, based on the PHMM specified by Tables 3.10 and 3.11. Use uniform probabilities for the random model, that is, the q_{X_i} that appear in the forward algorithm recursive relations are all equal and they sum to one.

a) EJG

b) GEECG

c) CGJEE

d) JJGECCG

11. Give the analogous results to Table 3.12 and Figure 3.6 for the following cases.

a) The sequence $X = (X_1, X_2, X_3)$ is emitted by a PHMM with $N = 3$.

b) The sequence $X = (X_1, X_2, X_3)$ is emitted by a PHMM with $N = 2$.

c) The sequence $X = (X_1, X_2)$ is emitted by a PHMM with $N = 3$.

12. Due to the logarithms in equation (3.8), PHMM scoring does not suffer from underflow. However, the exponentiation in this same equation could lead to overflow.

a) Apply the identity [47]

$$\log(p + q) = \log(p) + \log\left(1 + \exp\left(\log(q) - \log(p)\right)\right)$$

to equation (3.8) and simplify the result, if possible.

b) Is your answer to part a) an improvement, with respect to overflow, as compared to equation (3.8)? Explain.

Chapter 4

Principal Components of Principal Component Analysis

> *We talk on principal, but act on motivation.*
> — Walter Savage Landor

4.1 Introduction

In this chapter, we cover the basics of principal component analysis (PCA), which is a powerful machine learning technique based on methods from linear algebra. Geometrically, PCA finds the most significant dimensions in a dataset, which enables us to reduce the dimensionality of the problem, with a minimal loss of information. This is helpful, since real-world problems tend to suffer from the "curse of dimensionality."[1]

PCA relies on eigenvector analysis, which often utilizes the singular value decomposition (SVD). The terms PCA and SVD are sometimes used almost interchangeably. However, we'll refer to the general technique as PCA, while SVD is the most popular way to implement PCA.

Some sophisticated linear algebra lies just beneath the surface of PCA. However, it is possible to understand PCA well without digging too deeply into the mathematical background, and that's the strategy we follow here. As a result, this chapter should be easily accessible to anyone with basic mathematical knowledge and a desire to learn. In other words, don't let all of the fancy mathematics that undergirds PCA scare you away.

---

[1]Your multi-dimensional author has observed that as the dimensionality increases, the amount of data required to fill an equivalent fraction of space grows exponentially. Therefore, in higher-dimensional spaces, data will be more sparse, and hence statistically less significant, as compared to the same data in a lower-dimensional space.

4.2   Background

PCA can reveal structure that is not readily apparent from statistical analysis or other analytic techniques. Consequently, PCA can offer a different perspective on data, as compared to other machine learning techniques, most of which are ultimately statistical-based.

As mentioned above, PCA rests on a foundation of linear algebra. The theory underlying PCA is deep and involved, since it builds on fairly advanced mathematics. Here, we'll simply accept most of the necessary mathematical background as a given. This enables us to deal with the constructs required for PCA, without too much of a diversion into the mathematics.

As is the case for HMMs and PHMMs, in PCA we have a training phase and a scoring phase. And, as is typically the case, the training phase is the complex and challenging part. The scoring phase in PCA is particularly simple and generally extremely efficient. As a consequence, scoring is fast, efficient, and therefore practical—a fact that the reader should not lose sight of as we wade chest-deep into the details of the training phase.

In the next section, we discuss relevant background topics, including basic facts from linear algebra, and some very basic statistical concepts. From the field of linear algebra, the main things we need are eigenvalues and eigenvectors. From statistics, we discuss covariance, since the covariance matrix plays a fundamental role in PCA.[2] With this background in hand, we'll be prepared to turn our attention to PCA and the SVD technique that is typically used in its implementation.

4.2.1   A Brief Review of Linear Algebra

A *matrix* is an array of numbers and a *vector* is a one-dimensional matrix. Not surprisingly, a *row vector* is a vector that is written horizontally, while a *column vector* is written vertically. Usually, we restrict the use of the term matrix to two-dimensional arrays.

When dealing with vectors and matrices, a number is known as a *scalar*. By convention, we generally use capital letters for matrices and lower-case for scalars.[3]

An $n \times m$ matrix has n rows and m columns, and we'll write $A_{n \times m}$ when we want to emphasize the size of the matrix. We often denote the elements of a matrix by lower-case letters, with subscripts indicating the position of

---

[2]The reader who is intimately familiar with the relevant linear algebra and statistics is surely tempted to skip ahead to Section 4.3. However, your thorough author would thoroughly recommend this background material to all, and especially Section 4.2.3, where covariance matrices are discussed.

[3]Often, vectors are denoted using bold-face (lower-case) letters, or with an arrow over a letter, so as to distinguish them from scalars. We won't use either of these conventions and will instead rely on context to (hopefully) distinguish vectors from matrices and scalars.

the element in the matrix. For example,

$$A = \begin{pmatrix} a_{11} & a_{12} & a_{13} \\ a_{21} & a_{22} & a_{23} \end{pmatrix}$$

is a generic 2×3 matrix. For more compact notation, we can write $A = \{a_{ij}\}$, or slightly less compactly, but more informatively, $A_{n \times m} = \{a_{ij}\}$.

When multiplying a vector or matrix by a scalar, we simply multiply each element by the scalar. For example,

$$3 \begin{pmatrix} 1 \\ 2 \end{pmatrix} = \begin{pmatrix} 3 \\ 6 \end{pmatrix}.$$

Why is a scalar known as a scalar? I'm glad you asked. Multiplication by a scalar has the effect of stretching or shrinking a vector, and hence a scalar "scales" a vector.[4]

Matrix addition is defined for matrices with the same dimensions, and we simply add the corresponding elements. Addition of matrices and scalar multiplication are easy-peasy.

Matrix multiplication (i.e., the product of two matrices) is somewhat more complex and less intuitive. First, we define a special type of multiplication known as the *dot product*. Consider the vectors

$$x = \begin{pmatrix} x_1 & x_2 & \cdots & x_n \end{pmatrix} \text{ and } y = \begin{pmatrix} y_1 & y_2 & \cdots & y_n \end{pmatrix},$$

which are both of length n. The dot product of x and y, which is denoted as $x \cdot y$, is computed as

$$x \cdot y = x_1 y_1 + x_2 y_2 + \cdots + x_n y_n.$$

The dot product is only defined for vectors of the same length, and the result is a scalar, not a vector. Also, the vectors x and y are said to be *orthogonal* if they meet at a right angle, and orthogonal vectors satisfy $x \cdot y = 0$.

We can define matrix multiplication in terms of the dot product. Suppose we are given matrices $A_{m \times n}$ and $B_{k \times \ell}$. Then the product $C = AB$ is only defined when $n = k$, in which case the product C is $m \times \ell$. When the product is defined, the element in row i and column j of C, that is, c_{ij}, is given by the dot product of the ith row of A with the jth column of B.

For example, consider

$$A = \begin{pmatrix} -1 & 2 & 4 \\ 2 & -3 & -1 \end{pmatrix} \text{ and } B = \begin{pmatrix} 3 & 4 \\ 1 & 7 \\ -1 & 1 \end{pmatrix}.$$

---

[4]According to this description, it seems that it should be "scaler," not "scalar," which explains why mathematicians are not English majors.

Since A is 2×3 and B is 3×2, the product $C = AB$ is defined and C will be 2×2. In this case, we have

$$
C = AB = \begin{pmatrix} (-1 \quad 2 \quad 4) \cdot \begin{pmatrix} 3 \\ 1 \\ -1 \end{pmatrix} & (-1 \quad 2 \quad 4) \cdot \begin{pmatrix} 4 \\ 7 \\ 1 \end{pmatrix} \\ (2 \quad -3 \quad -1) \cdot \begin{pmatrix} 3 \\ 1 \\ -1 \end{pmatrix} & (2 \quad -3 \quad -1) \cdot \begin{pmatrix} 4 \\ 7 \\ 1 \end{pmatrix} \end{pmatrix}
$$

$$
= \begin{pmatrix} -5 & 14 \\ 4 & -14 \end{pmatrix}.
$$

In this case, the product BA is also defined, but $AB \neq BA$. In general, matrix multiplication is not commutative. In fact, it often happens that AB is defined, while BA is not (or vice versa).

A *square matrix* has an equal number of rows and columns,[5] while the $n \times n$ *identity matrix* I is a square matrix with 1s on the main diagonal and 0s elsewhere. For a given a square matrix A, if there exists a matrix B such that $AB = BA = I$, then we say that B is the *inverse* of A, and we denote the inverse of A as A^{-1}. Note that the inverse is not defined for non-square matrices, and even when A is square, the inverse A^{-1} need not exist.

The *transpose* of a matrix A, which is denoted A^T, is obtained by interchanging the rows and columns. For example, if

$$
A = \begin{pmatrix} 1 & 2 & 3 \\ -1 & -2 & 3 \end{pmatrix}
$$

then

$$
A^T = \begin{pmatrix} 1 & -1 \\ 2 & -2 \\ 3 & 3 \end{pmatrix}.
$$

The transpose of column vector is a row vector, and vice versa.

Given a set of vectors that are all of the same dimension, the *span*, or linear span, of these vectors consists of all linear combinations of the vectors, that is, all sums of scalar multiples. For example, given $x_{n \times 1}$, $y_{n \times 1}$, and $z_{n \times 1}$, any vector that can be written as

$$
\alpha x + \beta y + \gamma z
$$

for some scalars α, β, and γ, is in the span of x, y, z.

A *basis* is a minimal spanning set, that is, a basis spans a given space, and no set of fewer vectors can do so. For example, the vectors

$$
\begin{pmatrix} 1 \\ 0 \end{pmatrix} \text{ and } \begin{pmatrix} 0 \\ 1 \end{pmatrix}
$$

---

[5]In contrast, a square person is equal parts dull and boring.

form a basis for the plane. Why is this the case? Suppose that we are given any vector of the form $(\; x \quad y \;)^T$. Then we have

$$
\begin{pmatrix} x \\ y \end{pmatrix} = x \begin{pmatrix} 1 \\ 0 \end{pmatrix} + y \begin{pmatrix} 0 \\ 1 \end{pmatrix},
$$

which shows that the claimed basis spans the plane. Since no single vector can span the plane, this pair of vectors satisfies the definition of a basis. This basis is usually known as the *standard basis*, which implies that there are also non-standard bases. In fact, PCA training consists of finding a "better" basis for the given training data.

For a square matrix A, any non-zero vector x that satisfies

$$
Ax = \lambda x
$$

for some scalar λ is an *eigenvector* of A. The scalar λ is the *eigenvalue* associated with the eigenvector x. For example, consider the matrix

$$
A = \begin{pmatrix} 2 & 1 \\ 0 & -1 \end{pmatrix} \tag{4.1}
$$

Since

$$
\begin{pmatrix} 2 & 1 \\ 0 & -1 \end{pmatrix} \begin{pmatrix} 1 \\ 0 \end{pmatrix} = 2 \begin{pmatrix} 1 \\ 0 \end{pmatrix}
$$

it follows from the definitions that $x = (\; 1 \quad 0 \;)^T$ is an eigenvector of A, with corresponding eigenvalue $\lambda = 2$. It's easy to verify that any scalar multiple of an eigenvector is also an eigenvector with the same eigenvalue.

Consider the vector $x = (x_1, x_2, \ldots, x_n)$. The *length* of x, denoted as $||x||$, is computed as

$$
||x|| = \sqrt{x_1^2 + x_2^2 + \cdots + x_n^2} \, .
$$

In PCA, we'll want to normalize each eigenvector to be a *unit vector*. Given any non-zero vector x, the vector $w = x/||x||$ is a unit vector that points in the same direction as x. It follows that if x is an eigenvector with eigenvalue λ, then $w = x/||x||$ is also an eigenvector with the same eigenvalue λ. Thus, it's easy to convert any eigenvector into a unit eigenvector. While eigenvectors are not unique, unit eigenvectors are almost unique.

An eigenvalue λ of A must satisfy the matrix equation $\det(A - \lambda I) = 0$, where det is the *determinant* and I is the identity matrix. As mentioned above, the identity matrix is a square matrix with 1s on the main diagonal and 0 elsewhere.

For a 2×2 matrix, the determinant is just

$$
\det \begin{pmatrix} a & b \\ c & d \end{pmatrix} = ad - bc.
$$

For larger matrices, determinant computations are fairly involved, so we won't discuss the topic further here.

For the matrix A in (4.1) we have

$$\det(A - \lambda I) = \det\left[\begin{pmatrix} 2 & 1 \\ 0 & -1 \end{pmatrix} - \lambda \begin{pmatrix} 1 & 0 \\ 0 & 1 \end{pmatrix}\right]$$

$$= \det\begin{pmatrix} 2 - \lambda & 1 \\ 0 & -1 - \lambda \end{pmatrix}$$

$$= (2 - \lambda)(-1 - \lambda) = 0,$$

which yields the eigenvalues $\lambda_1 = 2$ and $\lambda_2 = -1$. Since

$$\begin{pmatrix} 2 & 1 \\ 0 & -1 \end{pmatrix}\begin{pmatrix} 1 \\ 0 \end{pmatrix} = 2 \begin{pmatrix} 1 \\ 0 \end{pmatrix}$$

we see (again) that $x = \begin{pmatrix} 1 & 0 \end{pmatrix}^T$ is an eigenvector of A corresponding to the eigenvalue $\lambda_1 = 2$.

4.2.2 Geometric View of Eigenvectors

For any eigenvector x of the matrix A, by definition we have $Ax = \lambda x$, where the eigenvalue λ is a scalar. Geometrically, this means that A stretches (or shrinks) the eigenvector x by λ, without changing its direction. Consequently, the magnitude[6] of an eigenvalue can be viewed as indicative of the significance of the corresponding eigenvector—the larger (in magnitude) the eigenvalue, the more significant the eigenvector.

As mentioned above, if x is an eigenvector of A, then so is βx for any scalar β. Also, if x and y are eigenvectors of A, then so is $x + y$. Therefore, the eigenvectors of A form a linear subspace. Not surprisingly, linear subspace spanned by the eigenvectors of A is known as the *eigenspace* of A.

Consider the matrix

$$A = \begin{pmatrix} 2 & 2 \\ 5 & -1 \end{pmatrix} \tag{4.2}$$

and the vector

$$x = \begin{pmatrix} 1 \\ 2 \end{pmatrix}.$$

The product is given by

$$Ax = \begin{pmatrix} 6 \\ 3 \end{pmatrix}.$$

Figure 4.1 illustrates the geometry behind this matrix multiplication.

---

[6]In PCA, the eigenvalues are non-negative, so we could talk of their "size" instead of their "magnitude," but magnitude sounds way more impressive.

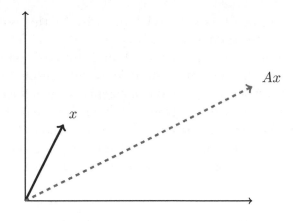

Figure 4.1: Matrix multiplication example

For the matrix A in (4.2) suppose that we compute Ax for the vector

$$x = \begin{pmatrix} 1 \\ 1 \end{pmatrix}.$$

Then, we find

$$Ax = \begin{pmatrix} 4 \\ 4 \end{pmatrix} = 4x.$$

For this particular matrix A and this specific column vector x, the effect of multiplication by A is the same as multiplication of x by the scalar 4. It follows that, by definition, x is an eigenvector of the matrix A with corresponding eigenvalue $\lambda = 4$. The geometry behind this matrix multiplication is illustrated in Figure 4.2.

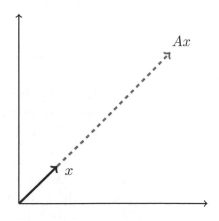

Figure 4.2: Eigenvector example

It's clear that eigenvectors are special, but why are they so important that we've spent three pages (and counting) discussing them? The fact is that we can form a basis from the eigenvectors of A, and this basis often reveals structure that is "hidden" in the matrix A, at least with respect to the standard basis. Furthermore, from the geometry of eigenvectors, it's clear that the relative effect of each eigenvector is given by the magnitude of its corresponding eigenvalue. This feature enables us to ignore uninteresting directions, and thereby reduce the dimensionality, often without any significant loss of information. Finally, there are efficient algorithms for generating eigenvectors and eigenvalues.

The next section covers some elementary facts from statistics. Specifically, we focus on the covariance matrix and explain why this particular matrix plays a critical role in PCA.

4.2.3   Covariance Matrix

Before we can discuss the covariance matrix, we need to define a few basic statistical concepts. Let $x = (\begin{array}{cccc} x_1 & x_2 & \ldots & x_n \end{array})$. Then the *mean*, denoted μ_x, is simply the average, that is,

$$\mu_x = \frac{x_1 + x_2 + \cdots + x_n}{n}.$$

Once we know the mean, the *variance* is computed as

$$\sigma_x^2 = \frac{(x_1 - \mu_x)^2 + (x_2 - \mu_x)^2 + \cdots + (x_n - \mu_x)^2}{n}.$$

The mean is a measure of central tendency, while the variance measures the spread of the data about the mean.

For two vectors $x = (\begin{array}{cccc} x_1 & x_2 & \ldots & x_n \end{array})$ and $y = (\begin{array}{cccc} y_1 & y_2 & \ldots & y_n \end{array})$, the *covariance* is defined as

$$\mathrm{cov}(x, y) = \frac{(x_1 - \mu_x)(y_1 - \mu_y) + \cdots + (x_n - \mu_x)(y_n - \mu_y)}{n}.$$

The covariance relates variations in x to those of y, relative to their respective means. Also, the variance is a special case of the covariance since

$$\sigma_x^2 = \mathrm{cov}(x, x).$$

Note that whenever x_i and y_i both lie on the same side of their respective means, then $x_i - \mu_x$ and $y_i - mu_y$ will both be of the same sign, and their contribution to $\mathrm{cov}(x, y)$ will be positive. On the other hand, if x_i and y_i lie on opposite sides of their respective means, then their contribution to $\mathrm{cov}(x, y)$ is negative. Therefore, a positive covariance implies that x and y tend to have a positive (linear) correlation (relative to their respective means), while a negative covariance implies a negative correlation.

If the means μ_x and μ_y are both 0, then the covariance simplifies to (essentially) a dot product,

$$\text{cov}(x,y) = \frac{x \cdot y}{n} = \frac{x_1 y_1 + x_2 y_2 + \cdots + x_n y_n}{n}.$$

By subtracting the mean from each term, we can modify the vector x so that its mean is 0, and similarly for the vector y. This is often done in practice to simplify covariance calculations.

For example, consider

$$x = \begin{pmatrix} -1 & 2 & 1 & -2 \end{pmatrix} \text{ and } y = \begin{pmatrix} 1 & -1 & 1 & -1 \end{pmatrix}.$$

Since the means are both 0, we have

$$\text{cov}(x,y) = \frac{(-1) \cdot 1 + 2 \cdot (-1) + 1 \cdot 1 + (-2) \cdot (-1)}{4} = \frac{0}{4} = 0.$$

When the covariance is 0, we say that x and y are *uncorrelated*, since there is no linear relationship between x and y.

As another example, consider

$$x = \begin{pmatrix} -1 & 2 & 1 & -2 \end{pmatrix} \text{ and } y = \begin{pmatrix} -1 & 1 & 1 & -1 \end{pmatrix}.$$

The covariance of these vectors is

$$\text{cov}(x,y) = \frac{(-1) \cdot (-1) + 2 \cdot 1 + 1 \cdot 1 + (-2) \cdot (-1)}{4} = \frac{6}{4} = \frac{3}{2}.$$

Since the covariance is positive, in this case we know that x and y tend to vary together in their corresponding elements. In contrast, a negative covariance would indicate that corresponding elements tend to vary opposite in sign of each other.

As an aside, it's interesting to note that a larger (in magnitude) covariance does not immediately imply a stronger correlation. To determine the strength of the correlation, we use the *correlation coefficient*

$$\rho_{x,y} = \frac{\text{cov}(x,y)}{\sigma_x \sigma_y},$$

which is a normalized version of the covariance. It's easy to verify that the correlation coefficient satisfies $-1 \leq \rho_{x,y} \leq 1$. Furthermore, $\rho_{x,y} = 1$ implies that x and y are collinear, i.e., the points (x_i, y_i) all lie on the same line, and the line has positive slope. Similarly, $\rho_{x,y} = -1$ means that x and y are collinear with negative slope. The smaller that $\rho_{x,y}$ is (in magnitude), the further x and y are from being collinear, and when $\rho_{x,y} = 0$ (which is equivalent to $\mathrm{cov}(x, y) = 0$), there is no linear relationship and we say that the vectors x and y are uncorrelated. Figure 6.5 in Chapter 6 includes several illustrative examples of the correlation coefficient.

Suppose that we repeat an experiment n times, where each experiment yields a set of m measurements. For example, each experiment might consist of measuring a person's height and weight.[7] Then we define A to be the $m \times n$ matrix obtained by letting each column be the measurements from one of these n experiments. Note that each row of A contains n measurements of the same type and, of course, the same is true of each column of A^T.

Assuming that each row of A has mean 0, the $m \times m$ *covariance matrix* is given by

$$C = \frac{1}{n} AA^T.$$

Why is $C = \{c_{ij}\}$ a covariance matrix? The diagonal element c_{ii} is the variance in measurement type i, while the off-diagonal element c_{ij}, where $i \neq j$, is the covariance of measurement type i with measurement type j. Consequently, the matrix C contains the variances of all measurement types, and all covariances between different measurement types. It's easily seen from the definition of covariance that C is symmetric, that is, we always have $c_{ij} = c_{ji}$.

What might an ideal covariance matrix C look like? If the variance is small, then the mean (which we have assumed is 0) tells the whole story. On the other hand, a large variance for a given measurement type implies that it carries more information (in some sense) than can be conveyed by the mean alone. Consequently, we can (and do) view a larger variance as indicative of more interesting data.

A covariance of 0 tells us that the corresponding measurement types are uncorrelated. This is the easiest case to deal with, since uncorrelated implies that there are is no linear relationship between the measurement types.[8] Therefore, it would seem that our ideal covariance matrix C would be diagonal (i.e., all covariances would be 0). In addition, we would like to see a few relatively large values on the diagonal (i.e., variances), with the remainder of the diagonal elements being relatively small. In this ideal case, the measurement types corresponding to the large diagonal elements would contain most of the useful information, and we would know that there are no interesting interactions between these measurements—at least to a first-order approximation. In such an ideal case, we could reduce the dimensionality of the problem, without any significant loss of information.

---

[7]We'll see that in the context of PCA, many things can be considered experiments, and measurement is also a highly flexible term.

[8]Intuitively, there is no "overlap" between the information contained in measurement types that are uncorrelated. That is, uncorrelated measurement types each provide information that cannot be readily obtained from the other.

Of course, we don't get to choose our experimental (i.e., training) data, so we have no control over the covariance matrix. But, by the magic of PCA, we can change to a new basis where the transformed covariance matrix will have many of the desirable properties just discussed. In such cases, we can reduce the dimensionality in this transformed space without any significant loss of information.

4.3   Principal Component Analysis

In this section, we discuss the ideas behind principal component analysis (PCA) from a fairly intuitive perspective. Here, we'll view PCA as representing the big picture, while singular value decomposition (SVD) is one concrete implementation of PCA.[9] Our goal in this section is to make it clear—from a high-level perspective—how eigenvalue-based techniques work and why they are useful.

Consider an $m \times n$ matrix B, where the ith column of B contains a set of measurements from the ith iteration of an experiment. That is, we have conducted n iterations of an experiment, with the same m types of measurements in each iteration, and we've collected the results in the matrix B. Then

$$
B = \begin{pmatrix}
b_{11} & b_{12} & \cdots & b_{1n} \\
b_{21} & b_{22} & \cdots & b_{2n} \\
\vdots & \vdots & \ddots & \vdots \\
b_{m1} & b_{m2} & \cdots & b_{mn}
\end{pmatrix},
$$

where each row of B contains n measurements of the same type, as does each column of B^T.

Let μ_i be the mean of the elements in row i of B, that is,

$$
\mu_i = \frac{1}{n} \sum_{j=1}^{n} b_{ij}.
$$

Define the $m \times n$ matrix $A = \{a_{ij}\}$ where

$$
a_{ij} = b_{ij} - \mu_i.
$$

Note that each row of A has mean 0 and, as discussed above, the $m \times m$ matrix

$$
C = \frac{1}{n} A A^T
$$

---

[9]This subject is sometimes presented with SVD as the more general case, while PCA is the more specific case. This view derives from the perspective of change of basis, since SVD is a general change of basis technique [127]. However, from your perspicacious author's perspective, it seems more appropriate to consider PCA as the general approach, with SVD being one specific implementation.

is the covariance matrix for the set of experiments under consideration. Again, the reason we call this the covariance matrix is because c_{ij}, for $i \neq j$, is the covariance of measurement type i with measurement type j, while c_{ii} is the variance of measurement type i.

As mentioned above, large variances are generally considered more interesting than small variances. A small variance implies that the mean contains virtually all of the information, while a large variance implies that more information than the mean is present. Geometrically, large variances can be viewed as representing the more significant directions in the data. Also, a covariance of 0 implies that the vectors are uncorrelated, while a non-zero covariance indicates redundancy. Therefore, from the perspective of dimensionality reduction, the ideal case is a covariance matrix with a few large elements on the diagonal, and all off-diagonal elements equal to zero.

Of course, we do not get to choose the covariance matrix, since it's determined from the data itself. But, we can transform a covariance matrix to a diagonal form, based on its eigenvalues, thereby revealing structure that would otherwise be hidden. In most cases, we can use this information to significantly reduce the dimensionality.

Before turning our attention to the details of PCA, we first consider a simple example that might clarify some of the ideas in the previous paragraphs. Suppose that we perform an experiment and obtain the results in the scatterplot in Figure 4.3 (a). In this case, the standard basis corresponding to the x and y axes may not be the most informative way to view the data. Instead, we might want to consider the line in Figure 4.3 (b), which captures the dominant information contained in the data, and also effectively reduces the dimensionality from two to one.[10] However, we do lose information by relying only on a one-dimensional representation of this data; specifically, we lose sight of the "spread" of the data about the line.

The line in Figure 4.3 is aligned with the direction of the largest variance in the data. PCA can be viewed as an extension of this approach, where we determine an entire basis from variances in the data, rather than a single dominant dimension. This resulting basis is likely to be much more informative than the standard basis. For the data in Figure 4.3, such a basis is illustrated in Figure 4.4, where the direction of each vector is determined by the structure of the data, while the magnitude of each vector quantifies the variance of the data in the given direction. From such a basis we can determine the dominant directions, and thereby reduce the dimensionality by eliminating less-informative directions. Again, all of this reasoning is based on the assumption that a lower variance implies less interesting data, which is intuitively appealing for many types of problems.

---

[10]The line in Figure 4.3 (b) might look like the linear regression line, but it's not; see Problem 16 in Chapter 7 for more information.

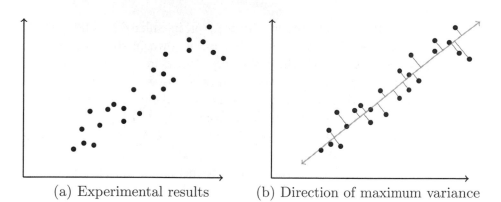

(a) Experimental results   (b) Direction of maximum variance

Figure 4.3: PCA and maximum variance

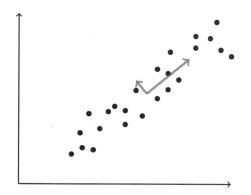

Figure 4.4: A better basis

The bottom line is that in PCA we align the basis vectors with the variances. Then we can reduce the dimensionality, while minimizing the information loss—assuming that large variances are most informative.

PCA training consists of diagonalizing the covariance matrix C. From the resulting diagonalized matrix, we can easily determine the most significant components—the *principal components*. Several linear algebraic techniques can be used to diagonalize a matrix. Regardless of the linear algebra, the basic idea behind PCA is the following.

1. Choose the direction with maximum variance.

2. Find the direction with maximum variance that is orthogonal to all previously selected directions.

3. If any dimensions remain, goto 2.

The vectors obtained by this process are defined as the principal components.

An analogy similar to the following is given in Shlens' excellent PCA tutorial [127]. Suppose that we want to explore a town in the Western United States. To do so, we employ the following algorithm. We begin by driving down the longest street. When we see another long street, we drive down it. After continuing this process for a while, it's likely that we will obtain a reasonably accurate map of the most important parts of the town, without having to explore all of the small side streets. In PCA, we obtain a basis by an analogous process. We can then eliminate the directions (i.e., basis elements) that are least informative, thereby reducing the dimensionality, while minimizing the information loss. This (roughly) corresponds to eliminating the shorter roads in Shlen's analogy.

It's important to realize that PCA relies on some strong assumptions. Specifically, we assume the following.

- Linearity — We rely on linear algebra techniques to determine the principal components. Consequently, if the underlying data is highly nonlinear, we may not obtain useful results.

- Large variances — We view large variances as the "signal," while small variances are treated as "noise." Intuitively, this is appealing, but it may not be valid for all problems.

- Orthogonality — We assume that the principal components are mutually orthogonal. This assumption makes the problem efficiently solvable. However, the optimal directions in the training data need not be orthogonal.

The orthogonality assumption is easy to state in terms of the road analogy mentioned above. That is, orthogonality implies that we can only make right-angle turns when exploring the town. However, it is certainly possible that some of the best roads to explore might not meet at right angles to each other. For example, we could expect good results using a PCA-like approach for a city that is laid out in a grid (e.g., Phoenix, Arizona), but if major roads meet at odd angles (e.g., Washington, DC), then the utility of a such a technique is far less certain.

With these assumptions in mind, we briefly discuss two examples [127] that illustrate cases where PCA will likely fail. First, consider data obtained by periodically measuring the position of a point on a Ferris wheel. An example of such data is given in Figure 4.5. For this data, we can reduce the dimensionality to a single angular variable by considering the problem in polar coordinates. However, such a coordinate system requires a nonlinear transformation. Since PCA is an inherently linear technique, we can only obtain a linear approximation to this transformation, and hence we would not expect good results in this case.

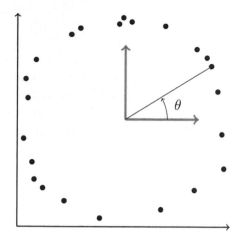

Figure 4.5: Ferris wheel data

As another example, suppose an experiment yields the data in Figure 4.6. For this data, the most informative directions are not mutually orthogonal. Since PCA assumes orthogonality, we would not expect to obtain particularly strong results for this case either.

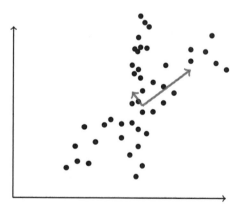

Figure 4.6: Non-orthogonal data

The third major assumption in PCA is that large variances are the most interesting. In the road analogy, this corresponds to driving on the longest roads. However, it is certainly possible that some short roads are among the most important in the town. For example, it's often the case that the most important street—which non-ironically often goes by the name of Main Street—is short, but has the majority of the most important businesses. In such cases, by focusing on the longer streets (which correspond to large variances in PCA), we might miss the most important street in town.

In spite of potential failures such as these, it can be shown that PCA is, in some sense, optimal for a large class of problems [127]. And, of course, there is extensive empirical evidence showing that the technique often works well in practice. In addition, some types of failures can be overcome by using kernel methods, which effectively embed a nonlinear transformation within the process. We won't discuss kernel methods here, but we do cover kernel methods in some detail in Chapter 5 when we discuss the "kernel trick," in the context of support vector machines.

To summarize, in PCA we'll perform the following steps [127].

1. Collect experimental results into an $m \times n$ matrix, where n is the number of experiments, and m is the number of measurements per experiment.

2. Subtract the mean of measurement type i from each element in row i to yield the matrix A.

3. Form the covariance matrix $C = \frac{1}{n} A A^T$.

4. Compute the eigenvalues and unit eigenvectors (typically, using the singular value decomposition) of the matrix C.

Why do we compute the eigenvectors of C in step 4? Since the matrix C is real-valued and symmetric, one of the more impressive results from linear algebra [7] tells us that we can write C as

$$C = EDE^T$$

where the columns of E are the eigenvectors[11] of C, the matrix D is diagonal, and D contains the corresponding eigenvalues of C. And, it can also be shown that $E^T = E^{-1}$. Therefore,

$$E^T C E = D,$$

which implies that the eigenvectors can be used to diagonalize the matrix C. In our discussion of the covariance matrix above, we claimed that the ideal case is a diagonal matrix C. However, we don't get to choose C, since it is determined by the data. But, by diagonalizing C, we reveal useful structure inherent in the data. Furthermore, the dominant eigenvalues are associated with the most informative directions in the transformed basis determined by this diagonalization process. That is, we can use the magnitude of the eigenvalues to reduce the dimensionality of the problem. This process often results in a dramatic reduction in dimensionality.

In the next section, we give a high-level overview of the well-known singular value decomposition (SVD) and show that it provides an ideal means

---

[11]The eigenvectors of a symmetric matrix, such as C, are mutually orthogonal, so the principal components will be orthogonal.

of diagonalizing the covariance matrix C. Then in Section 4.5 we discuss PCA training and scoring in detail. We follow up this discussion with an illuminating numerical example in Section 4.6.

4.4 SVD Basics

Singular value decomposition (SVD) [10, 128] is a matrix factorization (or decomposition) method. Specifically, the SVD of an $m \times n$ matrix M gives us

$$M = USV^T. \tag{4.3}$$

Here, U is $m \times m$ with columns consisting of the eigenvectors of MM^T, while V is $n \times n$ with columns consisting of the eigenvectors of M^TM. The matrix S is $m \times n$ and only has non-zero entries on its main diagonal, and we denote these so-called *singular values* as $\sigma_1, \sigma_2, \ldots, \sigma_k$, where $k = \min\{m, n\}$. The singular values are the square roots of the eigenvalues for both U and V. Furthermore, $U^TU = I$ where I is the $m \times m$ identity matrix. Therefore, the eigenvectors contained in U form an *orthonormal* set, which is just a fancy way of saying that they are mutually orthogonal and of length one. Similarly, $V^TV = I$ where I is the $n \times n$ identity matrix, and hence the eigenvectors in V are also an orthonormal set. Thus, the SVD factorization in (4.3) provides us everything (and more) that we need for PCA training.

To geometrically illustrate the SVD factorization, we can consider the action of a 2-dimensional shear matrix [8], as illustrated in the top row in Figure 4.7. Shear transformations can be used, for example, to convert a letter in a standard font to its italic or slanted form. The matrix M in Figure 4.7 stretches and rotates the unit disc, yielding an ellipse with the same area. By computing the SVD, we obtain the factorization $M = USV^T$, where, as illustrated in Figure 4.7, the matrices V^T and U are rotations, with S having the effect of scaling. Consequently, we see that the SVD factors the linear transformation M in a natural and intuitive way, at least in this particular case. For the purposes of PCA, the matrix U contains the essential information that we'll need for training and scoring. And we'll see that the matrices V and S are useful too.

4.5 All Together Now

We'll now discuss the PCA training (using SVD) and scoring phases in some detail. As previously mentioned, it is important to realize that "experiment" and "measurement" can both be taken in a very general sense, as we'll see in the PCA applications discussed in Chapter 11.

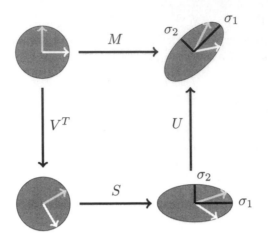

Figure 4.7: Matrix transformation using SVD

4.5.1   Training Phase

Here, we assume that the reader is familiar with the general concepts behind PCA and SVD as discussed above. With this background in mind, the PCA training phase consists of the following steps.

1. We are given a set of results from n experiment. Each experiment has m measurements, with the same types of measurements appearing in corresponding components of each experiment.

2. Let X_i be the vector of measurements from experiment i. Then X_i is of length m. For example, suppose that we first measure the height and then the weight of several humans. Then $m = 2$ and X_i is an ordered pair of the height and weight of the ith person in our sample. As another example, in facial recognition (see the "Eigenfaces" example discussed in Section 11.2 of Chapter 11), the X_i might consist of pixel values extracted from image i of the training set.

3. Let $e_i(X_j)$ denote the ith element of the training vector X_j. Then for each $j \in \{1, 2, \ldots, m\}$ we compute the mean

$$\mu_j = \frac{1}{n} \sum_{i=1}^{n} e_j(X_i).$$

Define the vector of means

$$\mu = \begin{pmatrix} \mu_1 \\ \mu_2 \\ \vdots \\ \mu_m \end{pmatrix} \tag{4.4}$$

and let $\widetilde{X}_i = X_i - \mu$. Finally, we define the matrix

$$A = (\begin{array}{cccc} \widetilde{X}_1 & \widetilde{X}_2 & \cdots & \widetilde{X}_n \end{array}),$$

that is, column i of A is the vector $\widetilde{X}_i$. By construction, the mean of the elements in any row of A is 0.

4. We want to determine the unit eigenvectors of the covariance matrix

$$C = \frac{1}{n} AA^T.$$

For more details on the covariance matrix, see Section 4.3 or [92].

We apply the SVD algorithm to obtain

$$A = USV^T$$

where the columns of U are the unit eigenvectors of AA^T, and the square roots of the eigenvalues are in the diagonal matrix S. Let u_i be the ith column of U and let σ_i be the corresponding singular value in S. Assuming that we have k non-zero singular values, which are contained in the matrix S, let $(u_1, u_2, \ldots, u_k)$ be the corresponding eigenvectors in U, with these vectors ordered by the magnitude of the singular values. That is, the singular value corresponding to u_1 is largest, the singular value corresponding to u_2 is the second largest, and so on. Then each u_i is a unit eigenvector of C with corresponding eigenvalue $\lambda_i = \sigma_i^2/n$.

5. As discussed in Section 4.2.2, the most significant eigenvectors are those corresponding to the eigenvalues of largest magnitude. Therefore, we will use the first ℓ unit eigenvectors, $u_1, u_2, \ldots, u_\ell$, for some $\ell \leq k$. The choice of ℓ could be determined experimentally or it can be based on the relative magnitudes of the eigenvalues, as discussed in Problem 9. Let

$$\widetilde{U} = (\begin{array}{cccc} u_1 & u_2 & \cdots & u_\ell \end{array}). \tag{4.5}$$

Then $\widetilde{U}$ is $m \times \ell$ and its columns are the ℓ dominant eigenvectors of C.

6. Recall that $\widetilde{X}_i$ is the ith column of the matrix A. We compute a scoring matrix by projecting each training vector $\widetilde{X}_i$ onto the eigenspace. Specifically, the $k \times n$ scoring matrix Δ is computed as

$$\Delta = \widetilde{U}^T A. \tag{4.6}$$

Let Δ_i be the ith column of Δ. It is easily verified that

$$\Delta_i = \begin{pmatrix} \widetilde{X}_i \cdot u_1 \\ \widetilde{X}_i \cdot u_2 \\ \vdots \\ \widetilde{X}_i \cdot u_\ell \end{pmatrix}$$

and we see that Δ_i is indeed the projection of $\widetilde{X}_i$ onto the eigenspace specified by the dominant eigenvectors of the covariance matrix C.

Next, we discuss how the scoring matrix Δ is used for scoring. Spoiler alert: The crucial step in the scoring process consists of projecting a vector onto the eigenspace determined by the matrix $\widetilde{U}$, which is the easy step in the training phase.

4.5.2 Scoring Phase

We assume that we've trained a model, which implies that $\widetilde{U}$ in (4.5) is known. In addition, we assume that the scoring matrix Δ in (4.6) has been determined.

Let Y be a sample that we want to score. By assumption, Y is from the same type of experiment as used in training and therefore the number and type of measurements in Y match those in the training vectors X_i. To compute the score of Y, we proceed as follows.

1. As when training, we first subtract the means, then project the resulting vector onto the eigenspace determined by $\widetilde{U}$. That is, we let $\widetilde{Y} = Y - \mu$, where μ is the vector of means in equation (4.4). Then we compute the weight vector

$$W = \begin{pmatrix} w_1 \\ w_2 \\ \vdots \\ w_\ell \end{pmatrix} = \widetilde{U}^T \widetilde{Y}.$$

Note that $w_i = \widetilde{Y} \cdot u_i$ and hence W is the projection of $\widetilde{Y}$ onto the eigenspace.

2. Next, let ε_i be the Euclidean distance from this weight vector W to column i of the scoring matrix Δ. That is,

$$\varepsilon_i = d(W, \Delta_i), \text{ for } i = 1, 2, \ldots, n.$$

3. Finally, the score is given by

$$\texttt{score}(Y) = \min_i \varepsilon_i.$$

Since each ε_i is a distance, we have $\texttt{score}(Y) \geq 0$. Furthermore, if Y happens to be an element of the training set, that is, if $Y = X_i$ for some i, then it is easy to see that $\texttt{score}(Y) = 0$. It's reassuring that when we score an element of the training set, we obtain the minimum possible score.

Although PCA training is somewhat complex and involved, the PCA scoring phase is extremely efficient, since each score only requires ℓ dot products (where ℓ is generally small) and n distance computations. In particular, no SVD or other expensive (or complex) linear algebra operations are used when computing scores.

Next, we consider a simple numerical example. This example illustrates both the training and scoring phases of PCA, using matrices that are small enough so that the results can be verified by relatively straightforward hand calculations.

4.6   A Numerical Example

Suppose we have a training set consisting of the four vectors

$$
X_1 = \begin{pmatrix} 2 \\ 1 \\ 0 \\ 3 \\ 1 \\ 1 \end{pmatrix}, \quad
X_2 = \begin{pmatrix} 2 \\ 3 \\ 1 \\ 2 \\ 3 \\ 0 \end{pmatrix}, \quad
X_3 = \begin{pmatrix} 1 \\ 0 \\ 3 \\ 3 \\ 1 \\ 1 \end{pmatrix}, \quad
X_4 = \begin{pmatrix} 2 \\ 3 \\ 1 \\ 0 \\ 3 \\ 2 \end{pmatrix}. \tag{4.7}
$$

These vectors could represent pixel values from image files, byte values from malware executables, opcodes extracted from malware samples, or other such data. Regardless of the source of the training data, the PCA process is as follows.

We first form the matrix

$$
B = \begin{pmatrix} X_1 & X_2 & X_3 & X_4 \end{pmatrix} = \begin{pmatrix}
2 & 2 & 1 & 2 \\
1 & 3 & 0 & 3 \\
0 & 1 & 3 & 1 \\
3 & 2 & 3 & 0 \\
1 & 3 & 1 & 3 \\
1 & 0 & 1 & 2
\end{pmatrix}.
$$

We then compute the mean of each row of B to obtain

$$
\mu = \begin{pmatrix} 7/4 \\ 7/4 \\ 5/4 \\ 2 \\ 2 \\ 1 \end{pmatrix} \tag{4.8}
$$

from which we determine the normalized training vectors $\tilde{X}_i = X_i - \mu$. For this example, we find

$$
\tilde{X}_1 = \begin{pmatrix} 1/4 \\ -3/4 \\ -5/4 \\ 1 \\ -1 \\ 0 \end{pmatrix}, \quad
\tilde{X}_2 = \begin{pmatrix} 1/4 \\ 5/4 \\ -1/4 \\ 0 \\ 1 \\ -1 \end{pmatrix}, \quad
\tilde{X}_3 = \begin{pmatrix} -3/4 \\ -7/4 \\ 7/4 \\ 1 \\ -1 \\ 0 \end{pmatrix}, \quad
\tilde{X}_4 = \begin{pmatrix} 1/4 \\ 5/4 \\ -1/4 \\ -2 \\ 1 \\ 1 \end{pmatrix}.
$$

This gives us the matrix

$$
A = \begin{pmatrix} \tilde{X}_1 & \tilde{X}_2 & \tilde{X}_3 & \tilde{X}_4 \end{pmatrix} =
\begin{pmatrix}
1/4 & 1/4 & -3/4 & 1/4 \\
-3/4 & 5/4 & -7/4 & 5/4 \\
-5/4 & -1/4 & 7/4 & -1/4 \\
1 & 0 & 1 & -2 \\
-1 & 1 & -1 & 1 \\
0 & -1 & 0 & 1
\end{pmatrix}.
$$

By construction, each row of A has mean 0.

For this example, the SVD yields $A = USV^T$ where[12]

$$
U = \begin{pmatrix}
0.1641 & 0.2443 & -0.0710 \\
0.6278 & 0.1070 & 0.2934 \\
-0.2604 & -0.8017 & 0.3952 \\
-0.5389 & 0.4277 & 0.3439 \\
0.4637 & -0.1373 & 0.3644 \\
0.0752 & -0.2904 & -0.7083
\end{pmatrix}
$$

and

$$
S = \begin{pmatrix}
4.0414 & 0 & 0 \\
0 & 2.2239 & 0 \\
0 & 0 & 1.7237
\end{pmatrix}
$$

and

$$
V = \begin{pmatrix}
-0.2739 & 0.6961 & -0.4364 \\
0.3166 & 0.2466 & 0.7674 \\
-0.6631 & -0.5434 & 0.1224 \\
0.6205 & -0.3993 & -0.4534
\end{pmatrix}.
$$

It follows that the nonzero eigenvalues of $C = \frac{1}{n} AA^T$ are

$$
\lambda_1 = 4.0833, \quad \lambda_2 = 1.2364, \quad \text{and} \quad \lambda_3 = 0.7428 \tag{4.9}
$$

---

[12]Here, we have omitted all eigenvalues of 0 and their corresponding eigenvectors, since these play no role in PCA. As a result, the matrices U, S, and V in this example do not quite agree with the descriptions given in Section 4.4. This issue is explored further in Problem 14 at the end of this chapter.

with corresponding unit eigenvectors

$$u_1 = \begin{pmatrix} 0.1641 \\ 0.6278 \\ -0.2604 \\ -0.5389 \\ 0.4637 \\ 0.0752 \end{pmatrix}, \quad u_2 = \begin{pmatrix} 0.2443 \\ 0.1070 \\ -0.8017 \\ 0.4277 \\ -0.1373 \\ -0.2904 \end{pmatrix}, \quad u_3 = \begin{pmatrix} -0.0710 \\ 0.2934 \\ 0.3952 \\ 0.3439 \\ 0.3644 \\ -0.7083 \end{pmatrix}. \quad (4.10)$$

These u_i are the principal components of C.

The scoring matrix is computed as $\Delta = U^T A$, which has the effect of projecting each of the normalized training vectors $\widetilde{X}_i$ onto the eigenspace. As above, we denote the ith column of Δ as Δ_i. Then we see that

$$\Delta_i = \begin{pmatrix} \widetilde{X}_i \cdot u_1 \\ \widetilde{X}_i \cdot u_2 \\ \widetilde{X}_i \cdot u_3 \end{pmatrix}$$

where "$\cdot$" is the dot product. For this particular example, we find

$$\Delta = \begin{pmatrix} -1.1069 & 1.2794 & -2.6800 & 2.5076 \\ 1.5480 & 0.5484 & -1.2085 & -0.8879 \\ -0.2583 & 1.4217 & -0.4807 & -0.6827 \end{pmatrix}. \quad (4.11)$$

Suppose that we choose to use only the two most significant principal components. Then the scoring matrix reduces to

$$\Delta = \begin{pmatrix} -1.1069 & 1.2794 & -2.6800 & 2.5076 \\ 1.5480 & 0.5484 & -1.2085 & -0.8879 \end{pmatrix}. \quad (4.12)$$

Now, suppose that we want to score a vector of the form

$$Y = \begin{pmatrix} y_1 & y_2 & y_3 & y_4 & y_5 & y_6 \end{pmatrix}^T$$

using the scoring matrix in (4.12). We first determine $\widetilde{Y} - \mu$, where μ is the vector of means in (4.8). Then we project $\widetilde{Y}$ onto the eigenspace determined in the training phase, that is, we compute

$$W = \begin{pmatrix} \widetilde{Y} \cdot u_1 \\ \widetilde{Y} \cdot u_2 \end{pmatrix}.$$

Finally, we compute the score as

$$\texttt{score}(Y) = \min_i \varepsilon_i$$

where ε_i is the Euclidean distance between W and the ith column of the scoring matrix, that is, $\varepsilon_i = d(W, \Delta_i)$. That is, we compute the minimum distance to any training vector, where all distance calculations are done in the projection space.

For example, suppose $Y = X_1 = (\ 2 \quad 1 \quad 0 \quad 3 \quad 1 \quad 1 \ )^T$. Then subtracting the mean vector, we have $\widetilde{Y} = Y - \mu = (\ 1/4 \quad -3/4 \quad -5/4 \quad 1 \quad -1 \quad 0 \ )^T$ and hence

$$W = \left(\begin{array}{c} \widetilde{Y} \cdot u_1 \\ \widetilde{Y} \cdot u_2 \end{array} \right) = \left(\begin{array}{c} \widetilde{X}_1 \cdot u_1 \\ \widetilde{X}_1 \cdot u_2 \end{array} \right) = \left(\begin{array}{c} -1.1069 \\ 1.5480 \end{array} \right).$$

Since W matches the first column of the scoring matrix (4.12), $\texttt{score}(Y) = 0$. It's clear that, in general, we obtain the minimum score of 0 for any element in the training set.

As another scoring example, suppose $Y = (\ 2 \quad 3 \quad 4 \quad 4 \quad -3 \quad -2 \ )^T$. In this case, $\widetilde{Y} = Y - \mu = (\ 1/4 \quad 5/4 \quad 11/4 \quad 2 \quad -5 \quad -3 \ )^T$ and we compute the projection

$$W = \left(\begin{array}{c} \widetilde{Y} \cdot u_1 \\ \widetilde{Y} \cdot u_2 \end{array} \right) = \left(\begin{array}{c} -0.2256 \\ -0.8712 \end{array} \right).$$

From the scoring matrix in (4.12), we find

$$\varepsilon_1 = 2.57, \ \ \varepsilon_2 = 2.07, \ \ \varepsilon_3 = 2.48, \ \ \varepsilon_4 = 2.73$$

where, again, $\varepsilon_i = d(W, \Delta_i)$. The score of Y is the minimum of these ε_i, and hence $\texttt{score}(Y) = 2.07$. Intuitively, this vector Y seems to be far from the training set, so it is reassuring that we obtain a relatively high score in this case.

4.7   The Bottom Line

PCA is a powerful and practical technique. The primary selling point of PCA is that it can often be used to dramatically reduce the dimensionality of a problem by eliminating redundancy, without any significant loss of information. This should be clear from the geometric intuition behind the technique.

Typically, in PCA we use a singular value decomposition (SVD) for training. That is, we use the SVD to obtain the necessary eigenvalues and unit eigenvectors from the training set.

Much sophisticated linear algebra underlies the PCA training phase and the work factor is not insignificant. But, training is usually one-time work, and the PCA scoring phase is extremely fast and efficient, which makes it practical for almost any application. So, don't let the mathematics behind PCA scare you away, as excellent results are often obtained, and the scoring phase is nothing short of simplicity itself.

Among the many available sources of information on PCA, Shlens tutorial [127] stands out, especially with respect to the intuition and motivation behind the technique. For a concise and readable mathematical treatment, the book chapter by Shalizi [125] is highly recommended. If you want a very brief and intuitive yet enlightening discussion of PCA, see [136].

4.8 Problems

1. Let

$$A = \begin{pmatrix} 1 & 0 & -2 \\ -2 & 3 & 1 \end{pmatrix}, \ B = \begin{pmatrix} 1 & -1 \\ 2 & -2 \\ 3 & 1 \end{pmatrix}, \ \text{and } C = \begin{pmatrix} 3 & 2 \\ -1 & -3 \\ 2 & -1 \end{pmatrix}.$$

Compute each of the following. If the operation is undefined, explain why it is undefined.

a) $2A$

b) $B + C$

c) $A + B$

d) AB

e) BA

f) BC

2. In this chapter, it is claimed that the main advantage of PCA is that it can be used to reduce the dimensionality of the training data.

a) Specifically, what are the advantages of reducing the dimensionality of the data?

b) Discuss in detail how PCA reduces the dimensionality of the data.

3. In the text, it is mentioned that PCA is somewhat analogous to constructing an approximate map of a town by driving on the longest streets. Discuss a different intuitive example that also illustrates the concepts behind PCA.

4. Let

$$A = \begin{pmatrix} 1 & 2 \\ 3 & 1 \\ 2 & 3 \end{pmatrix}.$$

Solve each of the following by hand.

a) Compute the covariance matrix $C = \frac{1}{2}AA^T$.

b) Determine the eigenvalues λ_1 and λ_2 of the matrix C in part a).

c) Find the corresponding unit eigenvectors for the eigenvalues you determined in part b). Verify that each is an eigenvector of C and that each is a vector of length one.

5. Recall that the covariance matrix is $C = \frac{1}{n}AA^T$. Suppose that we omit the factor of $1/n$, that is, we consider $\widehat{C} = AA^T$ instead of C.

   a) How do the eigenvalues and eigenvectors of $\widehat{C}$ compare to those of C?

   b) Show that we can easily obtain eigenvalues and eigenvectors of the covariance matrix C from those of $\widehat{C}$.

6. In Section 4.5.2 it is claimed that if $Y = X_i$, then $\mathrm{score}(Y) = 0$. That is, if Y is an element of the training set, then its score is the minimum possible. Prove that this is indeed the case and explain why this is a desirable feature of the score.

7. This problem deals with the eigenvalues and eigenvectors that appear in (4.9) and (4.10), respectively.

   a) Compute the matrix $C = \frac{1}{n}AA^T$.

   b) Verify that each putative eigenvector u_i and corresponding eigenvalue λ_i is actually an eigenvector and eigenvalue of C, i.e., verify that $Cu_i = \lambda_i u_i$.

   c) Verify that all of the eigenvectors u_i are unit vectors.

8. Recall that in PCA we have n training vectors, each of which is of length m. These training vectors form the columns of the $m \times n$ matrix A. The principal components are the unit eigenvectors of the covariance matrix $C = \frac{1}{n}AA^T$, which is $m \times m$. These eigenvectors can be obtained from the columns of the U matrix in the SVD, as given in equation (4.3).

   a) Suppose that we only have access to the V and S matrices from the SVD, not the U matrix. Show that we can easily determine the eigenvectors and eigenvalues of C. Hint: The columns of the V matrix in the SVD give us the eigenvectors of the $n \times n$ matrix $A^T A$, and we can easily determine the corresponding eigenvalues from singular values in S. Thus, we have $A^T A v_i = \lambda_i v_i$ where the eigenvalues v_i are the columns of V.

   b) In many applications, m is much larger than n. In such cases, why would it be advantageous to compute the eigenvalues of $A^T A$ instead of those of C?

c) For the example in Section 4.6, compute the eigenvalues and eigen-vectors of $A^T A$, and from these, derive the unit eigenvectors of C. Verify that your eigenvectors agree with those of AA^T, which appear in (4.10).

9. This problem considers the relationship between the total variance in the input space and the total variance in the PCA projection space, based on the numerical example in Section 4.6.

a) Determine the total variance in the input space for the example in Section 4.6. Hint: Form the covariance matrix $C = \frac{1}{n}AA^T$ and sum the variances that appear on the main diagonal. Note that $n = 4$ in this example.

b) Compute the total variance in the projection space and compare your answer to the result in part a). Hint: In PCA, the eigenvectors u_i are unit vectors. Explain why this implies that the eigenvalues must correspond to the variances in the projection space.

c) For the example in Section 4.6, suppose that we use a PCA score based on the single most dominant eigenvector. What percentage of the total variance is accounted for by such a score? If instead we use the two most dominant eigenvectors, what percentage of the total variance is accounted for by the PCA score? And, what percentage of the total variance is accounted for if we use all three non-trivial eigenvectors? In general, how can we determine the fraction of the variance that is accounted for by a PCA score that uses the ℓ most dominant eigenvalues, assuming that we have a total of k nontrivial eigenvalues?

10. Consider the scoring matrix Δ in equation (4.12), which is based on the training set given in equation (4.7) and the eigenvectors in equation (4.10). Use this scoring matrix to score each of the vectors

$$Y_1 = \begin{pmatrix} 2 \\ 3 \\ 1 \\ 0 \\ 3 \\ 2 \end{pmatrix}, \; Y_2 = \begin{pmatrix} -4 \\ -5 \\ 0 \\ 3 \\ 1 \\ -2 \end{pmatrix}, \; Y_3 = \begin{pmatrix} 2 \\ 3 \\ 0 \\ 1 \\ 3 \\ 2 \end{pmatrix}, \; Y_4 = \begin{pmatrix} 3 \\ 2 \\ 1 \\ 0 \\ 3 \\ 2 \end{pmatrix}.$$

11. In this problem, you will train and score using the PCA technique discussed in this chapter.

a) Train using the following set of vectors.

$$X_1 = \begin{pmatrix} 2 \\ -1 \\ 0 \\ 1 \\ 1 \\ -3 \\ 5 \\ 2 \end{pmatrix}, \quad X_2 = \begin{pmatrix} -2 \\ 3 \\ 2 \\ 3 \\ 0 \\ 2 \\ -1 \\ 1 \end{pmatrix}, \quad X_3 = \begin{pmatrix} -1 \\ 3 \\ 3 \\ 1 \\ -1 \\ 4 \\ 5 \\ 2 \end{pmatrix}, \quad X_4 = \begin{pmatrix} 3 \\ -1 \\ 0 \\ 3 \\ 2 \\ -1 \\ 3 \\ 0 \end{pmatrix}.$$

That is, form the matrix $B = \begin{pmatrix} X_1 & X_2 & X_3 & X_4 \end{pmatrix}$, then normalize so that each row has mean 0, and denote the resulting matrix as A. Determine the eigenvalues and unit eigenvectors of the covariance matrix $C = \frac{1}{n} A A^T$. Finally, generate the scoring matrix Δ, as in (4.11), based on the three most significant eigenvectors of C.

b) Use the scoring matrix from part a) to score each of the following.

$$Y_1 = \begin{pmatrix} 1 \\ 5 \\ 1 \\ 5 \\ 5 \\ 1 \\ 1 \\ 3 \end{pmatrix}, \quad Y_2 = \begin{pmatrix} -2 \\ 3 \\ 2 \\ 3 \\ 0 \\ 2 \\ -1 \\ 1 \end{pmatrix}, \quad Y_3 = \begin{pmatrix} 2 \\ -3 \\ 2 \\ 3 \\ 0 \\ 0 \\ 2 \\ -1 \end{pmatrix}, \quad Y_4 = \begin{pmatrix} 2 \\ -2 \\ 2 \\ 2 \\ -1 \\ 1 \\ 2 \\ 2 \end{pmatrix}.$$

12. When scoring using PCA, we generally use Euclidean distance, but other distance measures could be used.

a) Repeat Problem 11 using taxicab distance when scoring. The *taxicab distance* between two vectors

$$x = \begin{pmatrix} x_1 & x_2 & \cdots & x_n \end{pmatrix} \text{ and } y = \begin{pmatrix} y_1 & y_2 & \cdots & y_n \end{pmatrix}$$

is defined as

$$d(x, y) = \sum_{i=1}^{n} |x_i - y_i|.$$

b) Repeat Problem 11 using Mahalanobis distance when scoring. Given vectors

$$x = \begin{pmatrix} x_1 & x_2 & \cdots & x_n \end{pmatrix} \text{ and } y = \begin{pmatrix} y_1 & y_2 & \cdots & y_n \end{pmatrix}$$

and covariance matrix D, the *Mahalanobis distance* is defined as

$$d(x, y) = \sum_{i=1}^{n} (x - y) D^{-1} (x - y)^T.$$

For this problem, let D be the a diagonal matrix containing the eigenvalues of the A matrix in Problem 11, arranged in descending order of magnitude.

13. Suppose that we have a training set consisting of n malware samples, all of which belong to a given malware family, and we have m representative benign executable samples. Let M_1, M_2, ..., M_n be feature vectors extracted from the malware samples, and let B_1, B_2, ..., B_m be feature vectors extracted from the benign samples. Further, suppose that we want to classify a sample that does not belong to our training set. Let Y be the feature vector extracted from this sample. Perhaps the simplest possible classification method is to measure the distance from Y to each of the malware feature vectors M_i, for $i = 1, 2, \ldots, n$, and each of the benign feature vectors B_j, for $j = 1, 2, \ldots, m$, in the training set. We can then classify Y based on its nearest neighbor, that is, if Y is nearest to one of the vectors M_i, it is classified as malware; otherwise it is classified as benign. This nearest neighbor algorithm easily generalizes to the well-known k-nearest neighbor (k-NN) algorithm. The k-NN algorithm and several variants[13] are discussed in more detail Section 7.2 of Chapter 7.

It's possible—and possibly beneficial—to combine the nearest neighbor algorithm with PCA as follows. First, as in Section 4.5.1, determine the A matrix corresponding to the malware samples and project these onto the eigenspace to determine the scoring matrix $\Delta = \widetilde{U}^T A$. Also construct a matrix analogous to A using the benign data, and denote this matrix as $\widehat{A}$. Project this matrix onto the eigenspace to obtain $\nabla = \widetilde{U}^T \widehat{A}$. Then given a sample X to classify, we compute its weight vector $W = \widetilde{U}^T X$ and classify the sample based on the nearest column in Δ or ∇. That is, if W is nearest to Δ_i for some i, then X is classified as malware; on the other hand, if W is nearest to ∇_j for some j, then X is classified as benign. Note that this approach directly yields a classification, as opposed to a score. This is in contrast to the the standard PCA technique, which generates a score.

a) Recall the numerical example of PCA in Section 4.6. Use the scoring matrix Δ as given in (4.12) to score (in the usual PCA sense) the

---

[13]It would also be interesting to apply some of the variants of k-NN, as discussed in Section 7.2, to this problem. Your lawyerly author is virtually certain that there is no law against doing more work than is asked for in a problem.

representative malware samples

$$M_1 = \begin{pmatrix} 1 \\ -1 \\ 1 \\ -1 \\ -1 \\ 1 \end{pmatrix}, \quad M_2 = \begin{pmatrix} -2 \\ 2 \\ 2 \\ -1 \\ -2 \\ 2 \end{pmatrix}, \quad M_3 = \begin{pmatrix} 1 \\ 3 \\ 0 \\ 1 \\ 3 \\ 1 \end{pmatrix}, \quad M_4 = \begin{pmatrix} 2 \\ 3 \\ 1 \\ 1 \\ -2 \\ 0 \end{pmatrix}.$$

b) Compute the matrix ∇ based on the benign samples

$$B_1 = \begin{pmatrix} -1 \\ 2 \\ 1 \\ 2 \\ -1 \\ 0 \end{pmatrix}, \quad B_2 = \begin{pmatrix} -2 \\ 1 \\ 2 \\ 3 \\ 2 \\ 1 \end{pmatrix}, \quad B_3 = \begin{pmatrix} -1 \\ 3 \\ 0 \\ 1 \\ 3 \\ -1 \end{pmatrix}, \quad B_4 = \begin{pmatrix} 0 \\ 2 \\ 3 \\ 1 \\ 1 \\ -2 \end{pmatrix}.$$

Note that the same process is used to construct this matrix ∇ as was used to construct the scoring matrix Δ, except that the vectors B_i are used in place of the vectors M_i.

c) Based on the matrices Δ and ∇, classify each of the vectors

$$Y_1 = \begin{pmatrix} 1 \\ 5 \\ 1 \\ 5 \\ 5 \\ 1 \end{pmatrix}, \quad Y_2 = \begin{pmatrix} -2 \\ 3 \\ 2 \\ 3 \\ 0 \\ 2 \end{pmatrix}, \quad Y_3 = \begin{pmatrix} 2 \\ -3 \\ 2 \\ 3 \\ 0 \\ 0 \end{pmatrix}, \quad Y_4 = \begin{pmatrix} 2 \\ -2 \\ 2 \\ 2 \\ -1 \\ 1 \end{pmatrix}.$$

using the nearest neighbor algorithm. That is, if $W = \tilde{U}^T Y_i$ is nearest (as measured by Euclidean distance) to a column of Δ, classify it as malware, whereas if W is nearest to a column of ∇, classify it as benign.

14. In Section 4.4 we claimed that the SVD of an $m \times n$ matrix M gives us the factorization $M = USV^T$ where U is $m \times m$ and V is $n \times n$, while the diagonal matrix S is $m \times n$. We also claimed that $U^T U = I$ and $V^T V = I$. However, in the example in Section 4.6, we have $m = 6$ and $n = 4$, yet the given U matrix is 6×3, the S matrix is 3×3, and the V matrix is 4×3. For the remainder of this problem, refer to the example in Section 4.6.

a) Verify that $A = USV^T$.

b) Show that the covariance matrix C corresponding to A has three eigenvalues of 0. For the six eigenvectors of C, including those that correspond to eigenvalues of 0, determine a set of orthonormal eigenvectors and give the resulting 6×6 matrix U and 6×4 matrix S. Hint: Recall that orthonormal vectors are mutually orthogonal, and each is of length one. Include the eigenvectors in (4.10) in your set, and find three more mutually orthogonal unit eigenvectors corresponding to the zero eigenvalues. Note that for an eigenvalue of 0, the corresponding eigenvector x of C satisfies $Cx = 0$.

c) Similar to part b), determine the missing column of V.

d) For the matrices U and V that you determined in parts b) and c), respectively, verify that $U^T U = I$ and $V^T V = I$, for the appropriate size of identity matrices.

15. The Jacobi eigenvalue method [114] is a numerically stable and simple iterative technique for computing eigenvalues and eigenvectors of a matrix. The drawback is that it is inefficient, and hence it's only useful for relatively low-dimensional problems.

a) Implement the Jacobi eigenvalue method.

b) Use your code from part a) to compute the eigenvalues and eigenvectors of the matrix $C = \frac{1}{n} AA^T$ corresponding to the matrix A in Section 4.6.

c) Use the results of this problem to verify the scoring and training computations in Section 4.6.

16. In this problem, we consider using PCA for (lossy) data compression. Suppose that we are given data vectors X_i, for $i = 1, 2, \ldots, n$, where each vector is of length m. As discussed in this chapter, we can determine the principal components by forming the $m \times n$ matrix A where column i is $\widetilde{X}_i = X_i - \mu$, and μ is the vector of means. Use the SVD to factor A as $A = USV^T$, as discussed in Section 4.4. Then the columns of U are the principal components of the covariance matrix $C = \frac{1}{n} AA^T$. Let $\widetilde{U}$ be the $m \times \ell$ truncated version of U containing the ℓ dominant principal components of C.

a) Suppose that we compress the data as $\widehat{A} = \widetilde{U}^T A$ and decompress by computing $\widetilde{A} = \widetilde{U} \widehat{A}$, and then add the means to recover approximations to the original data vectors X_i. Does this approach make intuitive sense as a compression scheme? Why or why not?

b) What rate of compression does the method in part a) achieve?

c) Apply the compression scheme in part a) to the data in Section 4.6 with $\ell = 2$. That is, compress the data vectors in (4.7) based on the two most dominant principal components in (4.10). Decompress the result, add the means, and compare to the original data.

17. In the next chapter, we'll see that when training a linear support vector machine (SVM) we obtain a weight vector, where each weight corresponds to a specific feature in the input space—the larger the weight, the more the model relies on that feature. Thus, for SVM we can reduce the dimensionality by simply discarding lightly weighted features from the input space; see Problem 12 in Chapter 5 for more details. In PCA, we also reduce the dimensionality, but this reduction is not as straightforward to interpret with respect to the input space features. In effect, PCA generates new features in the projection space that are linear combinations of the input features.

Suppose that we train a model using PCA and we obtain the principal components (i.e., unit eigenvectors) $u_1, u_2, \ldots, u_k$, and the corresponding eigenvalues $\lambda_1, \lambda_2, \ldots, \lambda_k$. Each u_i determines a linear combination of the input variables, and this linear combination acts essentially as a new variable in the projection space. To determine the relative importance of input features with respect to a specific u_i, we only need to consider the elements of u_i. The larger the magnitude of an element in u_i, the greater the significance of the corresponding input feature, with the sign specifying positive or negative correlation. But, since u_i is a unit vector, it only specifies a direction, while the corresponding eigenvalue λ_i gives us the magnitude of the variance in that direction. Thus, to compare the relative importance of input variables across multiple principal components, we'll also need to account for the eigenvalues. We define the *component loading* vectors[14] as $\sqrt{\lambda_i}\, u_i$, for $i = 1, 2, \ldots, k$.

a) Consider the principal component u_1 in (4.10). Which input space feature with positive correlation has the greatest effect on the projection space feature determined by u_1? Which input space feature with negative correlation has the greatest effect on u_1? Overall, which input space feature has the greatest effect on u_1?

b) Compute the component loading vector corresponding to each of the three principal components u_1, u_2, u_3 in (4.10).

c) Suppose that we define a PCA score using only the two most significant principal components u_1 and u_2 in (4.10). For the resulting score, rank the relative importance of each of the six input features, based on the component loading vectors. Also, give a numerical "weight" to each input feature, based on its relative importance to the PCA score.

---

[14]Scalar projections give us squared distance in the projection space, which is why we use $\sqrt{\lambda_i}$ instead of λ_i for the component loading vectors; see also Problem 16 in Chapter 5.

Chapter 5

A Reassuring Introduction to Support Vector Machines

Vector! That's me, because I commit crimes with both
direction and magnitude. Oh yeah!
— Vector in *Despicable Me*

5.1 Introduction

All of the machine learning techniques we have considered so far (HMM, PHMM, and PCA) are typically used to generate scores. These scores can then be used to classify samples into one of two categories (i.e., the same type as the training data, or not), based on a threshold. In contrast, a support vector machine (SVM) directly generates a classification, rather than a score. In other words, with an SVM there is no need to score samples and construct a classifier, as this is built into the SVM process.[1]

SVMs are very powerful and have been successfully applied to a wide variety of applications. For example, in the context of malware detection, we could train an SVM on, say, opcodes extracted from members of a given malware family. Then the trained SVM could be used to classify samples as either malware of the type that the SVM was trained to detect, or not.

Due to the fact that an SVM generates a classification, it's also very natural to apply the technique to a set of scores, as opposed to the raw training data itself. For example, suppose that we've already generated an HMM score and a PCA score for each sample in a particular dataset. Determining a good method to combine these scores into one meta-score might be challenging. It

---

[1]Your non-standard author would like to note that, although it is not exactly standard practice, it is possible to generate a score from an SVM, rather than a classification. We discuss this briefly at the end of Section 5.3.1.

would be entirely reasonable to apply an SVM to such scores as a means
of generating a classification, rather than trying to devise an ad hoc score
combination. In this mode of usage, we can view SVMs as operating on a
"higher plane" than the individual scores.

As with most other machine learning techniques, it's possible to describe
SVMs from a very high-level perspective in simple terms. But, we've seen in
previous chapters that to really understand a machine learning technique we
must dig into the details, and in this respect, SVM is no exception. As in
previous chapters, our goal here is to present a sufficient level of detail so the
reader can understand what is really going on inside an SVM.

The big ideas behind SVMs are clear and intuitive. We'll get to these ideas
in a moment, but first we briefly discuss supervised and unsupervised learning. A *supervised* learning algorithm requires labeled training data. That is,
the training data must be categorized in advance. For example, in malware
detection the training data could consist of a set of samples that are known to
be malware of a particular type (or family), along with another representative
set of benign samples. Such labeled data is needed during the SVM training
process.

In contrast, an *unsupervised* algorithm deals with unlabeled data. In the
context of malware, an unsupervised algorithm could be applied to a set of
unlabeled samples; that is, we don't have to tell the algorithm which samples
are malware and which are benign. The benefit of an unsupervised algorithm
is that it can help us determine possible structure, so it is generally most
useful in cases where we don't know much about the data. A third category
of *semi-supervised* algorithms might also be considered. These are technically
supervised algorithms, but in some sense they require less supervision.

The clustering algorithms discussed in Chapter 6 provide classic examples
of unsupervised learning. For such algorithms, we generally have raw unlabeled data, and we hope that the resulting clusters might tell us something
interesting about the data. Such algorithms are typically used in a data exploration mode, where we are trying to pry some useful information out of a
stubborn dataset.

When training an HMM, for example, we usually provide data of the
specific type that we want the HMM to model. And, when generating scores
to determine a threshold, we certainly need labeled data. But in some cases,
we could train an HMM on unlabeled data and analyze the resulting model to
look for structure. This latter approach is used in the English text example
discussed in Section 9.2 of Chapter 9. This application could be viewed as
an unsupervised use of an HMM, since we simply train on text, without
any significant preprocessing or labeling. The resulting model provides us
with some useful information about the English language; specifically, in the
case of $N = 2$ hidden states, the B matrix clearly shows the split between
consonants and vowels.

SVMs are a supervised technique, since they require labeled data. Consequently, we must use preprocessed the training data that includes labels. Since SVMs are used for binary classification, the labels can be taken to be 0 and 1, or +1 and −1, for example. We'll see that for SVMs, it's convenient to use +1 and −1 for the class labels.

The big ideas behind SVMs are the following.

- Separating hyperplane — We separate the labeled data into two classes based on a hyperplane.

- Maximize the margin — When constructing the separating hyperplane, we maximize the margin, which is the separation between the two classes in the training set. Intuitively, this seems like a good idea.

- Work in a higher dimensional space — We often try to reduce the dimensionality of data, due to the dreaded curse of dimensionality.[2] However, in the context of SVMs, it's actually beneficial to work in a higher dimensional space. By moving the problem to a higher dimension, we have more space available, and hence there is a better chance of finding a separating hyperplane.

- Kernel trick — We'll use a kernel function to transform the data, with the goal of obtaining better separation. As the name suggests, this is the tricky part. While it's easy to understand the basic ideas behind SVMs from a few simple pictures, it's not so easy to understand how the kernel trick does its magic. Most of the details we provide in this chapter are aimed at making the kernel trick less tricky.

According to Bennett and Campbell [15], "SVMs are a rare example of a methodology where geometric intuition, elegant mathematics, theoretical guarantees, and practical algorithms meet."[3] In particular, the "geometric intuition" behind SVMs is an especially nice feature. In this chapter, we draw many illustrative pictures and, at least at a high level, these pictures really do tell the story.[4]

Suppose that we want to distinguish malware samples from benign samples based on the size (in KB) and entropy (in bits) of each sample. For the dataset under consideration, we plot the size and entropy, and obtain the results in Figure 5.1, where the solid circles correspond to malware samples and the hollow squares correspond to the benign samples. These results indicate that, on average, the malware samples in the training set are smaller and have lower entropy than the benign samples.

---

[2]Not to be confused with *The Curse of Frankenstein* [33].

[3]Your usually-disagreeable author quite agrees.

[4]They say that a picture is worth a thousand words. If that's true, then this chapter would be many times longer without the pictures.

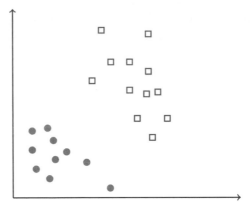

Figure 5.1: Scatterplot of training data

The goal when training an SVM is to find a separating hyperplane, where a *hyperplane* is defined as a subspace of one dimension less than the space in which we are working. For example, if our data lives in two-dimensional space, a hyperplane is just a line. And "separating" means exactly what it says, namely, that the hyperplane separates the two classes. If a separating hyperplane exists, we say the data is *linearly separable*. If our training data happens to be linearly separable, then any separating hyperplane could be used as the basis for subsequent classification.

The data in Figure 5.1 is clearly linearly separable—two distinct separating hyperplanes are illustrated in Figure 5.2. Whichever separating hyperplane we select will be used for classification. That is, for any sample that we subsequently want to classify, we simply plot its position in the (x, y)-plane and classify it based on the side of the separating hyperplane on which it lies.

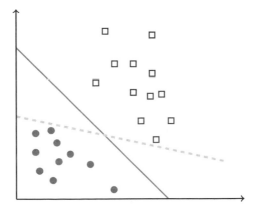

Figure 5.2: Separating hyperplanes

For the example in Figure 5.2, which separating hyperplane is better, the solid line or the dashed line? Intuitively it seems a good idea to separate the training data by equally splitting the distance between the two sets. From this perspective, the solid line in Figure 5.2 is better than the dashed line, since it provides a larger margin for error.

When training a support vector machine, we choose a separating hyperplane that maximizes the margin, where the *margin* is defined as the minimum distance between the hyperplane and any element of the training set. For our current example, the optimal hyperplane (in the SVM sense) is given by the solid line in Figure 5.3. And, by definition, the length of the arrows represent the margin. It follows that the solid line is the optimal separating hyperplane, since any variation from this line will result in a smaller margin. Furthermore, the space between the dashed lines is a "no man's land" where the training data provides no information. By choosing a separating hyperplane that maximizes the margin, we have given ourselves the largest possible margin for error, with respect to the training data. Of course, we are assuming that errors are equally likely, and equal in magnitude, in either direction.

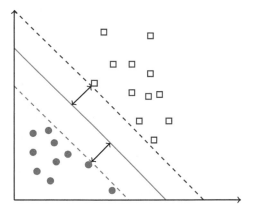

Figure 5.3: Maximizing the margin

What could possibly go wrong? For one thing, we have no guarantee that the data itself is linearly separable—it can (and often does) happen that no separating hyperplane exists. For example, the training data in Figure 5.4, is not linearly separable.

SVMs employ two techniques to deal with training data that is not linearly separable. A *soft margin* allows for some classification errors when determining a separating hyperplane. The more classification errors we can tolerate, in general, the larger the margin. In SVMs, there is a user-defined parameter that specifies the softness of the margin. In practice, the value of this parameter could be determined by trial and error.

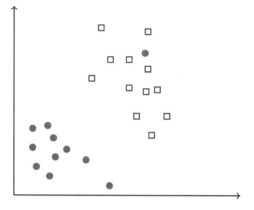

Figure 5.4: Not linearly separable

Another technique employed in SVM training is to map the input data to a *feature space* where the problem of constructing a separating hyperplane is more tractable. In practical application, this generally involves transforming the input data to a feature space of higher dimension. As discussed above, the idea is that by moving the problem to a higher dimensional space, we can often improve the linear separability.

For example, consider the data on the left-hand side of Figure 5.5. Even allowing for a (very) soft margin, we can't obtain reasonable linear separation, although, as illustrated, a parabola can be used to easily separate the data. The transformation ϕ maps the input space (on the left) to a feature space (on the right) where the problem becomes linearly separable. Note that in Figure 5.5, the dimension of the feature space is the same as that of the input space. However, in SVM training, we typically use a transformation ϕ that maps the data into a higher dimensional space. Again, by working in a higher dimensional space, there will generally be a much better chance that a separating hyperplane exists.

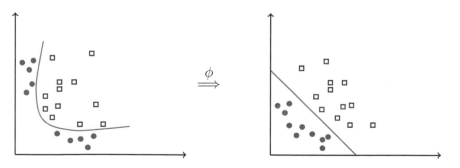

Figure 5.5: Transformation to linearly separable

Figure 5.6 illustrates the benefit of transforming to a higher dimension. In this example, the input space (left-hand side) is not linearly separable, but after transforming to the feature space (right-hand side), we can easily construct a hyperplane that separates the sets.[5]

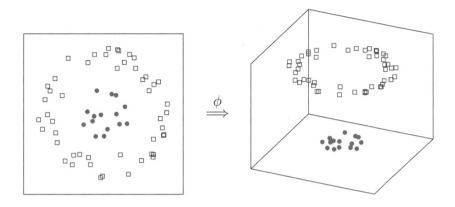

Figure 5.6: Transformation from 2-d to 3-d

Recall that one of the major selling points of PCA is that it reduces the dimensionality of the data. How can it be a good idea to reduce the dimensionality in PCA, and also a good idea to increase the dimensionality in SVM? In higher dimensional space, it's harder to distinguish statistically significant events—data points tend to be more sparse, so far more data is required to detect statistically meaningful information. PCA helps with this problem by moving the data to a lower dimension, where features are more prominent in a statistical sense. In contrast, with SVMs we stand the supposed curse of dimensionality on its head. Specifically, by injecting the input data into a higher dimensional feature space, we can spread the data out, thus making it easier to distinguish between the two classes.[6]

Another aspect of the curse of dimensionality is that computations tend to become more expensive in higher dimensions. For SVMs, a critical issue is whether we can gain the benefit of working in a higher dimensional space without paying a significant price. In fact, with SVMs, we are able to work in the input space, and the transformation to the feature space happens behind the scenes. In fact, no explicit transformation to the feature space is required, yet we gain a benefit of better separability. This amazing feat—known as the kernel trick [74]—is one of the rare cases in life where we get to have our cake and eat it too.

---

[5]In 3-dimensional space, a hyperplane is not hyper, as it's just a plane.

[6]From this discussion, it might seem that PCA and SVM are essentially opposites. However, there are actually some deep connections between the two techniques—see Section 7.6 of Chapter 7 for more details.

While the basic ideas behind SVMs are fairly easy to appreciate, to truly understand how the kernel trick works requires significant effort. Our primary goal for the remainder of this chapter is to clarify the kernel trick.

Next, we turn our attention to the general problem of constrained optimization using Lagrange multipliers. With this background in hand, we'll be positioned to delve into the details of SVMs and, in particular, we can elucidate the kernel trick.

5.2   Constrained Optimization

In a *constrained optimization* problem, our goal is to maximize (or minimize) a function, subject to a constraint, or set of constraints. For example, suppose that we want to solve the problem

$$\text{Maximize: } f(x, y)$$
$$\text{Subject to: } g(x, y) = c. \tag{5.1}$$

where c is a constant. We call $f(x, y)$ the *objective function*, and $g(x, y) = c$ is the *constraint*. A solution (x, y) to this problem is a point at which the constraint is satisfied, i.e., $g(x, y) = c$, and the function $f(x, y)$ is as large as possible. Another way to view this is that $g(x, y) = c$ defines a feasible region, and we maximize $f(x, y)$ over this feasible region.

As a concrete example, consider the problem

$$\text{Maximize: } f(x, y) = 16 - (x^2 + y^2)$$
$$\text{Subject to: } 2x - y = -4 \tag{5.2}$$

The graph of the objective function $f(x, y) = 16 - (x^2 + y^2)$ appears in Figure 5.7.

In Figure 5.8 (a), we have graphed the constraint in (5.2) and sliced away the front part of $f(x, y)$ to more clearly illustrate the intersection. The solution to the optimization problem in (5.2) is the highest point on the intersection of these two surfaces. In this case, the intersection consists of the black curve in Figure 5.8 (b) and, hence the problem boils down to finding the maximum point on this curve.

Next, we want to find a general strategy for solving a constrained optimization problem of the form (5.1). Lagrange multipliers provide us with a powerful technique for dealing with such problems. To motivate the central idea behind Lagrange multipliers, consider the function [76]

$$J(x, y) = f(x, y) + I(x, y) \tag{5.3}$$

where

$$I(x, y) = \begin{cases} 0 & \text{if } g(x, y) = c \\ -\infty & \text{otherwise.} \end{cases}$$

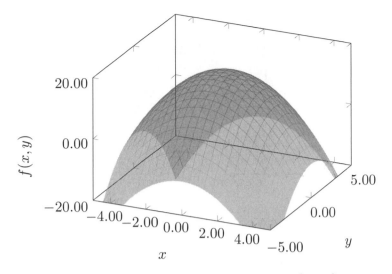

Figure 5.7: Graph of $f(x,y) = 16 - (x^2 + y^2)$

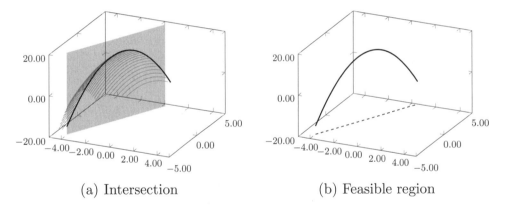

(a) Intersection   (b) Feasible region

Figure 5.8: Constrained optimization example

For all points that satisfy the constraint in (5.1), we have $J(x,y) = f(x,y)$, while at the points that do not satisfy the constraint, $J(x,y) = -\infty$. It's clear that a point (x,y) that maximizes $J(x,y)$ solves the constrained optimization problem (5.1). That is, a solution to (5.1) can be obtained by solving

$$\max_{(x,y)} J(x,y).$$

Note that via $J(x,y)$, we have converted the constrained optimization in (5.1) into an unconstrained optimization problem. Next, we discuss the method of Lagrange multipliers, which also transforms a constrained optimization problem into an unconstrained optimization, but it does so using a much nicer function than $J(x,y)$.

5.2.1   Lagrange Multipliers

Conceptually, the function $J(x,y)$ in (5.3) does exactly what we want. However, from a mathematical perspective, this function is extremely difficult to work with—for one thing it's wildly discontinuous. Can we obtain a similar effect as $J(x,y)$, but with a continuous function? Let's try something really simple, namely, a function that is linear in the constraint. We define the *Lagrangian* as

$$L(x,y,\lambda) = f(x,y) + \lambda\big(g(x,y) - c\big). \qquad (5.4)$$

Note that just like the function $J(x,y)$ in (5.3), whenever $g(x,y) = c$, the Lagrangian L is identical to $f(x,y)$. At points where $g(x,y) \neq c$, the function $J(x,y)$ applies a uniform penalty of $-\infty$ while the Lagrangian applies a penalty that approaches $-\infty$ as λ approaches ∞ (in case $g(x,y) < c$) or as λ approaches $-\infty$ (in case $g(x,y) > c$). Consequently, for any fixed point (x,y), we have

$$\min_{\lambda} L(x,y,\lambda) = J(x,y). \qquad (5.5)$$

Applying the max over (x,y) to both sides of (5.5), we find

$$\max_{(x,y)} \min_{\lambda} L(x,y,\lambda) = \max_{(x,y)} J(x,y).$$

Since $\max J(x,y)$ solves the constrained optimization problem in (5.1), it follows that

$$\max_{(x,y)} \min_{\lambda} L(x,y,\lambda) \qquad (5.6)$$

also solves the problem in (5.1).

As mentioned above, whenever $g(x,y) \neq c$, the min in (5.6) yields $-\infty$. On the other hand, if $g(x,y) = c$, then the min has no effect and we are left with $\max f(x,y)$. This is precisely the same effect produced by the function $J(x,y)$ in (5.3). The advantage of using the Lagrangian is that it is a nice function of the parameter λ (in fact, the Lagrangian is linear in λ), unlike the evil discontinuous function $J(x,y)$. The bottom line is that we can apply optimization techniques from calculus to the Lagrangian, which is not an option with a discontinuous function such as $J(x,y)$.

We won't solve our constrained optimization problem by directly using the min max point of view as given in (5.6). This form of the problem is provided simply to show that the Lagrangian encodes the information needed to solve the original constrained optimization problem. To actually solve the problem, we'll apply some elementary calculus—which we can do, since the Lagrangian is a nice smooth function. When we do so, we'll see that defining the Lagrangian as a linear function in λ was a particularly good idea. The big idea here is that by using the Lagrangian, we convert a constrained optimization problem into an unconstrained optimization problem, which we can solve by applying powerful tools from calculus.

Speaking of calculus, we know that the way to solve a maximization problem involving a smooth function of one variable x is to compute its derivative, set the result equal to zero, and solve for x. Such a solution x is known as a stationary point, and it must occur at a (local) peak or valley in the graph of the function. We can then use the second derivative test to determine whether the point corresponds to a (local) maximum or minimum.

For a function of several variables, the analog of the first derivative is the *gradient*. To compute the gradient of the Lagrangian, we compute the partial derivatives of L with respect to x, y, and λ and find the points where all of the resulting equations are equal to 0. Any such point is a stationary point and, as such, is a candidate for the desired maximum (or minimum).

When we compute the partial derivatives of equation (5.4) with respect to x and y, we obtain

$$\frac{\partial L}{\partial x} = \frac{\partial f(x,y)}{\partial x} + \lambda \frac{\partial g(x,y)}{\partial x} = 0$$

and

$$\frac{\partial L}{\partial y} = \frac{\partial f(x,y)}{\partial y} + \lambda \frac{\partial g(x,y)}{\partial y} = 0,$$

respectively. On the other hand, taking the partial derivative of L with respect to λ yields

$$\frac{\partial L}{\partial \lambda} = g(x,y) - c = 0$$

or, equivalently,

$$g(x,y) = c.$$

Hence, the form of the Lagrangian ensures that the constraint is satisfied when we apply the usual optimization technique from calculus. This is a major benefit to having the constraint appear as a linear function of λ in L.

To summarize, computing partial derivatives of the Langrangian L with respect to x and y, and setting the resulting expressions equal to 0 enables us to find the max (or min) of the objective function $f(x,y)$. Also, computing the partial derivative of the Lagrangian L with respect to λ ensures that the constraints are satisfied. Therefore, any solution that satisfies all of these conditions solves the original constrained optimization problem in equation (5.1).

For the example in Figure 5.8, the Lagrangian is

$$L(x,y,\lambda) = 16 - (x^2 + y^2) + \lambda(2x - y + 4). \qquad (5.7)$$

Computing the partial derivatives, we find

$$\frac{\partial L}{\partial x} = -2x + 2\lambda = 0$$

$$\frac{\partial L}{\partial y} = -2y - \lambda = 0$$

$$\frac{\partial L}{\partial \lambda} = 2x - y + 4 = 0.$$

Solving this system of equations, we determine the stationary point

$$(x, y, \lambda) = (-8/5, 4/5, -8/5),$$

which yields the maximum value of

$$f(x, y) = f(-8/5, 4/5) = 64/5 = 12.8.$$

It's easy to verify that the solution $(x, y) = (-8/5, 4/5)$ does indeed satisfy the constraint $2x - y = -4$.

In general, there can be multiple stationary points. The desired solution to the Lagrangian must occur at one of these stationary points. Also, note that we can easily generalize the Lagrangian to more variables and more constraints. With n variables, which we denote as $x_1, x_2, \ldots, x_n$, and m constraints of the form $g_i(x_1, x_2, \ldots, x_n) = c_i$, for $i = 1, 2, \ldots, m$, the Lagrangian can be written as

$$L(x_1, x_2, \ldots, x_n, \lambda_1, \lambda_2, \ldots, \lambda_m)$$
$$= f(x_1, x_2, \ldots, x_n) + \sum_{i=1}^{m} \lambda_i(g_i(x_1, x_2, \ldots, x_n) - c_i)$$

or, more succinctly,

$$L(x, \lambda) = f(x) + \sum_{i=1}^{m} \lambda_i(g_i(x) - c_i)$$

where $x = (x_1, x_2, \ldots, x_n)$ and $\lambda = (\lambda_1, \lambda_2, \ldots, \lambda_m)$. In this general case, the Lagrangian L is a function of $n + m$ variables, and hence we'll need to solve a system of $n + m$ equations to determine the stationary points.

Before moving on to bigger and better things, let's consider a slightly more substantive example that highlights some of the strengths of Lagrange multipliers. Note that the example in Figure 5.8 has a very nice and intuitive geometric interpretation—many such geometric examples can be found in the literature. In contrast, the example that we now discuss does not lend itself to pretty pictures, but does yield an interesting result.

Consider a discrete probability distribution on n points. By the definition of a probability distribution, we have $p = (p_1, p_2, \ldots, p_n)$, where $0 \le p_i \le 1$ for $i = 1, 2, \ldots, n$, and $\sum p_i = 1$. Suppose we want to determine which probability distribution of this form has the maximum entropy. In this case, the entropy is given by

$$f(p) = \sum_{i=1}^{n} p_i \log_2 p_i$$

and our goal is to maximize $f(p)$ subject to the constraints

$$0 \le p_i \le 1 \text{ for } i = 1, 2, \ldots, n \tag{5.8}$$

and

$$p_1 + p_2 + \cdots + p_n = 1.$$

We'll solve the simpler problem

$$\text{Maximize: } f(p) = \sum_{i=1}^{n} p_i \log_2 p_i$$

$$\text{Subject to: } \sum_{i=1}^{n} p_i = 1 \tag{5.9}$$

using Lagrange multipliers. Once we've solved this problem, we'll consider the role of the additional constraints in (5.8).

For the constrained optimization problem in (5.9), the Lagrangian is given by

$$L(p_1, p_2, \ldots, p_n, \lambda) = \sum_{i=1}^{n} p_i \log_2 p_i + \lambda \left(\sum_{i=1}^{n} p_i - 1 \right).$$

Computing the partial derivatives, we find

$$\frac{\partial L}{\partial p_i} = \log_2 p_i + \frac{1}{\ln 2} + \lambda, \text{ for } i = 1, 2, \ldots, n$$

and

$$\frac{\partial L}{\partial \lambda} = \sum_{i=1}^{n} p_i - 1.$$

Setting these equal to 0 we have

$$p_i = 2^{-(\lambda + 1/\ln 2)} = \frac{1}{e} 2^{-\lambda}, \text{ for } i = 1, 2, \ldots, n \tag{5.10}$$

and

$$\sum_{i=1}^{n} p_i = 1. \tag{5.11}$$

Although (5.10) might look intimidating, the fact that the right-hand side is independent of i tells us that $p_1 = p_2 = \cdots = p_n$, regardless of the value of λ. This result, together with (5.11), implies that

$$p_1 = p_2 = \cdots = p_n = \frac{1}{n}.$$

And, for this solution, we see that the additional constraints in (5.8) are also satisfied.[7] This result tells us that to maximize the entropy (i.e., the uncertainty), we need to draw samples from a uniform distribution.[8]

5.2.2 Lagrangian Duality

Before diving more deeply into SVMs, we need to discuss the important concept of *Lagrangian duality* [37]. For any constrained optimization problem, there is a so-called dual version of the problem, where the sense of the original problem is reversed. That is, the dual of a max problem is a min problem, and vice versa. In general, solving the dual version will provide a bound on the solution for the *primal problem*, as the original version of the problem is known.[9] However, in the special case of Lagrange multipliers, a solution to the dual problem provides an exact solution to the primal problem.

To motivate the concept of duality, observe that reversing the order of the max and min in equation (5.6) gives us

$$\min_{\lambda} \max_{(x,y)} L(x, y, \lambda). \tag{5.12}$$

The notion of duality can be viewed as arising from reversing the order of these operations. We want to look more closely at the relationship between the dual problem in (5.12) and the primal problem in (5.6).

From equation (5.5), it follows that for any value of λ we have

$$L(x, y, \lambda) \geq J(x, y)$$

where $J(x, y)$ is defined in (5.3). Therefore,

$$\max_{(x,y)} L(x, y, \lambda) \geq \max_{(x,y)} J(x, y)$$

holds true for all λ, which implies

$$\min_{\lambda} \max_{(x,y)} L(x, y, \lambda) \geq \max_{(x,y)} J(x, y).$$

Furthermore, the left-hand side of this expression is the tightest upper bound on the function $J(x, y)$ that we can obtain using the function L. We previously showed that $\max J(x, y)$ is a solution to the primal problem, as is

$$\max_{(x,y)} \min_{\lambda} L(x, y, \lambda).$$

---

[7]For a good time, try to solve for λ in terms of n and show directly that $p_i = 1/n$. But, whatever you do, don't call 867-5309.

[8]Your cryptic author would like to note that this result implies that we want to choose cryptographic keys uniformly. This will make the attacker's job more difficult—in terms of an exhaustive key search—than if we choose keys according to any other distribution.

[9]Obviously, the original problem requires a cool name too, otherwise it might lose its self-esteem.

It follows that

$$\min_{\lambda} \max_{(x,y)} L(x, y, \lambda) \geq \max_{(x,y)} \min_{\lambda} L(x, y, \lambda), \qquad (5.13)$$

which shows that a solution to the dual problem provides an upper bound on any solution to the primal problem.

We have just shown that when the primal problem is a max, the dual problem is a min, and a solution to the dual provides an upper bound on a solution to the primal problem. On the other hand, if the primal problem is a max, then the dual is a min that provides a lower bound on the solution to the primal problem.

While a bound on the solution might be useful in some situations, an exact solution would be much better. Fortunately, for Lagrange multipliers, a solution to the dual problem provides an exact solution to the primal problem. And, best of all, it's often easier to deal with the dual problem. But, to show that equality holds requires some fancy math that, while very interesting, would take us too far afield.[10] Therefore, we'll simply discuss an example and show that equality holds in this specific case.

Consider again the example in (5.2), which is illustrated in Figures 5.7 and 5.8. In this case, the Lagrangian is

$$L(x, y, \lambda) = 16 - (x^2 + y^2) + \lambda(2x - y + 4).$$

For the dual problem, we first compute the max of L with respect to (x, y). Taking the necessary partial derivatives yields

$$\frac{\partial L}{\partial x} = -2x + 2\lambda = 0$$

$$\frac{\partial L}{\partial y} = -2y - \lambda = 0,$$

which implies

$$x = \lambda \text{ and } y = -\lambda/2. \qquad (5.14)$$

Substituting these values into $L(x, y, \lambda)$, we obtain

$$L(\lambda) = 16 - (\lambda^2 + (-\lambda/2)^2) + \lambda(2\lambda + \lambda/2 + 4) = \frac{5}{4}\lambda^2 + 4\lambda + 16.$$

To complete the solution to this dual problem, we minimize $L(\lambda)$ by the usual methods of calculus. That is, we compute the first derivative and set it equal to 0, which gives us

$$\frac{dL}{d\lambda} = \frac{5}{2}\lambda + 4 = 0.$$

---

[10]Executive summary: For convex functions, the *duality gap* (the difference between the solution obtained via the primal problem and that obtained from the dual problem) is 0. For reasonable objective functions, the Lagrangian is convex.

Solving, we have $\lambda = -8/5$. Substituting this value of λ into (5.14), we obtain the point $(x, y) = (-8/5, 4/5)$, which is the same result we found when solving the primal version of this problem in Section 5.2.1. The second derivative test can be used to verify that we have indeed found a minimum of the function $L(\lambda)$.

This example illustrates the process we follow to convert the primal version of a Lagrange multiplier problem into its dual. That is, we use the partial derivative equations to solve for the variables x and y in terms of λ. Then we write the Lagrangian as a function of λ only, that is, $L(\lambda)$. If the primal problem is a maximization problem, the dual problem consists of minimizing $L(\lambda)$, and vice versa. In any case, the constraint involving $g(x, y)$ seemingly vanishes from the problem.

In practice, it is often easier to deal with the dual version of a Lagrange multipliers problem. Below, we make use of the dual problem when deriving the SVM training process.[11]

Obviously, Lagrange multipliers and Lagrangian duality are totally awesome. But, you may ask yourself,[12] what does any of this awesomeness have to do with SVMs? Next, we will show that training an SVM can be viewed as a constrained optimization problem. And by using Lagrange multipliers—and solving via the dual problem—the kernel trick becomes a lot less tricky. The bottom line is that Lagrange multipliers enable us to derive the SVM training process, while simultaneously clarifying the trickiest aspect of the entire SVM technique.

5.3   A Closer Look at SVM

Let $X_1, X_2, \ldots, X_n$ be a set of data points. In general, each X_i could be a point in n-dimensional space, but to keep the notation simple, we'll assume that each X_i is a point in the plane, that is, $X_i = (x_i, y_i)$. For example, if we consider houses in Silicon Valley, we might measure

$$x_i = \text{price of house } i$$

and

$$y_i = \frac{1}{\text{age of house } i}.$$

Since we only consider binary classification, let $z_i \in \{-1, +1\}$ be the classification of X_i. For example, we might classify a house as safe (+1) or

---

[11]Believe it or not, the HMM training process and the PCA training process can also be derived using Lagrange multipliers.

[12]And you may ask yourself, well, how did I get here? And you may ask yourself, how do I work this? And you may ask yourself, where is that large automobile? And so on [144].

unsafe (-1) based on our estimate of the likelihood that it will survive a major earthquake.

Suppose that we obtain the training data in Figure 5.9, where the hollow squares are the points X_i for which $z_i = +1$ (house is expected to survive a major earthquake), and the solid circles are the X_i at which $z_i = -1$ (house is not expected to survive a major earthquake). The data shows that for the houses in our sample, those that are older and less expensive are generally less likely to survive an earthquake.

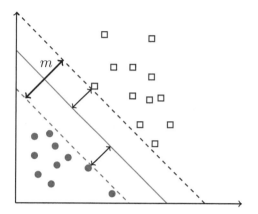

Figure 5.9: Linearly separable example

The equation of the solid line in Figure 5.9 can be written as

$$w_1 x + w_2 y + b = 0$$

for some $W = (w_1, w_2)$ and b. And we can write the equation of the upper dashed line as

$$w_1 x + w_2 y + b = +1$$

and, similarly, the equation of the lower dashed line can be written as

$$w_1 x + w_2 y + b = -1.$$

For any hollow square in Figure 5.9, its coordinates $X = (x, y)$ satisfy

$$w_1 x + w_2 y + b \geq +1$$

while each of the solid circles $X = (x, y)$ satisfy

$$w_1 x + w_2 y + b \leq -1.$$

The ultimate goal of training an SVM is to determine the parameters W and b that define the separating hyperplane, as illustrated in Figure 5.9 . Once these parameters have been determined, we can classify any given point X. Specifically, when scoring,[13] we classify $X = (x, y)$ as type z where

$$z = \begin{cases} +1 & \text{if } w_1 x + w_2 y + b \geq 0 \\ -1 & \text{otherwise.} \end{cases}$$

That is, we classify the point X as being of the same type as the hollow squares (earthquake safe) in Figure 5.9 provided that $w_1 x + w_2 y + b \geq 0$; otherwise it is classified as the same type as the solid circles (not earthquake safe).

From this high level perspective, the SVM training phase consists of determining the equation of a separating hyperplane. Then during the scoring phase, we use this separating hyperplane to classify data points.

Of course, when training, we also want to maximize the margin, and we will have to deal with kernel functions. Next, we discuss the plain vanilla version of SVM training and scoring in more detail. Then we'll slowly work our way up to the kernel trick.

5.3.1   Training and Scoring

Assuming we are in the ideal case, as illustrated in Figure 5.9, how do we train an SVM? When training, we must determine the equation of the separating hyperplane, which for the example in Figure 5.9 consists of determining the parameters $W = (w_1, w_2)$ and b that define the solid line.

Given a linear equation of the form

$$\alpha x + \beta y + \gamma = 0$$

its distance from the origin is

$$\frac{|\gamma|}{\sqrt{\alpha^2 + \beta^2}}.$$

Therefore, the distance from the origin to the upper dashed line in Figure 5.9 is $|1 - b|/||W||$, where $||W|| = \sqrt{w_1^2 + w_2^2}$. Similarly, the distance from the origin to the lower dashed line is $|-1 - b|/||W||$. It follows that the size of the margin in Figure 5.9 is $m = 2/||W||$.

Now we can specify the SVM training process. Suppose that we are given data points $X_1, X_2, \ldots, X_n$, where each $X_i = (x_i, y_i)$, and we are also given the corresponding classifications z_i, where $z_i \in \{-1, +1\}$. We want to find

---

[13]Your pedantic author would like to point out that when "scoring" with an SVM, we don't actually compute a score, but instead we determine a classification. Therefore, in this chapter it would be more accurate to use "classify" instead of "score." However, to be consistent with other sections of the book, we'll stick with the terms training and scoring.

the equations corresponding to the upper dashed line $w_1x + w_2y + b = +1$ and the lower dashed line $w_1x + w_2y + b = -1$ in Figure 5.9, so that the margin $m = 2/||W||$ is maximized. Since $z_i \in \{-1, +1\}$, the conditions on W and b can be written succinctly as

$$z_i(w_1x_i + w_2y_i + b) \geq 1 \text{ for all } i.$$

It follows that the SVM training problem will be solved, provided we can solve the constrained optimization problem

$$\text{Maximize: } m = \frac{2}{||W||}$$
$$\text{Subject to: } z_i(w_1x_i + w_2y_i + b) \geq 1 \text{ for } i = 1, 2, \ldots, n. \tag{5.15}$$

The known unknowns here are $W = (w_1, w_2)$ and b.

It is convenient to restate the maximization problem in (5.15) as

$$\text{Minimize: } F(W) = \frac{||W||^2}{2} = \frac{w_1^2 + w_2^2}{2}$$
$$\text{Subject to: } 1 - z_i(w_1x_i + w_2y_i + b) \leq 0 \text{ for } i = 1, 2, \ldots, n. \tag{5.16}$$

For this form of the problem, the Lagrangian is

$$L(w_1, w_2, b, \lambda) = \frac{w_1^2 + w_2^2}{2} + \sum_{i=1}^{n} \lambda_i\big(1 - z_i(w_1x_i + w_2y_i + b)\big). \tag{5.17}$$

Computing partial derivatives yields

$$\frac{\partial L}{\partial w_1} = w_1 - \sum_{i=1}^{n} \lambda_i z_i x_i = 0$$
$$\frac{\partial L}{\partial w_2} = w_2 - \sum_{i=1}^{n} \lambda_i z_i y_i = 0$$
$$\frac{\partial L}{\partial b} = \sum_{i=1}^{n} \lambda_i z_i = 0 \tag{5.18}$$
$$\frac{\partial L}{\partial \lambda_i} = 1 - z_i(w_1x_i + w_2y_i + b) = 0, \text{ for } i = 1, 2, \ldots, n.$$

In addition to recovering the constraints, the partial derivative equations yield

$$W = \sum_{i=1}^{n} \lambda_i z_i X_i \tag{5.19}$$

and

$$\sum_{i=1}^{n} \lambda_i z_i = 0.$$

Substituting these expressions into the Lagrangian, we find

$$L(\lambda) = \sum_{i=1}^{n} \lambda_i - \frac{1}{2} \sum_{i=1}^{n} \sum_{j=1}^{n} \lambda_i \lambda_j z_i z_j (X_i \cdot X_j) \tag{5.20}$$

where $X_i \cdot X_j$ is the dot product,

$$X_i \cdot X_j = (x_i, y_i) \cdot (x_j, y_j) = x_i x_j + y_i y_j.$$

For simplicity, we are assuming 2-dimensional data vectors throughout this discussion, but all of the machinery works for data of any dimension.

We'll solve the dual form of (5.16), which is

$$\text{Maximize: } \sum_{i=1}^{n} \lambda_i - \frac{1}{2} \sum_{i=1}^{n} \sum_{j=1}^{n} \lambda_i \lambda_j z_i z_j (X_i \cdot X_j)$$

$$\text{Subject to: } \sum_{i=1}^{n} \lambda_i z_i = 0.$$

A solution to this problem gives us the λ_i, for $i = 1, 2, \ldots, n$. And once the λ_i are known, we can use the expressions derived from the partial derivatives in (5.18) to determine W and b (note that x_i, y_i and z_i are known from the training data). Recall that when W and b have been determined, we have found the separating hyperplane (e.g., the solid line in Figure 5.9), and hence the SVM has been trained.

Now let's consider the scoring phase. Given a trained SVM and a data point $X = (x, y)$ that we want to classify, we need to determine on which side of the separating hyperplane it resides. Let

$$f(X) = w_1 x + w_2 y + b = W \cdot X + b. \tag{5.20}$$

If we have $f(X) \geq 0$, then we classify X as type $+1$, otherwise X is classified as type -1.

We note in passing that $f(X)$ in equation (5.20) could be used as a score. That is, instead of classifying X directly based on whether $f(X) > 0$ or not, we could simply define $\text{score}(X) = f(X)$. This score could then be used to determine a threshold based on a test set, or to compute ROC curves—topics that are discussed in detail in Chapter 8. Or we could classify X with the SVM, then use this score to assign a confidence factor to the classification. In any case, in its standard usage, an SVM is designed to directly provide a classification rather than a score.

5.3.2   Scoring Revisited

Given a trained SVM, there is a slightly different—and ultimately better—way to score $X = (x, y)$. Observe that in (5.19), we have $W = \sum \lambda_i z_i X_i$. We can therefore rewrite the function $f(X)$ in (5.20) as

$$f(X) = \sum_{i=1}^{n} \lambda_i z_i (X_i \cdot X) + b. \tag{5.21}$$

Using this form of $f(X)$, there is no need to explicitly compute W. Below, we'll see that there is another, more significant, advantage to the version of $f(X)$ in (5.21).

5.3.3 Support Vectors

The sum in (5.21) is nominally over the range $i = 1, 2, \ldots, n$. However, this is misleading, since, typically, for almost all i we'll find that $\lambda_i = 0$. In fact, from the form of the Lagrangian in (5.17), it is apparent that $\lambda_i \neq 0$ only for those cases where

$$z_i(w_1 x_i + w_2 y_i + b) = 1.$$

In other words, the only nonzero λ_i are those that correspond to the X_i in the training set that lie on the line

$$w_1 x_i + w_2 y_i + b = +1$$

or on the line

$$w_1 x_i + w_2 y_i + b = -1.$$

Geometrically, these are the points that fall exactly on one of the dashed lines in Figure 5.10. Training data points that lie on either of these lines are known as *support vectors*.

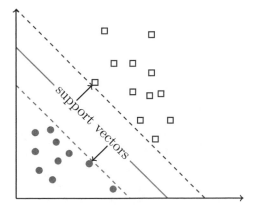

Figure 5.10: Support vectors

Suppose that there are exactly s support vectors. Then we can rewrite equation (5.21) as[14]

$$f(X) = \sum_{i=1}^{s} \lambda_i z_i (X_i \bullet X) + b \qquad (5.22)$$

where, in general, s is much smaller than n. Note that for the illustrative example in Figure 5.10, we have $n = 22$, while there are only $s = 2$ support vectors. It bears repeating that only the support vectors are relevant in the scoring phase. And, since s is typically small, scoring is highly efficient, even in cases where the training set is large.[15] Below, we'll see that we can take further advantage of the support vectors.

It should not be surprising that support vectors play a critical role in a technique that goes by the name of support vector machines. But what about the "machine" part of a support vector machine? This should become clear in the next section.

5.3.4   Training and Scoring Re-revisited

In Section 5.1, we mentioned the concept of a soft margin, where we allow for some classification errors when training, in exchange for a larger margin. An example of a soft margin appears in Figure 5.11. Note that there are two types of errors illustrated in Figure 5.11, namely, a misclassification and a correct classification that is within the margin.

To account for errors due to a soft margin, in the formulation of the training problem we can introduce *slack variables*, denoted ε_i, where $\varepsilon_i \in \{0, 1\}$. The use of slack variables is a standard tool in constrained optimization.

With slack variables included, the primal problem can be written as

$$\text{Minimize: } F(W) = \frac{||W||^2}{2} + C \sum_{i=1}^{n} \varepsilon_i \qquad (5.23)$$

Subject to: $w_1 x_i + w_2 y_i + b \geq z_i (1 - \varepsilon_i)$ for $i = 1, 2, \ldots, n$.

Recall that $z_i \in \{-1, +1\}$ and hence for any index i such that $z_i = +1$, the corresponding constraint in (5.23) is

$$w_1 x_i + w_2 y_i + b \geq +1 - \varepsilon_i.$$

---

[14]There is a slight abuse of notation in equation (5.22), as the λ_i, z_i, and X_i will not typically correspond to the first s indices in equation (5.21). Here, we have chosen to keep the notation simple, with the understanding that the indices have been rearranged so that the support vectors come first.

[15]This is somewhat reminiscent of PCA, in the sense that the underlying math is fairly difficult and training is relatively complex, but scoring is simple and highly efficient.

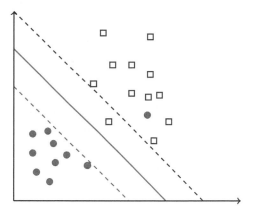

Figure 5.11: Errors and soft margin

On the other hand, if $z_i = -1$, then constraint i is

$$w_1 x_i + w_2 y_i + b \leq -1 + \varepsilon_i.$$

After introducing Lagrange multipliers and computing partial derivatives, we find that the dual version of (5.23) is

$$\text{Maximize: } L(\lambda) = \sum_{i=1}^{n} \lambda_i - \frac{1}{2} \sum_{i=1}^{n} \sum_{j=1}^{n} \lambda_i \lambda_j z_i z_j (X_i \cdot X_j)$$

$$\text{Subject to: } C \geq \lambda_i \geq 0 \text{ for } i = 1, 2, \ldots, n \text{ and } \sum_{i=1}^{n} \lambda_i z_i = 0.$$

(5.24)

Observe that this dual problem is the same as in the case without slack variables, except for the additional constraints of the form $C \geq \lambda_i$. Here, $C > 0$ is a user-specified *regularization parameter* that relates to the softness of the margin. If $C = \infty$, then $C \geq \lambda_i$ does not affect the problem, and we have a hard margin. Conversely, the smaller the value of C, the softer the margin, that is, the more classification errors that will be tolerated in training. Also, note that C only appears in training—when scoring, we can still use equation (5.22), which was derived without slack variables.

The optimization in (5.24) is a *quadratic programming* problem, since the problem consists of optimizing a quadratic function subject to linear constraints. Due to the inequality constraints in (5.24), the solution is fairly challenging. In Section 5.5, we briefly discuss one (slightly simplified) method for solving this specific type of quadratic programming problem.

5.3.5 The Kernel Trick

So far, we have dealt with the case where our data is linearly separable, or nearly so. We have shown how to deal with a soft margin, where we allow training errors, which has the effect of enlarging the margin. But, the real "wow factor" with SVM lies in the kernel trick, which allows us to improve the separability by working in a higher dimensional space. Perhaps the trickiest part of the kernel trick is that we are able to do so without paying any significant penalty, with respect to efficiency.

Before presenting the kernel trick, we briefly summarize training and scoring for the linearly separable case. Recall that the training data is denoted as $X_1, X_2, \ldots, X_n$. To simplify some of the notation, we'll again assume that $X_i = (x_i, y_i)$, although the same approach carries over for training vectors of any dimension.

From (5.24), we see that an SVM is trained by maximizing the objective function

$$\sum_{i=1}^{n} \lambda_i - \frac{1}{2} \sum_{i=1}^{n} \sum_{j=1}^{n} \lambda_i \lambda_j z_i z_j (X_i \cdot X_j) \tag{5.25}$$

subject to a set of linear constraints. Note that this objective function involves the dot products $X_i \cdot X_j$.

From (5.22) we see that to score any X, we can use the function

$$f(X) = \sum_{i=1}^{s} \lambda_i z_i (X_i \cdot X) + b \tag{5.26}$$

where the sum is over the s support vectors. Note that the dot product also play a crucial role when scoring.

Any function that allows us to "multiply" two vectors together to obtain a scalar is known as an *inner product*. The dot product is the Volkswagen of inner products, that is, it's the most basic version. In fact, we can use a fancier Cadillac version of an inner product in the SVM training and scoring equations, and all of the math still works. But, is there any possible advantage to using a more general inner product? The answer is an emphatic yes, since some choices of the inner product will effectively enable us to work in a higher dimensional space which, as we have previously noted, often improves the separability. The use of more general inner products is the essence of the kernel trick.

Let's consider a specific example to illustrate how we can use a more general inner product to our advantage. Define

$$\phi(X) = \phi(x, y) = \left(1, \sqrt{2}\,x, \sqrt{2}\,y, x^2, y^2, \sqrt{2}\,xy\right). \tag{5.27}$$

Observe that ϕ maps a 2-dimensional input vector to a 5-dimensional output vector. Also, for $X_i = (x_i, y_i)$ and $X_j = (x_j, y_j)$, we have

$$\phi(X_i) \cdot \phi(X_j) = (1 + x_i x_j + y_i y_j)^2.$$

Then the *kernel function*

$$K(X_i, X_j) = (1 + x_i x_j + y_i y_j)^2 \tag{5.28}$$

is simply the composition of the function ϕ in (5.27) and the dot product.

Again, the kernel function K in (5.28) maps a 2-dimensional input vector to a vector into 5-dimensional feature space (via the function ϕ), where the dot product is computed. If we have made a good choice for K then the training data will be easier to separate in this higher-dimensional feature space.

Intuitively, it might seem that we must pay a high price in terms of computational complexity to work in a higher dimensional space. Fortunately, such is not the case. If we simply substitute the kernel function K in (5.28) into the training equation (5.25) and scoring equation (5.26), we obtain

$$\sum_{i=1}^{n} \lambda_i - \frac{1}{2} \sum_{i=1}^{n} \sum_{j=1}^{n} \lambda_i \lambda_j z_i z_j K(X_i, X_j)$$

and

$$f(X) = \sum_{i=1}^{s} \lambda_i z_i K(X_i, X) + b,$$

respectively. It is easily verified that all other aspects of training and scoring are unchanged. The net effect here is that we have transformed our training and scoring computations to a higher dimensional feature space, with only a minimal increase in the computational cost.

One interesting aspect of a kernel transformation is that we only need to know the kernel function K, and we never have to deal directly with the mapping function ϕ. In fact, we don't have to know anything about the function ϕ, since it does not explicitly appear in the problem.

There are a variety of standard kernel functions used in practice, almost all of which seem to have really cool names. Families of popular kernel functions include the following.

- Linear kernel[16]

$$K(X_i, X_j) = X_i \cdot X_j$$

- Polynomial learning machine

$$K(X_i, X_j) = (X_i \cdot X_j + 1)^p \tag{5.29}$$

- Gaussian radial basis function (RBF)[17]

$$K(X_i, X_j) = e^{-(X_i - X_j) \cdot (X_i - X_j)/(2\sigma^2)} \tag{5.30}$$

---

[16]Sorry, linear kernel, but you do not have a cool name.

[17]The radial basis function is sometimes given as $K(X_i, X_j) = e^{-\gamma(X_i - X_j) \cdot (X_i - X_j)}$. In this form, the parameter is $\gamma = 1/(2\sigma^2)$.

- Two-layer perceptron

$$K(X_i, X_j) = \tanh\big(\beta_0(X_i \cdot X_j) + \beta_1\big)$$

While there are some general rule-of-thumb guidelines for choosing the kernel function, the proper choice is more art than science.[18]   Evidently, choosing the correct kernel function is the real trick to the kernel trick.

5.4   All Together Now

In previous sections, we've taken several intermediate steps towards the ultimate SVM algorithm. For clarity, in this section we summarize the general training and scoring algorithms.

We are given a set of training vectors $X_1, X_2, \ldots, X_n$ and a corresponding set of classifications $z_1, z_2, \ldots, z_n$, where $z_i \in \{-1, +1\}$. We select a kernel function K and a regularization parameter $C > 0$, where C is related to the softness of the margin. Using these values, we solve the optimization problem

$$\text{Maximize: } L(\lambda) = \sum_{i=1}^{n} \lambda_i - \frac{1}{2}\sum_{i=1}^{n}\sum_{j=1}^{n} \lambda_i \lambda_j z_i z_j K(X_i, X_j)$$

$$\text{Subject to: } C \geq \lambda_i \geq 0 \text{ for } i = 1, 2, \ldots, n \text{ and } \sum_{i=1}^{n} \lambda_i z_i = 0 \tag{5.31}$$

to obtain $\lambda_1, \lambda_2, \ldots, \lambda_n$ and b.

Once we've trained the model, to score a given vector X, we compute

$$f(X) = \sum_{i=1}^{s} \lambda_i z_i K(X_i, X) + b. \tag{5.32}$$

Then the classification of X, which we denote as $c(X)$, is given by

$$c(X) = \begin{cases} +1 & \text{if } f(X) > 0 \\ -1 & \text{otherwise.} \end{cases} \tag{5.33}$$

To finish beating this dead horse, we restate the training and scoring algorithms in a more compact form.

- Training: Given data points $X_1, X_2, \ldots, X_n$ and the corresponding classifications $z_1, z_2, \ldots, z_n$, where $z_i \in \{-1, 1\}$.

  1. Select a kernel function K and parameter C.

---

[18]In practice, your inartistic author would recommend trial and error—experiment with different kernel functions and parameters to determine which works best.

2. Solve the optimization problem in (5.31) for $\lambda_1, \lambda_2, \ldots, \lambda_n$ and b.

- Scoring: Given X that we want to score.

  1. Compute $f(X)$ using (5.32).
  2. Classify X according to (5.33).

5.5 A Note on Quadratic Programming

Training an SVM requires that we solve a challenging quadratic programming problem. There are several methods available to solve such problems—here we outline a simplified version of one algorithm.

Recall that SVM training data is of the form (X_i, z_i), for $i = 1, 2, \ldots, n$, where each $z_i \in \{-1, +1\}$. Throughout this section, we'll assume that a linear kernel is used, although the same technique works for other kernel functions. For a linear kernel, the SVM training problem consists of determining the λ_i and b in the scoring function

$$f(X) = \sum_{i=1}^{n} \lambda_i z_i (X_i \cdot X) + b$$

where the λ_i can be derived from the optimization problem

$$\text{Maximize: } L(\lambda) = \sum_{i=1}^{n} \lambda_i - \frac{1}{2} \sum_{i=1}^{n} \sum_{j=1}^{n} \lambda_i \lambda_j z_i z_j (X_i \cdot X_j)$$

$$\text{Subject to: } C \geq \lambda_i \geq 0 \text{ for } i = 1, 2, \ldots, n \text{ and } \sum_{i=1}^{n} \lambda_i z_i = 0.$$

Sequential minimal optimization (SMO) is a popular algorithm for solving the SVM training problem [108]. At each step of the SMO algorithm, we select an ordered pair (λ_i, λ_j), and optimize with respect to this pair, keeping all other λ_k constant.

Much of the SMO algorithm deals with clever heuristics to choose the pairs (λ_i, λ_j) in a way that is likely to reduce the overall work. Here, we consider a simplified version of the SMO technique that we'll refer to as SSMO to distinguish it from the full SMO algorithm. The SSMO algorithm described in this section is similar to that found in [104].

Our version of the SSMO algorithm is listed in Algorithm 5.1. In the remainder of this section, we discuss the various steps in this algorithm in some detail. However, much of the derivation and verification of the algorithm is left as an exercise; see, for example, Problem 14.

Algorithm 5.1 SSMO algorithm

1: **Given:**

       Labeled training data (X_i, z_i) for $i = 1, 2, \ldots, n$

       Regularization parameter $C > 0$

2: **Initialize:**

       $\lambda_1 = \lambda_2 = \cdots = \lambda_n = 0$ and $b = 0$

       ε = numerical tolerance

3: **repeat**

4:      Select indices $i, j \in \{1, 2, \ldots, n\}$, with $i \neq j$

5:      $d = 2(X_i \bullet X_j) - (X_i \bullet X_i) - (X_j \bullet X_j)$

6:      **if** $|d| > \varepsilon$ **then**

7:          $E_i = f(X_i) - z_i$ and $E_j = f(X_j) - z_j$

8:          $\widetilde{\lambda}_i = \lambda_i$ and $\widetilde{\lambda}_j = \lambda_j$

9:          $\lambda_j = \lambda_j - \left(z_j(E_i - E_j)/d\right)$

10:         **if** $z_i = z_j$ **then**

11:             $\ell = \max\{0, \lambda_i + \lambda_j - C\}$

12:             $h = \min\{C, \lambda_i + \lambda_j\}$

13:         **else**

14:             $\ell = \max\{0, \lambda_j - \lambda_i\}$

15:             $h = \min\{C, C + \lambda_j - \lambda_i\}$

16:         **end if**

17:         $\lambda_j = \begin{cases} h & \text{if } \lambda_j > h \\ \lambda_j & \text{if } \ell \leq \lambda_j \leq h \\ \ell & \text{if } \lambda_j < \ell \end{cases}$

18:         $\lambda_i = \lambda_i + z_i z_j (\widetilde{\lambda}_j - \lambda_j)$

19:         $b_i = b - E_i - z_i(\lambda_i - \widetilde{\lambda}_i)(X_i \bullet X_i) - z_j(\lambda_j - \widetilde{\lambda}_j)(X_i \bullet X_j)$

20:         $b_j = b - E_j - z_i(\lambda_i - \widetilde{\lambda}_i)(X_i \bullet X_j) - z_j(\lambda_j - \widetilde{\lambda}_j)(X_j \bullet X_j)$

21:         $b = \begin{cases} b_i & \text{if } 0 < \lambda_i < C \\ b_j & \text{if } 0 < \lambda_j < C \\ \dfrac{b_i + b_j}{2} & \text{otherwise} \end{cases}$

22:      **end if**

23: **until** Stopping criteria is met

24: **return** $\lambda_1, \lambda_2, \ldots, \lambda_n$ and b

---

In Algorithm 5.1, we do not specify the method used to select the ordered pairs (λ_i, λ_j). Throughout this discussion, we'll assume that these pairs are selected in some straightforward way, and that we also have a (simple) stopping criteria. Problem 15 at the end of this chapter considers specific methods for selecting the pairs (λ_i, λ_j).

Given a pair (λ_i, λ_j), we're going to first update λ_j, then use this new λ_j to update λ_i. But first, we need to save the current values, so we let $\widetilde{\lambda}_i = \lambda_i$

and $\widetilde{\lambda}_j = \lambda_j$. Next, as a consequence of the constraint $C \geq \lambda_j \geq 0$, we have the bounds $\ell \leq \lambda_j \leq h$, where

$$\ell = \begin{cases} \max\{0, \lambda_j - \lambda_i\} & \text{if } z_i \neq z_j \\ \max\{0, \lambda_i + \lambda_j - C\} & \text{if } z_i = z_j \end{cases}$$

and

$$h = \begin{cases} \min\{C, C + \lambda_j - \lambda_i\} & \text{if } z_i \neq z_j \\ \min\{C, \lambda_i + \lambda_j\} & \text{if } z_i = z_j. \end{cases}$$

Next, we update λ_j so that it maximizes the objective function $L(\lambda)$, where we assume that all other λ_k are fixed. Treating this as an unconstrained optimization problem, a solution is given by

$$\lambda_j = \lambda_j - \frac{z_j(E_i - E_j)}{d} \tag{5.34}$$

where

$$E_k = f(X_k) - z_k \tag{5.35}$$

and

$$d = 2(X_i \bullet X_j) - (X_i \bullet X_i) - (X_j \bullet X_j). \tag{5.36}$$

Since we optimized without considering the bounds ℓ and h, it is possible that our computed value of λ_j is outside of the closed interval specified by ℓ and h. Thus, to enforce the requirement that $\ell \leq \lambda_j \leq h$, we'll "clip" λ_j, that is,

$$\lambda_j = \begin{cases} h & \text{if } \lambda_j > h \\ \lambda_j & \text{if } \ell \leq \lambda_j \leq h \\ \ell & \text{if } \lambda_j < \ell. \end{cases}$$

The quantity E_k is essentially the error that occurs when using our current estimates for the parameters λ and b when computing the score of X_k. Also, it is possible that $d = 0$ in (5.36), in which case equation (5.34) is undefined. The SMO algorithm deals with this case, but in the SSMO algorithm, we'll simply skip any pair (λ_i, λ_j) for which $|d| < \varepsilon$, where ε is a specified numerical tolerance.

Having updated λ_j, we now update the other half of the ordered pair, namely, λ_i. This update is computed as

$$\lambda_i = \lambda_i + z_i z_j(\widetilde{\lambda}_j - \lambda_j).$$

Recall that $\widetilde{\lambda}_j$ is the "old" value of λ_j before it was updated by the process discussed above.

At this point, we have computed an updated pair (λ_i, λ_j). To complete this iteration of the SSMO algorithm, we'll update the parameter b that appears in the scoring function $f(X)$.

It can be shown that any optimal solution to the SVM training problem must satisfy the so-called Karush-Kuhn-Tucker (KKT) conditions [139]. The KKT conditions—which are necessary and sufficient for the SVM training problem—state that for each λ_i, one of the following holds:

$$\text{If } \lambda_i = 0 \text{ then } z_i f(X_i) \geq 1.$$
$$\text{If } \lambda_i = C \text{ then } z_i f(X_i) \leq 1. \qquad (5.37)$$
$$\text{If } 0 < \lambda_i < C \text{ then } z_i f(X_i) = 1.$$

We'll modify b in the scoring function $f(X)$ so that the KKT conditions in (5.37) are satisfied for our newly-updated pair (λ_i, λ_j). Let

$$b_i = b - E_i - z_i(\lambda_i - \widetilde{\lambda}_i)(X_i \bullet X_i) - z_j(\lambda_j - \widetilde{\lambda}_j)(X_i \bullet X_j) \qquad (5.38)$$

and

$$b_j = b - E_j - z_i(\lambda_i - \widetilde{\lambda}_i)(X_i \bullet X_j) - z_j(\lambda_j - \widetilde{\lambda}_j)(X_j \bullet X_j) \qquad (5.39)$$

where E_i and E_j are the error terms defined by (5.35). It can be verified that the KKT conditions are satisfied for both λ_i and λ_j, provided that we let

$$b = \begin{cases} b_i & \text{if } 0 < \lambda_i < C \\ b_j & \text{if } 0 < \lambda_j < C \\ \dfrac{b_i + b_j}{2} & \text{otherwise.} \end{cases} \qquad (5.40)$$

It is not difficult to show that whenever $0 < \lambda_i < C$ and $0 < \lambda_j < C$ both hold, then $b_i = b_j$, and hence there is no ambiguity in (5.40). Also, if both λ_i and λ_j are at a boundary, that is, $(\lambda_i, \lambda_j) \in \{(0,0), (0,C), (C,0), (C,C)\}$, then any b between b_i and b_j will satisfy the KKT conditions. In such cases, we've chosen to let b be the midpoint between b_i and b_j.

5.6   The Bottom Line

Support vector machines are, from a high level perspective, fairly intuitive and straightforward. But, to really understand the process is not easy, requiring a deep immersion in Lagrange multipliers. In this chapter, we have tried to provide enough detail so that the reader can understand what is going on behind the scenes, but without so much rigor as to cause permanent scarring [75], let alone rigor mortis.

For supervised learning problems, SVMs are extremely popular, and with good reason. The intuition behind the technique is appealing, the theoretical foundation is sound, efficient algorithms exist, and strong results are often obtained in practice. What more could we possibly ask for from a machine learning technique?

Some of the inherent strengths of SVMs include the following.

- When training, we obtain a global maximum.

- During training, we can trade off errors for an increased margin via the parameter C.

- The kernel trick is very powerful and can lead to much better results than we could otherwise hope to achieve.

In the world of machine learning, nothing is perfect.[19] For SVMs, perhaps the biggest practical issue is choosing an appropriate kernel function K.

For more information on SVMs, see [32, 64, 84], or Berwick's delightfully titled tutorial [17]. The paper [1] discusses an interesting connection between SVMs and HMMs that the authors cleverly refer to as hidden Markov support vector machines.

5.7 Problems

1. Use the Lagrangian dual to solve the problem illustrated in Figure 5.8. The Lagrangian for this problem is given in equation (5.7). Hint: Take the partial derivatives of L with respect to x and y and set them equal to zero. Use the resulting equations to solve for x and y in terms of λ and substitute these into L to obtain $L(\lambda)$, that is, write L as a function of λ only. Minimize $L(\lambda)$ subject to the constraint $\lambda \geq 0$ and verify that you actually obtain a minimum of $L(\lambda)$.

2. Solve the maximization problem (5.9) using the Lagrangian dual. The hint given in Problem 1 might prove helpful.

3. Explicitly solve (5.10) and (5.11) to show that $p_i = 1/n$ for all i. Hint: Solve for λ in terms of n, then substitute into (5.10).

4. Derive equation (5.20), and verify that the form given in the book is correct. Show your work.

5. Repeat the analysis of the dual problem as given in equations (5.4) through (5.13) for the case where the primal problem is a constrained minimization, instead of a maximization.

6. In Section 5.3 we claim that the equation of the separating hyperplane (i.e., line) in Figure 5.9 can be written as $w_1 x + w_2 y + b = 0$, while the equations for the "margin" lines are $w_1 x + w_2 y + b = +1$ for the upper dashed line and $w_1 x + w_2 y + b = -1$ for the lower dashed line. The

---

[19]No machine learning technique is perfect, regardless of what your local random forester might say.

purpose of this problem is to verify that these equations can always be written in this way.

Let $a_1 x + a_2 y = \alpha$ be the equation of the upper margin line. Since the lower margin line is parallel, it can be written as $a_1 x + a_2 y = \beta$, where $\alpha > \beta$. The y-intercept of the upper line is α/a_2 and the lower line is β/a_2. The y-intercept for the separating hyperplane must be at the midpoint, which is $(\beta + \alpha)/(2a_2)$. It follows that the separating hyperplane can be written as $a_1 x + a_2 y = (\beta + \alpha)/2$. Find w_1, w_2, and b for which the equations of the separating hyperplane and the margin lines are as stated above. That is, determine w_1, w_2, and b in terms of a_1, a_2, α, and β so that the equation of the separating hyperplane is $w_1 x + w_2 y + b = 0$ and the margin lines are $w_1 x + w_2 y + b = +1$ and $w_1 x + w_2 y + b = -1$.

7. Derive the dual problem (5.24) from the primal problem (5.23). Show your work.

8. Consider the constrained optimization problem in equation (5.31).

    a) Verify that this equation can be rewritten in matrix form as

$$\text{Maximize: } \mathbf{1}^T \boldsymbol{\lambda} - \frac{1}{2} \boldsymbol{\lambda}^T P \boldsymbol{\lambda}$$

$$\text{Subject to: } \mathbf{C} \geq \boldsymbol{\lambda} \geq \mathbf{0} \text{ and } \mathbf{z}^T \boldsymbol{\lambda} = 0$$

    where

$$\mathbf{0} = \begin{pmatrix} 0 \\ 0 \\ \vdots \\ 0 \end{pmatrix}, \quad \mathbf{1} = \begin{pmatrix} 1 \\ 1 \\ \vdots \\ 1 \end{pmatrix}, \quad \mathbf{C} = \begin{pmatrix} C \\ C \\ \vdots \\ C \end{pmatrix}, \quad \mathbf{z} = \begin{pmatrix} z_1 \\ z_2 \\ \vdots \\ z_n \end{pmatrix}, \quad \boldsymbol{\lambda} = \begin{pmatrix} \lambda_1 \\ \lambda_2 \\ \vdots \\ \lambda_n \end{pmatrix}$$

    and

$$P = \begin{pmatrix} z_1 z_1 K(X_1, X_1) & z_1 z_2 K(X_1, X_2) & \cdots & z_1 z_n K(X_1, X_n) \\ z_2 z_1 K(X_2, X_1) & z_2 z_2 K(X_2, X_2) & \cdots & z_2 z_n K(X_2, X_n) \\ \vdots & \vdots & \ddots & \vdots \\ z_n z_1 K(X_n, X_1) & z_n z_2 K(X_n, X_2) & \cdots & z_n z_n K(X_n, X_n) \end{pmatrix}.$$

    b) Discuss possible advantages or disadvantages of this matrix form as compared to (5.31).

9. Suppose that we are given a training set $X_1, X_2, \ldots, X_n$, with corresponding classifications $z_1, z_2, \ldots, z_n$, where $z_i \in \{-1, +1\}$ for all i, and we train a linear SVM on this data.

a) For a linear SVM, the scoring function is given in (5.21). For this case, explicitly determine the weight associated with each component of a scored vector.

b) Explain how we could use the SVM weights to reduce the dimensionality of the training data.

c) If we want to reduce the dimensionality, what are the advantages and disadvantages of SVM, as compared to PCA.[20]

10. HMM, simple substitution distance (SSD) [126], and opcode graph similarity (OGS) [118] scores for each of 40 malware samples and 40 benign samples can be found in the file `malwareBenignScores.txt` at the textbook website. For each part of this problem, train an SVM using the first 20 malware samples and the first 20 benign samples in this dataset. Then test each SVM using the next 20 samples in the malware dataset and the next 20 samples in the benign dataset. In each case, determine the accuracy.

a) Let $C = 1$ and for the kernel function select the polynomial learning machine in equation (5.29) with $p = 2$.

b) Let $C = 3$ and for the kernel function select the polynomial learning machine in equation (5.29) with $p = 2$.

c) Let $C = 1$ and for the kernel function select the polynomial learning machine in equation (5.29) with $p = 4$.

d) Let $C = 3$ and for the kernel function select the polynomial learning machine in equation (5.29) with $p = 4$.

11. The Gaussian radial basis function (RBF) in equation (5.30) includes a shape parameter σ. For this problem, we want to consider the interaction between the RBF shape parameter σ and the SVM regularization parameter C. Using the same data as in Problem 10, and the RBF kernel in equation (5.30), perform a grid search over each combination of $C \in \{1, 2, 3, 4\}$ and $\sigma \in \{2, 3, 4, 5\}$. That is, for each of these 16 test cases, train an SVM using the first 20 malware samples and the first 20 benign samples, then test the resulting SVM using the next 20 samples in each dataset. Determine the accuracy in each case and clearly indicate the best result obtained over this grid search.

12. For the sake of efficiency, we generally want to use fewer features when scoring, but we also do not want to significantly reduce the effectiveness of our classification technique. A method known as recursive feature

---
[20]In Section 7.6 of Chapter 7, we discuss various connections between SVM and PCA.

elimination (RFE) [58] is one approach for reducing the number of features while minimizing any reduction in the accuracy of the resulting classifier.[21]

a) Train a linear SVM using the first 20 malware and the first 20 benign samples, based on the HMM, SSD, and OGS scores that are given in the dataset in Problem 10. Determine the accuracy based on the next 20 samples in each set, and list the SVM weights corresponding to each feature, namely, the HMM, SSD, and OGS scores.

b) Perform RFE based on the data in Problem 10, and at each step, list the SVM weights and give the accuracy for the reduced model. Hint: Eliminate the feature with the lowest weight from part a), and recompute a linear SVM using the two remaining scores. Then, eliminate the feature with the lowest weight from this SVM and train a linear SVM using the one remaining feature.

13. Suppose that we have determined the parameters λ_i that appear in the SVM training problem. How do we then determine the parameters b and s that appear in (5.33)?

14. At each iteration of the SSMO algorithm, as discussed in Section 5.5, we select an ordered pair of Lagrange multipliers (λ_i, λ_j), and we update this pair, while keeping all other λ_k fixed. We use these updated values to modify b, thus updating the scoring function $f(X)$. In this process, the intermediate values b_i in equation (5.38) and b_j in equation (5.39) are computed. Then b is updated according to (5.40). Note that in these equations, λ_i and λ_j are the updated values, while $\widetilde{\lambda}_i$ and $\widetilde{\lambda}_j$ are the old values for these Lagrange multipliers, i.e., the values of λ_i and λ_j before they were updated in the current step of the algorithm.

a) In the text it is claimed that whenever the updated pair (λ_i, λ_j) satisfies both $0 < \lambda_i < C$ and $0 < \lambda_j < C$, then $b_i = b_j$. Verify that this is the case.

b) Show that for $(\lambda_i, \lambda_j) \in \{(0,0), (0,C), (C,0), (C,C)\}$, any value of b between b_i and b_j will satisfy the Karush-Kuhn-Tucker (KKT) conditions.

c) Verify that the KKT conditions as given in (5.37) are satisfied for the updated pair (λ_i, λ_j), and scoring function $f(X)$.

15. Suppose that we are given the following training data.

---

[21]In fact, in some cases, feature reduction can actually improve the accuracy of a classifier by, in effect, removing noise.

i	(x_i, y_i)	z_i
1	$(3,3)$	$+1$
2	$(3,4)$	$+1$
3	$(2,3)$	$+1$
4	$(1,1)$	-1
5	$(1,3)$	-1
6	$(2,2)$	-1

Plotting these points in the plane, we obtain the following, where the hollow squares correspond to the $+1$ cases and the solid circles are the -1 cases.

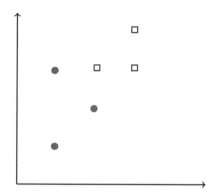

a) Implement the SSMO algorithm in Section 5.5 and solve for the unknown parameters $\lambda_1, \lambda_2, \ldots, \lambda_6$ and b using a linear kernel. Also, let $C = 2.5$ and $\varepsilon = 0.00001$. Select the ordered pairs (λ_i, λ_j) as follows

$$
\begin{aligned}
&\text{row 1:} && (\lambda_1, \lambda_2)\ (\lambda_2, \lambda_3)\ (\lambda_3, \lambda_4)\ (\lambda_4, \lambda_5)\ (\lambda_5, \lambda_6) \\
&\text{row 2:} && (\lambda_1, \lambda_3)\ (\lambda_2, \lambda_4)\ (\lambda_3, \lambda_5)\ (\lambda_4, \lambda_6) \\
&\text{row 3:} && (\lambda_1, \lambda_4)\ (\lambda_2, \lambda_5)\ (\lambda_3, \lambda_6) \\
&\text{row 4:} && (\lambda_1, \lambda_5)\ (\lambda_2, \lambda_6) \\
&\text{row 5:} && (\lambda_1, \lambda_6) \\
&\text{row 6:} && (\lambda_2, \lambda_1)\ (\lambda_3, \lambda_2)\ (\lambda_4, \lambda_3)\ (\lambda_5, \lambda_4)\ (\lambda_6, \lambda_5) \\
&\text{row 7:} && (\lambda_3, \lambda_1)\ (\lambda_4, \lambda_2)\ (\lambda_5, \lambda_3)\ (\lambda_6, \lambda_4) \\
&\text{row 8:} && (\lambda_4, \lambda_1)\ (\lambda_5, \lambda_2)\ (\lambda_6, \lambda_3) \\
&\text{row 9:} && (\lambda_5, \lambda_1)\ (\lambda_6, \lambda_2) \\
&\text{row 10:} && (\lambda_6, \lambda_1)
\end{aligned}
$$

Repeat this pattern 10 times, unless one entire pass through the list is made with no modification to any λ_i. Discuss your results.

b) Repeat part b), but select the pairs (λ_i, λ_j) as follows: The index i is chosen in sequence, that is, $i = 1, 2, \ldots, 6$. The corresponding index j is chosen at random, with the restriction that $j \neq i$. Generate 1000 pairs (λ_i, λ_j) using this approach, repeating $i = 1, 2, \ldots, 6$ as necessary.

c) Graph the separating hyperplane corresponding to your solution in part b) and on a separate graph, plot your solution to part c). On each graph, include the data points from part a).

16. In this problem, we use Lagrange multipliers to prove that the training process used in principal component analysis (PCA) maximizes the variance [125]. Recall from Chapter 4 that PCA is based on the notion that large variances correspond to the most informative and interesting aspects of the training data. Let X_i, for $i = 1, 2, \ldots, n$, be training vectors, where each vector is of length m. In PCA, each X_i can be viewed as corresponding to an "experiment" with m "measurements." Let $\widetilde{X}_i = X_i - \mu$, where μ is the vector of means in equation (4.4) on page 80. Form the $m \times n$ matrix A, where the columns of A are these normalized training vectors $\widetilde{X}_i$. Due to the normalization, each row of A has mean 0. Then $C = \frac{1}{n} A A^T$ is the covariance matrix for the given data. PCA training is based on the eigenvalues and unit eigenvectors of the matrix C. The normalized training vectors $\widetilde{X}_i$ are then projected onto the resulting eigenspace to form a scoring matrix based on the most dominant eigenvectors.

a) Let u be a unit vector. The *scalar projection* of a vector y onto u is given by the dot product $y \cdot u$, while the projection vector is αu where $\alpha = y \cdot u$. Note that since u is a unit vector, the scalar projection is the length of the the projection vector.[22] Then the projection of a normalized training vector $\widetilde{X}_i$ onto the unit vector u is given by $(\widetilde{X}_i \cdot u) u$. Show that the projected training vectors have mean 0, that is, verify that

$$\frac{1}{n} \sum_{i=1}^{n} (\widetilde{X}_i \cdot u) u = \begin{pmatrix} 0 \\ 0 \\ \vdots \\ 0 \end{pmatrix}.$$

b) When using the projection $(\widetilde{X}_i \cdot u) u$ instead of $\widetilde{X}_i$, the (squared) error that is introduced is $||\widetilde{X}_i - (\widetilde{X}_i \cdot u) u||^2$, where $||y||^2 = y \cdot y$. Verify that

$$||\widetilde{X}_i - (\widetilde{X}_i \cdot u) u||^2 = \widetilde{X}_i \cdot \widetilde{X}_i - (\widetilde{X}_i \cdot u)^2.$$

---

[22]See Problem 10 in Chapter 7 for more details on the relationship between a scalar projection and its projection vector.

Hint: Use the fact that u is a unit vector.

c) The *mean squared error* (MSE) that is introduced by projecting onto u is given by

$$\text{MSE}(u) = \frac{1}{n} \sum_{i=1}^{n} (\widetilde{X}_i \cdot \widetilde{X}_i - (\widetilde{X}_i \cdot u)^2)$$

$$= \frac{1}{n} \sum_{i=1}^{n} \widetilde{X}_i \cdot \widetilde{X}_i - \frac{1}{n} \sum_{i=1}^{n} (\widetilde{X}_i \cdot u)^2.$$

Show that minimizing $\text{MSE}(u)$ is equivalent to maximizing the variance. Hint: Use the fact that, in general, $\mu_{y^2} = \mu_y^2 + \sigma_y^2$, that is, the mean of a squared variable is the square of the mean of the (unsquared) variable, plus the variance of the (unsquared) variable. Also make use of the result from part a).

d) Instead of projecting onto a single unit vector u, in PCA we typically project onto a set of orthogonal unit vectors, say, $u_1, u_2, \ldots, u_\ell$. In such a case, the projection of the training vector $\widetilde{X}_i$ is

$$\sum_{j=1}^{\ell} (\widetilde{X}_i \cdot u_j) u_j.$$

Verify that the MSE of this sum is equal to the sum of the MSE for each component. This result implies that by maximizing the variance of each individual component, we will maximize the overall variance. Hint: The solution to Problem 9 in Chapter 4 might be helpful.

e) Maximize the variance using Lagrange multipliers and show that the optimal result is given by the eigenvectors of the covariance matrix C. Hint: We have

$$\sigma_u^2 = \frac{1}{n} \sum_{i=1}^{n} (\widetilde{X}_i \cdot u)^2,$$

which can be written in matrix form as

$$\sigma_u^2 = \frac{1}{n} uA(uA)^T = u\frac{AA^T}{n}u^T = uCu^T.$$

Since we only consider unit vectors, we have the constrained optimization problem

$$\text{Maximize: } \sigma_u^2 = uCu^T$$
$$\text{Subject to: } u \cdot u = 1.$$

The Lagrangian for this problem is

$$L(u, \lambda) = uCu^T + \lambda\big((u \cdot u) - 1\big).$$

Compute partial derivatives $\partial L(u, \lambda)/\partial\lambda$ and $\partial L(u, \lambda)/\partial u$, where u is a vector of length m, set the resulting equations equal to zero, and solve the unknowns.

Chapter 6

A Comprehensible Collection of Clustering Concepts

You cannot eat a cluster of grapes at once,
but it is very easy if you eat them one by one.
— Jacques Roumain

6.1 Introduction

The goal of clustering is to group objects in some meaningful way. Clustering and cluster analysis is generally used in a data exploration mode, where the objective is to learn something about the data itself. As with all of the machine learning techniques discussed in this book, the clustering techniques in this chapter are used in a wide variety of applications.

We'll focus our attention on two popular techniques, namely, K-means and EM clustering. The K-means algorithm is easy to understand and is extremely popular. The expectation maximization (EM) algorithm is less easy and consequently less widely used, but it can give more refined results in many cases. We also discuss the issue of measuring cluster quality. But, before we get to the main topics of the chapter, we present an overview, along with a quick look at a few relevant background topics.

6.2 Overview and Background

Clustering techniques can be classified in many different ways. For example, *intrinsic* approaches work with the raw data and can be considered a form of unsupervised learning. On the other hand, an *extrinsic* clustering technique requires class labels and, therefore, can be viewed as a type of supervised learning.

We can also cluster clustering techniques into *agglomerative* and *divisive*. As the name implies, an agglomerative approach starts with many small clusters, which are coalesced into fewer and larger clusters. In contrast, a divisive approach begins with large clusters that are split into smaller clusters. Agglomerative can be equated with a bottom-up approach, whereas divisive is a top-down strategy.

A particularly important clustering dichotomy is *hierarchical* versus *partitional*. In hierarchical clustering, there are parent-child relationships between elements—such relationships can be illustrated via a *dendrogram*, such as that in Figure 6.1.

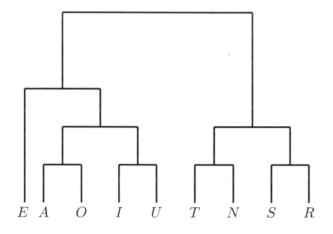

Figure 6.1: Dendrogram

Given a function that defines a distance between clusters (a topic we discuss in a moment), a hierarchical clustering algorithm could be as simple as Algorithm 6.1. While there is no law against using a hierarchical approach, it may be somewhat disconcerting that such techniques are entirely ad hoc, as there is no real theory underlying such an algorithm. In contrast, even the simplest partitional clustering algorithm (i.e., K-means) has some theoretical underpinnings.

Before moving on to discuss K-means in detail, we briefly mention a couple of relevant background topics. First, we need some way to measure distance between data points. The Euclidean distance between the vectors $x = (x_1, x_2, \ldots, x_n)$ and $y = (y_1, y_2, \ldots, y_n)$, which is defined as

$$d(x, y) = \sqrt{(x_1 - y_1)^2 + (x_2 - y_2)^2 + \cdots + (x_n - y_n)^2},$$

will feature prominently in our discussion of K-means clustering. However, other distance measures can certainly be used. For example, *Manhattan distance* (or taxicab distance) is also widely used. The Manhattan distance

---

Algorithm 6.1 Hierarchical clustering

1: **Given:**
         Data points $x_1, x_2, \ldots, x_n$ to cluster
         Number of clusters K, where $K \leq n$
2: **Initialize:**
         n clusters, each of size 1
3: Let $m = n$
4: **while** $m > K$ **do**
5:     Find two nearest clusters and merge
6:     $m = m - 1$
7: **end while**

---

between x and y is given by

$$d(x, y) = |x_1 - y_1| + |x_2 - y_2| + \cdots + |x_n - y_n|.$$

In the plane, this corresponds to the distance a taxicab travels between points in a place like Manhattan where only right-angle turns are allowed, and thus the name. The relationship between Euclidean distance and Manhattan distance is illustrated in Figure 6.2.

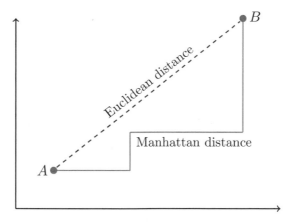

Figure 6.2: Euclidean vs Manhattan distance

There are other less intuitive measures of distance that can be useful when analyzing data. For example, Mahalanobis distance is a statistical measure that accounts for mean and covariance. Another statistical-based distance can be obtained by use of the χ^2 statistic. And even less intuitively, a simple substitution cipher can be used to define a "decryption" distance that is not limited to ciphertext. This latter distance function has been used with success in the context of malware detection [126]. There are innumerable other distance measures that may be useful in certain applications.

Next, we discuss K-means clustering. The K-means algorithm is easy to implement, easy to understand, and it is undoubtedly the most widely used clustering technique in the known universe.

6.3 K-Means

In this section, we first discuss a generic approach to clustering. We then consider how to implement such an approach, which leads us naturally to the K-means algorithm.

Suppose that we are given the n data points $X_1, X_2, \ldots, X_n$, where each of the X_i is (typically) a vector of m real numbers. For example, if we want to analyze home sales in a particular area, we might have

$$X_i = (\text{sale price of house } i, \text{ size of house } i)$$

in which case $m = 2$. As another example, we could analyze a set of malware samples based on, say, seven distinct scores, denoted $s_1, s_2, \ldots, s_7$. Then each data point would be of the form

$$X_i = (s_1, s_2, s_3, \ldots, s_7).$$

We'll assume that the desired number of clusters K is specified in advance. Then we want to partition our n data points $X_1, X_2, \ldots, X_n$ into K clusters. We also assume that we have a distance function $d(X_i, X_j)$ that is defined for all pairs of data points.

Again, we'll require that each data point X_i belongs to exactly one cluster.[1] Furthermore, we also associate a *centroid* with each cluster, where the centroid can be viewed as representative of its cluster—intuitively, a centroid is the center of mass of its cluster. In K-means, centroids need not be actual data points. In any case, we'll denote the clusters as C_j with the corresponding centroid denoted as c_j.

Now suppose that we have clustered our n data points. Then we have a set of K centroids,

$$c_1, c_2, c_3, \ldots, c_K$$

and each data point is associated with exactly one centroid. Let centroid(X_i) denote the (unique) centroid of the cluster to which X_i belongs. The centroids determine the clusters, in the sense that whenever we have

$$c_j = \text{centroid}(X_i),$$

then X_i belongs to cluster C_j.

---

[1]Some clustering algorithms allow for a "soft" assignment of points to clusters, in which case points can be viewed as partially belonging to multiple clusters. But, your simple-minded author would like to keep things as simple as possible, at least for now.

Before we can cluster data based on the outline above, we need to answer the following two basic questions.

1. How do we determine the centroids c_j?

2. How do we determine the clusters? That is, we need to specify the function centroid(X_i), which assigns data points to centroids and has the effect of determining the clusters.

Of course, there are many ways to answer these questions. As a trivial example, we could simply select centroids at random and then assign points to centroids at random. However, such an approach is sure to be useless in our quest to obtain meaningful clusters.

At the very least, we need a method to compare clusterings, that is, we must have a way to determine whether one clustering is better than another. For now, we'll focus on a simple method for measuring cluster quality. In Section 6.4 we revisit this issue of measuring cluster quality.

Intuitively, it seems clear that the more compact a cluster, the better. Of course, this will depend on the data points X_i and the number of clusters K. Since the data is given, and we assume that K has been specified, at this point we have no control over the X_i or K. But, we do have control over the centroids c_j and the assignment of points to centroids via the function centroid(X_i). The choice of centroids and the assignment of points to centroids will clearly influence the compactness (or "shape") of the resulting clusters.

How can we measure the compactness of a given set of clusters? Let's define

$$\text{distortion} = \sum_{i=1}^{n} d\big(X_i, \text{centroid}(X_i)\big). \tag{6.1}$$

Intuitively, the smaller the distortion, the better, since a smaller distortion implies that individual clusters are more compact.[2]

For example, consider the data in Figure 6.3, where the same data points are clustered in two different ways. Given reasonable centroids, it's clear that the clustering on the left-hand side in Figure 6.3 has a smaller distortion than that on the right-hand side. Therefore, we would say that the left-hand clustering is superior, at least with respect to the measure of distortion.

Since we've decided that a smaller distortion is better, let's try to minimize the distortion. First, we note that the distortion depends on K, since more clusters means more centroids and, all else being equal, the larger the value

---

[2]In addition to having compact clusters, we might also want a large separation between clusters. However, such separation is not (directly) accounted for in K-means. In the next section, we consider measures of cluster quality that also take into account cluster separation.

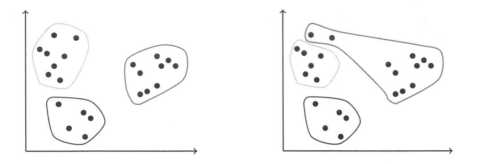

Figure 6.3: Distortion

of K, the closer each point will tend to be to its centroid. Hence, we write distortion$_K$ to emphasize the dependence on the parameter K. As mentioned above, we assume that K is specified in advance.

The problem we want to solve can be stated precisely as follows.

$$\text{Given: } K \text{ and data points } X_1, X_2, \ldots, X_n$$
$$\text{Minimize: distortion}_K = \sum_{i=1}^{n} d\big(X_i, \text{centroid}(X_i)\big). \tag{6.2}$$

Finding an exact solution to this problem is NP-complete. But, that doesn't rule out the possibility of an efficient approximate solution. In fact, we will now derive a very simple, iterative approximation.

We claim that a solution to (6.2) must satisfy the following two conditions.

Condition 1 Each X_i is clustered according to its nearest centroid. That is, if the data point X_i belongs to cluster C_j, then $d(X_i, c_j) \leq d(X_i, c_\ell)$ for all $\ell \in \{1, 2, \ldots, K\}$, where the c_ℓ are the centroids.

Condition 2 Each centroid is located at the center of its cluster.

To verify the necessity of Condition 1, suppose that X_i is in cluster C_j and that $d(X_i, c_\ell) < d(X_i, c_j)$ for some ℓ. Then by simply reassigning X_i to cluster ℓ, we will reduce distortion$_K$. Condition 2 also seems intuitively clear, but it's not entirely straightforward to prove.[3] In any case, these two conditions suggest an approximation algorithm—and not just any approximation algorithm, but one that is wildly popular, widely used, and often highly effective in practice.

From Condition 1, we see that given any clustering for which there are points that are not clustered based on their nearest centroid, we can improve the clustering by simply reassigning such data points to their nearest centroid.

---

[3] Predictably, your predictable author has left the proof as an exercise.

By Condition 2, we always want the centroids to be at the center of the clusters. So, given any clustering, we may improve it—and we cannot un-improve it—by performing either of the following two steps.

Step 1 Assign each data point to its nearest centroid.

Step 2 Recompute the centroids so that each lies at the center of its respective cluster.

It's clear that nothing can be gained by applying Step 1 more than once in succession, and the same holds true for Step 2. However, by alternating between these two steps, we obtain an iterative process that yields a series of solutions that will generally tend to improve, and even in the worst case, the solution cannot get worse. This is precisely the K-means algorithm [97], which we state somewhat more precisely as Algorithm 6.2.

Algorithm 6.2 K-means clustering

1: **Given:**
   Data points $X_1, X_2, \ldots, X_n$ to cluster
   Number of clusters K
2: **Initialize:**
   Partition $X_1, X_2, \ldots, X_n$ into clusters $C_1, C_2, \ldots, C_K$
3: **while** stopping criteria is not met **do**
4:    **for** $j = 1$ to K **do**
5:       Let centroid c_j be the center of cluster C_j
6:    **end for**
7:    **for** $i = 1$ to n **do**
8:       Assign X_i to cluster C_j so that $d(X_i, c_j) \leq d(X_i, c_\ell)$
          for all $\ell \in \{1, 2, \ldots, K\}$
9:    **end for**
10: **end while**

The stopping criteria in Algorithm 6.2 could be that distortion$_K$ improves (i.e., decreases) by less than a set threshold, or that the centroids don't change by much, or we could simply run the algorithm for a fixed number of iterations. Regardless of the stopping criteria used, we would always want to set a maximum number of iterations to avoid spinning our wheels for too long.

Algorithm 6.2 is a hill climb, and hence K-means is only assured of finding local maximum. And, as with any hill climb, the maximum we obtain will depend on our choice for the initial conditions. For K-means, the initial conditions correspond to the initial selection of centroids. Therefore, it can be beneficial to repeat the algorithm multiple times with different initializations of the centroids.

Instead of the random initialization specified in Algorithm 6.2, we might want to uniformly space the initial centroids. Recall that each X_i is a vector of length m. Let a_1 be the minimum value of the first component over the set of all X_i. For example, if

$$X_i = (\text{sale price of house } i, \ \text{size of house } i)$$

then a_1 is the minimum sale price of any house in our dataset. Similarly, define a_2 through a_m as the minimum values in components 2 through m. Also, let A_1 be the maximum value of the first component, and so on through A_m. Then given K, we can let

$$\tilde{a}_i = \frac{A_i - a_i}{K + 1}, \ \text{for } i = 1, 2, \ldots, m.$$

Then for $\ell = 1, 2, \ldots, K$, we select the initial centroids as

$$\text{centroid}(\ell) = \big(a_1 + \ell \cdot \tilde{a}_1, a_2 + \ell \cdot \tilde{a}_2, \ldots, a_m + \ell \cdot \tilde{a}_m\big).$$

Note that in each dimension, we are simply dividing the range of values into $K+1$ equal-sized segments. By this process, we select the initial centroids so that they are uniformly spaced throughout the range of the data. Of course, other initialization strategies could be used.

In practice we might want to repeat the K-means process multiple times and retain the best result. But to do so, we must have some way to compare different clusterings. So, how can we compare different clusterings? And what about the related issue of choosing a reasonable (ideally, optimal) value of K? We could rely on distortion$_K$, as defined above. However, there are some important aspects of clustering that are ignored by this measure. In the next section, we discuss other measures of cluster quality that can be useful in practice. These cluster quality measures are independent of the clustering technique used.

Before moving on to discuss cluster quality in general, we note in passing that there are several variations on the popular K-means algorithm. Two such variants are K-medoids and fuzzy K-means. Recall that in K-means, the centroids need not be actual data points. In contrast, for K-medoids, we require the centroids to be data points. That is, we select the data point that is closest to the center as the centroid. Also, recall that in K-means, each data point resides in exactly one cluster. In fuzzy K-means, we allow each data point to have a "degree of membership" with respect to each cluster. In this way, the boundaries between clusters are less distinct—and hence the name fuzzy K-means. There are certainly many other sensible variations on the K-means algorithm.

6.4 Measuring Cluster Quality

Suppose that we invent a new malware detection score, and we want to quantify its effectiveness. We could apply the score to a set of malware (of the type that the score is designed to detect) and a representative set of benign samples. Then we could measure the accuracy or use ROC analysis to determine the effectiveness of our proposed score, as discussed in Chapter 8. The assumption is that, in general, the score will perform similar to the way it performs on the test set—a reasonable assumption if the test set is truly representative. The point here is that when we want to measure the effectiveness of any binary classifier, we have many well-defined tools for doing so.

Now, suppose that we apply a clustering technique to a dataset and we want to determine the effectiveness, or quality of the results [69]. Can we simply apply the same tools as we use for a binary classifier? Unfortunately, the answer is generally no. When we have a test set of labeled data (e.g., malware and benign), we can then measure the quality of our score relative to this test set—the ideal case is perfect classification, and we can measure how far our results are from this ideal. In contrast, clustering is typically used in data exploration mode, where we don't really know what an ideal result would look like. And, even if we do have a reasonable test case, it may not be straightforward to define a meaningful score. Hence, tools such as ROC analysis are generally not directly applicable, although there are some exceptions [3].

Fortunately, all is not lost. Given a set of clusters, we can measure characteristics of the clusters—compactness within clusters, and the spread between clusters, for example. Then we can compare the actual results to an idealized clustering. That is, we can compare our clusters against something that, in general, seems "really good." Recall that in the case where we train a model and score samples, the ideal result is complete separation between the match and no-match scores. However, clustering is more challenging since the optimal clusters for one dataset might be completely different from those for another dataset. In addition, we might obtain more meaningful results for clusters that are further from the ideal. For example, in a given dataset, the most natural clusters might be quite spread out, and yet, generically, we would prefer compact clusters. Also, it is possible that there is no useful information contained in a dataset, yet we might still obtain clusters that look strong, relative to some particular measure. The bottom line is that measuring the success of clustering is inherently difficult, primarily because we generally don't know what constitutes an optimal result.

The first thing that we might want to consider is whether the data is inherently "clusterable," that is, whether some sort of natural clustering might actually exist. For example, the data in Figure 6.4 (a) looks to be much more cluster-friendly than the data that appears in Figure 6.4 (b).

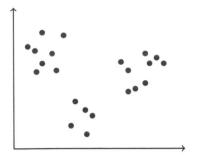

(a) Suitable for clustering   (b) Not as well-suited for clustering

Figure 6.4: Clusterability

However, in higher dimensions, where we cannot easily visualize data points, it's bound to be more difficult to determine whether the data naturally separates into reasonable clusters. In any case, for the clustering applications considered in Chapter 13, we'll take an experimentalist approach. That is, we'll simply cluster the data, varying the number of clusters, and then analyze the results to see which appears to be most useful. This is typical of the way that clustering is generally used in practice.

Having obtained a set of clusters, we can attempt to validate the clusters. That is, we can use various measures to tell us whether the clusters appear to be reasonable or not. There are two general approaches to this cluster validation problem, namely, *external validation* and *internal validation*. Any external validation is based on something that we know beforehand about the data, while internal validation is based solely on the topology or shape of the clusters themselves. For example, the measure of distortion, which we defined in equation (6.1), is clearly an internal measurement, since it is based entirely on the compactness of the clusters, and it does not rely on any properties of the underlying data. We'll consider both internal and external validation methods, but we put the most emphasis on internal validation, since that's the more challenging case.

Recall that we wrote distortion$_K$ to emphasize that the distortion depends on the number of clusters. For most—if not all—of the validation methods we discuss below, there is some dependence on the number of clusters. For simplicity, we'll ignore any dependence on the number of clusters, but it's important to realize that due to such dependence, the problem of selecting the (near) optimal number of clusters is also difficult. Furthermore, for any given measure of cluster quality, it may not be easy to directly compare results when the numbers of clusters varies. The bottom line is that the methods discussed here will not necessarily help us to resolve the sticky issue of the best choice for the number of clusters K.

6.4.1 Internal Validation

Internal validation relies on the shape or topology of the clusters themselves, not on the type of data points found within the clusters. While there are many possible topological measurements, we'll only consider cluster correlation, similarity matrix, sum of squares error, and the silhouette coefficient.

6.4.1.1 Correlation

Given any two vectors $X = (x_1, x_2, \ldots, x_m)$ and $Y = (y_1, y_2, \ldots, y_m)$, the Pearson *correlation coefficient* is defined as

$$r_{XY} = \frac{\text{cov}(X, Y)}{\sigma_X \sigma_Y} = \frac{\sum\limits_{i=1}^{m}(x_i - \mu_X)(y_i - \mu_Y)}{\sqrt{\sum\limits_{i=1}^{m}(x_i - \mu_X)^2 \sum\limits_{i=1}^{m}(y_i - \mu_Y)^2}}$$

where $\text{cov}(X, Y)$ is the covariance of X and Y (see Section 4.2 of Chapter 4 for a discussion of covariance), μ_X is the sample mean of the x_i, and σ_X^2 is the sample variance of the x_i, with μ_Y and σ_Y^2 defined similarly. It can be shown that $-1 \leq r_{XY} \leq 1$. Furthermore, there is a relationship between linear regression and the correlation coefficient (see Section 7.9 of Chapter 7 for a discussion of linear regression). Specifically, if $r_{XY} = 1$, then all data points lie on a regression line with positive slope, while $r_{XY} = -1$ implies that all data points lie on a regression line with negative slope. On the other hand, for $0 < r_{XY} < 1$, the regression line has positive slope, but points are dispersed about the line—the closer r_{XY} is to 0, the greater the dispersion. Similar comments hold for $-1 < r_{XY} < 0$, except the slope of the regression line is negative. These different cases are illustrated in Figure 6.5. The relationship between regression and correlation can be useful when trying to interpret correlation results.

Now, we show how the correlation coefficient can be used as an intrinsic measure of cluster quality. Let $X_1, X_2, \ldots, X_n$ be a dataset, with each data point assigned to one of K clusters. Let $D = \{d_{ij}\}$ be the $n \times n$ distance matrix defined by

$$d_{ij} = d(X_i, X_j). \tag{6.3}$$

We also define the $n \times n$ adjacency matrix A where

$$a_{ij} = \begin{cases} 1 & \text{if } X_i \text{ and } X_j \text{ belong to the same cluster} \\ 0 & \text{otherwise.} \end{cases}$$

Ideally, we want the distance d_{ij} to be small when $a_{ij} = 1$ and large otherwise. That is, in the ideal case, we want a large inverse correlation between the

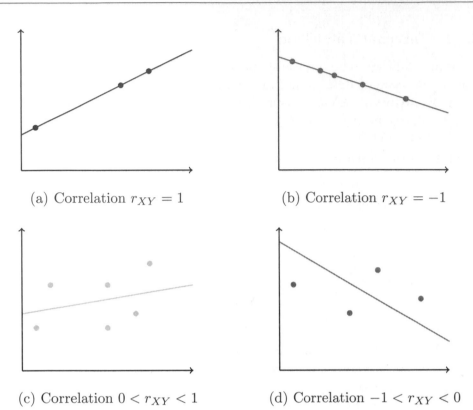

(a) Correlation $r_{XY} = 1$ (b) Correlation $r_{XY} = -1$

(c) Correlation $0 < r_{XY} < 1$ (d) Correlation $-1 < r_{XY} < 0$

Figure 6.5: Correlation coefficient and regression line examples

elements of these two matrices This sounds like a job for the correlation coefficient, so we compute

$$r_{AD} = \frac{\text{cov}(A, D)}{\sigma_A \sigma_D} = \frac{\sum_{i,j=1}^{n} (a_{ij} - \mu_A)(d_{ij} - \mu_D)}{\sqrt{\sum_{i,j=1}^{n} (a_{ij} - \mu_A)^2 \sum_{i,j-1}^{n} (d_{ij} - \mu_D)^2}}. \tag{6.4}$$

Note that the closer that r_{AD} is to -1, the closer we are to the ideal case, where the inverse correlation between the corresponding elements of the adjacency matrix A and the distance matrix D is as large as possible.

In Figure 6.6 we give two clustering examples along with their correlation coefficients r_{AD}. In these examples, the clustering with the larger correlation coefficient, which appears in Figure 6.6 (a), does indeed appear to be much better than the clustering with the lower correlation coefficient, which is given in Figure 6.6 (b).

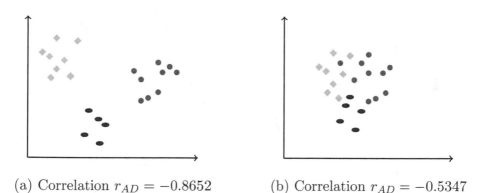

(a) Correlation $r_{AD} = -0.8652$ (b) Correlation $r_{AD} = -0.5347$

Figure 6.6: Correlation coefficient examples

6.4.1.2   Similarity Matrix

Another useful measure of intrinsic cluster quality is based on a similarity matrix. For this measure, we generate a similarity matrix, then group the rows and columns by cluster and, finally, generate a heatmap for the resulting matrix. This provides a visual representation of the clusters, where sharp breaks (in color) between clusters are a good sign.

To generate a similarity matrix, we first need to decide what to use as a similarity measure. While there are many possibilities, perhaps the most obvious would be the same distance matrix $D = \{d_{ij}\}$ as defined in equation (6.3). For this similarity matrix, the resulting *heatmap* provides a visual representation of the correlation. The heatmaps corresponding to Figures 6.6 (a) and (b) are given in Figures 6.7 (a) and (b), respectively.

For the heatmaps in Figures 6.7 (a) and (b), rows and columns 1 through 8 correspond to the diamonds in Figures 6.6 (a) and (b), respectively, while rows and columns 9 through 13 correspond to the ovals, and the last 10 rows and columns correspond to the circles. Note that when viewed in color, this particular heatmap uses blue to represent close distances, while red is used for the farthest distances.[4]

Comparing Figures 6.7 (a) and (b), we see that the clusters for (a) have smaller intra-cluster spacing in comparison to their inter-cluster spacing and hence we would consider (a) a better result than (b). Of course, in this example, it's obvious from the the clusters in Figure 6.6 that (a) is superior to (b). However, in dimensions greater than three, we would not have the luxury of viewing the clusters in such a manner. Regardless of the number of dimensions, we can always use this heatmap technique to obtain a visual representation of cluster quality. Specifically, a heatmap gives us a useful view of intra-cluster versus inter-cluster spacing.

---

[4]Your munificent author has generously made all images in this book available in color on the textbook website.

X	1	2	3	4	5	6	7	8	9	10	11	12	13	14	15	16	17	18	19	20	21	22	23
1						1.61			2.17	2.25	1.71	2.49	2.81	3.28	3.50	3.82	4.46	4.46	3.96	3.20	2.97	3.86	4.23
2									2.23	2.42	1.77	2.55	2.94	3.16	3.37	3.67	4.25	4.25	3.75	3.01	2.75	3.62	4.00
3						1.61		1.44	1.72	2.01		2.03	2.48	2.61	2.83	3.13	3.76	3.76	3.26	2.50	2.27	3.16	3.53
4								0.83	2.31	2.63	1.88	2.61	3.09	2.97	3.16	3.42	3.92	3.92	3.42	2.72	2.42	3.25	3.65
5									2.73	2.93	2.28	3.05	3.46	3.56	3.75	4.92	4.52	4.52	4.03	3.32	3.03	3.85	4.26
6	1.61								2.75	3.21	2.38	3.02	3.59	3.01	3.14	3.32	3.64	3.64	3.16	2.57	2.21	2.92	3.35
7							1.31		3.01	3.18	2.55	3.33	3.72	3.85	4.04	4.30	4.79	4.79	4.29	3.60	3.30	4.11	4.52
8			1.44						3.13	3.45	2.71	3.43	3.92	3.66	3.82	4.02	4.39	4.39	3.91	3.29	2.94	3.68	4.10
9	2.17	2.23	1.72	2.31	2.73	2.75	3.01	3.13						1.63	1.90	2.30	3.21	3.21	2.79	2.05	2.11	2.90	3.11
10	2.25	2.42	2.01	2.63	2.93	3.21	3.18	3.45						2.33	2.60	3.00	3.92	3.92	3.52	2.79	2.85	3.64	3.84
11	1.71	1.77	1.26	1.88	2.28	2.38	2.55	2.71						1.88	2.15	2.53	3.38	3.38	2.93	2.15	2.13	2.98	3.24
12	2.49	2.55	2.03	2.61	3.05	3.02	3.33	3.43						1.51	1.78	2.18	3.11	3.11	2.72	2.03	2.15	2.87	3.04
13	2.81	2.94	2.48	3.09	3.46	3.59	3.72	3.92						2.09	2.33	2.73	3.68	3.68	3.33	2.68	2.82	3.51	3.65
14	3.28	3.16	2.61	2.97	3.56	3.01	3.85	3.66	1.63	2.33	1.88	1.51	2.09			1.60	1.60	1.26				1.47	1.56
15	3.50	3.37	2.83	3.16	3.75	3.14	4.04	3.82	1.90	2.60	2.15	1.78	2.33							0.79			
16	3.82	3.67	3.13	3.42	4.02	3.32	4.30	4.02	2.30	3.00	2.53	2.18	2.73				0.96	0.96					
17	4.46	4.25	3.76	3.92	4.52	3.64	4.79	4.39	3.21	3.92	3.38	3.11	3.68	1.60		0.96				1.27	1.50		
18	4.46	4.25	3.76	3.92	4.52	3.64	4.79	4.39	3.21	3.92	3.38	3.11	3.68	1.60		0.96				1.27	1.50		
19	3.96	3.75	3.26	3.42	4.03	3.16	4.29	4.29	2.79	3.52	2.93	2.72	3.33										
20	3.20	3.01	2.50	2.72	3.32	2.57	3.60	3.29	2.05	2.79	2.15	2.03	2.68										
21	2.97	2.75	2.27	2.42	3.03	2.21	3.30	2.94	2.11	2.85	2.13	2.15	2.82				1.50	1.50					
22	3.86	3.62	3.16	3.25	3.85	2.92	4.11	3.68	2.90	3.64	2.98	2.87	3.51	1.48									0.45
23	4.23	4.00	3.53	3.65	4.26	3.35	4.52	4.10	3.11	3.84	3.24	3.04	3.65	1.56									

(a) Heatmap corresponding to Figure 6.6 (a)

X	1	2	3	4	5	6	7	8	9	10	11	12	13	14	15	16	17	18	19	20	21	22	23
1				0.85		1.53	0.95	1.41		1.01	0.80	1.32	1.56	1.46	1.70	2.05	2.11	2.42	1.66	1.10	1.23	1.66	2.05
2						1.17		1.10			1.31	1.70	1.35	1.55	1.86	1.82	2.12	1.35			0.89	1.31	1.70
3				0.86	1.05	1.55	1.30	1.61			0.87	1.17	1.05	1.30	1.68	1.84	2.16	1.45	0.93		1.35	1.57	1.96
4	0.85		0.86				0.89	0.83	1.00	1.55		1.36	1.90	1.24	1.37	1.60	1.41	1.69	0.91			0.82	1.20
5			1.05			1.01		0.76	1.30	1.72	1.17	1.80	2.21	1.78	1.95	2.20	2.00	2.26	1.50	1.02		1.31	1.66
6	1.53	1.17	1.55		1.01		1.17		1.66	2.23	1.35	1.89	2.51	1.63	1.66	1.73	1.25	1.43		0.74			
7	0.95		1.30	0.89		1.17			1.57	1.95	1.45	2.09	2.47	2.07	2.21	2.48	2.25	2.50	1.75	1.30		1.52	1.83
8	1.41	1.10	1.61						1.81	2.31	1.57	2.19	2.72	2.03	2.12	2.26	1.85	2.04	1.39	1.13		1.03	1.25
9				1.00	1.30	1.66	1.57	1.81					0.92	0.81	1.08	1.47	1.74	2.06	1.40	0.95	1.51	1.60	1.97
10	1.01	1.23		1.55	1.72	2.23	1.95	2.31			0.92			1.22	1.48	1.89	2.27	2.58	1.97	1.53	2.05	2.18	2.55
11	0.80				1.17	1.35	1.45	1.57		0.92			1.17		0.90	1.26	1.43	1.75	1.07		1.25	1.26	1.63
12	1.32	1.31		1.36	1.80	1.89	2.09	2.19							1.07	1.54	1.84	1.37	1.13	1.86	1.70	2.02
13	1.56	1.70	1.17	1.90	2.21	2.51	2.47	2.72			1.17			1.10	1.30	1.67	2.21	2.51	2.05	1.75	2.11	2.36	2.69
14	1.46	1.35	1.05	1.24	1.78	1.63	2.07	2.03	0.81	1.22			1.10				1.12	1.42	1.00	0.90	1.68	1.37	1.65
15	1.70	1.55	1.30	1.37	1.95	1.66	2.24	2.12	1.08	1.48	0.90		1.30				0.93	1.21	0.93	0.99	1.77	1.35	1.57
16	2.05	1.86	1.68	1.60	2.20	1.73	2.48	2.26	1.47	1.89	1.26	1.07	1.67					0.91	0.92	1.19	1.91	1.35	1.48
17	2.11	1.82	1.84	1.41	2.00	1.25	2.25	1.85	1.74	2.27	1.43	1.54	2.21	1.12	0.93	0.71				1.03	1.54	0.83	0.82
18	2.42	2.12	2.16	1.69	2.26	1.43	2.50	2.04	2.06	2.58	1.75	1.84	2.51	1.42	1.21	0.91				1.33	1.76	1.01	0.87
19	1.66	1.35	1.45	0.91	1.50	0.92	1.75	1.39	1.40	1.97	1.07	1.37	2.05	1.00	0.93	0.92				1.06			1.03
20	1.10		0.93		1.02		1.30	1.13	0.95	1.53		1.13	1.75	0.90	0.99	1.19	1.03	1.33					1.03
21	1.23	0.89	1.35						1.51	2.05	1.25	1.86	2.41	1.68	1.77	1.91	1.54	1.76	1.06				1.04
22	1.66	1.31	1.57	0.82	1.31		1.52	1.03	1.60	2.18	1.26	1.70	2.36	1.37	1.35	1.35	0.83	1.01			0.75		
23	2.05	1.70	1.96	1.20	1.66		1.83	1.25	1.97	2.55	1.63	2.02	2.69	1.65	1.57	1.48	0.82	0.87		1.03	1.04		

(b) Heatmap corresponding to Figure 6.6 (b)

Figure 6.7: Heatmaps

6.4.1.3   Sum of Squared Error

Another approach to measuring cluster quality is to compute a residual sum of squares (RSS) error term, which is also known as a sum of squared errors (SSE). Whichever name we call it, it's just what it sounds like—we sum the squared error terms. RSS is a general concept, which can be applied to any error function we select. For example, using distance as our "error" function, the RSS is equivalent to distortion, as defined above in equation (6.1), assuming that we use Euclidean distance. Of course, other error measures could be used in an SSE calculation.

6.4.1.4   Silhouette Coefficient

Ideally, we want each cluster to be *cohesive*, in the sense that the points within a cluster are close together. In addition, we would like the points in different clusters to exhibit *separation*. That is, the more cohesive the individual clusters and the more separation between the clusters, the better. Of course, we've seen these concepts before—for example, distortion can be considered a measure of cohesion, while the heatmaps in Figure 6.7 provide a visual representation of both cohesion and separation. Here, we provide formulae for explicitly computing cohesion and separation relative to a given data point. Then we combine these quantities into a single number to obtain the so-called silhouette coefficient of the point. Finally, we argue that the average silhouette coefficient provides a sensible measure of cluster quality.[5]

Suppose that we have a set of n data points $X_1, X_2, \ldots, X_n$ partitioned into K clusters, $C_1, C_2, \ldots, C_K$. Let M_i be the number of elements in cluster C_i. Then $M_1 + M_2 + \cdots + M_K = n$.

Select a point X_i. Then $X_i \in C_j$ for some $j \in \{1, 2, \ldots, K\}$. Let a be the average distance from X_i to all other points in its cluster C_j. That is,

$$a = \frac{1}{M_j - 1} \sum_{\substack{Y \in C_j \\ Y \neq X_i}} d(X_i, Y). \tag{6.5}$$

In the degenerate case where $M_j = 1$, let $a = 0$. Also, for each cluster C_ℓ, such that $\ell \neq j$, let b_ℓ be the average distance from X_i to all points in cluster C_ℓ. That is,

$$b_\ell = \frac{1}{M_\ell} \sum_{Y \in C_\ell} d(X_i, Y).$$

Finally, we let b be the smallest of the b_ℓ. Then

$$b = \min_{\substack{\ell \in \{1,2,\ldots,K\} \\ \ell \neq j}} b_\ell. \tag{6.6}$$

The a in (6.5) is a measure of the cohesion of cluster C_j, relative to the point X_i, and b in (6.6) provides a measure of the separation relative to the point X_i.

We define the *silhouette coefficient* of X_i as

$$S(X_i) = \frac{b - a}{\max(a, b)}.$$

For any reasonable clustering, we expect that $b > a$, in which case

$$S(X_i) = 1 - \frac{a}{b}.$$

---

[5] Even if you don't believe that the silhouette coefficient is the best intrinsic measure of cluster quality, you have to admit that it's got the coolest name.

For example, consider the clusters in Figure 6.8. In this case, a is the average length of the lines connecting X_i to the other points (i.e., the squares) in its cluster, C_1. Also, b_2 is the average length of the lines from X_i to the points (i.e., ovals) in C_2, and b_3 is the average length of the lines from X_i to the points (i.e., circles) in C_3. Letting $b = \min\{b_2, b_3\}$, the silhouette coefficient for x_i is given by $S(x_i) = 1 - a/b$.

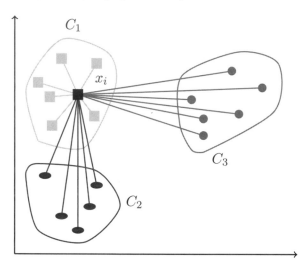

Figure 6.8: Silhouette coefficient example

If X_i is much closer to the points in its own cluster, as compared to its distance to any other cluster, then a is much less than b, and $S(X_i) \approx 1$. On the other hand, if X_i is relatively far from points in its own cluster and close to points in at least one other cluster, then $S(X_i)$ will be close to 0. Therefore, the larger the silhouette coefficient $S(X_i)$, the better.

The average silhouette coefficient

$$\frac{1}{n} \sum_{i=1}^{n} S(X_i)$$

provides an intrinsic measure of the overall quality of a given clustering.

The bottom line is that the average silhouette coefficient combines cohesion and separation into a single number. This provides a useful intrinsic measure of cluster quality.

6.4.2   External Validation

External validation means that we measure quality based on some inherent feature or features of the data within clusters. In contrast, the internal measures discussed above rely on the topology or shape of clusters, without making any reference to the actual nature of the data within the clusters.

It makes sense to use external measures, provided that we know something about the data.

For example, suppose that we have labeled data points derived from several different malware families, and we partition this data into K clusters. We could use internal measures, such as the silhouette coefficient, to measure the quality of the clusters based on their topology. However, since we have labeled data, we know which family each point corresponds to, and we can use this information to determine the quality of our clusters. This is somewhat akin to the typical process used to evaluate a model derived based on a labeled training set.

Assuming that we have labeled data, what external properties should we measure? Intuitively, it seems clear that we would like the data within a cluster to be as uniform as possible. We'll briefly discuss two measures that we can use to quantify the uniformity of clusters.

Entropy is a general measure of uncertainty or randomness—the higher the entropy, the greater the randomness. Low entropy within clusters and high entropy between clusters would indicate good clustering results, while the converse would indicate questionable results.

As above, let $X_1, X_2, \ldots, X_n$ be the data points, and let $C_1, C_2, \ldots, C_K$ be the clusters. And, let M_j be the number of elements in cluster C_j and define M_{ij} to be the number of elements of type i in cluster C_j. Then we have $i \in \{1, 2, \ldots, \ell\}$, where ℓ is the number of different types of data in the overall dataset.

The probability of data of type i in cluster j is given by $p_{ij} = M_{ij}/M_j$ and hence the entropy of cluster C_j is given by

$$E_j = - \sum_{i=1}^{\ell} p_{ij} \log(p_{ij}).$$

Then the (weighted) intra-cluster entropy is computed as

$$E = \frac{1}{n} \sum_{i=1}^{K} M_j E_j.$$

The smaller that E is, the better, since this indicates more uniformity within the clusters.

Purity is another useful measure. With the same notation as above, define the purity of cluster C_j as $U_j = \max_i p_{ij}$. If $U_j = 1$, then C_j consists of a single type of data, while the closer that U_j is to 0, the less uniform the cluster. The overall (weighted) purity is given by

$$U = \frac{1}{n} \sum_{j=1}^{K} M_j U_j.$$

As with an individual cluster, a purity of $U = 1$ is optimal, while the closer that U is to 0, the less the clusters reflect the characteristics of the data.

Figure 6.9 gives two examples of entropy and purity calculations, where the color of a point indicates its type. In both cases, there are three types of data, denoted by ovals, circles, and diamonds, and three clusters. By any internal measure, the clusterings in Figures 6.9 (a) and (b) will yield identical results. But, using our knowledge of the type of data represented by each point, we can see that the clustering in Figure 6.9 (a) is far superior to that in Figure 6.9 (b), and both the entropy score E and purity score U support this observation. Again, in these examples it's easy to see which clustering is better. However, in higher dimensions where we cannot directly visualize clusters, we can still use the measures E and U to enable us to quantify cluster quality.

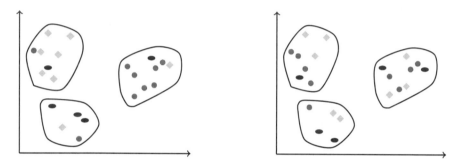

(a) $E = 0.7632$ and $U = 0.7272$ (b) $E = 1.0280$ and $U = 0.4545$

Figure 6.9: Entropy and purity examples

6.4.3 Visualizing Clusters

When clustering based on 2-dimensional data, as in the examples above, the resulting clusters can be drawn in the plane. And for 3-dimensional vectors, we can draw the clusters in space. However, for higher dimensions, we can't draw straightforward pictures of clusters, so it's natural to consider whether there is any effective way to illustrate higher dimensional clusters. In this section, we present a simple and practical method for visualizing clusters of labeled data that works well for any number of dimensions and any number of clusters.

Figure 6.10 illustrates a three-cluster clustering, while Figure 6.11 gives a *stacked column chart* for the data in Figure 6.10. Of course, in this case, we could simply look at the actual clusters, but that's not an option with high-dimensional data. And, in any case, a stacked column chart gives us an easy and intuitive way to view the distribution of the different data types within each cluster.

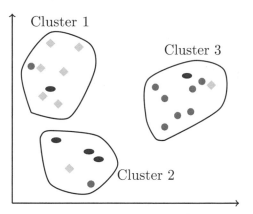

Figure 6.10: Three clusters

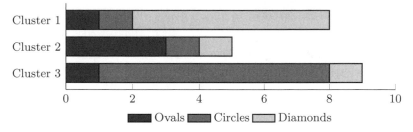

Figure 6.11: Stacked column chart for clusters in Figure 6.10

Figure 6.12 gives a more realistic example of a stacked column chart [106]. This example is derived from a clustering that consists of 10 clusters based on 4-dimensional scores. Because of the 4-dimensional scores, we cannot draw pictures of the actual clusters. Nevertheless, the stacked column chart gives us an intuitive and useful way to visualize the distribution of the different types of data within the clusters. In this case, the clustered data consists of samples from three different malware families (Zeroaccess, Zbot, and Winwebsec; see Section 10.3 for a description of these families), as well as benign samples, where the mapping of families to colors is given in the legend below the chart.

6.5 EM Clustering

Any clustering technique must rely on some measure of distance. If the underlying data is drawn from multiple probability distributions, then it would seem eminently sensible to use these probability distributions to measure "distance." However, there is a catch: Almost surely we don't know much (if anything) about these probability distributions. After all, we typically use clustering because we don't know much about the data itself. This is where the expectation maximization (EM) algorithm comes to the rescue. We can

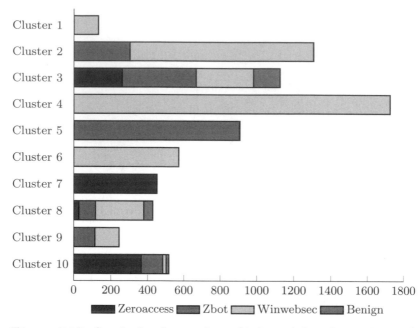

Figure 6.12: Stacked column chart (4-d model with 10 clusters)

use EM to determine the relevant parameters (typically, mean and variance) of unknown probability distributions. And, best of all, EM has much in common with hidden Markov models, while also being surprisingly similar to K-means clustering.

Figure 6.13 contains eruption data for Old Faithful, the famous geyser in Yellowstone National Park. This data includes duration of an eruption and wait time between consecutive eruptions. The result of clustering this data using the EM algorithm (based on Gaussian distributions) is given in Figure 6.13. The concentric ellipses in Figure 6.13 are centered at the means, with the axes (and shading) determined by the the standard deviations. In effect, K-means only generates circular clusters, whereas EM with Gaussian distributions generates elliptic clusters of differing shapes and orientations. In this sense, EM is much more general than K-means. And, by using other probability distributions, such as the hypergeometric distribution [65], we can generate clusters having an even greater variety of shapes.

Of course, we could apply K-means clustering to the data in Figure 6.13, in which case the cluster boundaries would be circles. By scaling the data, we could obtain elliptical instead of circular clusters via K-means. However, all of the resulting ellipses would be aligned in the same way, with the major and minor axes all pointing in the same directions. In effect, EM allows us to scale and orient each cluster independent of the other clusters.

As mentioned above, one obvious difficulty with clustering based on probability distributions is that the distributions are almost certainly not known

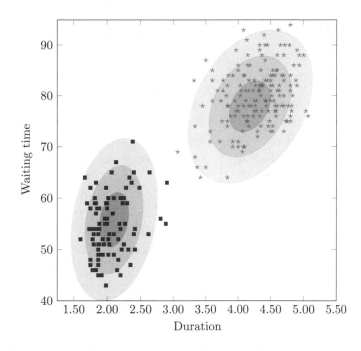

Figure 6.13: EM clustering of Old Faithful eruption data

in advance. In fact, we probably do not even know what type of probability distribution (Gaussian, hypergeometric, etc.) will yield the best results. Thus, we'll need to cluster based on some "hidden" information. This sounds vaguely similar to hidden Markov models and, in fact, EM clustering and HMMs are fairly closely related.

A process of expectation maximization is at the heart of Baum-Welch re-estimation, which is used to train an HMM. Furthermore, the EM clustering algorithm bears some striking similarities to the K-means algorithm, as discussed in Section 6.3, above. As with K-means, in EM clustering, we have an optimization problem where any exact algorithm is infeasible. Also as in K-means, the practical version of EM clustering uses a hill climb that alternates between two distinct steps.

For K-means, we alternate between the following two steps.

Step 1 Recompute clusters based on the current centroids.

Step 2 Recompute the centroids based on the current clusters.

Another way to view K-means is that Step 1 determines the "shape" (or size) of the clusters, while Step 2 re-estimates the parameters (i.e., the centroids).

Perhaps not surprisingly, in EM clustering, we have an expectation (E) step and a maximization (M) step. These two steps can be summarized as follows.

E step Recompute the probabilities needed in the M step.

M step Recompute maximum likelihood estimators for the parameters of the distributions (as discussed below).

In the E step, we compute the "shape" of the various clusters based on our current estimate of the probability distributions. This is analogous to Step 1 in the K-means algorithm. Then in the M step, we re-estimate the parameters of the probability distributions.[6] The M step is analogous to Step 2 in the K-means algorithm.

In K-means, we make a "hard" decision in Step 1, in the sense that each data point must be assigned to a cluster before we can recompute the centroids. In contrast, the E step in the EM algorithm only assigns probabilities, which can be viewed as making "soft" assignments of points to clusters. With EM, every point has a probability relative to each cluster, which can be viewed as a fuzzy approach to clustering. Typically, we assign a point to the cluster for which its probability is largest, but it might also be reasonable in some cases to split points between clusters, based on the relative probabilities.

Before turning our attention to a simple EM example—which is followed by a more realistic example and the general algorithm—we first consider some relevant statistical concepts. In particular, we need to discuss the concept of a maximum likelihood estimator (MLE).

6.5.1 Maximum Likelihood Estimator

Suppose that we flip a coin 10 times and obtain the outcome

$$X = \text{HHHHTHHHTT}. \tag{6.7}$$

We want to determine the most likely value of the bias (if any) for this coin, that is, we want to determine $P(\text{H})$, based on X.

A series of coin flips follows a binomial distribution, so that

$$P(k \text{ heads in } n \text{ trials}) = f(p) = \binom{n}{k} p^k (1-p)^{n-k}$$

where p is the probability of heads on any one flip of the coin. The *likelihood function* for X in (6.7) is

$$\mathcal{L}_X(\theta) = \binom{10}{7} \theta^7 (1-\theta)^3$$

and for this example, the log likelihood function is

$$l_X(\theta) = c + 7 \log \theta + 3 \log (1-\theta). \tag{6.8}$$

---

[6]The parameters we want to determine are the mean and variance (or functions thereof) for each probability distribution.

Since $\mathcal{L}$ is an increasing function, the maximum likelihood estimator (MLE) of θ can be obtained by maximizing $l_X(\theta)$ with respect to θ.

Using elementary calculus, we compute the MLE by taking the first derivative, setting the result equal to 0, and solving. For the log likelihood function in (6.8), we have

$$\frac{dl}{d\theta} = \frac{7}{\theta} - \frac{3}{1-\theta} = 0,$$

which yields an MLE of $\theta = 0.7$, that is, $P(\text{H}) = 0.7$. This should be no surprise, since we obtained heads on seven out of ten flips of the coin. Note that the MLE of 0.7 in this example does not mean that the coin is necessarily biased in such a way that it will return H with probability 0.7 consistently—in fact, a fair coin will give us seven heads out of ten flips almost 12% of the time. But, we can say that based on the available data, the most likely scenario is that the coin has a bias of 0.7 to heads. In the EM algorithm, we find the parameters of probability distributions using MLEs.

6.5.2 An Easy EM Example

EM can be viewed as a method for determining the MLE when some nontrivial information is missing. To illustrate the concepts behind the EM algorithm, we begin with an elementary example, which closely follows that in [45]. Then we will turn our attention to a more complex (and realistic) scenario.

Suppose that we have two coins, denoted A and B, and we perform the following experiment. One coin is selected at random and flipped ten times. This is repeated five times, giving us a total of 50 coin flips. Our goal is to estimate

$$P_A(\text{H}) = \text{probability that coin } A \text{ lands on H}$$

and

$$P_B(\text{H}) = \text{probability that coin } B \text{ lands on H}$$

based on the result of the 50 coin flips in our experiment.

If we know which coin was selected in each of the five iterations, we can easily compute the MLEs—to compute the MLE for $P_A(\text{H})$, we simply divide the number of heads that appeared when coin A was flipped by the total number of times that the coin was flipped, and similarly for B. For example, suppose we obtain the results in Table 6.1. Since coin A turned up H for 24 of its 30 flips and coin B yielded H for nine of its 20 flips, we obtain the MLEs

$$P_A(\text{H}) = 24/30 = 0.8 \text{ and } P_B(\text{H}) = 9/20 = 0.45.$$

This agrees perfectly with common sense.[7]

---

[7]Your uncommonly sensible author would like to emphasize that common sense is not all that common, and, ironically, uncommon sense is also uncommon.

Table 6.1: Coin flipping with known coin

Coin	Outcome	Total
A	HTHHHHHTHH	8 H and 2 T
B	HTTTHHTHTH	5 H and 5 T
A	HHHHTHHHHH	9 H and 1 T
B	HTHTTTHHTT	4 H and 6 T
A	THHHTHHHTH	7 H and 3 T

The problem is much more interesting—and much more relevant for our purposes—when we don't know which coin was flipped. Suppose that the first column in Table 6.1 is "hidden." Then we only have the information in Table 6.2. Above, we saw that determining the MLEs is trivial if we know which coin was selected at each iteration. But at first blush, it might seem that we have little hope of determining the relevant parameters when the coin selection is hidden.

Table 6.2: Coin flipping with unknown coin

Coin	Outcome	Total
unknown	HTHHHHHTHH	8 H and 2 T
unknown	HTTTHHTHTH	5 H and 5 T
unknown	HHHHTHHHHH	9 H and 1 T
unknown	HTHTTTHHTT	4 H and 6 T
unknown	THHHTHHHTH	7 H and 3 T

Assuming that we are only given the information in Table 6.2, can we obtain reasonable estimates for the parameters $P_A(\text{H})$ and $P_B(\text{H})$? One possible approach is to append the observed sequences of heads and tails and train an HMM with $N = 2$ hidden states on the resulting super-sequence. If the model converges, the final B matrix would contain the probabilities that we're looking for.[8] However, there are a few problems with using an HMM in this situation. For one thing, it would likely require far more data than 50 coin flips before the model would reliably converge (or, alternatively, a vast number of random restarts [16]). And, even if such an HMM converged, it's very "heavy artillery" for this particular task. In contrast, the EM algorithm offers a simple iterative process to determine the relevant parameters.

---

[8]Your clear-headed author believes that it should be clear from Chapter 2 that Baum-Welch re-estimation, which is used to train an HMM, is an EM technique.

Next, we illustrate the first few steps of the EM iterative process for this coin flipping example. Then we formalize the process, which will make it easier to apply in more interesting cases, such as Gaussian mixture problems, which seem to be the most popular application of the EM algorithm.

For the coin flipping example in Table 6.2, suppose that we initialize the parameters as $P_A(\text{H}) = 0.6$ and $P_B(\text{H}) = 0.5$. Then the E step of the EM algorithm consists of computing the expected number of heads for each coin, using our current estimates for the parameters $P_A(\text{H})$ and $P_B(\text{H})$.

Let $P(A)$ denote the probability that the coin flipped was A, and similarly for $P(B)$. Now, consider the first row in Table 6.2, where we obtained eight heads and two tails, and let

$$a = 0.6^8 \cdot 0.4^2 \text{ and } b = 0.5^8 \cdot 0.5^2.$$

Under the assumption that $P_A(\text{H}) = 0.6$ and $P_B(\text{H}) = 0.5$, the first row in Table 6.2 implies

$$P(A) = \frac{a}{a+b} \approx 0.73 \text{ and } P(B) = \frac{b}{a+b} \approx 0.27.$$

Repeating this calculation for each row in Table 6.2 gives us the results in Table 6.3.

Table 6.3: Probability of A and B

Outcome	$P(A)$	$P(B)$
8 H and 2 T	0.73	0.27
5 H and 5 T	0.45	0.55
9 H and 1 T	0.80	0.20
4 H and 6 T	0.35	0.65
7 H and 3 T	0.65	0.35

Applying the results in the first row of Table 6.3 to the first row in Table 6.2, we obtain the expected values

$$E_A(\text{H}) = 0.73 \cdot 8 = 5.84$$
$$E_A(\text{T}) = 0.73 \cdot 2 = 1.46$$
$$E_B(\text{H}) = 0.27 \cdot 8 = 2.16$$
$$E_B(\text{T}) = 0.27 \cdot 2 = 0.54$$

where $E_A(\text{H})$ is the expected number of heads for coin A and $E_B(\text{H})$ is the expected number of heads for coin B. Similarly, by applying the results in the second row of Table 6.3 to the second row in Table 6.2, we obtain the expectations

$$E_A(\text{H}) = 0.45 \cdot 5 = 2.25$$
$$E_A(\text{T}) = 0.45 \cdot 5 = 2.25$$
$$E_B(\text{H}) = 0.55 \cdot 5 = 2.75$$
$$E_B(\text{T}) = 0.55 \cdot 5 = 2.75$$

and so on. These numbers are summarized in Table 6.4.

Table 6.4: Expected numbers of H and T

Outcome	$P(A)$	$P(B)$	$E_A(\text{H})$	$E_A(\text{T})$	$E_B(\text{H})$	$E_B(\text{T})$
8 H and 2 T	0.7335	0.2665	5.8677	1.4669	2.1323	0.5331
5 H and 5 T	0.4491	0.5509	2.2457	2.2457	2.7543	2.7543
9 H and 1 T	0.8050	0.1950	7.2449	0.8050	1.7551	0.1950
4 H and 6 T	0.3522	0.6478	1.4086	2.1129	2.5914	3.8871
7 H and 3 T	0.6472	0.3528	4.5305	1.9416	2.4695	1.0584
totals	—	—	21.2975	8.5722	11.7025	8.4278

At this point, we have finished computing expectations based on our current estimates of $P_A(\text{H})$ and $P_B(\text{H})$. This completes the first E step of the EM algorithm.

For the M step, we use the results in Table 6.4 to re-estimate the parameters $P_A(\text{H})$ and $P_B(\text{H})$. From Bayes' formula, we have

$$P_A(\text{H}) = \frac{21.2975}{21.2975 + 8.5722} \approx 0.7130$$

$$P_B(\text{H}) = \frac{11.7025}{11.7025 + 8.4278} \approx 0.5813.$$

(6.9)

Next, we repeat the E step using the updated probabilities in (6.9). Then for the M step we recompute $P_A(\text{H})$ and $P_B(\text{H})$ using the expectations obtained from the E step, and so on. This iterative process continues until convergence, or until a specified maximum number of iterations is reached. For this particular example, the process converges to

$$P_A(\text{H}) = 0.7968 \text{ and } P_B(\text{H}) = 0.5196.$$

This coin flipping example is a binomial mixture, since the overall distribution is a combination of two binomial distributions. In practice, Gaussian mixture models are most often used. A Gaussian (or normal) distribution is significantly more complex than a binomial distribution. Consequently, it's worth our while to take a closer look at the process just described, to express the E and M steps in more general terms. This will make it a breeze to deal with a Gaussian mixture model, which is our ultimate goal.[9] Of course, the EM technique can be applied to other probability distributions as well.

6.5.3   EM Algorithm

In this section, we present the EM algorithm in its general form. As we derive the notation, we continually relate it back to the simple coin flipping example in the previous section. Consequently, this section will surely be far more meaningful to a reader who has read (and understood) the example in Section 6.5.2.

To simplify the notation, we'll assume that we have a mixture consisting of two distributions, although it's easy to generalize to more distributions. We'll also assume that the distributions are of the same type but, of course, the parameters can differ. In addition to the distributions, there are mixture parameters, denoted as τ_1 and τ_2, which specify the fraction of samples that were drawn from the respective distributions. Since we're assuming there are only two distributions, and we are confident that no samples will disappear into the ether, we have $\tau_2 = 1 - \tau_1$. For the coin example in Section 6.5.2, we note that $\tau_1 = P(A)$ is the fraction of times that the A coin was selected, while $\tau_2 = P(B)$ is the fraction of times that the B coin was selected. And, of course, $\tau_1 + \tau_2 = 1$.

We denote the relevant parameters of the first distribution as θ_1 and the parameters of the second distribution as θ_2. We let $\tau = \begin{pmatrix} \tau_1 & \tau_2 \end{pmatrix}$ and $\theta = \begin{pmatrix} \theta_1 & \theta_2 \end{pmatrix}$. Then the parameters τ and θ together determine the mixture model. In the coin flipping example in the previous section, we had $\theta_1 = P_A(\text{H})$ and $\theta_2 = P_B(\text{H})$. However, for more complex distributions, typically θ_j is a vector of parameters involving the mean and variance of the jth distribution.

Let $f_1(X_i, \theta_1)$ be the probability function for the first distribution under consideration, and $f_2(X_i, \theta_2)$ be the probability function for the second distribution. For the coin flipping example in Section 6.5.2, these functions can be written as

$$f_j(X_i, \theta_j) = \binom{10}{X_i} \theta_j^{X_i} (1 - \theta_j)^{10 - X_i}, \text{ for } j = 1, 2 \text{ and } i = 1, 2, 3, 4, 5$$

where X_i is interpreted as the number of heads observed in the 10 coin flips that constitute the ith experiment.

At this point, we have all of the necessary notation to describe the E and M steps that together define the EM algorithm. After we present the general

---

[9]For now, you will have to trust your trustworthy author on this point.

case, we'll illustrate the algorithm using the coin example in Section 6.5.2, followed by a more interesting example involving Gaussian distributions.

E step This is easy.[10] Given our current estimates for τ and θ, we use Bayes' formula to compute

$$p_{j,i} = \frac{\tau_j \, f(X_i, \theta_j)}{\tau_1 \, f(X_i, \theta_1) + \tau_2 \, f(X_i, \theta_2)} \tag{6.10}$$

for $j = 1, 2$ and $i = 1, 2, \ldots, n$, where n is the number of experiments (i.e., data points). Here, $p_{j,i}$ can be interpreted as our best guess—based on our current estimates for the parameters—for the probability of outcome X_i under distribution j. Perhaps a more clustering-centric viewpoint is that $p_{j,i}$ is the "part" of X_i that "belongs" to cluster j, where cluster j is defined in terms of the jth distribution. We note in passing that $p_{1,i} + p_{2,i} = 1$ for $i = 1, 2, \ldots, n$.

M step In this step, we use the freshly minted $p_{j,i}$ from the E step above, as computed using equation (6.10), to re-estimate the parameters τ and θ. First, consider $\tau = (\tau_1, \tau_2)$. Recall that τ_j is the fraction of the samples from distribution j. Based on the current values of $p_{j,i}$, our best estimate is

$$\tau_j = \frac{\displaystyle\sum_{i=1}^{n} p_{j,i}}{\displaystyle\sum_{i=1}^{n} p_{1,i} + \sum_{i=1}^{n} p_{2,i}}.$$

Since $p_{1,i} + p_{2,i} = 1$ for all i, this expression simplifies to

$$\tau_j = \frac{1}{n} \sum_{i=1}^{n} p_{j,i}. \tag{6.11}$$

It's easily verified that $\tau_1 + \tau_2 = 1$, as required. Similarly, based on the current values of $p_{j,i}$, our best estimates for the means μ_1 and μ_2 are given by

$$\mu_j = \sum_{i=1}^{n} p_{j,i} \, X_i \Big/ \sum_{i=1}^{n} p_{j,i}. \tag{6.12}$$

And once these means have been computed, we can similarly estimate the variances σ_1^2 and σ_2^2 via

$$\sigma_j^2 = \sum_{i=1}^{n} p_{j,i} (X_i - \mu_j)^2 \Big/ \sum_{i=1}^{n} p_{j,i}. \tag{6.13}$$

---

[10]Maybe the "E" in EM really stands for "easy."

For any distributions, each parameter in θ_j that we re-estimate will be some function of the mean μ_j and variance σ_j^2. Of course, the precise function of the mean and variance will depend on the specific type of probability distributions under consideration.

The mean of a binomial distribution is $\mu = Np$, where N is the number of trials per experiment and, in the case of coin flipping, $p = P(\text{H})$. Recall that for the coin flipping example in Section 6.5.2, we have $N = 10$, while $P_A(\text{H})$ and $P_B(\text{H})$ are the parameters of interest. Consequently, computing the means in the M step is sufficient for this particular case. On the other hand, for a Gaussian distribution, $\theta = (\mu, \sigma^2)$ and hence we would need to compute both the means and variances in the M step.

Iterating the EM process yields a sequence of parameters τ and θ that converge to a (local) maximum. We can define clusters based on the resulting distributions by simply assigning each data point to its most probable distribution. Or, we could allow for soft margins, where each data point is effectively split between clusters, based on the relative probability with respect to each distribution.

Next, we illustrate the EM algorithm using the same coin flipping example that we considered in the previous section. In the following section, we consider a Gaussian mixture problem which, as previously noted, is the case most often seen in practice.

As in Section 6.5.2, we begin with the experimental results in Table 6.2, which can be restated as

$$
\begin{aligned}
&\text{Experiment 1: 8 H and 2 T} \\
&\text{Experiment 2: 5 H and 5 T} \\
&\text{Experiment 3: 9 H and 1 T} \\
&\text{Experiment 4: 4 H and 6 T} \\
&\text{Experiment 5: 7 H and 3 T.}
\end{aligned} \tag{6.14}
$$

More succinctly, we can simply specify the number of times H occurs in each experiment, which gives us

$$(X_1, X_2, \ldots, X_5) = (8, 5, 9, 4, 7).$$

So that we can compare our results, let's make the same initial guess for the parameters as in Section 6.5.2, that is, $P_A(\text{H}) = 0.6$ and $P_B(\text{H}) = 0.5$. Then we initialize the EM algorithm with $\theta_1 = 0.6$ and $\theta_2 = 0.5$. We also need to initialize τ_1 and τ_2, which specify how the data is split between the distributions (i.e., clusters). So suppose that we initialize $\tau_1 = 0.7$, which implies $\tau_2 = 0.3$. Using these initial values and (6.14), the first E step of the EM algorithm yields the results in Table 6.5.

Table 6.5: Initial E step of EM algorithm

$$p_{1,1} = 0.7(0.6^8 \cdot 0.4^2)/(0.7(0.6^8 \cdot 0.4^2) + 0.3(0.5^8 \cdot 0.5^2)) = 0.8652$$
$$p_{2,1} = 0.3(0.5^8 \cdot 0.5^2)/(0.7(0.6^8 \cdot 0.4^2) + 0.3(0.5^8 \cdot 0.5^2)) = 0.1348$$
$$p_{1,2} = 0.7(0.6^5 \cdot 0.4^5)/(0.7(0.6^5 \cdot 0.4^5) + 0.3(0.5^5 \cdot 0.5^5)) = 0.6554$$
$$p_{2,2} = 0.3(0.5^5 \cdot 0.5^5)/(0.7(0.6^5 \cdot 0.4^5) + 0.3(0.5^5 \cdot 0.5^5)) = 0.3445$$
$$p_{1,3} = 0.7(0.6^9 \cdot 0.4^1)/(0.7(0.6^9 \cdot 0.4^1) + 0.3(0.5^9 \cdot 0.5^1)) = 0.9059$$
$$p_{2,3} = 0.3(0.5^9 \cdot 0.5^1)/(0.7(0.6^9 \cdot 0.4^1) + 0.3(0.5^9 \cdot 0.5^1)) = 0.0941$$
$$p_{1,4} = 0.7(0.6^4 \cdot 0.4^6)/(0.7(0.6^4 \cdot 0.4^6) + 0.3(0.5^4 \cdot 0.5^6)) = 0.5592$$
$$p_{2,4} = 0.3(0.5^4 \cdot 0.5^6)/(0.7(0.6^4 \cdot 0.4^6) + 0.3(0.5^4 \cdot 0.5^6)) = 0.4408$$
$$p_{1,5} = 0.7(0.6^7 \cdot 0.4^3)/(0.7(0.6^7 \cdot 0.4^3) + 0.3(0.5^7 \cdot 0.5^3)) = 0.8106$$
$$p_{2,5} = 0.3(0.5^7 \cdot 0.5^3)/(0.7(0.6^7 \cdot 0.4^3) + 0.3(0.5^7 \cdot 0.5^3)) = 0.1894$$

For the first M step, we re-estimate the parameters using the probabilities $p_{j,i}$ in Table 6.5. From equation (6.11), we find that the re-estimated mixture parameters are

$$\tau_1 = \frac{1}{5} \sum_{i=1}^{5} p_{1,i}$$
$$= \frac{0.8652 + 0.6554 + 0.9059 + 0.5592 + 0.8106}{5} = 0.7593$$

and

$$\tau_2 = \frac{1}{5} \sum_{i=1}^{5} p_{2,i}$$
$$= \frac{0.1348 + 0.3445 + 0.0941 + 0.4408 + 0.1894}{5} = 0.2407.$$

Alternatively, we could compute τ_1 as above, and use the fact that $\tau_2 = 1 - \tau_1$ to determine τ_2. In any case, we have

$$\tau = (\ \tau_1 \quad \tau_2\ ) = (\ 0.7593 \quad 0.2407\ ).$$

From (6.12), the re-estimated means are

$$\mu_1 = \sum_{i=1}^{5} p_{1,i} X_i \Big/ \sum_{i=1}^{5} p_{1,i}$$
$$= \frac{0.8652 \cdot 8 + 0.6554 \cdot 5 + 0.9059 \cdot 9 + 0.5592 \cdot 4 + 0.8106 \cdot 7}{0.7593 \cdot 5} = 6.9180$$

and

$$\mu_2 = \sum_{i=1}^{5} p_{2,i} X_i \bigg/ \sum_{i=1}^{5} p_{2,i}$$

$$= \frac{0.1348 \cdot 8 + 0.3445 \cdot 5 + 0.0941 \cdot 9 + 0.4408 \cdot 4 + 0.1894 \cdot 7}{0.2407 \cdot 5} = 5.5969.$$

At this point, we have re-estimated the means as

$$\mu = (\begin{array}{cc} \mu_1 & \mu_2 \end{array}) = (\begin{array}{cc} 6.9180 & 5.5969 \end{array})$$

The parameters of interest are $\theta_1 = P_A(\text{H})$ and $\theta_1 = P_B(\text{H})$. Since we have a binomial distribution with $N = 10$ in this example, the updated values for these parameters are

$$\theta = (\begin{array}{cc} \theta_1 & \theta_2 \end{array}) = (\begin{array}{cc} \mu_1/10 & \mu_2/10 \end{array}) = (\begin{array}{cc} 0.6918 & 0.5597 \end{array}).$$

Furthermore, these are the only parameters of interest, so we don't need to compute the variances in this case.

Continuing, in this example the iterative EM process converges with

$$\tau = (\begin{array}{cc} \tau_1 & \tau_2 \end{array}) = (\begin{array}{cc} 0.5228 & 0.4772 \end{array})$$

and

$$\theta = (\begin{array}{cc} \theta_1 & \theta_2 \end{array}) = (\begin{array}{cc} 0.7934 & 0.5139 \end{array}). \tag{6.15}$$

We can now use the distributions determined in (6.15) to cluster our data. However, clustering 1-dimensional data is not very interesting, so we omit this step. Next, we'll consider a 2-dimensional example involving Gaussian distributions, where the resulting clusters are sure to yield pretty pictures.

6.5.4 Gaussian Mixture Example

Suppose that we want to cluster data based on a combination of normal distributions. To be cool like our statistician friends, we'll call these *Gaussian distributions*.

A Gaussian distribution has a probability density function of the form

$$f(x, \mu, \sigma) = \frac{1}{\sigma\sqrt{2\pi}} e^{-(x-\mu)^2/(2\sigma^2)}$$

where μ is the mean and σ^2 is the variance. This is a particularly useful distribution, since the central limit theorem tells us that most things converge to this distribution as the sample size grows.

Consider the data in Figure 6.14, which is a subset of the Old Faithful data in Figure 6.13. For this particular example, the raw data is given in Table 6.6. Our goal is to use the EM algorithm, as stated in Section 6.5.3, to cluster this data. We'll make the assumption that the data consists of a mixture drawn from two Gaussian distributions. Thus, we'll need to determine the parameters for two distributions, and these distributions will, in turn, determine the clusters.

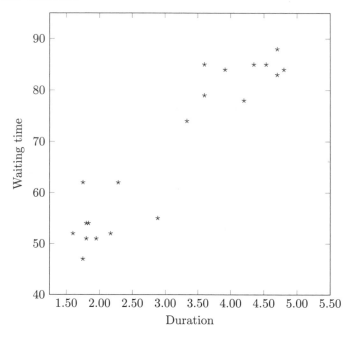

Figure 6.14: Old Faithful data for Gaussian mixture example

Since the data in Table 6.6 is 2-dimensional, we must consider a mixture of bivariate Gaussian distributions [36]. The probability function for a bivariate Gaussian can be written as

$$f(x, y, \theta) = \frac{1}{2\pi\sigma_x\sigma_y\sqrt{1-\rho^2}} e^{-z/2} \tag{6.16}$$

where

$$z = \frac{1}{(1-\rho^2)} \left(\frac{(x-\mu_x)^2}{\sigma_x^2} - \frac{2\rho(x-\mu_x)(y-\mu_y)}{\sigma_x\sigma_y} + \frac{(y-\mu_y)^2}{\sigma_y^2} \right).$$

and

$$\rho = \frac{\text{cov}(x, y)}{\sigma_x\sigma_y}.$$

Recall that $\text{cov}(x, y)$ is the covariance of x and y, which measures the variation of x relative to y (and vice versa). For for more details on the covariance, see Section 4.2 of Chapter 4.

Table 6.6: Old Faithful data

Case	Duration	Wait	Case	Duration	Wait
1	3.600	79	11	1.600	52
2	1.800	54	12	4.350	85
3	2.283	62	13	3.917	84
4	3.333	74	14	4.200	78
5	2.883	55	15	1.750	62
6	4.533	85	16	1.800	51
7	1.950	51	17	4.700	83
8	1.833	54	18	2.167	52
9	4.700	88	19	4.800	84
10	3.600	85	20	1.750	47

We can express a multivariate Gaussian distribution in a more compact (and convenient) form using matrix notation. For the n-dimensional case,

$$f(X, \theta) = \frac{1}{\sqrt{(2\pi)^n \det(S)}} \, e^{-\frac{1}{2}(X-\mu)^T S^{-1}(X-\mu)}. \tag{6.17}$$

For the 2-dimensional case, this simplifies slightly to

$$f(X, \theta) = \frac{1}{2\pi\sqrt{\det(S)}} \, e^{-\frac{1}{2}(X-\mu)^T S^{-1}(X-\mu)} \tag{6.18}$$

where

$$X = \begin{pmatrix} x \\ y \end{pmatrix} \text{ and } \mu = \begin{pmatrix} \mu_x \\ \mu_y \end{pmatrix}$$

and the covariance matrix S is given by

$$S = \begin{pmatrix} s_{11} & s_{12} \\ s_{21} & s_{22} \end{pmatrix} = \begin{pmatrix} \sigma_x^2 & \rho\sigma_x\sigma_y \\ \rho\sigma_x\sigma_y & \sigma_y^2 \end{pmatrix}. \tag{6.19}$$

From (6.19), it follows that

$$\rho = \frac{s_{12}}{\sqrt{s_{11}s_{22}}}.$$

In addition, since S is 2×2, its determinant is easily computed as

$$\det(S) = s_{11}s_{22} - s_{12}s_{21}$$

and the inverse of S is given by

$$S^{-1} = \frac{1}{\det(S)} \begin{pmatrix} s_{22} & -s_{12} \\ -s_{21} & s_{11} \end{pmatrix}.$$

By the definition of the inverse, $SS^{-1} = S^{-1}S = I$, where I is the identity matrix. It will be convenient to work with the matrix form in the EM algorithm, which we now present for the 2-dimensional case. This easily generalizes to n dimensions.

From equation (6.17), it's apparent that the parameters that we want to estimate are

$$\theta = (\,\mu \quad S\,)$$

where $\mu = (\,\mu_x \quad \mu_y\,)^T$. Since S is symmetric, it is sufficient to determine

$$(s_{11}, s_{22}, s_{12}) = (\sigma_x^2, \sigma_y^2, \rho\sigma_x\sigma_y).$$

Also, since S has three parameters and μ has two, we see that θ contains a total of five parameters. This is the same number of parameters as in the non-matrix form (6.16), where ρ is the fifth parameter.[11]

Since we are considering a mixture of two bivariate normal distributions, we'll estimate the parameters

$$\theta_1 = (\,\mu_1 \quad S_1\,) \text{ and } \theta_2 = (\,\mu_2 \quad S_2\,)$$

and we'll also need to determine the mixture parameters, which are denoted as $\tau = (\,\tau_1 \quad \tau_2\,)$, where $\tau_1 + \tau_2 = 1$.

Although the bivariate normal looks complicated, for the EM algorithm, we use the function $f(X, \theta)$ in (6.17) in the same way that we used the much simpler probability function in the previous section. That is, the EM algorithm itself is essentially the same—we just plug in a different probability function, depending on the assumed type of distribution. And Gaussian distributions are a popular choice, thanks to the central limit theorem.

As mentioned above, for bivariate and higher dimensional Gaussian distributions, it's more convenient to use the matrix versions of equations (6.10) through (6.13). We now explicitly restate the EM algorithm for the case of a bivariate Gaussian mixture problem, using matrix notation.

E step Given our current estimates for τ and the parameters θ_1 and θ_2, we use Bayes' formula to compute

$$p_{j,i} = \frac{\tau_j\, f(X_i, \theta_j)}{\tau_1\, f(X_i, \theta_1) + \tau_2\, f(X_i, \theta_2)}$$

for $j = 1, 2$ and $i = 1, 2, \ldots, n$. For bivariate Gaussian distributions, the function f is given in equation (6.18). Note that this version of the E step is similar to that given in equation (6.10), except that here the data X_i is multi-dimensional and the probability function is more complex.

---

[11]This fifth parameter is not to be confused with the fifth Beatle [91].

M step We compute

$$\tau_j = \frac{1}{n}\sum_{i=1}^{n} p_{j,i}. \tag{6.20}$$

This part of the M step is identical to the version in equation (6.11).

For $j = 1, 2$, the means are computed as

$$\mu_j = \sum_{i=1}^{n} p_{j,i}\, X_i \Bigg/ \sum_{i=1}^{n} p_{j,i}. \tag{6.21}$$

While this formula looks similar to that given in equation (6.12), here each X_i is a vector, so we compute a vector of means μ_j. In the bivariate case, $\mu_j = (\ \mu_x \quad \mu_y\ )$, where μ_x and μ_y are the means in the x and y components, respectively, under the jth distribution.

Once the mean vectors μ_j have been computed, we then estimate the covariance matrices as

$$S_j = \sum_{i=1}^{n} p_{j,i}(X_i - \mu_j)(X_i - \mu_j)^T \Bigg/ \sum_{i=1}^{n} p_{j,i}. \tag{6.22}$$

In the bivariate case, $X_i - \mu_j$ is a 2×1 column vector and $(X_i - \mu_j)^T$ is a 1×2 row vector, so that the product S_j in equation (6.22) is indeed a 2×2 matrix. In general, we obtain an $m \times m$ covariance matrix, where the data that is being clustered is m-dimensional.

Now, we apply the EM clustering algorithm to the Old Faithful data in Table 6.6, treating it as a Gaussian mixture problem. We denote the data in Table 6.6 as $X_i = (x_i, y_i)$, where the x_i component is the duration and the y_i component is the waiting time. Since the data is 2-dimensional, we'll need to use bivariate Gaussian distributions. To keep things simple, we'll split this data into $K = 2$ clusters, which implies that we have to determine the parameters for a pair of bivariate Gaussian distributions.

For the data in Table 6.6, the mean duration is about 3.08 and the mean of waiting time is 68.25. The variance in the x_i component is about 1.39 while the variance of the y_i is 221.1875. We use these values as a (very rough) guide for selecting the initial parameters for the EM algorithm.

Suppose that our initial guess for the parameters is

$$\theta_1 = (\ \mu_1 \quad S_1\ ) = \left(\begin{pmatrix} 2.5 \\ 65.0 \end{pmatrix} \begin{pmatrix} 1.0 & 5.0 \\ 5.0 & 100.0 \end{pmatrix} \right) \tag{6.23}$$

and

$$\theta_2 = (\ \mu_2 \quad S_2\ ) = \left(\begin{pmatrix} 3.5 \\ 70.0 \end{pmatrix} \begin{pmatrix} 2.0 & 10.0 \\ 10.0 & 200.0 \end{pmatrix} \right). \tag{6.24}$$

Recall that the correlation coefficient ρ must satisfy $-1 < \rho < 1$. We verify that this condition holds for the matrix S_1 where

$$\rho_1 = \frac{s_{12}}{\sqrt{s_{11}s_{22}}} = 0.5.$$

It's easy to verify that for the initial S_2 matrix, we have $\rho_2 = 0.5$. To complete the parameter initialization, we let $\tau = \begin{pmatrix} \tau_1 & \tau_2 \end{pmatrix} = \begin{pmatrix} 0.6 & 0.4 \end{pmatrix}$. Using these parameters, the first E step of the EM algorithm yields the results in Table 6.7.

Table 6.7: First E step using the data in Table 6.6

$p_{1,1} = 0.5635$	$p_{1,6} = 0.2643$	$p_{1,11} = 0.7950$	$p_{1,16} = 0.7701$
$p_{2,1} = 0.4365$	$p_{2,6} = 0.7357$	$p_{2,11} = 0.2050$	$p_{2,16} = 0.2299$
$p_{1,2} = 0.8004$	$p_{1,7} = 0.7551$	$p_{1,12} = 0.3064$	$p_{1,17} = 0.2451$
$p_{2,2} = 0.1997$	$p_{2,7} = 0.2449$	$p_{2,12} = 0.6936$	$p_{2,17} = 0.7549$
$p_{1,3} = 0.8074$	$p_{1,8} = 0.7982$	$p_{1,13} = 0.4170$	$p_{1,18} = 0.7425$
$p_{2,3} = 0.1926$	$p_{2,8} = 0.2018$	$p_{2,13} = 0.5830$	$p_{2,18} = 0.2575$
$p_{1,4} = 0.6639$	$p_{1,9} = 0.1913$	$p_{1,14} = 0.4277$	$p_{1,19} = 0.2123$
$p_{2,4} = 0.3361$	$p_{2,9} = 0.8087$	$p_{2,14} = 0.5723$	$p_{2,19} = 0.7877$
$p_{1,5} = 0.6564$	$p_{1,10} = 0.4490$	$p_{1,15} = 0.8294$	$p_{1,20} = 0.7122$
$p_{2,5} = 0.3436$	$p_{2,10} = 0.5510$	$p_{2,15} = 0.1706$	$p_{2,20} = 0.2878$

In the first M-step of the EM algorithm, we use the values in Table 6.7 to re-estimate the parameters. Specifically, to re-estimate $\tau = \begin{pmatrix} \tau_1 & \tau_2 \end{pmatrix}$, we use equation (6.20) and to re-estimate $\theta = \begin{pmatrix} \theta_1 & \theta_2 \end{pmatrix}$, we use equations (6.21) and (6.22). In this example, we find that the re-estimated parameters are

$$\tau = \begin{pmatrix} \tau_1 & \tau_2 \end{pmatrix} = \begin{pmatrix} 0.5704 & 0.4296 \end{pmatrix}$$

and

$$\theta_1 = \begin{pmatrix} \mu_1 & S_1 \end{pmatrix} = \left(\begin{pmatrix} 2.6269 \\ 63.0160 \end{pmatrix} \begin{pmatrix} 1.0548 & 12.7306 \\ 12.7306 & 181.5183 \end{pmatrix} \right)$$

and

$$\theta_2 = \begin{pmatrix} \mu_2 & S_2 \end{pmatrix} = \left(\begin{pmatrix} 3.6756 \\ 75.1981 \end{pmatrix} \begin{pmatrix} 1.2119 & 14.1108 \\ 14.1108 & 189.2046 \end{pmatrix} \right).$$

After 100 iterations, the EM process converges with

$$\tau = \begin{pmatrix} \tau_1 & \tau_2 \end{pmatrix} = \begin{pmatrix} 0.5001 & 0.4999 \end{pmatrix}$$

and

$$\theta_1 = \begin{pmatrix} \mu_1 & S_1 \end{pmatrix} = \left(\begin{pmatrix} 1.9819 \\ 54.0049 \end{pmatrix} \begin{pmatrix} 0.1284 & 0.4178 \\ 0.4178 & 20.4931 \end{pmatrix} \right) \qquad (6.25)$$

and

$$\theta_2 = \begin{pmatrix} \mu_2 & S_2 \end{pmatrix} = \left(\begin{pmatrix} 4.1735 \\ 82.5021 \end{pmatrix} \begin{pmatrix} 0.2537 & 1.2638 \\ 1.2638 & 15.8362 \end{pmatrix} \right). \qquad (6.26)$$

For these converged parameters we have $\rho_1 = 0.2576$ and $\rho_2 = 0.6305$. The clusters determined by these distributions are given in Figure 6.15, where the hollow square is the cluster centroid specified by the mean μ_1 and the solid square is the cluster centroid given by the mean μ_2. The darker shaded regions are within one standard deviation of their respective means, while the lighter shaded regions are between one and two standard deviations from the corresponding means.

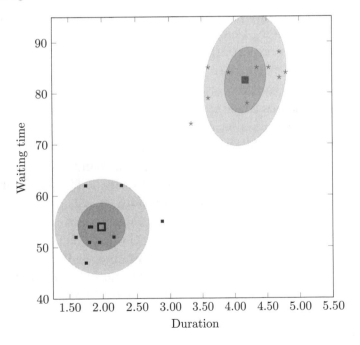

Figure 6.15: EM clusters for Old Faithful data

As an aside, we note that each shaded region in Figure 6.15 is bounded by an ellipse of the form

$$\frac{(x - \mu_x)^2}{\sigma_x^2} - \frac{2\rho(x - \mu_x)(y - \mu_y)}{\sigma_x \sigma_y} + \frac{(y - \mu_y)^2}{\sigma_y^2} = c$$

for some constant c. For the lower-left cluster, the values of the parameters are determined by the converged values of θ_1 in equation (6.25), and for the upper-right cluster, the values are derived from θ_2 in equation (6.26).

While a picture such as that in Figure 6.15 is interesting, it is not necessary for clustering—which is fortunate, since it is not so easy to draw pictures when working in four or more dimensions. Using the converge parameters, we can easily compute the probability of each point with respect to each derived probability distribution. Points can then be assigned to clusters based on the distribution that yields the highest probability.

6.6   The Bottom Line

In this chapter, we considered a wide variety of topics related to clustering. Clustering techniques are generally used in a data exploration mode, where we don't know much about the data and we are, in effect, fishing for any interesting or useful structure.

The K-means algorithm provides an easy and intuitive method for clustering. In comparison, the EM clustering algorithm is certainly more complex, but it also allows for more variations in cluster shape, and hence should produce better results in many cases.

We also considered various methods for measuring the quality of clusters. While all such measures have inherent limitations, it's often necessary to quantitatively compare different clusterings, so that we can experiment with different parameters and different clustering techniques.

Additional sources of information on clustering can be found at [65, 94, 96, 147]. Online animations are useful for visualizing the clustering process. For the K-means algorithm, the series of animations at [123] might be especially helpful. For EM clustering, a very good animation based on the Old Faithful data can be found at [49]. Also, see [81] for an interactive animation that can be used to explore the dependence of clusters on the placement of the initial centroids. Finally, [60] has several nice animations for density-based clustering, which we briefly discuss in Problem 16, below.

6.7   Problems

1. Suppose that we have a clustering that is optimal with respect to the distortion, that is, distortion$_K$ is minimized.

   a) Assuming that the data is 1-dimensional and $K = 1$, prove that each centroid c_j must be located at the center of its cluster. Hint: Since there is a single cluster, the distortion is given by

$$f(c) = \sum_{i=1}^{n} d(X_i, c)$$

where c is the centroid and $X_1, X_2, \ldots, X_n$ are the elements in the dataset. Let $d(x, y)$ be the squared Euclidean distance and minimize $f(c)$. Note that each X_i is a number, not a vector.[12]

b) Repeat part a) for the case where $K > 1$, again assuming that the data is 1-dimensional.

2. Consider the correlation coefficient r_{AD} as defined in equation (6.4).

a) With respect to clustering, why is $r_{AD} = -1$ the ideal case?

b) Suppose that r_{AD} is near 1. What does this say about the clusters?

3. This problem deals with the residual sum of squares (RSS).

a) Define an error function different from that in equation (6.1).

b) Compute the RSS for the data points in Figure 6.6 (a) using your error function from part a).

c) Compute the RSS for the data points in Figure 6.6 (b) using your error function from part a).

4. Compute the entropy and purity for both of the clusterings below.

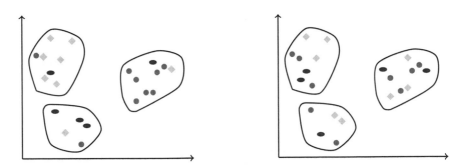

5. Implement the K-means clustering algorithm by writing your own computer program.

a) Use your K-means clustering program with $K = 2$ to cluster the Old Faithful eruption data in Table 6.6.

---

[12]If you have completed Chapter 5 (in particular, the material on Lagrangian duality), this problem should be a piece of cake.

b) Use your K-means clustering program with $K = 3$ to cluster the Old Faithful eruption data in Table 6.6.

6. Intuitively, we would like to have clusters that are individually compact, and spaced far apart from each other. In Section 6.3 we saw that K-means is focused on generating compact clusters, without directly dealing with the spacing between clusters. In this problem, we consider a measure that combines both the compactness and spacing between clusters, and we use this measure as the "distance" in K-means.

Suppose that $K > 1$ clusters $C_1, C_2, \ldots, C_K$ are specified, along with corresponding centroids $c_1, c_2, \ldots, c_K$. As in K-means, we'll update the centroids to be the centers of the clusters. But, when recomputing the clusters, we will use the following approach, rather than simply assigning each point to its nearest centroid.

For a given data point X, let $s = \sum d(X, c_i)$ and let

$$p_i = \frac{1}{K-1}\left(1 - \frac{d(X, c_i)}{s}\right)$$

for $i = 1, 2, \ldots, K$, where $d(x, y)$ is Euclidean distance. If p_i is large, then the distance from X to c_i is small, relative to its distance to the other centroids c_j. Conversely, if p_i is small, then X is far from c_i, as compared to the other centroids c_j. Thus, we'll assign X to the cluster that yields the largest probability p_i. That is, we reassign X so that $c_i = \text{centroid}(X)$ where $i = \text{argmax}_j\, p_j$.

a) Show that for any X, the corresponding $p_1, p_2, \ldots, p_K$ satisfy the conditions of a discrete probability distribution.

b) Repeat Problem 5 using the clustering technique outlined in this problem instead of K-means.

c) Comment on the effectiveness of this clustering approach, as compared to K-means.

7. Compute the probabilities $p_{j,i}$ corresponding to those in Table 6.5 for the second E step of the coin flipping example in Section 6.5.3.

8. Write your own program to implement the EM clustering algorithm, as given in Section 6.5.3.

a) Use your implementation of the EM algorithm to verify that the binomial example in Section 6.5.3 converges to

$$\theta = (\,\theta_1 \quad \theta_2\,) = (\,0.7934 \quad 0.5139\,)$$

when the parameters are initialized as

$$\theta = (\theta_1 \quad \theta_2) = (0.6 \quad 0.5)$$
$$\tau = (\tau_1 \quad \tau_2) = (0.7 \quad 0.3).$$

b) Using the same data as in part a), test your implementation of the EM algorithm with at least three different initializations and compare the final θ you obtain in each case to that obtained in part a).

9. For the EM coin flipping example in Section 6.5.3, we initialized

$$\theta = (\theta_1 \quad \theta_2) = (0.6 \quad 0.5)$$
$$\tau = (\tau_1 \quad \tau_2) = (0.7 \quad 0.3).$$

Using these initializations, how many iterations of the EM algorithm are required before both θ_1 and θ_2 are within 10% of their converged values in equation (6.15)?

10. Verify that in the case of a bivariate Gaussian distribution, the matrix form in (6.17) is equivalent to the formula given in equation (6.16).

11. Consider the Gaussian mixture problem in Section 6.5.4.

a) Compute all $p_{j,i}$ for the second iteration of the EM algorithm.

b) Use the $p_{j,i}$ you computed in part a) to re-estimate θ_1 and θ_2.

12. For the Gaussian mixture example in Section 6.5.4, verify $\rho_1 = 0.2576$ and $\rho_2 = 0.6305$ for θ_1 and θ_2 in (6.25) and (6.26), respectively.

13. Use the EM algorithm to cluster the Old Faithful eruption data in Table 6.6 as follows.

a) Use two clusters with the initial values for θ_1 given in equation (6.23) and the initial values for θ_2 given in equation (6.24).

b) Use two clusters and a different set of initial values than in part a).

c) Use three clusters and your choice of initial values.

d) Graphically compare your EM results from part a) of this problem to the K-means results from part a) of Problem 5. Comment on the observed similarities and differences.

14. Consider the Gaussian mixture example in Section 6.5.4. In this case, our initial estimates for the parameters were not close to the final converged values.

a) Why should we have known in advance that our choices for parameters were not likely to be close to the converged values?

b) Outline a better way to initialize the parameters, and explain why your initialization method is superior to that used for the Gaussian mixture example in Section 6.5.4.

15. Discuss the relative advantages and disadvantages of EM clustering as compared to K-means.

16. Rather than relying only on distance (as in K-means) or probability (as in EM), we might instead cluster points based on density. That is, we can determine clusters based on the areas where points tend to bunch together. DBSCAN is the best-known example of such a *density-based clustering* strategy.

In DBSCAN, there are two parameters, a positive integer m that specifies the minimum number of data points in a "core" neighborhood, and a parameter $\varepsilon > 0$ that determines the neighborhood size. Based on these parameters, every point in the dataset can be classified as follows.

- Core point — We say that X is a core point provided that m or more data points are within a distance of ε of X, where X itself is included among these m points.

- Reachable point — The point X is said to be reachable if it satisfies $d(X, Y) \leq \varepsilon$ for some core point Y. Note that any core point is also a reachable point, but not all reachable points are core points.

- Outlier — Any X that is not a reachable point is classified as an outlier. The outliers are often viewed as noise.

In the DBSCAN algorithm, we randomly select a point X that has not previously been visited. If X is not a core point, simply mark it as visited and select another non-visited point X. If the selected point X is a core point, then we grow a cluster based on X by including all points in the ε neighborhood of X. Furthermore, for each core point Y included in this manner, we iterate the process, that is, we include all points in the ε neighborhood of Y, thus extending the cluster based on the core points in neighborhoods of neighbors. This continues until no more points can be added to the cluster. In this way, all reachable points are added to this X-based cluster. Only core points are used to extend a cluster to additional neighborhoods. Thus, we can view the non-core reachable points as being on the edge of the cluster. Finally, the algorithm terminates when there are no more unvisited points to select from when attempting to initiate a new cluster.

Unlike K-means and EM clustering, for DBSCAN, we do not specify the number of clusters. Another major distinction is that with DBSCAN, outlier points are not assigned to any cluster. And, recall that K-means clusters are round, while EM clusters based on Gaussian distributions are elliptical. In contrast, a DBSCAN cluster can be of any arbitrary shape, since clusters are based on the local density of points, not on a fixed topology.

a) In DBSCAN, a previously visited point can be added to a cluster. Clearly explain how this could happen.

b) The DBSCAN algorithm is not entirely deterministic. Explain how a point X could be assigned to different clusters depending on the order in which points are selected.

c) Implement the DBSCAN algorithm and use your program to cluster the data below, which can be found in the file `dbscan.txt` on the textbook website. Test each of the 4 pairs of parameters

$$(\varepsilon, m) \in \{(0.6, 3), (0.75, 4), (1.0, 5), (2.0, 10)\}.$$

In each case, plot the clusters, list the number of elements in each cluster, and give the number of outliers.

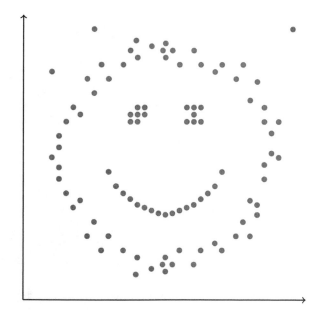

Chapter 7

Many Mini Topics

> *Nothing is particularly hard if you divide it into small jobs.*
> — Henry Ford

7.1 Introduction

In this chapter, we briefly discuss several techniques related to machine learning. Some of these topics are here because they are simply too simple to warrant an entire chapter (e.g., k-nearest neighbor). Ironically, some topics are included in this chapter because they are too big (e.g., neural networks) and would require an entire book to cover at a reasonable depth. In any case, everything discussed here is sure to be useful in some situations.

7.2 k-Nearest Neighbors

The k-nearest neighbor (k-NN) algorithm is perhaps the simplest machine learning technique known to man.[1] Given a training set of labeled data and a distance function, k-NN classifies a point X based on the k elements of the training set that are nearest to X.

Consider the training data in Figure 7.1. This training set consists of 10 elements of the "solid circle" type, and and eight elements of the "hollow square" type.

Suppose that we want to classify the solid diamond that is labeled as X in Figure 7.2 (a) using 1-NN (i.e., k-NN, with $k = 1$, which is also known simply as the nearest neighbor algorithm). Since the nearest point to X is the hollow square labeled b, Figure 7.2 (a) shows that for this case, we would classify X as type "hollow square." On the other hand, suppose that we want

---

[1]Not to mention woman.

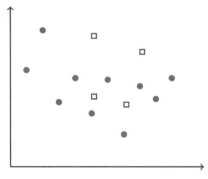

Figure 7.1: Labeled training data

to classify X using 3-NN. In Figure 7.2 (b), we see that the three nearest data points to X (with respect to Euclidean distance) consist of one hollow square and two solid circles—labeled b, r_1, and r_2, respectively. Since the majority of the three nearest points in the training set are solid circles, using 3-NN, we would classify X as being of the same type as the solid circles.

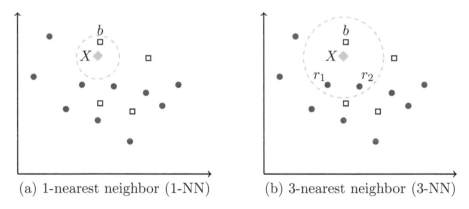

(a) 1-nearest neighbor (1-NN)   (b) 3-nearest neighbor (3-NN)

Figure 7.2: k-NN examples

It is reasonable to weight the nearest neighbors based on their relative frequency in the training set. Consider again the example of 3-NN given in Figure 7.2 (b). Since there are ten solid circles and only eight hollow squares, we could weight each hollow square by a factor of 1, with each solid circle being weighted by 1.25. Then for this example, the point X would have a "square" score of 2 and a "circle" score of 1.25, and hence X would be classified as of square type in the $k = 3$ case.

Intuitively, when classifying using k-NN, we might also want to weight the nearest neighbors based on their distance to X. That is, the closer data points should count for more. Consider again the example in Figure 7.2 (b), and let $d_0 = 1/d(X, b)$, and $d_1 = 1/d(X, r_1)$, and $d_2 = 1/d(X, r_2)$, where we are using the Euclidean distance. If we weight the data points using this measure, we would classify X as being of the square type, provided that we have $d_0 > d_1 + d_2$, which appears to be the case in Figure 7.2 (b). Of course, we could combine this approach with a normalization based on relative frequencies, as discussed in the previous paragraph. Various other measures could be used too, including statistical measures, or other scores, such as those based on various machine learning techniques.

A related approach would be to classify based on a fixed radius. This would have the potential advantage of using more data points in areas where the density is high, and less data points when the data is sparse.

Note that in k-NN, there is no explicit training phase—once we have a training set in hand, the training phase is complete. It doesn't get any simpler than that. While scoring is also conceptually simple, it could be computationally expensive to determine the distances to all data points each time we want to compute a score. Fortunately, there are nearest neighbor search algorithms that make this problem tractable; see, for example, Knuth's *post office problem* [77]. However, the use of such techniques does, perhaps, slightly negate one of the primary selling points of k-NN, namely, its inherent simplicity.

For k-NN, it can be proved that as the number of data points in the training set goes to infinity, the error rate approaches optimal, in a well-defined sense. Unfortunately, the optimal k also increases with the data size.

Thanks to its simplicity, k-NN can easily be combined with other machine learning techniques. For example, in Problem 13 of Chapter 4, we consider the use of k-NN for scoring within the context of principal component analysis (PCA). We might also, for example, use PCA or a support vector machine (SVM) to reduce the dimensionality of the data, then use k-NN for classification on the resulting, lower-dimensional data.

7.3 Neural Networks

Neural networks (also known as artificial neural networks) are a class of machine learning techniques that attempt to model interconnected neurons of the brain. Here, we only consider one example of a neural network, and even then we take a very high-level perspective. To provide any reasonable level of detail on neural networks is a book-length undertaking.

The human brain is able to learn,[2] whereas the ability to learn is not exactly a strength of computers. The neurons in the human brain have a high degree of interconnectivity that is thought to allow for massive parallelism. The brain also has some ability to self-organize and includes a high degree of

---

[2]A politician's brain being the obvious exception.

fault-tolerance. These features provide humans with the ability to generalize based on experience. It seems reasonable to try to obtain such features in a computing system by modeling the brain at the level of neurons. That, in a minuscule nutshell, is the basic idea behind neural networks.

While there are many different types of neural networks, in this section, we'll only discuss one—the multilayer perceptron (MLP).[3] An MLP is a supervised learning technique that includes an input layer, one or more hidden layers, and an output layer, with each layer fully connected to the preceding layer. An illustration of an MLP with two hidden layers is given in Figure 7.3.

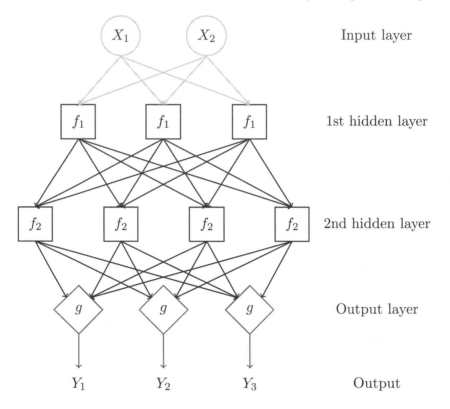

Figure 7.3: MLP with two hidden layers

Any number of nodes can appear in a layer. The functions used in an MLP must be nonlinear—otherwise it would be trivial to replace multiple layers with a single layer. The functions f_i at the intermediate layers are typically smooth versions of step functions. For example, the hyperbolic tangent function $f(x) = \tanh(x)$ is a popular choice.

Each edge in an MLP represents a weight—the purpose of training is to determine these weights. Given a set of weights, we can measure the accuracy of the MLP by computing scores on labeled test data.

---

[3]Your hip author is sure that MLPs have the coolest name of any neural network.

A technique known as *back-propagation* is used to train an MLP. The basic intuition behind the back-propagation algorithm is that we make small modifications to the weights in such a way that the measured error decreases. Typically, there are a large number of weights to determine, so making random modifications is unlikely to be a good strategy. Instead, modifications to the weights are made so that the error reduction is large, which tends to speed convergence. Determining optimal weight modifications sounds like a job for calculus (partial derivatives, in particular), and such is indeed the case. The back-propagation algorithm requires quite a bit of calculus, but perhaps the most challenging part is the notation. In any case, we omit the details here.

While undoubtedly useful in many situations, Neural networks seem to be almost synonymous with the field of artificial intelligence (AI). Perhaps this is unavoidable, given that Neural networks model aspects of the brain, and it would seem that if we can do that effectively, then truly intelligent machines can't be far behind.[4] However, it's worth noting that biology is not always an ideal model for engineering. For example, birds flap their wings to fly, but humans fly (mostly) in fixed-wing aircraft. Outside of a few early (and failed) prototypes, airplanes do not flap their wings—at least not intentionally. Attempting to construct intelligent systems by modeling neural interactions within the brain might one day be seen as akin to trying to build an airplane that flies by flapping its wings.

In machine learning, we often derive a model that can be viewed as representing an intermediate "layer" between the input and the output, and deriving this model is the whole point of training. For example, in HMMs, the training phase determines a (hidden) Markov process that models the observations. From this perspective, it's not clear that neural networks are all that unique in comparison to various other machine learning techniques. In a similar vein, it is interesting to note that in [31], it is shown that MLPs are closely related to SVMs.

Another issue with neural networks is that it's often difficult to derive any meaningful meaning from a trained model. This is in stark contrast to various other machine learning techniques, for which we can sometimes gain useful insights into the underlying problem by analyzing a model. For example, in Section 9.2 of Chapter 9 we trained an HMM on English text, and we observed that the B matrix reveals a great deal about the English language. And there are other examples—the weights of a linear SVM can reveal the relative importance of the various inputs, while PCA can be used in a similar (although somewhat less intuitive) manner. However, due to the

---

[4]At this point, your naturally intelligent author feels compelled to admit that he is skeptical of the prospects for "strong" artificial intelligence. Your jaded author has noticed that the big breakthrough in AI always seems to be just around the corner. A cynic might conclude that AI researchers are trying to circumnavigate an apeirogon.

complex interactions in the intermediate layers, it's difficult to extract such information from neural networks.

And, not surprisingly, neural networks must deal with many of the same issues that arise with other machine learning algorithms. For example, when determining the parameters of an MLP, we can only be assured of finding a local maximum, and there are likely to be a large number of local maximums. We discussed this issue in the context of HMMs in Chapter 2, and it arises in one form or another in most other techniques that we have considered. The bottom line here is that it is undoubtedly wise to view neural networks as another useful weapon in the machine learning arsenal, rather than as some sort of universal solvent.

Neural networks have a long—if somewhat rocky—history and there is a wealth of good information available. Kriesel's introduction to the subject [80] is recommended. A highly informative discussion of back-propagation can be found in [105].

7.4 Boosting

Boosting is a process whereby we combine multiple (weak) classifiers into one (much stronger) classifier [117]. Of course, many machine learning techniques can be applied to a set of classifiers, with the goal of making a stronger classifier—we discussed such a meta-scoring approach based on SVMs in Chapter 5. But the beauty of boosting is that the individual classifiers can be extremely weak—anything that is better than flipping a coin is useful. And provided that we have a sufficient number of non-random classifiers, boosting can be used to construct an arbitrarily strong classifier.

The best-known boosting algorithm is *AdaBoost*, which is a clever shorthand for adaptive boosting. At each iteration of AdaBoost, we use a greedy strategy, in the sense that we select the individual classifier—and its associated weight—that improves our overall classifier the most. And it's an adaptive approach, since we build up the classifier over a sequence of iterations.

7.4.1 Football Analogy

To illustrate the AdaBoost process, let's consider the problem of building the best football team possible from a collection of average players.[5] One reasonable way to organize a team would be to select the best player at each position from your collection of players. But, suppose that your best quarterback is terrible, while your best receiver is also one of your best players

---

[5]If you don't know much about American football, don't worry. All you need to know is that it's like rugby, except that a ball is used instead of a watermelon. Also, in football the quarterback throws the ball to a receiver on his same team, who is supposed to catch it.

at several other positions. If you put your best receiver at receiver, he won't catch any passes, because your quarterback is terrible. So, it would seem to make more sense to put your best receiver at some other position where he is also very good. In other words, the best overall team might not have each player playing at his best position.

The following adaptive strategy could be used to try to assemble the best possible team from a collection of average players.

1. Select the best player and determine his role on the team.

2. Determine the biggest weakness remaining on the team.

3. From the remaining players, choose the one who can best improve on the weakness identified in step 2.

4. Decide exactly what role the newly selected player will fill.

5. If the team is not yet complete, goto 2.

Note that this strategy does not assure us of obtaining the best possible team—that might require an exhaustive search over all possible teams. But, this adaptive approach is likely to produce a better team than the naïve approach of simply selecting the best player at each position. And the weaker the individual players, the better this algorithm is likely to do, as compared to the naïve strategy.

7.4.2 AdaBoost

AdaBoost is somewhat analogous to building your football team using the adaptive strategy outlined in the previous section. At each iteration, we'll identify the biggest weakness in the classifier that we have constructed so far. Then we'll determine which of the remaining available classifiers will help the most with respect to this weakness. Finally, we determine the optimal way to merge this newly-selected classifier into our overall classifier.

Using an adaptive approach, we can combine a large number of weak classifiers to obtain a result that is much stronger than any of the individual classifiers. The AdaBoost algorithm that we describe below is efficient and easy to implement.

But before discussing AdaBoost in more detail, we note that in practice, boosting may not achieve the seemingly too-good-to-be-true results that the theory promises. Unfortunately, boosting algorithms tend to be extremely sensitive to noise. The reason for this sensitivity should become clear after we discuss the AdaBoost algorithm.

As mentioned above, AdaBoost is the most popular boosting technique and it uses an iterative, greedy approach. Now, we describe this algorithm in more detail.

Suppose that we have a labeled training set of size n, denoted (X_i, z_i), for $i = 1, 2, \ldots, n$, where X_i is the ith data point, with corresponding label (i.e., classification) z_i. Since we are dealing with a binary classification problem, we'll assume that each $z_i \in \{-1, +1\}$. In addition, we assume that there are L (weak) classifiers, denoted c_ℓ, for $\ell = 1, 2, \ldots, L$, where each c_ℓ assigns a label (either $+1$ or -1) to each X_i. An example of such training data is illustrated in Table 7.1. Note that an entry of $+1$ in row i, column ℓ in Table 7.1 indicates that classifier c_ℓ correctly classifies data point X_i (based on its label z_i), while a -1 indicates that the classifier misclassifies the data point. Our goal is to construct a classifier $C(X)$ as a weighted combination of the c_ℓ. Of course, we want $C(X)$ to be as strong as possible, that is, we want $C(X)$ to correctly classify as many of training vectors X_i as possible.

Table 7.1: Classifiers

Data	Label	Classifiers			
		c_1	c_2	$\cdots$	c_L
X_1	z_1	-1	$+1$	$\cdots$	$+1$
X_2	z_2	$+1$	-1	$\cdots$	-1
X_3	z_3	-1	-1	$\cdots$	$+1$
$\vdots$	$\vdots$	$\vdots$	$\vdots$	$\vdots$	$\vdots$
X_n	z_n	-1	$+1$	$\cdots$	-1

The classifiers c_ℓ can be weak, i.e., the number of $+1$ elements in row ℓ might be only marginally greater than the number of -1 entries. And note that if the number of misclassifications exceeds the number of correct classifications in a given row (i.e., the number of -1s exceed the number of $+1$s), then we can simply reverse the sense of the classifier to obtain a classifier with more $+1$s than -1s. But, a classifier cannot be perfectly random, that is, we cannot use a classifier for which the number of $+1$ and -1 are exactly equal. In other words, the only classifiers that are not usable for boosting are those that are indistinguishable from flipping a fair coin.

Since AdaBoost is an iterative algorithm, we'll generate a series of classifiers, $C_1, C_2, \ldots, C_M$, where the final classifier is $C = C_M$. Furthermore, each classifier is of the form

$$C_m(X_i) = a_1 k_1(X_i) + a_2 k_2(X_i) + \cdots + a_m k_m(X_i)$$

where each k_j is a distinct element selected from the set of classifiers c_ℓ, for $\ell = 1, 2, \ldots, L$, and each a_j is a non-negative weight. Furthermore, we'll select the classifiers and weights so that

$$C_m(X_i) = C_{m-1}(X_i) + a_m k_m(X_i).$$

That is, at each iteration, we add another classifier k_m from the unused c_ℓ and determine a new weight a_m. In terms of the football analogy discussed above, we select one of the remaining players, and we determine his role. This is a greedy approach, since we choose k_m and a_m to maximize the improvement at each step.

In AdaBoost, we use an exponential *loss function*. A loss function is like a score, except that the smaller the loss, the better, whereas larger scores are better. Specifically, the loss (or error) function at step m is defined as

$$E_m = \sum_{i=1}^{n} e^{-z_i \left(C_{m-1}(X_i) + \alpha_m k_m(X_i) \right)}$$

where k_m is chosen from among the unused c_j and $a_m > 0$ is to be determined. Equivalently, we can write the loss function as

$$E_m = \sum_{i=1}^{n} w_i \, e^{-z_i \alpha_m k_m(X_i)} \tag{7.1}$$

where

$$w_i = e^{-z_i C_{m-1}(X_i)}.$$

Equation (7.1) can be rewritten as

$$E_m = \sum_{z_i = k_m(X_i)} w_i \, e^{-\alpha_m} + \sum_{z_i \neq k_m(X_i)} w_i \, e^{\alpha_m}$$

which we can rewrite as

$$E_m = W_1 e^{-\alpha_m} + W_2 \, e^{\alpha_m} \tag{7.2}$$

where

$$W_1 = \sum_{z_i = k_m(X_i)} w_i \text{ and } W_2 = \sum_{z_i \neq k_m(X_i)} w_i. \tag{7.3}$$

Then

$$e^{\alpha_m} E_m = W_1 + W_2 \, e^{2\alpha_m}$$

and it follows that

$$e^{\alpha_m} E_m = (W_1 + W_2) + W_2 \left(e^{2\alpha_m} - 1 \right).$$

Letting $W = W_1 + W_2$, we have

$$e^{\alpha_m} E_m = W + W_2 \left(e^{2\alpha_m} - 1 \right).$$

From the definitions of W_1 and W_2, we see that any increase in W_1 is offset by precisely the same decrease in W_2, and vice versa. Consequently, W is fixed for this iteration. Then, regardless of the value of α_m, we'll want to choose k_m so that W_2 is minimized.

Once we have selected k_m, we determine the corresponding weight α_m. But note that once k_m is specified, both W_1 and W_2 are known. From equation (7.2), we see that

$$\frac{dE_m}{d\alpha_m} = -W_1 e^{-\alpha_m} + W_2\, e^{\alpha_m}.$$

Setting this equal to zero and solving for α_m, we find

$$\alpha_m = \frac{1}{2}\, \ln\left(\frac{1 - r_m}{r_m}\right) \tag{7.4}$$

where

$$r_m = W_2/W.$$

To summarize, iteration m of the AdaBoost algorithm consists of the following steps, where "misses" are incorrect classifications and "hits" are correct classifications.

1. Select k_m from among the unused classifiers c_ℓ so that W_2 in equation (7.3) is minimized. That is, we select the k_m that minimizes the number of misses, with respect to our training data.

2. After selecting k_m, compute W_2 and $W = W_1 + W_2$. Note that W_2 is the number of misses, while W_1 is the number of hits.

3. Determine α_m using equation (7.4).

In the football analogy, choosing k_m corresponds to selecting the player— from among those not yet selected—who can help the team the most. And determining α_m corresponds (roughly) to putting the selected player at the position that does the most good for the team.

As previously mentioned, errors in the training data can be an Achilles heel for AdaBoost. This is fairly clear from the algorithm, as an error in one step will tend to snowball in subsequent iterations. It is also interesting to note that as a consequence of the exponential weighting function, outliers can have excessive influence on the final classifier.

7.5   Random Forest

A random forest is a clever generalization of a decision tree. A decision tree is a simple tree structure that can be constructed from labeled training data. A trained decision tree can be used to efficiently classify data.

Decision trees are extremely simple and require little data to construct. In addition, decision trees are intuitive and easy to combine with other techniques. This all sounds pretty good, so why do we need a generalization? The primary drawback to a decision tree is that it will tend to overfit the training data, which is usually undesirable in any learning algorithms.

In this section, we'll first discuss decision trees. Then we'll consider ways to generalize such trees, with the aim of reducing the tendency to overfit.

To illustrate a decision tree, suppose that we have a labeled training set consisting of malware samples and benign samples. From this training set, we observe that malware samples tend to be smaller in size and have higher entropy, as compared to benign samples. We could use this information to construct the decision tree in Figure 7.4, where the thresholds for "large" versus "small" (size) and "high" versus "low" (entropy) would be based on the training data. This decision tree could then be used to classify any sample as either malware or benign, based on its size and entropy.

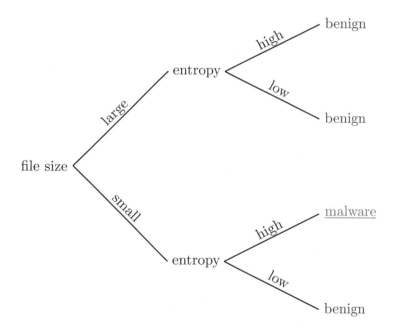

Figure 7.4: Decision tree example

Of course, we might want to consider features in a different order. For example, the two features of file size and entropy, as illustrated in Figure 7.4, could be instead considered in the opposite order, as illustrated in Figure 7.5.

Is there any reason to choose one ordering of the features over another? Observe that in Figure 7.4, a "large" sample will always be classified as benign regardless of its entropy, whereas for the feature ordering in Figure 7.5, a "low" entropy sample will always be classified as benign. In general, splits

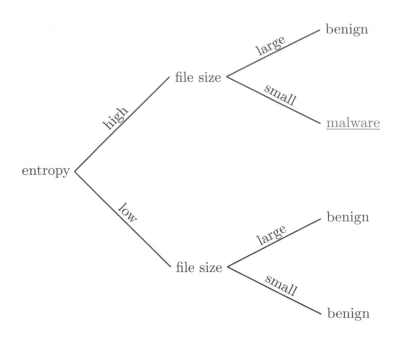

Figure 7.5: Features in different order

made closer to the root will tend to have more impact on the final classification. Therefore, we want to make decisions that are based on more distinguishing information closer to the root of the tree. In this way, the decisions for which the training data is less useful are made later in the process, where such decisions will have less influence on the final classification.

The *information gain* provided by a feature can be defined as the expected reduction in entropy when we branch on that feature. In the context of a decision tree, information gain can be computed as the entropy of the parent node minus the average weighted entropy of its child nodes. We can measure the information gain for each feature, and select features in a greedy manner based on this measure. In this way, features with the highest gain will be closest to the root. This is desirable, since we'll reduce the entropy as rapidly as possible, which would enable us to simplify the tree by trimming features that provide little or no gain.

To illustrate the concept of information gain, consider the training data in Table 7.2, where the 10 malware samples are denoted X_i and the 10 benign samples as Y_i. Also, $S(X)$ is the size of sample X (in, say, KB), $H(X)$ is the entropy of X (in bits), and $D(X)$ is the number of distinct opcodes.

If we construct a single decision tree from the data in Table 7.2, it would be reasonable to select 115 for the threshold between large and small file size; similarly, it would be reasonable to select 5.5 for the threshold between high and low entropy, and we could use 27.5 for the threshold between the number

Table 7.2: Training data

i	Malware			Benign		
	$S(X_i)$	$H(X_i)$	$D(X_i)$	$S(Y_i)$	$H(Y_i)$	$D(Y_i)$
1	120	7	32	120	4	22
2	120	7	28	130	5	23
3	100	6	34	140	5	26
4	130	5	33	100	5	21
5	100	6	35	110	6	20
6	100	5	27	140	7	20
7	100	6	32	140	3	28
8	120	6	33	100	4	21
9	100	8	32	100	4	24
10	110	6	34	120	7	25
Average	110	6	32	120	5	23

of distinct opcodes. Then when constructing a decision tree, we could use these values as the thresholds.

For example, based only on a file size threshold of 115, we would classify the elements of the training set

$$T_m = \{X_3, X_5, X_6, X_7, X_9, X_{10}, Y_4, Y_5, Y_8, Y_9\}$$

as malware, while the elements

$$T_b = \{X_1, X_2, X_4, X_8, Y_1, Y_2, Y_3, Y_6, Y_7, Y_{10}\}$$

would all be classified as benign. The entropy of this split is

$$H(T_m) = H(T_b) = -\frac{3}{5} \cdot \log_2\left(\frac{3}{5}\right) - \frac{2}{5} \cdot \log_2\left(\frac{2}{5}\right) = 0.9710.$$

Since we have an equal number of malware and benign samples, the root node has entropy of 1.0. Then, the information gain for the size feature S is given by

$$G_S = 1.0 - 0.9710 = 0.0290.$$

Similar calculations show that the gain for the entropy feature H is given by $G_H = 0.1952$, while for opcodes D the gain is $G_D = 0.5310$. Hence, we would want to use D as our first branch in a decision tree.

Among the advantages of decision trees are simplicity and clarity, where by clarity we mean that the tree itself is informative. As we have seen in previous chapters, this is not always the case for machine learning models.

Of course, there are also some disadvantages to decisions trees, chief of which is a tendency to overfit the training data. That is, the simple and intuitive nature of the tree structure captures the information in the training data too well, in the sense that it does not generalize. In machine learning, this is undesirable, as the training data is only a representative sample, and we want our models to capture the significant properties of this data.

One way to generalize a decision tree is to train multiple trees. We could select different (and overlapping) subsets of the training data and construct a tree for each subsct, then use a majority vote of the resulting trees to determine the classification. This is known as *bagging* the observations, and such a strategy is less likely to overfit since it tends to better generalize the training data.

In a random forest, the idea of bagging is taken one step further—in addition to bagging the observations, we also bag the features. That is, we construct multiple decision trees from selections (with replacement) of the training data, and also for various selections of the features (i.e., various subsets and orderings of the features). Then for classification, we combine the output from all of the resulting decision trees to obtain the final classification. For example, we could generate t decision trees, where t is odd, with each based on a different subset of features and data. Then we could use a simple majority vote of the resulting trees for classification.

As previously mentioned, a significant advantage of a random forest is that it's not prone to overfitting. However, random forests do lose some of the inherent simplicity and intuitiveness that make decision trees so appealing.

Suppose that we are given a sample U of unknown type that we want to classify as either malware or benign. Further, suppose that we want to classify based on the decision tree in Figure 7.5, while using the training data in Table 7.2 to set the thresholds for entropy and size. As discussed above, we'll use 5.5 as our threshold between high and low entropy, and 115 as the threshold between large and small file size. Suppose that we determine that $H(U) = 7$ and $S(U) = 116$. Then based on our decision tree, this sample U would be classified as benign. However, this classification might be considered suspect, since U is clearly in the malware range with respect to entropy, and it's just barely above the threshold with respect to size.

We now generalize our single decision tree to multiple (bagged) decision trees, again based on the data in Table 7.2. Suppose that we construct three decision trees, using the five-element subsets[6]

$$A = \{1, 2, 3, 5, 10\}, \ B = \{3, 5, 7, 9, 10\}, \text{ and } C = \{1, 2, 6, 8, 10\}. \quad (7.5)$$

The relevant training data for subset A is listed in Table 7.3.

---

[6]Of course, the malware and benign sets could be selected independently, but we'll keep the notation simple in this example.

Table 7.3: Subset A

i	Malware		Benign	
	$S(X_i)$	$H(X_i)$	$S(Y_i)$	$H(Y_i)$
1	120	7	120	4
2	120	7	130	5
3	100	6	140	5
5	100	6	110	6
10	110	6	120	7
Average	110	6.4	124	5.4

Based on Table 7.3, we would set the entropy threshold at 5.9 and the size threshold would be 117. With these thresholds applied to the decision tree in Figure 7.5, we would classify U as malware. It is also easy to show that for a decision tree based on the B subset, sample U would be classified as benign and for the C subset, U would again be classified as malware. Thus, a majority vote from these three decision trees classifies U as malware, whereas it was classified as benign by a single decision tree based on all of the training data. To extend this approach to a random forest, we would also use bagging at the level of classifiers, that is, we would select subsets (and orderings) of the available classifiers, as well as the data. This is further explored in the exercises at the end of this chapter.

Finally, we note that there is an interesting connection between k-NN, which is discussed in Section 7.2, and random forests. Suppose that we have a labeled training set (X_i, z_i), for $i = 1, 2, \ldots, n$, with each $z_i \in \{-1, +1\}$, and suppose that we are given a sample X to classify.

For k-NN, we can define the weight function

$$W_k(X_i, X) = \begin{cases} 1 & \text{if } X_i \text{ is one of the } k \text{ nearest neighbors to } X \\ 0 & \text{otherwise.} \end{cases}$$

We could then compute

$$\texttt{score}_k(X) = \sum_{i=1}^{n} z_i W_k(X_i, X)$$

and we would classify X as type $+1$ provided that $\texttt{score}_k(X) > 0$, and as type -1 if $\texttt{score}_k(X) < 0$.

Now, for the same training set, suppose that we use a decision tree instead. Then we can define

$$W_t(X_i, X) = \begin{cases} 1 & \text{if } X_i \text{ is on the same leaf node as } X \\ 0 & \text{otherwise.} \end{cases}$$

With this weight function, we compute

$$\texttt{score}_t(X) = \sum_{i=1}^{n} z_i \, W_t(X_i, X) \tag{7.6}$$

and the decision tree classifies X as type $+1$, provided that $\texttt{score}_t(X) > 0$, and of type -1 if $\texttt{score}_t(X) < 0$.

From this perspective, we see that k-NN and decision trees are both neighborhood-based classification algorithms, but with different neighborhood structures. Since a random forest is a collection of decision trees, a random forest is also a neighborhood-based classification technique, but with a relatively complex neighborhood structure. This topic is explored further in the problems at the end of the chapter.

For an intuitive and almost unbelievably easy to read (and understand) discussion of random forests, see [27]. For the basics on random forests, a good source is [20]. In addition, a gentle and practical introduction to the topic can be found in [86]. For an in-depth discussion of the connection between random forests and k-NN (and other similar algorithms), see [87].

7.6   Linear Discriminant Analysis

In linear discriminant analysis (LDA), we classify data points based on a separating hyperplane. Perhaps not surprisingly, quadratic discriminant analysis (QDA) can be viewed as separating the data using a quadratic surface, instead of the (linear) hyperplane of LDA. As a result, QDA can sometimes provide more accurate results, as illustrated in Figure 7.6. The tradeoff is that there are more parameters to estimate in QDA, which requires more work and more training data. In practice, LDA often works surprisingly well. In the remainder of this section, we'll only consider LDA, not QDA.

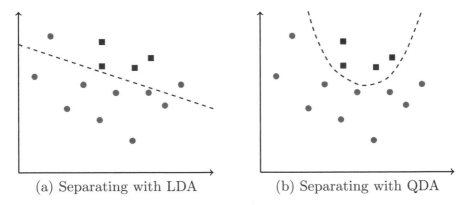

(a) Separating with LDA   (b) Separating with QDA

Figure 7.6: LDA vs QDA

We first discuss the LDA training process in some detail. Our presentation draws from a variety of sources, most notably Farag and Elhabian [50] and Welling [163]. We conclude this section with a detailed example, which should serve to illustrate the concepts.

LDA can be viewed as something of a hybrid between PCA and SVM. As with PCA, we can view LDA as a method to reduce the dimensionality of the training data. The LDA training process relies on a covariance-like matrix, which is an obvious similarity to PCA, as discussed in Chapter 4. However, in contrast to PCA (but similar to SVM), with LDA we directly discriminate between two (or more) classes of data. And, as mentioned above, we can view LDA as constructing a separating hyperplane, which sounds eerily similar to a linear SVM.

In fact, we'll derive the LDA training process based on Lagrange multipliers (as with SVM) and eigenvector analysis (as with PCA). However, in LDA there is nothing comparable to the kernel trick, which plays a prominent role in SVM. Instead, LDA relies on a fairly direct and relatively simple means of projecting the training data onto a hyperplane.

Recall that in PCA, we train on a set of n vectors, where each vector contains m components, that is, we have n column vectors, where each vector is of length m. We then subtract the mean for each data type and construct the covariance matrix C. The eigenvalues and eigenvectors of C generally yield a more informative basis, which enables us to reduce the dimensionality by, in effect, reducing noise in the data. Then the PCA score for a given vector is obtained by projecting the vector onto this new basis and comparing the result (within the eigenspace) to vectors in the training set.[7]

In LDA, we'll see that the setup is somewhat similar to PCA, that is, we have column vectors of training samples, we subtract the means, we form a covariance-like matrix, and so on. However, in contrast to PCA, with LDA we have labeled training data, which implies that there are (at least) two distinct classes of vectors. The goal in LDA is to project these vectors onto a hyperplane, where the within-class separation is small, but the between-class separation is large, as measured in the projection space.[8] To measure the between-class separation, we'll rely on the sample means, and to measure the within-class separation, we'll rely on the sample *scatter*, which is related to the variances. Of course, we don't get to choose the means or the scatter, since they're determined from the training data. But, we do get to choose the hyperplane, which gives us some control over the means and scatter within the projection space.

---

[7]If any of this paragraph is terra incognita, it would be a good time to review Chapter 4.

[8]Based on this description, your easily tempted author is sorely tempted to discuss connections between LDA and clustering. He would then, no doubt, relate clustering concepts (specifically, cohesion and separation) to within-class and between-class separation in LDA. However, your foreshadowing author will avoid this temptation, at least for now.

For this discussion, we'll assume that there are only two classes. Specifically, our training set consists of the two classes

$$X_1, X_2, \ldots, X_m \text{ and } Y_1, Y_2, \ldots, Y_n \tag{7.7}$$

where each X_i and Y_j is a vector of ℓ real numbers. LDA generalizes fairly easily to more than two classes.

To illustrate the LDA projection process, consider the examples that appear in Figures 7.7 (a) and (b). In Figure 7.7 (a), we have projected the two classes (circles and squares) onto a hyperplane where the classes are not well-separated. In contrast, the projected data in Figure 7.7 (b) is better separated. In LDA, we want to project the training data onto the hyperplane that "best" separates the training sets, as determined by a measure that incorporates both between-class separation (which, ideally, should be large) and the within-class spread (which, ideally, should be small).

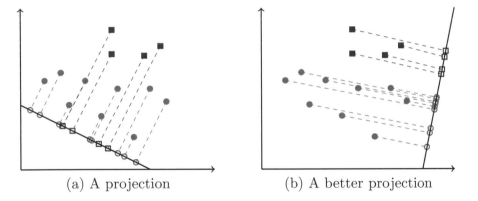

(a) A projection   (b) A better projection

Figure 7.7: Projecting onto hyperplanes

At first blush, it might seem better to determine the LDA projection based solely on maximizing the separation between the projected means. While such an approach would be simple to implement, the examples in Figure 7.8 show that this can yield poor results. The projection onto the x-axis in Figure 7.8 (a) better separates the means, yet the projection in Figure 7.8 (b) yields better separation between the classes. This example shows that it is not sufficient to maximize the separation between the means—we'll also need to account for the (projected) within-class scatter.

In our discussion of cluster quality in Section 6.4 of Chapter 6, we considered cohesion (i.e., compactness of clusters) and separation (i.e., spacing between clusters). Using only the means when determining an LDA-like projecting hyperplane would be somewhat analogous to attempting to cluster based only on the separation between clusters, while ignoring the cohesiveness of the resulting clusters. In contrast, K-means clustering is based only on the cohesiveness of the clusters, and does not (directly) account for separation

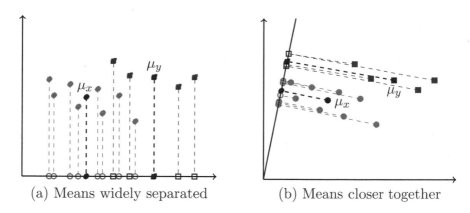

(a) Means widely separated   (b) Means closer together

Figure 7.8: Projecting the means

between clusters. Of course, clustering is an unsupervised technique, whereas LDA uses labeled data, so we can't take these analogies too far—although it's tempting to try.

The crucial question is: How should we account for both the between-class separation (based on the means) and the within-class cohesion (based on the scatter) when determining the LDA hyperplane? The technique used in LDA is fairly straightforward, but before we can describe the process, we need some additional notation.

Assume that we have two classes of data, as specified in equation (7.7). We'll project the data—both the X and the Y classes—onto a hyperplane. As in the discussion of PCA in Chapter 4, we represent the projection of the vector X as

$$w \cdot X = w^T X, \text{ where } X = \begin{pmatrix} x_1 \\ x_2 \\ \vdots \\ x_\ell \end{pmatrix} \text{ and } w = \begin{pmatrix} w_1 \\ w_2 \\ \vdots \\ w_\ell \end{pmatrix}$$

for some coefficient vector w. Note that X is a given training vector, while the projection w is to be determined (see Problem 10 at the end of this chapter for more details on this projection).

For the classes in equation (7.7), the sample means are given by

$$\mu_x = \frac{1}{m} \sum_{i=1}^{m} X_i \text{ and } \mu_y = \frac{1}{n} \sum_{i=1}^{n} Y_i.$$

The means μ_x and μ_y are both vectors of length ℓ, where each component is simply the mean in that particular dimension. Then the scatter within each class is computed as

$$s_x^2 = \sum_{i=1}^{m}(X_i - \mu_x)^T(X_i - \mu_x) \text{ and } s_y^2 = \sum_{i=1}^{n}(Y_i - \mu_y)^T(Y_i - \mu_y).$$

Whereas the means are vectors, the scatter is a scalar.

In the projection space determined by the vector w, the mean for the X dataset is

$$\widehat{\mu}_x = \frac{1}{m}\sum_{i=1}^{m}w^TX_i = w^T\frac{1}{m}\sum_{i=1}^{m}X_i = w^T\mu_x$$

and a similar calculation yields the projected mean for the Y dataset which, not surprisingly, we denote as $\widehat{\mu}_y$.

The scatter for the projected X dataset is given by

$$\widehat{s}_x^2 = \sum_{i=1}^{m}(w^TX_i - \widehat{\mu}_x)^2 = \sum_{i=1}^{m}(w^T(X_i - \mu_x))^2$$

and a similar calculation gives us the scatter for the projected Y dataset, which we denote as $\widehat{s}_y^2$. Note that in the projection space, both the mean and the scatter are scalars.

If our only concern was the distance between the respective means in the projection space, then the w that we want is $\text{argmax}\, M(w)$ where[9]

$$M(w) = (\widehat{\mu}_x - \widehat{\mu}_y)^2 = (w^T(\mu_x - \mu_y))^2.$$

However, Figure 7.8 shows that maximizing the separation between the means is not enough—we also need to account for the scatter within each class.

Alternatively, suppose that we are only concerned with minimizing the sum of the within-class scatter. Then the desired weight vector w is given by $\text{argmin}\, C(w)$, where

$$C(w) = \widehat{s}_x^2 + \widehat{s}_y^2.$$

Since $\text{argmin}\, C(w) = \text{argmax}(1/C(w))$, we could instead solve for this w via the maximization of $1/C(w)$.

In case that $\text{argmax}\, M(w) = \text{argmin}\, C(w)$, the resulting w would solve the LDA training problem. However, in general this will not be the case, so we need to determine a tradeoff between these two extreme solutions. To keep things simple, in LDA, we deal with the function

$$J(w) = \frac{M(w)}{C(w)} = \frac{(\widehat{\mu}_x - \widehat{\mu}_y)^2}{\widehat{s}_x^2 + \widehat{s}_y^2}, \tag{7.8}$$

---

[9]Defining $M(w)$ to be the squared distance between the means makes the math easier.

which is simply the product of $M(w)$ and $1/C(w)$. Then $\operatorname{argmax} J(w)$ will be our desired solution.

The function $J(w)$ is known as the *Fisher discriminant*. While there are many possible ways to maximize the function $J(w)$, below we'll outline an approach that serves to highlight the similarities between LDA and PCA, and, to a lesser extent, SVM.

Maximizing $J(w)$ in (7.8) requires balancing a large distance between the (projected) means and a small scatter within each class. Figure 7.8 (a) gives an example that would yield a relatively large value for $M(w)$, but would not fare so well with respect to $J(w)$, since $C(w)$ is fairly large. In contrast, Figure 7.8 (b) would not do as well with respect to $M(w)$, but it will yield a larger value for $J(w)$, due to the smaller scatter within both of the classes, which gives a smaller value for $C(w)$.

As an aside, we note that the function $J(w)$ is somewhat reminiscent of the silhouette coefficient from clustering, which is discussed in Section 6.4 of Chapter 6. Recall that the silhouette coefficient is a single number that accounts for both the between-cluster spacing and the within-cluster compactness.

Now let's consider equation (7.8) in more detail. Expanding, we have

$$J(w) = \frac{\left(w^T(\mu_x - \mu_y)\right)^2}{\sum_{i=1}^{m}\left(w^T(X_i - \mu_x)\right)^2 + \sum_{i=1}^{n}\left(w^T(Y_i - \mu_y)\right)^2}.$$

Define the *within-class scatter* matrices as

$$S_x = \sum_{i=1}^{m}(X_i - \mu_x)(X_i - \mu_x)^T \text{ and } S_y = \sum_{i=1}^{n}(Y_i - \mu_y)(Y_i - \mu_y)^T.$$

Then S_x and S_y are essentially the covariance matrices for the X and Y classes, respectively.[10] The total *within-class scatter* is defined as

$$S_W = S_x + S_y.$$

We also define the *between-class scatter* matrix as

$$S_B = (\mu_x - \mu_y)(\mu_x - \mu_y)^T.$$

The scatter matrices S_x, S_y, S_W, and S_B are all defined in ℓ-dimensional input space, not in the projection space. Of course, all of these matrices have analogs in the projection space. For example, if we define

$$\widehat{S}_B = (\widehat{\mu}_x - \widehat{\mu}_y)^2$$

---

[10]In fact, the only difference between these scatter matrices and covariance matrices is a normalizing factor that appears in the covariance matrix; see Section 4.2.3 of Chapter 4 for more information on covariance matrices.

then it is a straightforward exercise to show that

$$\widehat{S}_B = w^T S_B w. \tag{7.9}$$

Similarly, we define

$$\widehat{S}_W = \widehat{s}_x^2 + \widehat{s}_y^2$$

and it is easily verified that

$$\widehat{S}_W = w^T S_W w. \tag{7.10}$$

Using the results in the previous paragraph, we can rewrite equation (7.8) in terms of scatter matrices as

$$J(w) = \frac{(\widehat{\mu}_x - \widehat{\mu}_y)^2}{\widehat{s}_x^2 + \widehat{s}_y^2} = \frac{w^T S_B w}{w^T S_W w}.$$

In this form, it's easy to see that if a vector w maximizes $J(w)$, then all scalar multiples $\alpha\, w$ will also maximize $J(w)$. Hence, we can restrict our choice of w so that $w^T S_W w = 1$. Then the problem can be restated as

$$\begin{aligned} &\text{Maximize: } J(w) = w^T S_B w \\ &\text{Subject to: } w^T S_W w = 1. \end{aligned} \tag{7.11}$$

Note that in this form, LDA looks similar to the generic constrained optimization problem in equation (5.1) of Chapter 5. In fact, this problem can also be solved using Lagrange multipliers. Specifically, the Lagrangian in this case can be written as

$$L(w, \lambda) = w^T S_B w + \lambda\big(w^T S_W w - 1\big).$$

This formulation of the problem certainly evokes SVM, which we discussed in Chapter 5.

We're not done evoking just yet. It's easy to see that the constrained optimization problem

$$\begin{aligned} &\text{Minimize: } J(w) = -\frac{1}{2} w^T S_B w \\ &\text{Subject to: } \frac{1}{2} w^T S_W w = 1 \end{aligned}$$

is equivalent to that in (7.11). In this form, the Lagrangian is

$$L(w, \lambda) = -\frac{1}{2} w^T S_B w + \frac{1}{2} \lambda\big(w^T S_W w - 1\big). \tag{7.12}$$

We now use elementary calculus to maximize the Lagrangian in (7.12) with respect to w. That is, we compute the derivative with respect to w and set the resulting equation equal to zero. Doing so, we obtain

$$-2 \cdot \frac{1}{2} \cdot S_B w + \lambda \cdot 2 \cdot \frac{1}{2} \cdot S_W w = -S_B w + \lambda S_W w = 0,$$

which gives us the intriguing equation

$$S_B w = \lambda S_W w. \qquad (7.13)$$

Assuming that S_W^{-1} exists, we can rewrite this equation as

$$S w = \lambda w \qquad (7.14)$$

where $S = S_W^{-1} S_B$. In this form, it's clear that a solution w is an eigenvector[11] of S. This form of the solution shows that there is certainly a close connection between LDA and PCA.

Before we leave this topic, let's rewrite the Lagrangian in (7.12) in its dual form. For the dual problem, we obtain the equation

$$L(\lambda) = c_1 + c_2 \lambda \qquad (7.15)$$

where c_1 and c_2 are constants, with $c_2 > 0$. Since the primal problem was a minimization, the dual is a maximization (see Section 5.2.1 of Chapter 5). Furthermore, we've already shown that λ must be an eigenvalue. Therefore, the Lagrangian in (7.15) is maximized when we choose λ as the largest eigenvalue of S. This is just about as strong an evocation of PCA as we could possibly expect in the case of labeled data.[12]

It is interesting to note that while PCA is focused on the variance, LDA separates the datasets based primarily on the means. Therefore, training data with similar means will be hard to classify using LDA, even in cases where the variances are highly distinguishing. This is in contrast to PCA, where the largest variances correspond to the most significant eigenvectors. Of course, the underlying problems are different—in PCA we construct a score that models the data, whereas in LDA we determine a classifier that distinguishes between labeled datasets.

To illustrate the LDA technique, we now consider a simple numerical example in some detail. Suppose that we are given the training data in Table 7.4. First, we need to compute the input space mean vectors μ_x and μ_y.

---

[11] In its original form in equation (7.13), this is a generalized eigenvalue problem. But for the purpose of evoking, the form in equation (7.14) can't be beat.

[12] Perhaps your overly qualified author should qualify this statement slightly. It would be more precise to say that LDA is most closely related to the special case of PCA where we only retain the most significant eigenvector.

Table 7.4: LDA example data

i	X_i	Y_i
1	(1.25,3.00)	(2.75,3.50)
2	(1.50,2.00)	(3.25,3.00)
3	(2.00,2.75)	(4.50,2.75)
4	(2.25,2.00)	(3.50,4.75)
5	(2.00,0.50)	—
6	(3.25,0.75)	—
7	(3.50,2.25)	—
8	(4.25,0.75)	—

For the training data in Table 7.4, we have

$$\mu_x = \frac{1}{8}\sum_{i=1}^{8} X_i^T = \left(\begin{array}{c} 2.50 \\ 1.75 \end{array}\right) \text{ and } \mu_y = \frac{1}{4}\sum_{i=1}^{4} Y_i^T = \left(\begin{array}{c} 3.50 \\ 3.50 \end{array}\right).$$

Next, we compute the within-class scatter matrices

$$S_x = \sum_{i=1}^{8}(X_i - \mu_x)(X_i - \mu_x)^T = \left(\begin{array}{cc} 7.7500 & -3.7500 \\ -3.7500 & 6.5000 \end{array}\right)$$

and

$$S_y = \sum_{i=1}^{4}(Y_i - \mu_y)(Y_i - \mu_y)^T = \left(\begin{array}{cc} 1.6250 & -0.6250 \\ -0.6250 & 2.3750 \end{array}\right).$$

This gives us the overall within-class scatter matrix

$$S_W = S_x + S_y = \left(\begin{array}{cc} 9.3750 & -4.3750 \\ -4.3750 & 8.8750 \end{array}\right).$$

Also, since

$$\mu_x - \mu_y = \left(\begin{array}{c} -1.00 \\ -1.75 \end{array}\right),$$

the between class scatter matrix is

$$S_B = (\mu_x - \mu_y)(\mu_x - \mu_y)^T = \left(\begin{array}{cc} 1.0000 & 1.7500 \\ 1.7500 & 3.0625 \end{array}\right).$$

It is easily verified that the inverse of S_W is given by

$$S_W^{-1} = \left(\begin{array}{cc} 0.1385 & 0.0683 \\ 0.0683 & 0.1463 \end{array}\right)$$

and it follows that

$$S = S_W^{-1} S_B = \begin{pmatrix} 0.2580 & 0.4515 \\ 0.3243 & 0.5676 \end{pmatrix}.$$

From equation (7.14), we see that the desired solution must be an eigenvector of S. Solving for the eigenvectors, we find

$$w_1 = \begin{pmatrix} -0.6225 \\ -0.7826 \end{pmatrix} \text{ and } w_2 = \begin{pmatrix} -0.8683 \\ 0.4961 \end{pmatrix}$$

with corresponding eigenvalues $\lambda_1 = 0.8256$ and $\lambda_2 = 0.00002$. Note that w_1 has a slope of

$$m_1 = 0.7826/0.6225 = 1.2572$$

while the slope of w_2 is

$$m_2 = -0.4961/0.8683 = -0.5713.$$

In Figures 7.9 (a) and (b), we have projected the data from Table 7.4 onto the hyperplanes determined by w_1 and w_2, respectively. Since w_1 corresponds to the largest eigenvalue, we expect better results in Figure 7.9 (a), and this is indeed the case. In fact, for this particular example, we have ideal separation when using w_1, while w_2 produces poor results.

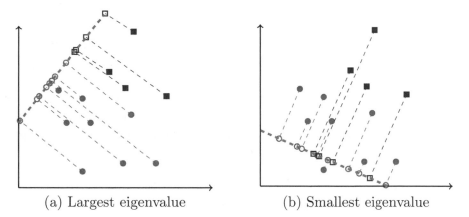

(a) Largest eigenvalue   (b) Smallest eigenvalue

Figure 7.9: Projections of data in Table 7.4

It's not difficult to generalize LDA to the case where there are more than two classes. Supposing that we have c classes, then the vector w in our discussion above is replaced by a matrix with $c - 1$ columns. Each column determines a hyperplane and these hyperplanes are used to partition the projection space.

For additional details on the generalization of LDA to more than two classes—and for additional insights into many other topics discussed in this section—see Farag and Elhabian [50]. There are several other good sources for LDA, including Welling [163], as well as [13] and [116].

7.7   Vector Quantization

Vector quantization (VQ), is a form of clustering where we have a so-called *codebook* of vectors,[13] each of which is viewed as a prototype for a collection of other vectors. A codebook vector can be viewed as an approximation of all of its associated vectors.

Rounding to the nearest integer is a particularly simple, one-dimensional example of VQ, where the integers serve as the codebook, with non-integers approximated by the nearest (in the rounding sense) integer. Rounding as VQ is illustrated in Figure 7.10, where, for example, the integer 1 is an element of the codebook, and its associated "vectors" consist of all numbers in the interval from 0.5 to 1.5 (including 0.5, but not 1.5, since we're assuming that we round up, as usual).

Figure 7.10: Rounding as VQ

From a clustering perspective, the prototype vectors in VQ can be viewed as centroids, with the set of vectors associated with a particular codebook prototype representing a cluster. While there are many approaches to VQ clustering, here we describe one simple and popular technique, namely, the Linde-Buzo-Gray (LBG) algorithm.

In the LBG algorithm, we are given a set of real-valued training vectors X_i, for $i = 1, 2, \ldots, n$, and the desired number of prototype vectors K is specified. We also specify a (small) value ε, which serves to determine the stopping criteria. Then the algorithm proceeds as follows.

1. Select distinct initial codebook vectors c_i, for $i = 1, 2, \ldots, K$, from among the training vectors X_i.

2. Initialize the *distortion* as $D_0 = 0$, and let $k = 0$. Also, denote cluster i as C_i, for $i = 1, 2, \ldots, K$, where c_i is assigned to cluster C_i.

3. Assign each of the n training vectors X_i to clusters as follows: The vector X_i is assigned to cluster C_j provided that $d(X_i, c_j) \leq d(X_i, c_\ell)$ for all $\ell \neq j$. That is, we assign vectors to clusters based on the nearest codebook vector.

4. Update each codebook vector by letting c_i be the average of the vectors

---

[13]These VQ codebook vectors are not to be confused with a codebook cipher [137].

in C_i. That is,

$$c_i = \frac{1}{|C_i|} \sum_{X_j \in C_i} X_j$$

where $|C_i|$ is the number of vectors in cluster C_i.

5. Compute the distortion

$$D_{k+1} = \sum_{i=1}^{K} \sum_{X_j \in C_i} d(c_i, X_j).$$

6. If $(D_{k+1} - D_k)/D_k > \varepsilon$, let $k = k + 1$ and goto step 3.

7. Output the codebook consisting of c_i, for $i = 1, 2, \ldots, K$, and the corresponding clusters C_i, for $i = 1, 2, \ldots, K$.

In practice, we would probably also want to test for a maximum number of iterations in step 6.

The LBG algorithm as just described is essentially the same as the well-known K-means clustering algorithm, which is discussed in Section 6.3 of Chapter 6. However, VQ is somewhat more general than K-means, since other measures of distortion can be used. That is, we can view K-means as a special case of VQ.

For a thorough introduction to VQ, see [56]. Also, the online tutorial [154] has an excellent two-dimensional animation illustrating the VQ process.

7.8   Naïve Bayes

Why is naïve Bayes naïve? And, for that matter, why is it Bayes? In naïve Bayes, we naïvely make a strong independence assumption. In many real-world applications, such an assumption is unlikely to be valid, but by assuming independence, the problem is greatly simplified. And we often obtain very good results in practice.

How much does this "naïve" assumption of independence simplify the problem? Suppose that we are given a set of n vectors $X_1, X_2, \ldots, X_n$, where each vector contains m elements. Furthermore, assume that across the n vectors, the mean in each component is 0. Then the independence assumption of naïve Bayes implies that all covariances are 0, that is, for $i \neq j$, $\mathrm{cov}(X_i, X_j) = 0$ (see Section 4.2.3 of Chapter 4 for a discussion of covariance and the covariance matrix). If these covariances are all 0, it follows that the covariance matrix is diagonal, in which case, the $n \times n$ covariance matrix has only n parameters, consisting of the variances. In contrast, the full $n \times n$ covariance matrix has n^2 parameters, which includes all covariances. The upshot is that this independence assumption implies that we only need to consider means and variances, not covariances.

Naïve Bayes is Bayes because it relies on Bayes' formula, which states

$$P(A \mid B) = \frac{P(B \mid A)P(A)}{P(B)}.$$

We can further break down the denominator to obtain

$$P(A \mid B) = \frac{P(B \mid A)P(A)}{P(B \mid A)P(A) + P(B \mid \neg A)P(\neg A)}$$

where $\neg A$ is the complement of A. In its most general form, we have

$$P(A_i \mid B) = \frac{P(B \mid A_i)P(A_i)}{\sum_j P(B \mid A_j)P(A_j)}$$

where the sets A_j partition the sample space.

As an application of Bayes' formula, consider a test for an illegal drug. Suppose that when we test someone who uses the drug, the test is positive 98% of the time, that is, the true positive rate is 0.98. Also, suppose that if we test someone who does not use the drug, the result will be negative 99% of the time, i.e., the true negative rate is 0.99. Finally, assume that in the tested population, about 5 out of every 1000 people actually use this illegal drug. Define the events

$$A = \{\text{a person uses the illegal drug}\}$$

and

$$B = \{\text{a person tests positive for the illegal drug}\}.$$

Then by Bayes' formula,

$$\begin{aligned}
P(A \mid B) &= \frac{P(B \mid A)P(A)}{P(B \mid A)P(A) + P(B \mid \neg A)P(\neg A)} \\
&= \frac{0.98 \cdot 0.005}{0.98 \cdot 0.005 + 0.01 \cdot 0.995} \approx 0.33.
\end{aligned}$$

This calculation shows that under the given scenario, there is only about a one in three chance that someone who tests positive actually uses the illegal drug. For our purposes, the crucial observation here is that directly computing $P(A \mid B)$ is difficult, but computing $P(B \mid A)$ is easy and, via Bayes' formula, we can determine $P(A \mid B)$ from $P(B \mid A)$.

Why is any of this relevant? Suppose that we want to determine the "best" state vector X based on an observation $\mathcal{O}$. Then we want to determine the X

that maximizes $P(X \mid \mathcal{O})$, over the possible choices of X. Under the naïve Bayes assumption, we have

$$P(X \mid \mathcal{O}) = \frac{P(\mathcal{O} \mid X)P(X)}{P(\mathcal{O})}$$

where X is a state. In general, it is difficult to compute $P(X \mid \mathcal{O})$ directly, but, as the example above illustrates, it may be easy to compute $P(\mathcal{O} \mid X)$, and $P(X)$ is generally also an easy calculation. Consequently, we can find the optimal X by computing $P(\mathcal{O} \mid X)P(X)$ for each X, and then select the X that gives us the biggest result. Note that in this scenario, there is no need to compute $P(\mathcal{O})$, since it's constant for any choice of X.

In Section 7.10, we'll show that there is a connection between the forward algorithm for HMMs and naïve Bayes. But first, we take a brief look at regression analysis.

7.9   Regression Analysis

In machine learning, *regression* is often contrasted with classification. In a classification problem, we classify samples into two or more categories. However, in regression, we don't regress.[14] Instead, regression can be viewed as providing a score (or probability) rather than a direct classification. The HMM process could be viewed as a form of regression, since an HMM generates a score, in contrast to, say, an SVM, which directly provides a classification. More generally, regression analysis can be viewed as a method for reasoning about the relationship between two or more things.

In this section, we first consider linear regression, which is simple and often highly effective. Then we turn our attention to logistic regression, which is more useful for certain types of problems.

Suppose that we obtain data on recent house sales in some particular location, and we plot the house size (x-axis) versus the selling price (y-axis), obtaining the scatterplot in Figure 7.11 (a). As expected, the data shows that larger houses tend to cost more than smaller houses.[15] While this might be a useful insight, it would be better if we could quantify the relationship between house price and size, which appears to be roughly linear.

In *linear regression*, we determine a linear model that best fits the given data, in the sense that the model minimizes the sum of the squared error terms. This problem can be efficiently solved using the linear least squares algorithm [98].

In Figure 7.11 (b) we include the regression line for the housing data in Figure 7.11 (a). This regression line could be used, for example, as an aid in

---

[14] And we don't digress either.
[15] Except in California, where all houses cost more.

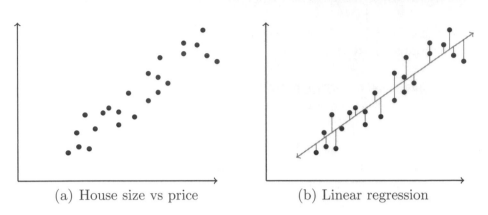

(a) House size vs price   (b) Linear regression

Figure 7.11: Regression line

setting the sale price for a house, or the line could be used to determine how a recent sale compared to the typical price for a house of its size. In effect, this regression line has reduced 2-dimensional data to a single dimension.

In a binary classification problem, there are only two possible outcomes. For example, we might classify software samples as either malware or benign. While linear regression is a simple and intuitive method, it is not ideal for binary classification problems, since there are only two outcomes (say, 0 and 1), with no cases in between. An example of such data appears in Figure 7.12 (a), along with the regression line.

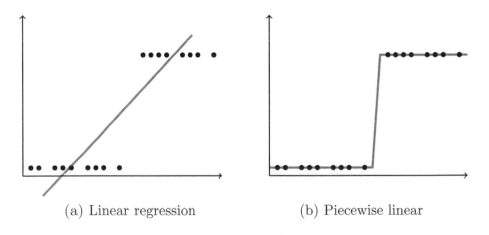

(a) Linear regression   (b) Piecewise linear

Figure 7.12: Regression examples

The regression line in Figure 7.12 (a) is not particularly useful. The problem is that the data is bunched up around 0 and 1, while the line is uniformly spaced between 0 and 1. A better solution might be obtained if we change the regression line to some other function. Intuitively, we want a function that doesn't waste too much "effort" in the area between 0 and 1, since nothing interesting is happening there. A possible solution is the piecewise linear function illustrated in Figure 7.12 (b). However, this function is not smooth, which is sure to complicate the mathematics.

The *logistic function* is defined as

$$F(t) = \frac{1}{1 + e^{-t}}.$$

The graph of this function appears in Figure 7.13. Note that the logistic function is defined for all t, and $0 < F(t) < 1$. Also, the logistic function is smooth and could serve as a reasonable approximation to the piecewise linear function in Figure 7.12 (b). Furthermore, since the range of this function is between 0 and 1, we can interpret $F(t)$ in terms of probabilities, which opens the door to the use of various statistical techniques.

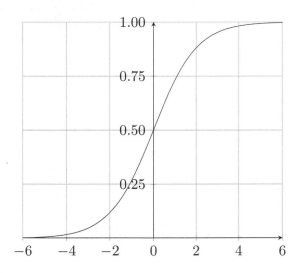

Figure 7.13: Logistic function

In *logistic regression* [124], we use the logistic function $F(t)$ to model our data, where t is a linear function in the data. For example, if each point X is a single numeric value, then $t = b_0 + b_1 X$ and we can write the logistic function as

$$F(X) = \frac{1}{1 + e^{-(b_0 + b_1 X)}}$$

where the parameters b_0 and b_1 are to be determined so that the function fits the data. In general, we have $X = (\begin{array}{cccc} x_1 & x_2 & \ldots & x_m \end{array})$ with each x_i being a numeric value. In this more general case, let $t = b_0 + b_1 x_1 + \cdots + b_m x_m$, and we have

$$F(X) = \frac{1}{1 + e^{-(b_0 + b_1 x_1 + \cdots + b_m x_m)}}. \tag{7.16}$$

As mentioned above, for linear regression, we can use the linear least squares algorithm to solve for the parameters of the regression line. The analogous process in logistic regression is significantly more complex. We won't go into much detail here, but the basic idea is to use a maximum likelihood estimation.

For any X, we can interpret the logistic function $F(X)$ as the probability p that X belongs to the class associated with "1" in the underlying binary classification problem. Then $1 - p = 1 - F(X)$ is the probability that X belongs to the class associated with "0." Thus, the parameters of the logistic function can be derived from a maximum likelihood estimator[16] based on the probability function defined by the logistic function $F(X)$. This maximum likelihood problem—which must be solved by a numerical approximation technique such as Newton's method—gives us the desired parameters of the logistic function, namely, $(b_0, b_1, \ldots, b_m)$.

Again, the "training" phase in logistic regression is considerably more complex than that used in linear regression. It is also interesting to compare logistic regression to naïve Bayes. In naïve Bayes, we make an independence assumption, which makes the resulting (simplified) problem relatively easy to solve. In contrast, for logistic regression we directly model the relevant parameters with no simplifying assumption. As a result, the underlying logistic regression problem remains difficult, but we work around this difficulty to some extent by using approximation techniques. Thus, from a high level perspective, we might say that logistic regression provides an approximate solution to an exact problem, whereas naïve Bayes gives us an exact solution to an approximate problem.

7.10   Conditional Random Fields

In this section, we assume that the reader is familiar with the discussion of hidden Markov models in Chapter 2. Here, we'll view a conditional random field (CRF) as a generalization of an HMM.

The graph structure of an HMM is illustrated in Figure 7.14. This graph structure highlights the fact that the current observation depends only on the current state, and the current state only depends on the previous state.

By viewing an HMM from the graph perspective in Figure 7.14, it's clear that a wide variety of other graph structures could be considered. However, the further we stray from the standard HMM graph structure, the more difficult it may be to find efficient algorithms. And, of course, efficiency is a crucial feature that makes HMMs so useful in practice. With this in mind, we'll want to begin by considering relatively minor modifications.

---

[16]The likelihood function and other topics related to maximum likelihood estimation are discussed in some detail in Section 6.5.1 of Chapter 6.

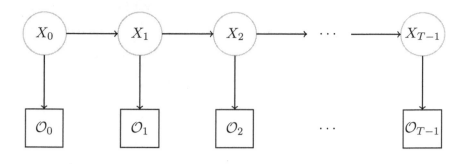

Figure 7.14: Graph structure of HMM

To motivate CRFs, suppose that we want to model the behavior of an airplane pilot. The observations could include the speed of the airplane, its altitude, and other physical measurements. We could model the pilot's behavior as the hidden state. Using an HMM, each hidden state can only depend on the previous hidden state. Such a model could reveal some useful information about the pilot's behavior, but it's virtually certain that the current observation also affect the pilot's behavior. By allowing the hidden state to depend on the current observation, we could take advantage of this information and we might thereby hope to create a significantly stronger model. Below, we'll consider this and various other generalizations of HMMs.

7.10.1   Linear Chain CRF

The simplest case of a CRF is a *linear chain CRF*, where we replace the linear directed graph structure of an HMM with an undirected graph. The graph structure of a linear chain CRF is illustrated in Figure 7.15. A linear chain CRF includes all of the features of an HMM, and also allows for additional interactions between states and observations. For example, in a linear chain CRF, the observation $\mathcal{O}_i$ can influence the state X_i, which is not allowed in a standard HMM. This could be far more realistic in some problems, such as when modeling the actions of an airplane pilot, as discussed above.

More general CRFs can include other dependencies between states and observations. However, linear chain CRFs are the most commonly used in practice, since the algorithms are more tractable than in more general cases.

Our goal in this section is to briefly consider some of the connections between HMMs and CRFs.[17] In this discussion, we assume that the reader is familiar with naïve Bayes and logistic regression—if not, now would be a good time to review Sections 7.8 and 7.9.

---

[17]We'll see that from a high-level perspective, HMMs and CRFs can be significantly different. However, the results obtained in practice might not differ by much; for such an example, see [110].

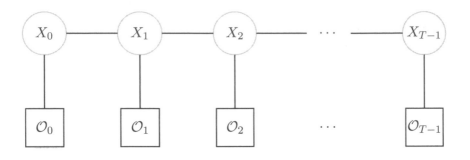

Figure 7.15: Linear chain CRF

First, let's consider the big picture. Ideally, we want to know $P(X, \mathcal{O})$, that is, we want to model the joint probability distribution of the (hidden) states X and the observations $\mathcal{O}$. This distribution contains information on all possible interactions between states and observations. In other words, $P(X, \mathcal{O})$ provides as complete a picture as it is possible to obtain. The bad news is that $P(X, \mathcal{O})$ involves a vast number of parameters, making the training problem intractable for almost any realistic scenario. The good news is that much of the information contained in the joint distribution of $P(X, \mathcal{O})$ is likely irrelevant for most applications. For example, we probably don't care about arbitrary interactions between observations, and hence there is no need to waste our time and effort trying to model such interactions.

A time-honored strategy for making a difficult problem tractable is to simplify. While there are many possible ways to simplify $P(X, \mathcal{O})$, we'll consider two general approaches—one motivated by naïve Bayes and another motivated by regression-like analysis. In both of these approaches, we'll focus on conditional probabilities of the form $P(X \mid \mathcal{O})$. This conditional probability approach is simpler and it makes sense whether training or scoring, since the observation sequence is known.

7.10.2   Generative vs Discriminative Models

Again, ideally, we might like to model $P(X, \mathcal{O})$, where $\mathcal{O}$ is an observation sequence and X is a state sequence. But, $P(X, \mathcal{O})$ is too complex, with too many parameters, so instead we model $P(X \mid \mathcal{O})$. This latter problem is feasible, and we often obtain good results in practice.

One general approach to modeling $P(X \mid \mathcal{O})$ is to consider further simplification of the problem. Under the naïve Bayes (independence) assumption, we can model $P(X \mid \mathcal{O})$ as $P(\mathcal{O} \mid X)P(X)$, which does indeed simplify the problem, while retaining the most significant aspects of the probability distribution. An alternative approach is to approximate $P(X \mid \mathcal{O})$, which is analogous to the approach used in logistic regression.

Models that use $P(\mathcal{O}\,|\,X)P(X)$ in place of $P(X\,|\,\mathcal{O})$ (as in naïve Bayes) are said to be *generative models*, while those that attempt to directly model (via approximation) the parameters of $P(X\,|\,\mathcal{O})$ (as in logistic regression) are known as *discriminative models*. Consequently, we can view naïve Bayes and logistic regression as a *generative-discriminative pair*.

As with anything in life, there are tradeoffs between generative and discriminative models.[18] In the discriminative case, since we model $P(X\,|\,\mathcal{O})$ directly, no effort is "wasted" on modeling $P(\mathcal{O})$, which is often not of interest. That is, we don't usually care about how the observations relate to each other—we want to know how the observations relate to the states and (possibly) how the states relate to each other. From this perspective, the discriminative case is focused on the things that matter most. However, for the generative case, we have very efficient algorithms, which might swing the pendulum in favor of a generative approach. That is, discriminative models might have the upper hand in theory, but in practice, generative models may have some advantages.

Recall that in HMM Problem 2, we uncover the best hidden state sequence X, where "best" is defined as maximizing the expected number of correct states. A quick review of Section 2.5 in Chapter 2 shows that when solving HMM Problem 2, we use the forward algorithm (or α-pass). In equation (2.9), which is the basis for the derivation of the forward algorithm, we substitute $P(\mathcal{O}\,|\,X,\lambda)P(X\,|\,\lambda)$ for $P(X,\mathcal{O}\,|\,\lambda)$. where $\lambda = (A,B,\pi)$ is the model. Ignoring the dependence on the model λ, this follows from the same independence assumption that we make in naïve Bayes. In this sense, HMMs are intimately related to naïve Bayes. In fact, we can view HMM Problem 2 as the sequential version of naïve Bayes.

We also claim that there is a similar connection between logistic regression and (linear chain) CRFs. However, to see this connection requires digging into the CRF algorithms. We won't go into that level of detail here, since doing so would take us too far afield—the interested reader can consult [140]. Instead, we simply note that in a linear chain CRF, the conditional probabilities can be computed from an expression of the form

$$P(X\,|\,\mathcal{O}) = \frac{1}{Z(\mathcal{O},W)}\,\exp\!\left(\sum_{j=1}^{n} w_j F_j(\mathcal{O},X)\right) \qquad (7.17)$$

where $W = \begin{pmatrix} w_1 & w_2 & \ldots & w_n \end{pmatrix}$ is a weight vector and Z is a normalizing factor, chosen so that the result is a probability. The F_j in equation (7.17) are referred to as feature functions. To draw out the analogy to logistic regression, a feature function can be viewed as the analog of a term of the form $e^{b_j x_j}$, which appears in the logistic function in equation (7.16).

---

[18]Sadly, it seems that there really is no such thing as a free lunch, and this is especially true when it is your cheapskate author's turn to buy.

For CRFs, equation (7.17) implies that given an observation sequence $\mathcal{O}$, the optimal state sequence X can be determined by

$$\operatorname*{argmax}_{X} P(X \mid \mathcal{O}) = \operatorname*{argmax}_{X} \sum_{j=1}^{n} w_j F_j(\mathcal{O}, X).$$

This form is the CRF analog to logistic regression as discussed in Section 7.9.

To summarize, we can say that naïve Bayes and logistic regression are one example of a generative-discriminative pair. Since an HMM can be viewed as a sequential version of naïve Bayes and a linear chain CRF can be viewed as a sequential version of logistic regression, HMMs and linear chain CRFs are another generative-discriminative pair. It's natural to ask whether there are any other such pairs.

In fact, general CRFs can apply to arbitrary (undirected) graph structures, not just (undirected) linear chains. As discussed above, an HMM can be viewed as the directed graph analog of a linear chain CRF. The directed linear chain view of an HMM, as illustrated in Figure 7.14, can also be generalized to arbitrary directed graph structures. Such a generalization of an HMM is known as a *generative directed model*. Thus, we have yet another generative-discriminative pair. Figure 7.16 shows the relationships between the three generative-discriminative pairs discussed in this section.

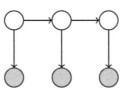
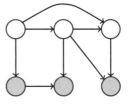

Naïve bayes   Hidden Markov model   Generative directed model

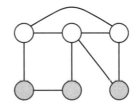

Logistic regression   Linear chain CRF   Conditional random field

Figure 7.16: Generative-discriminative pairs

According to the renowned Edwin Chen, generative models tend to give better results when data is limited, while discriminative models are preferred for larger datasets. A discussion of this topic—and additional insights into the relative advantages and disadvantages of various techniques—can be found in Chen's blog at [29].

7.10.3 The Bottom Line on CRFs

In this section, we argued that an HMM can be viewed as a a sequential version of naïve Bayes. Similarly, a linear chain CRF can be seen as a sequential version of logistic regression. Since logistic regression and naïve Bayes form a generative-discriminative pair, we can view HMMs and linear chain CRFs as another (in some sense, higher-order) generative-discriminative pair. We can extend this concept of generative-discriminative pairs to the case of general CRFs and generative directed models.

The bottom line here is that conditional random fields can be viewed as generalizing hidden Markov models to more complex graph structures. Linear chain CRFs are the most common type of CRF used in practice, which is undoubtedly due to the fact that the algorithms are most efficient in this case.

For further information on CRFs and related topics, see [28, 44, 48, 78, 82, 110, 161]. For a book-length discussion of CRFs, see [140], and for a generalization to "hidden" CRFs, see [112].

7.11 Problems

1. Plot each of the following points in the plane using the indicated color. Then determine the decision boundary for k-nearest neighbors (k-NN) in the case where $k = 3$. That is, shade all areas red for which a point would be classified as of type "red," and shade all areas blue for which a point would be classified as being type "blue."

color	point	color	point
red	(0.5,3.00)	blue	(0.5,1.75)
red	(1.0,4.25)	blue	(1.5,1.50)
red	(1.5,2.00)	blue	(2.5,4.00)
red	(2.0,2.75)	blue	(2.5,2.10)
red	(2.5,1.65)	blue	(3.0,1.50)
red	(3.0,2.70)	blue	(3.5,1.85)
red	(3.5,1.00)	blue	(4.0,3.50)
red	(4.0,2.50)	blue	(5.0,1.45)
red	(4.5,2.10)	—	—
red	(5.0,2.75)	—	—

2. Figure 7.3 provides an illustration of a multilayer perceptron (MLP). Give a similar high-level illustration for each of the following types of neural networks. For each, discuss the similarities to—and differences from—an MLP. Also discuss the training process that is typically used.

a) Recurrent neural network (RNN).

b) Self-organizing map (SOM).

c) Radial basis function (RBF) network.

3. For the following set of classifiers c_i, determine the AdaBoost classifier $C(X)$, as specified in Section 7.4.2.

Data	Label	Classifiers				
		c_1	c_2	c_3	c_4	c_5
X_1	+1	−1	−1	−1	+1	+1
X_2	−1	−1	−1	+1	+1	+1
X_3	−1	−1	−1	+1	−1	−1
X_4	+1	−1	−1	−1	+1	+1
X_5	+1	−1	+1	+1	+1	−1
X_6	+1	−1	+1	−1	+1	−1
X_7	+1	−1	−1	+1	−1	+1
X_8	−1	−1	+1	+1	−1	−1
X_9	+1	+1	+1	−1	+1	−1
X_{10}	−1	+1	−1	+1	−1	+1

a) In addition to the final classifier $C(X)$, at each iteration, state which of the classifiers c_i was selected, give W_1, W_2, and W, and the weight α_m that was computed using (7.4). Also, give the the classifier $C_m(X)$ at each iteration.

b) Based on the training data, determine the accuracy of each classifier $C_i(X)$, and the final classifier $C(X)$.

4. In Section 7.5, we discussed a random forest based on the data in Table 7.2, and the three subsets denoted A, B, and C in equation (7.5). Construct decision trees for each of the following three cases.

i) Subset A and features S and H.

ii) Subset B and features S and D.

iii) Subset C and features H and D.

Use the resulting random forest and a majority vote to classify each of the following samples.

Sample	$S(V_i)$	$H(V_i)$	$D(V_i)$
V_1	100	7	27
V_2	130	7	28
V_3	115	4	30
V_4	105	4	35
V_5	140	6	20

5. At the end of Section 7.5, we discussed the connection between k-NN and decision trees. Extend this result to show that a similarly close connection exists between k-NN and random forests. Hint: Assume that you have a random forest consisting of m decision trees. Generalize the scoring function in equation (7.6).

6. This problem deals with the derivation of the matrix form of the Fisher discriminant in Section 7.6.

   a) Verify that equation (7.9) is correct.
   b) Verify that equation (7.10) is correct.

7. This problem deals with the Lagrangian that appears in our analysis of LDA training in Section 7.6.

   a) Verify that when we maximize the Lagrangian in (7.12), we obtain the matrix equation in (7.13). Note that $w = (w_1, w_2, \ldots, w_\ell)$ is a vector in these equations.
   b) Verify that the dual version of the Lagrangian in equation (7.12) is of the form in (7.15), as claimed in the book.
   c) Explicitly determine the constants c_1 and c_2 in (7.15), and verify that $c_2 > 0$.

8. In Section 7.6, we compared and contrasted LDA and PCA.

   a) Provide a graph of a labeled dataset in the plane for which we would expect good results from LDA, but PCA would likely yield an inaccurate model of the data. For PCA, treat the data as unlabeled.
   b) Provide a graph of a labeled dataset in the plane for which we would expect poor results from LDA, but PCA would likely yield an accurate model of the data. For PCA, treat the data as unlabeled.

9. In Section 7.6, we discussed two different geometric views of LDA; see, for example, Figures 7.6 (a) and 7.7 (a). Explain why these two views of LDA are not contradictory.

10. Let $y = mx$ be the equation of a given line through the origin, and let (x_0, y_0) be a point not on the line.

   a) Show that the orthogonal projection of the point $(\; x_0 \quad y_0\;)$ onto the line $y = mx$ intersects at $(\; x \quad y\;) = c(\; 1 \quad m\;)$, where

$$
c = \frac{(\; x_0 \quad y_0\;)\begin{pmatrix} 1 \\ m \end{pmatrix}}{(\; 1 \quad m\;)\begin{pmatrix} 1 \\ m \end{pmatrix}}.
$$

That is, show that the perpendicular bisector of the line $y = mx$ from the point $(\, x_0 \quad y_0 \,)$ is at $(\, x \quad y \,) = c(\, 1 \quad m \,)$, for the value of c specified above.

b) Recall that in our discussion of LDA in Section 7.6, we define the "projection" of the vector X in terms of a dot product $w \cdot X = w^T X$, where in the 2-dimensional case, $w = (\, w_1 \quad w_2 \,)^T$. For the specific case considered in this problem (i.e., projecting onto a line of the form $y = mx$), explicitly determine w_1 and w_2 in terms m. Hint: The result of any dot product is a scalar, and a scalar obviously cannot represent a projection vector. Hence, the situation is somewhat more subtle than was explained in Section 7.6. We actually want to find a weight vector $w = (\, w_1 \quad w_2 \,)^T$ so that when we measure distance between the scalars $w^T X_1$ and $w^T X_2$, we obtain the same result as we would have obtained had we projected X_1 and X_2 and measured the distance between the resulting vectors. To solve this part of the problem, assume that you are given two vectors $X_1 = (\, x_1 \quad y_1 \,)^T$ and $X_2 = (\, x_2 \quad y_2 \,)^T$. Project each of these onto the line $y = mx$ using the result in part a), and compute the distance between these projected vectors. Next, compute the dot product of of X_1 with the weight vector $w = (\, w_1 \quad w_2 \,)^T$ and the dot product of X_2 with w, then find the distance between the resulting scalars. Equate the coefficients in the two distance expressions to determine w_1 and w_2, in terms of m. For simplicity, use the squared Euclidean distance.

11. From Section 7.6, we see that LDA training consists of maximizing the Fisher discriminant, as defined in equation (7.8). For simplicity, in this problem, we'll consider the case where the training data is 2-dimensional, in which case $w = (\, w_1 \quad w_2 \,)^T$. Maximize $J(w)$ in (7.8) directly by computing partial derivatives with respect to w_1 and w_2, setting the resulting equations equal to zero, and solving for w. Verify that your solution is equivalent to the form of the solution that appears in Section 7.6, specifically, in equation (7.13).

12. Consider the following LDA-based clustering strategy. Suppose that we have unlabeled data that we want to cluster. Initially, we split the data into two random sets. We then apply LDA to this data and compute $J(w)$, as given in equation (7.8). We proceed via a hill climb, where we swap a pair of elements between the two sets, retaining the modified partition only for those cases where $J(w)$ has increased. And, whenever the score improves, we start over from the beginning of the swapping routine. We continue until all possible swaps have been tested without any improvement in the score. The final partition is our clustering. Note that once we partition the elements, the number of elements in

each set does not change.[19]

a) Test this clustering approach using the data in Table 7.4, where one of the initial sets consist of $X_1, X_2, \ldots, X_8$ and the other initial set consists of Y_1, Y_2, Y_3, Y_4. Give your final clustering and also give the scores for the initial partition and the final clustering.

b) Again test this clustering approach using the data in Table 7.4, but let one of the initial sets be $X_1, X_2, X_3, X_4, Y_1, Y_2, Y_3, Y_4$ and let the other initial set be X_5, X_6, X_7, X_8. Give your final clustering and also give the scores for the initial partition and the final clustering.

c) Explain how you could modify this clustering strategy so that the size of each cluster can vary from the initial partition.

13. In Section 7.7, we showed that K-means can be viewed as a special case of the vector quantization (VQ). algorithm. Also, in Section 6.5 of Chapter 6, we showed that there is a very close connection between K-means and EM clustering. Explain why EM clustering is also a special case of the VQ algorithm.

14. DBSCAN, which is discussed in Problem 16 of Chapter 6, is the best-known density-based clustering algorithm. As discussed in Section 7.7, both K-means and EM clustering can be viewed as special cases of vector quantization (VQ). Is density-based clustering also a special case of VQ? Why or why not?

15. Repeat the example in Section 7.8, assuming the TPR is 0.99 and the TNR is 0.98, with all other assumptions unchanged.

16. Consider the linear regression example in Figure 7.11. This same data is used to illustrate principal component analysis (PCA) in Figure 4.3 in Chapter 4. Below, we have overlaid the regression line in Figure 7.11 (b) with the line representing the first principal component that is given in Figure 4.3 (b).

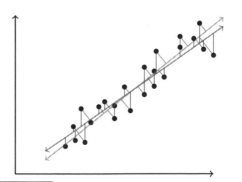

a) In this example, the regression line and the line determined by the first principal component are similar, but not identical. Why do they differ?

b) Comment on the relative advantages and disadvantages of modeling a dataset using linear regression as compared to the first principal component.

17. Figure 7.16 gives examples of a generative directed model and a general CRF, each with three hidden states, showing some of the many possible interconnections between states and observations. Provide illustrations of a generative directed model and a general CRF, each with two hidden states, showing all possible interconnections in each case.

Chapter 8

Data Analysis

The goal is to turn data into information,
and information into insight.
— Carly Fiorina

If you torture the data long enough, it will confess.
— Ronald Coase

8.1 Introduction

In this chapter, we'll consider some of the issues that arise when testing and evaluating an experimental technique. Our primary goal is to quantify the effectiveness of a given scoring or classification strategy, which is critically important when comparing experimental results. The issues considered here are generic to most such experimental situations, but to make things concrete, we'll assume that we want to test a malware detection technique. Specifically, we assume that the goal is to distinguish members of a specific malware family from benign code.

Ideally, we would like to directly compare our new results to previous work. However, this may not be possible for a variety of reasons. For one thing, our proposed score might apply to a new malware family for which no other score is available. And even if other comparable scores do exist, we would need to test on precisely the same dataset, which might not be feasible. In addition, we might want to take into account factors other than scoring success. For example, a malware score that relies on dynamic analysis (via code execution or emulation) could have an advantage over a score that only uses static analysis. But, a score that uses static analysis is likely more efficient to compute. And a faster score might be preferred, even if the results are slightly worse than those obtained with a more costly score.

For these reasons and more, we'd like to have a way to measure the effectiveness of a score, independent of any other score. That is, we don't want to have a method that only tells us that score A is better than score B when both are tested on a specific dataset Z. Instead, we want a method that tells us score A yields a numerical result of x when it is applied to dataset X, while score B yields a numerical result of y when it is applied to dataset Y. Ideally, we want the numerical results x and y to have some intuitive interpretation in terms of, say, detection rates. Given such numerical results, we can reasonably compare a new malware detection technique to a wide variety of existing techniques, and possibly even to existing anti-virus products. This will also enable us to quantify the tradeoff between different scores, based on other relevant factors, such as efficiency.

8.2   Experimental Design

We'll assume that we have a set of malware samples, all of which belong to a given family.[1] In addition, we have a representative collection of samples of benign code.

We want to test a malware score, so we'll refer to the malware dataset as the *match* set and the benign dataset as the *nomatch* set. The match set is partitioned into a *training* set and a *test* set. Not surprisingly, the training set is used to train a model, while the test set and the nomatch set are used to evaluate the resulting score. Note that we cannot test the score on the training set, since that would be cheating. An assumption here is that the malware we see in practice will be similar to the training set, but not identical—if it was identical, we'd probably just perform a signature scan. Also, we are assuming that the nomatch set is truly representative of the benign samples that will be scored in practice.

The overall experiment consists of a *training phase* and a *scoring phase*. During the training phase, we use the training data to determine the parameters of the model. During the scoring phase, we score match data—in the form of the test data—and the nomatch data. The results from the scoring phase are used to determine the strength of the model, i.e., the quality of the proposed score. Of course, for this to have any validity, the data used in the scoring phase must be representative of the data that we'll actually see in practice.

A scatterplot of the scores provides a visual representation of our experimental results. An example of such a scatterplot of is given in Figure 8.1, where we have 10 match scores and 10 nomatch scores.

---

[1]More generally, the malware could be of a similar type or related in some specific way. However, the broader the family, the more difficult the detection problem. To simplify the presentation, here we assume the malware is from a single, well-defined family.

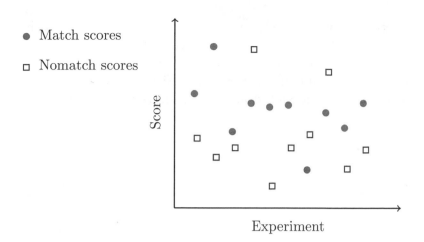

Figure 8.1: Scatterplot of scores

There are some potential pitfalls with the approach described so far. First, how should we partition the match set? It's possible that there is some biased data in this set, and we would like to minimize the chance of this data skewing our results. Second, the size of the match dataset is often small, relative to the nomatch set. Consequently, we would like to get as much information as possible from a limited match dataset. A technique known as *cross validation* enables us to deal with both of these issues.

Let S be the match set and let

$$U_0, U_1, \ldots, U_{n-1}$$

be a partition of S, where each U_i is of equal size. By the definition of a partition, each element of S is contained in exactly one U_i. Not surprisingly, n-fold cross validation consists of n distinct "folds." For the first fold, we let the test set be U_0, while the training set consists of

$$U_1 \cup U_2 \cup \cdots \cup U_{n-1}.$$

Using these sets, we train a model that is then used to compute scores on the test and nomatch sets. For the second fold, we repeat the process, with U_1 as the test set and

$$U_0 \cup U_2 \cup U_3 \cup \cdots \cup U_{n-1}$$

as the training set. The third through n^{th} folds are similar.

Note that if S has M elements, then with n-fold cross validation, we obtain M match scores. Also, if the number of nomatch elements is $\widetilde{M}$, then the total number of nomatch scores is $n\widetilde{M}$.

Again, cross validation serves (at least) two useful purposes. First, any bias in the data is smoothed by the partitioning, and second, we maximize the number of scores obtained from a given dataset.

In practice, we would likely want to use our experimental scoring results to set a *threshold*. In the ideal case, all of the match scores would be on one side of the threshold, and all of the nomatch scores on the other, so that the selected threshold would yield perfect separation. However, typically no such threshold exists—typical and ideal cases are illustrated in Figure 8.2.

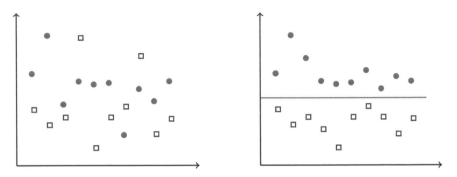

Figure 8.2: Thresholding is easy ... sometimes

For any given threshold, we can determine the accuracy of the scoring technique. Next, we discuss the concept of accuracy in some detail.

8.3 Accuracy

Suppose that we have developed a score to detect a specific type of malware. In addition, suppose that based on testing, we have determined a threshold for the score. Finally, suppose that scores greater than the threshold indicate malware, while scores below the threshold indicate benign.[2] Then when we score any given sample of code, precisely one of the four following outcomes will occur.

- True positive (TP) — The scored sample is malware and its score is above the threshold, so it is (correctly) classified as malware.

- True negative (TN) — The scored sample is not malware and its score is below the threshold, so it is (correctly) classified as not malware.

- False positive (FP) — The scored sample is not malware, but its score is above the threshold. In this case, the code is incorrectly classified as "positive," i.e., malware.

---

[2]Depending on the type of score, it could be the case that lower scores indicate malware and higher scores indicate benign code. In this discussion we assume that the higher the score, the stronger the indication of malware.

- False negative (FN) — The scored sample is malware, but its score is below the threshold. In this case, the code is incorrectly classified as "negative," i.e., not malware.

These four cases are illustrated in Figure 8.3, where the two "true" outcomes indicate correct classification, and the two "false" outcomes indicate incorrect classification. For a specific experiment, filling in the numbers for each type of outcome in Figure 8.3 yields a *confusion matrix*.[3]

	Malware	Not malware
High score	**TP**	**FP**
Low score	**FN**	**TN**

Figure 8.3: Confusion matrix

We can append "R" to any of TP, TN, FP, and FN to indicate the corresponding rate. For example,

$$\text{TPR} = \frac{\text{TP}}{P} = \frac{\text{TP}}{\text{TP}+\text{FN}} \text{ and } \text{TNR} = \frac{\text{TN}}{N} = \frac{\text{TN}}{\text{TN}+\text{FP}}$$

where P is the total number of positive cases and N is the total number of negative cases. The TPR is known as the *sensitivity*, while TNR is the *specificity*. These terms seem to have originated with medical testing. In the case of a medical test, the sensitivity is the fraction of those classified as sick—with respect to the particular condition being tested—who are actually sick, while specificity is the fraction of those who do not have the condition and are correctly classified as such. In the case of malware detection, sensitivity is the fraction of malware samples tested that are classified as malware, while the specificity is the fraction of benign samples tested that are correctly classified as benign.

There is an inherent tradeoff between sensitivity and specificity. For example, a trivial test that simply classifies everything as malware will have a sensitivity of 1.0 (the best possible), but a specificity of 0.0 (the worst possible). On the other hand, a test that classifies everything as not malware will have a sensitivity of 0.0, but a specificity of 1.0.

[3] Even your easily baffled author finds the confusion matrix less than confusing.

We define the *accuracy* of a classification scheme as

$$\text{accuracy} = \frac{\text{TP} + \text{TN}}{P + N}. \qquad (8.1)$$

If we never misclassify, then the sensitivity and specificity are both 1.0, and we obtain an accuracy of 1.0. On the other hand, if everything is misclassified, then the accuracy is 0.0. However, if we have a binary classifier that misclassifies everything, we can simply reverse the classification criteria, and everything will be classified correctly. It follows that the accuracy can never be less than 0.5. And, of course, the higher the accuracy, the better we expect the classifier to perform in practice.

In real-world application, it's often the case that the number of (negative) nomatch samples available is much, much larger than the number of (positive) match samples. For example, if we routinely test for a rare medical condition, then even if we are selective in applying the test, it is highly likely that the vast majority of subjects tested will be nomatch cases, with a relatively small number of matches. Similarly, when testing for a specific type of malware, it is virtually certain that the vast majority of samples are not malware of the particular type that the test was designed to detect. In cases such as these, the accuracy formula in (8.1) will tend to be dominated by N and TN, with the results on positive cases having little influence. To account for this *imbalance problem*, we can instead use the *balanced accuracy*, which is

$$\text{balanced accuracy} = \frac{\text{TPR} + \text{TNR}}{2} = \frac{1}{2}\left(\frac{\text{TP}}{P} + \frac{\text{TN}}{N}\right).$$

In the balanced accuracy calculation, we weight both data sets equally, regardless of their relative sizes. We discuss the imbalance problem in more detail in Section 8.5.

For any real-world application, we must determine a threshold before we can actually use a scoring method for classification. Accuracy (or balanced accuracy) is a useful measure of the expected effectiveness of the classification scheme, relative to a given threshold. However, when we are in research mode—as opposed to real-world application mode—we don't want to rely on the experimenter's selection of a parameter (such as a threshold) to determine the quality of the detection scheme. Reliance on such a parameter might give misleading results when comparing different experiments, due to the fact that different researchers chose their parameters in different ways.

Of course, we could try to choose the threshold in some specified (or optimal) way, which would enable direct comparison between different techniques. For example, we might require that the threshold be chosen so that the sensitivity equals the specificity. But regardless of how we set a threshold, there are many situations where, in practice, we would want to choose a different threshold.

Consider, for example, a commercial anti-virus (AV) product. It is a little-known fact[4] that AV products invariably set thresholds that reduce the FPR to a very small number, at the expense of a relatively large FNR. While this might seem counterintuitive, in the context of malware detection, false positives are generally obvious and annoy users, while infections caused by false negatives often go unnoticed. Any commercial AV vendor must keep their customers happy.

Often, malware researchers compare their experimental detection schemes against commercial AV products using accuracy as the measure of quality. Doing so, these researchers mistakenly conclude that their technique is far superior to methods used in commercial AV scanners. However, if the AV vendor had simply chosen to set their threshold so that the FPR and FNR were closer to being in balance, the accuracy would likely have been much more favorable for their AV product—and the researcher's work would appear to be less impressive in comparison.

The bottom line is that it's risky to rely on accuracy when comparing different detection strategies. This is primarily due to the fact that accuracy depends on the particular threshold selected, and different thresholds make sense in different situations. In the next section, we discuss ROC curves, which enable us to directly compare different classification techniques by removing any specific threshold from consideration. In effect, ROC analysis considers all possible thresholds simultaneously, thus removing the threshold as a variable. This is particularly useful when comparing experimental techniques.

8.4 ROC Curves

Receiver operating characteristic (ROC) curves might sound like a topic from electrical engineering, but that's only because it is. The concept originated with radar engineers during World War II, and ROC curves are now widely used in many fields. Given a binary classifier, we construct an ROC curve by plotting the TPR versus the FPR as the threshold varies through the range of data values. Equivalently, but more fancy-sounding, we plot $1 - $ specificity versus sensitivity as the threshold varies.

To illustrate the process, consider again the scatterplot in Figure 8.1. For any given threshold, we'll classify the points below the threshold as nomatch (i.e., not malware) and those above as match (i.e., malware). Based on the resulting classifications, we compute the TPR and FPR, which yields a point on the ROC curve.

---

[4]According to your overly optimistic author, this book is destined to become a best-seller, at which point there will no longer be any little-known facts in it.

In Figure 8.4 we illustrate one specific threshold and we plot the corresponding point on the ROC curve. For the given threshold, we have

$$\text{TPR} = \text{sensitivity} = 0.7$$

since seven of the 10 positive cases (solid circles) are correctly classified. For this same threshold, only two of the 10 negative cases (hollow squares) are classified incorrectly, so that

$$\text{FPR} = 1 - \text{specificity} = 0.2.$$

Hence, the ROC curve for this scatterplot passes through the point in the plane given by $(x, y) = (0.2, 0.7)$, as illustrated in the right-hand side of Figure 8.4.

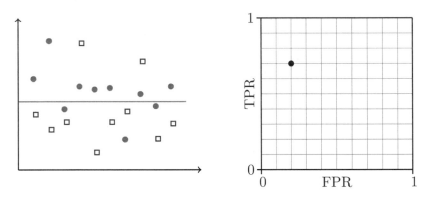

Figure 8.4: Scatterplot and a point on the ROC curve

If we place the threshold below the lowest point in the scatterplot in Figure 8.4, then TPR = 1 and FPR = 1, and if we place the threshold above the highest point, then TPR = 0 and FPR = 0. Consequently, an ROC curve always includes the points $(0, 0)$ and $(1, 1)$. In Figure 8.5, we give the ROC curve corresponding to the scatterplot in Figure 8.4.

On the left-hand side in Figure 8.6, the shaded region illustrates the area under the curve (AUC) for the ROC curve in Figure 8.5. In this example, the AUC is 0.75. In general the AUC varies between 0.0 and 1.0, with an AUC of 1.0 indicating ideal separation, that is, a threshold exists such that no false positives or false negatives occur. An AUC of 0.5 indicates that the binary classifier is no better than flipping a coin. In fact, the AUC gives the probability that a randomly selected match case scores higher than a randomly selected nomatch case [19]. Note that whenever we have an AUC of $x < 0.5$, we can simply reverse the match and nomatch criteria to obtain a classifier with an AUC of $1.0 - x > 0.5$. In other words, no binary classifier can do worse than flipping a fair coin.

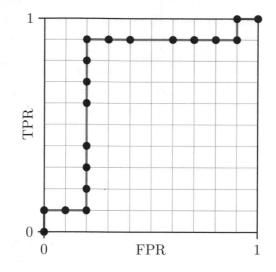

Figure 8.5: ROC curve example

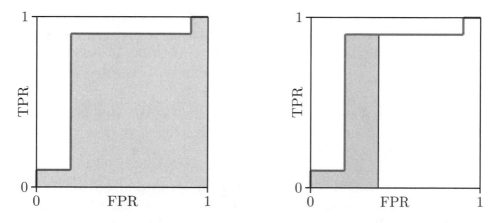

Figure 8.6: Area under ROC curve (AUC) and AUC_p

In some cases, we might want to exclude results with a high FPR (equivalently, $1 -$ specificity). In such cases, we can use the *partial AUC*, denoted AUC_p, in place of the AUC. When computing AUC_p, any FPR results greater than the specified value of p are ignored. We normalize AUC_p so that like the AUC, the result is within the range of 0 to 1.

The shaded region on the right-hand side of Figure 8.6 illustrates the case of $AUC_{0.4}$. In this particular example, we have

$$AUC_{0.4} = 0.2/0.4 = 0.5.$$

Sometimes, instead of the notation AUC_p, authors will define a "useful region." For the AUC_p example in Figure 8.6, such misguided authors would say that the useful region is the region where FPR < 0.4.

We note in passing that some equally misguided authors claim that the AUC tends to overstate the accuracy of experiments. However, the AUC is not a measure of accuracy, so this claim is dubious, at best. As previously mentioned, the AUC measures the probability that a randomly selected positive instance scores higher than a randomly selected negative instance—nothing more nor less. The beauty of the AUC is that it allows us to directly compare different experimental results.

8.5   Imbalance Problem

As mentioned above, in many real-world applications, the sizes of the match and nomatch sets are far out of balance. For example, if we have a score that tests for a particular type of malware, then it is almost certain that we will test a large number of benign samples for every malware sample. In such a situation, the number of negative (nomatch) cases would tend to be much larger than the set of positive (match) cases.

When setting a threshold, we should take account of any imbalance. To illustrate why this is so, suppose that for a given malware test, the selected threshold results in a sensitivity of 0.99 and a specificity of 0.98. Then we have

$$\text{TPR} = 0.99 \text{ and } \text{FPR} = 0.02.$$

Furthermore, suppose that only about 1 out of each 1000 samples tested are malware of the specific type that this test is designed to detect.[5] Finally, suppose that when scanning a system, we expect to scan 100,000 samples.

Under the scenario in the previous paragraph, we expect to test 100 malware samples. Since $\text{TPR} = 0.99$, of these 100 malware samples, we detect 99, with 1 being misclassified as benign. In addition, we test 99,900 negative samples. Since $\text{FPR} = 0.02$, of these negative samples, we classify 97,902 as benign and 1998 as malware. These results are summarized in the form of a confusion matrix in Figure 8.7.

In this example, we classified 97,903 samples as benign, of which 97,902 are actually are benign. Therefore, when we classify a sample as benign, the probability that this is the correct classification is

$$\frac{97,902}{97,903} > 0.9999,$$

which is certainly impressive. However, the probability that a sample classified as malware is actually malware is only

$$\frac{99}{99 + 1998} = \frac{99}{2097} < 0.0475.$$

---

[5]Your imbalanced author has noticed that in reality, the imbalance is often much greater than this, which only serves to make the problem worse.

	Malware	Not malware
High score	TP = 99	FP = 1998
Low score	FN = 1	TN = 97,902

Figure 8.7: Confusion matrix

Consequently, more than 95% of the samples classified as malware are not actually malware. The resulting high number of false positives is sure to cause users to lose confidence in any malware scanner that uses this test.

Can we improve on this dismal situation? Since there is an inherent tradeoff between sensitivity and specificity, suppose that we select a different threshold for which

$$\text{TPR} = 0.92 \text{ and } \text{FPR} = 0.0003.$$

Using the same numbers as above (i.e., we test 100,000 samples, with 1 in 1000 actually being malware), when we classify a sample as benign, the probability that it is correctly classified still exceeds 0.9999. In this case, the probability that a sample classified as malware is actually malware is now greater than 0.75, whereas this rate was less than 0.05 for our previous choice of threshold. This illustrates the importance of carefully selecting a threshold for use in practice. This example also illustrates the difficulty in relying on a specific threshold when comparing scoring techniques.

While we could choose a threshold that drives the FPR even lower, at some point we will pay a significant price in terms of the number of false negatives. It is usually a better idea to develop a secondary test that we apply to samples that are classified as malware by our primary test. This gives us the best of both worlds—few malware samples classified as benign and few benign samples ultimately classified as malware. We would want to balance the work between the primary and secondary tests, so that the optimal threshold will also depend on the cost of these tests.

If we want to explicitly analyze the effect of various levels of imbalance, ROC curves are of little use. In such cases (and others), it may be more informative to employ precision-recall curves.

8.6   PR Curves

Precision-recall (PR) curves are an alternative to ROC analysis for experimental data [35]. There are many connections between PR and ROC curves,[6] but in certain cases, PR curves might be preferred. Recall that when the nomatch set is large relative to the match set, the nomatch class will dominate the ROC analysis. However, we are likely more interested in the behavior of a score on the match class. This is a case where PR analysis can prove useful.

We define recall to be the fraction of the match cases that are classified correctly, and precision is the fraction of elements classified as positive that actually belong to the match set. More precisely,

$$\text{recall} = \frac{\text{TP}}{\text{TP} + \text{FN}} \text{ and } \text{precision} = \frac{\text{TP}}{\text{TP} + \text{FP}}.$$

Observe that recall is the same as the TPR, but precision is something we have not seen previously—in particular, it's not the same as the FPR, which we used when constructing ROC curves. Also note that TN does not appear in either formula, and hence true negatives play no (direct) role when computing a PR curve. Again, this may be useful if we want to focus our attention on the positive set, particularly when the positive set is dwarfed by a relatively large negative set.

Analogous to ROC analysis, to generate a PR curve, we plot the recall and precision pairs as the threshold varies through the range of values in a given scatterplot. To illustrate the process, we consider the same data used for the ROC curve example in Section 8.4.

For the data and threshold in Figure 8.8, we have TP = 7, FN = 3, FP = 2, and hence

$$\text{recall} = \frac{7}{7+3} = 0.7 \text{ and } \text{precision} = \frac{7}{7+2} \approx 0.7778.$$

On the right-hand side of Figure 8.8 we have plotted the point $(0.7, 0.7778)$ in the plane specified by

$$(x, y) = (\text{recall}, \text{precision}).$$

The complete PR curve corresponding to the data in Figure 8.8 appears in Figure 8.9. In this example, we have simply connected the dots between points. While this is valid for ROC curves, it is known that such linear interpolation will yield a slightly larger value for the area under the PR curve, which we denote as AUC-PR, than a more careful analysis would provide [35]. Nevertheless, for simplicity, we'll simply connect the dots when we want to compute the area under the PR curve.

---

[6]For example, if a curve "dominates" in ROC space, it also dominates in PR space, and vice versa [35].

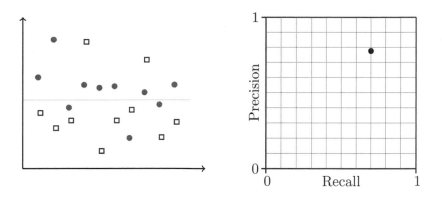

Figure 8.8: Scatterplot and a point on the PR curve

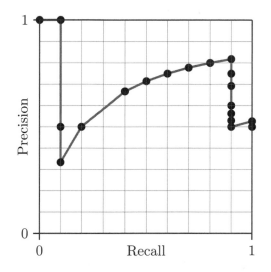

Figure 8.9: PR curve example

For the example in Figure 8.9, the AUC-PR is about 0.69. In the ideal case, where there is no overlap between the match and nomatch scores, the AUC-PR is 1.0, which agrees with the AUC from ROC analysis. Also, the larger the AUC-PR, the better the classifier. The potential advantages of AUC-PR are explored further in the problems at the end of the chapter.

8.7 The Bottom Line

It is important to design your experiments properly. Cross validation is almost always a good idea, where 5-fold and 10-fold cross validation seem to be used most often. ROC curves and PR curves are useful when comparing results from different experiments. In particular, we can use the AUC, AUC_p, or AUC-PR to quantify the differences in various experimental results.

When using a score in practice, we need to set a threshold, and this can be somewhat tricky. For example, a significant imbalance in the sizes of the experimental datasets will affect the accuracy, and hence this must be taken into account when setting a threshold. In practice, it's often best to develop secondary tests—if so, it is necessary to properly account for the primary and secondary work factors when determining the threshold and the overall work factor.

8.8   Problems

1. The topic of n-fold cross validation is discussed in Section 8.2.

   a) Show that when n-fold cross validation is used, we obtain exactly M match scores, where M is the size of the match set.

   b) Assuming that the nomatch set is of size N and we do n-fold cross validation, how many total nomatch scores are computed?

   c) In practice, it's common to use either $n = 5$ or $n = 10$. What is the advantage of 5-fold cross validation over 10-fold? What is the advantage of 10-fold cross validation over 5-fold?

2. Suppose that we design a malware classification strategy based on flipping a coin. That is, given a sample that we want to classify, we flip a coin and if the result is heads, we classify the sample as malware; otherwise we classify the sample as benign.

   a) If we test an equal number of malware and benign samples, what is the expected FPR, TPR, accuracy, and balanced accuracy?

   b) If we test P malware samples and N benign samples, what is the expected FPR, TPR, accuracy, and balanced accuracy?

3. This problem deals with ROC curves.

   a) For each point in Figure 8.5, draw the corresponding threshold on the scatterplot that appears on the left-hand side of Figure 8.4.

   b) Draw the ROC curve for the scatterplot that appears on the right-hand side in Figure 8.2, and compute the AUC.

4. This problem deals with the partial AUC, which we denote as AUC_p, where $0 < p < 1$.

   a) Determine $\text{AUC}_{0.1}$ for the example in Figure 8.6.

   b) Determine $\text{AUC}_{0.3}$ for the example in Figure 8.6.

   c) Determine $\text{AUC}_{0.5}$ for the example in Figure 8.6.

5. Repeat the analysis in Section 8.5, assuming that we have selected a threshold for which TPR = 0.90 and FPR = 0.0001.

6. Suppose that for a given experiment, TP = 98, FN = 2, TN = 8500, and FP = 1500.

   a) Compute the accuracy.

   b) Compute the balanced accuracy.

7. For the following scatterplot, draw the corresponding ROC curve, compute the area under the ROC curve (AUC), and compute the partial area under the curve, $AUC_{0.1}$.

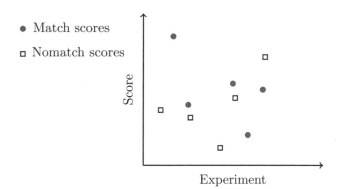

8. Using the same scatterplot as in Problem 7, draw the PR curve and compute the area under the PR curve, AUC-PR, using linear interpolation between points on the curve.

9. For the scatterplot in Problem 7, the match and nomatch sets are in balance. In many real-world applications, there is a gross imbalance between these sets. For example, in malware detection, we might expect to score thousands of benign samples for each malware sample scored. In such cases, we would like to take this imbalance into account when analyzing the score. However, it might be too costly or time-consuming to generate scores for a vast number of samples. Assuming that we have balanced match and nomatch sets, and the nomatch set is representative, we can simulate an imbalance by simply duplicating the nomatch scores. This can be viewed as upsampling from the nomatch distribution. Use the scatterplot in Problem 7 to answer the following.

   a) Duplicate each nomatch score 10 times. Draw the ROC curve and compute the AUC. Draw the PR curve and compute the AUC-PR.

   b) Duplicate each nomatch score 100 times. Draw the ROC curve and compute the AUC. Draw the PR curve and compute the AUC-PR.

10. Suppose that we have developed a test for a specific type of malware. Further, suppose that for the threshold that we have chosen, we find that TPR $= 0.95$ and FPR $= 0.01$. Further still, suppose that we expect 1 out of every 1000 files tested will be malware of this specific type. Furthermost, assume that we test 200,000 files.

   a) What fraction of the files classified as benign are actually benign?

   b) What fraction of the files classified as malware are actually malware?

   c) We could improve on these results by either changing the threshold to reduce the false positive rate, or by performing a secondary test on each sample that is classified as malware. Discuss the pros and cons of both of these approaches.

11. This problem highlights a difference between ROC and PR curves.

   a) Prove that there is a linear relationship between the TPR and FPR. This implies that linear interpolation between points on an ROC curve will yield an accurate value for the AUC.

   b) Prove that the relationship between precision and recall is not linear. This implies that linear interpolation between points on a PR curve will not yield an accurate value for AUC-PR.

   c) Prove that linear interpolation between points on a PR curve will overestimate the AUC-PR.

12. Suppose that we adjust the parameters of a scoring algorithm so as to optimize the AUC. Show that, in general, this will not optimize the AUC-PR. Hint: Give examples of two sets of experimental results, where the number of positive and negative instances is the same in both cases, and the AUC is greater in the first case, but the AUC-PR is greater in the second. For such a situation, if we were to optimize the AUC, we would choose the parameters corresponding to the first experiment, but this would decrease the AUC-PR.

Part II

Applications

Chapter 9

HMM Applications

My powers are ordinary. Only my application brings me success.
— Isaac Newton

9.1 Introduction

In this chapter, we consider three applications of hidden Markov models (HMMs). First, we discuss the use of HMMs in English text analysis. Then we turn our attention to an information security application where we apply HMMs to the malware detection problem. Specifically, we show that HMMs can be used to detect types of malware that cannot possibly be detected using standard signature-based techniques. Finally, we build on the English text analysis application to show that HMMs are a powerful tool for breaking classic substitution ciphers. Among other things, this latter example highlights the potential benefit of multiple random restarts when training an HMM.

9.2 English Text Analysis

English text analysis is a classic application of HMMs, which appears to have been first considered by Cave and Neuwirth [25]. This application nicely illustrates the strength of HMMs and it requires no background in any specialized field, such as speech processing or information security.

Suppose that Marvin the Martian [90] obtains a large body of English text. Marvin, who has a working knowledge of HMMs, but no knowledge of English, would like to determine something about the structure of this mysterious writing system. A reasonable question he might ask is whether the characters can be partitioned into sets, where each set is different in some significant (statistical) sense.

Marvin might reasonably attempt the following. To focus on the main symbols, he removes all punctuation, numbers, etc., and converts all letters to lower case. This leaves 26 distinct letters and word-space, for a total of 27 symbols. He then assumes that there is an underlying Markov process (of order one) with two hidden states. For each of these two hidden states, he assumes that the 27 symbols are observed according to fixed probability distributions.

This defines an HMM with $N = 2$ and $M = 27$, where the state transition probabilities of the A matrix and the observation probabilities of the B matrix are unknown, and the observations $\mathcal{O}_t$ consist of the series of characters Marvin has extracted from the text. To find the most probable A and B matrices, Marvin must solve HMM Problem 3, which is discussed in Chapter 2.

We have trained such an HMM, using the first $T = 50,000$ observations from the Brown Corpus,[1] which is available at [21]. We initialized each element of π and A randomly to approximately $1/2$. For one specific iteration of this experiment, the precise values used were

$$\pi = \begin{pmatrix} 0.51316 & 0.48684 \end{pmatrix}$$

and

$$A = \begin{pmatrix} 0.47468 & 0.52532 \\ 0.51656 & 0.48344 \end{pmatrix}.$$

Each element of B was initialized to approximately $1/27$. The values in the initial B matrix (more precisely, the transpose of B) appear in the second and third columns of Table 9.1.

After the initial iteration, we find

$$\log\big(P(\mathcal{O}\,|\lambda)\big) = -165097.29$$

and after 100 iterations,

$$\log\big(P(\mathcal{O}\,|\,\lambda)\big) = -137305.28.$$

These model scores indicate that training has improved the model significantly over these 100 iterations.[2]

In this particular experiment, after 100 iterations, the model $\lambda = (A, B, \pi)$ has converged to

$$\pi = \begin{pmatrix} 0.00000 & 1.00000 \end{pmatrix}$$

---

[1]Officially, it is the Brown University Standard Corpus of Present-Day American English, and it includes various texts totaling about 1,000,000 words. Here "Present-Day" actually means 1961.

[2]Provided the model actually converges, we typically see $\log\big(P(\mathcal{O}\,|\lambda)\big)$ improve very slowly over an initial series of iterations, followed by a period of rapid convergence, followed again by only negligible improvement. Once we reach this second plateau, the hill climb is typically complete.

Table 9.1: Initial and final B^T

	Initial		Final	
a	0.03735	0.03909	0.13845	0.00075
b	0.03408	0.03537	0.00000	0.02311
c	0.03455	0.03537	0.00062	0.05614
d	0.03828	0.03909	0.00000	0.06937
e	0.03782	0.03583	0.21404	0.00000
f	0.03922	0.03630	0.00000	0.03559
g	0.03688	0.04048	0.00081	0.02724
h	0.03408	0.03537	0.00066	0.07278
i	0.03875	0.03816	0.12275	0.00000
j	0.04062	0.03909	0.00000	0.00365
k	0.03735	0.03490	0.00182	0.00703
l	0.03968	0.03723	0.00049	0.07231
m	0.03548	0.03537	0.00000	0.03889
n	0.03735	0.03909	0.00000	0.11461
o	0.04062	0.03397	0.13156	0.00000
p	0.03595	0.03397	0.00040	0.03674
q	0.03641	0.03816	0.00000	0.00153
r	0.03408	0.03676	0.00000	0.10225
s	0.04062	0.04048	0.00000	0.11042
t	0.03548	0.03443	0.01102	0.14392
u	0.03922	0.03537	0.04508	0.00000
v	0.04062	0.03955	0.00000	0.01621
w	0.03455	0.03816	0.00000	0.02303
x	0.03595	0.03723	0.00000	0.00447
y	0.03408	0.03769	0.00019	0.02587
z	0.03408	0.03955	0.00000	0.00110
space	0.03688	0.03397	0.33211	0.01298

and

$$A = \begin{pmatrix} 0.25596 & 0.74404 \\ 0.71571 & 0.28429 \end{pmatrix}$$

with the converged B^T appearing in the last two columns of Table 9.1.

The most interesting part of an HMM is generally the B matrix. Without having made any assumption about the two hidden states, the B matrix in Table 9.1 shows us that one hidden state consists of vowels while the other hidden state consists of consonants. Curiously, from this perspective, word-space acts more like a vowel, while y is not even sometimes a vowel.

Of course, anyone familiar with English would not be surprised that there is a significant distinction between vowels and consonants. But, the crucial point here is that the HMM has automatically extracted this statistically important distinction for us—it has "learned" to distinguish between consonants and vowels. And, thanks to HMMs, this feature of the language could be easily discovered by someone—such as Marvin the Martian—who previously had no knowledge whatsoever of the language.

Cave and Neuwirth [25] obtain additional results when considering HMMs with more than two hidden states. In fact, they are able to sensibly interpret the results for models with up to $N = 12$ hidden states.

Building on the results of this section, in Section 9.4 we'll show that HMMs can be used to break some types of classic ciphers. But before we get to that topic, we first apply HMMs to a challenging malware detection problem.

9.3 Detecting Undetectable Malware

In the field of malware detection, a *signature* typically consists of a string of bits that is present in a malware executable. Signature-based detection is by far the most popular method used by anti-virus (AV) software today [12].

Metamorphic malware uses code morphing as a means of evading signature detection [143]. Since there are innumerable ways to modify software without changing its function, metamorphism can be a highly effective tool for malware writers. In fact, the authors of [18] provide a rigorous proof that well-designed metamorphic malware can evade signature detection.[3] Even better, the proof is constructive in the sense that it can be used to design a metamorphic generator that is assured of producing code that is "undetectable," from the perspective of signature detection.

In the paper [157], a metamorphic generator is constructed that satisfies the conditions in [18], and it is verified that the resulting malware evades signature detection. However, it is also shown that the resulting malware is easily detectable using HMMs. Note that this does not contradict the result in [18]. Instead, these results serve to highlight a strength of machine learning, as compared to standard signature-based detection. In the remainder of this section, we'll discuss the results in [157] in more detail.

9.3.1 Background

As mentioned above, well-designed metamorphic malware cannot be reliably detected using signature-based techniques [52, 134, 167]. So it might seem strange that relatively few examples of metamorphic malware have actually appeared in the wild, and very few of these provide a high degree of metamorphism. For example, several hacker-produced metamorphic generators

---

[3]Actually, the authors of [18] prove that their morphed code can evade "static detection." However, they have a narrow definition of static detection that is essentially equivalent to the usual concept of signature detection.

are considered in [166], and it's shown that all can be detected with extremely high accuracy using HMMs. Such results suggest that the aspiring metamorphic virus writer faces some significant practical difficulties. Additional research [135] has shown that it's possible (although not easy) to produce highly metamorphic code that is immune to signature scanning and HMM-based detection.

As mentioned above, metamorphic viruses use obfuscation techniques to produce structurally different—but functionally equivalent—versions of code. Again, the virus writer's goal is to evade signature detection, since signature detection is the most widely used anti-virus method.

From a high-level perspective, code obfuscation techniques include substitution, transposition, insertion, and deletion [109]. The specific code obfuscations implemented in several hacker-produced examples of metamorphic malware are summarized in Table 9.2.

Table 9.2: Code obfuscation techniques [18]

	Evol	Zmist	Zperm	Regswap	MetaPHOR
Instruction substitution	—	—	—	✓	—
Instruction permutation	✓	✓	—	—	✓
Garbage code	✓	✓	—	—	✓
Variable substitution	✓	✓	—	✓	✓
Alter control flow	—	✓	✓	—	✓

Instructions that are executed but have no effect on the program logic are referred to as garbage instructions. Garbage instructions inserted between blocks of useful code provides a simple obfuscation strategy and is used in all of the virus generators listed in Table 9.2. While garbage code does not change program functionality, it will tend to increase the size of the code, which can be problematic if repeated over many generations. Viruses that contain garbage instructions are harder to detect using signatures since such instructions tend to break up code that could otherwise yield a signature. Carefully selected garbage code can also be used to defeat statistical-based detection techniques [88].

Instruction reordering is another common metamorphic technique. The instructions in code can be shuffled, with the control flow adjusted (via jump statements, for example) to make the code execute in the appropriate order. In this way, instructions are physically reordered within the code, without altering the actual control flow. Such reordering can also effectively break signatures. However, if too many jump instructions are inserted, this could serve as a simple heuristic to detect malware.

Instruction interchange is another useful obfuscation technique. The idea here is to replace an instruction or set of instructions with equivalent instructions. Code substitution is a powerful obfuscation technique, but it is also relatively difficult to implement, so is seldom seen in the wild.

Of the hacker-produced metamorphic generators analyzed in [166], the only one that provides a high degree of metamorphism is the Next Generation Virus Construction Kit (NGVCK) [160]. Table 9.3 provides snippets of functionally equivalent assembly code from different instances of NGVCK viruses.

Table 9.3: Code obfuscation in NGVCK

Base Version	
	call delta
delta:	pop ebp
	sub ebp, offset delta
Morphed Version 1	
	call delta
delta:	sub dword ptr[esp], offset delta
	pop eax
	mov ebp, eax
Morphed Version 2	
	add ecx, 0031751B ; junk
	call delta
delta:	sub dword ptr[esp], offset delta
	sub ebx,00000909 ; junk
	mov edx, [esp]
	xchg ecx, eax ; junk
	add esp, 00000004
	and ecx, 00005E44 ; junk
	xchg edx, ebp

9.3.2   Signature-Proof Metamorphic Generator

Next, we briefly discuss the metamorphic generator used in the experiments reported here; see [157] for more details. The paper [18] provides a rigorous proof that viruses generated following the approach we outline below cannot be efficiently detected using signature detection.

A seed virus (in the form of assembly code) is input to the metamorphic generator. The code of this seed virus is split into small blocks, where the number of instructions in each block is variable. For the experiments described below, the block size has been set to an average of six opcodes. Following the specification in [18], code blocks cannot end with a label, jump, or a NOP (do nothing) instruction. Also, a precondition on the seed virus is that the entire code must appear in the code section of the assembly file, which implies that viruses that hide code in their data section (for example) cannot be used as the seed.

After splitting the code into blocks, the blocks are randomly shuffled. Then labels are inserted and conditional jump instructions are added as needed to maintain the original control flow. Optionally, the generator in [157] allows garbage code to be inserted, where the amount of such garbage code is an adjustable parameter. The garbage instructions include various copy instructions and opaque predicates [30], with the garbage inserted between pairs of code blocks, after the block shuffling has been completed. This generator has been successfully tested with several virus families, as discussed in [157].

An HMM virus detection technique has been applied to the resulting metamorphic viruses, following the approach in [166]. Specifically, an HMM was trained on 200 distinct metamorphic copies of a given seed virus. The metamorphic engine generated asm files, each of which yields executable code having the same functionality as the seed virus. These 200 samples were assembled using the Borland Turbo TASM 5.0 assembler and linked using the Borland Turbo TLINK 7.1 linker to produce exe (i.e., executable) files. The exe files thus obtained were disassembled using IDA Pro [63], and opcode sequences were extracted.

While this might seem like a very roundabout approach for obtaining opcodes, it is much more realistic than simply taking the opcodes directly from the original asm files. In practice, we would only have access to exe files, which would then have to be disassembled to extract the opcodes needed for training and scoring. The experiments described here mimic this real-world scenario as closely as possible.

Finally, a representative set of benign programs consisting of 40 Cygwin utilities was used in each experiment. These same benign samples were used, for example, in the experiments reported in the papers [166] and [88].

9.3.3 Results

For the experiments considered here, NGVCK viruses were used as the seed viruses. Other virus families were also tested, with equally strong results obtained in all cases; see [157] for more details.

In each experiment that we conducted, popular anti-virus scanners detected the seed virus, but none of the viruses produced by our metamorphic generator were detected. That is, the metamorphic generator successfully defeated all commercial anti-virus products tested. This is not surprising, since signature detection is the primary tool used in such products, and these new-and-improved metamorphic viruses were designed to defeat signature scanning. In contrast, an HMM-based approach was able to easily distinguish the viruses from benign code. We now discuss these HMM experiments in more detail.

In various experiments, the number of distinct opcodes (i.e., M in the HMM) ranged from 40 to 42 and the total number of observations (i.e., T in the HMM) ranged from 41,472 to 42,151. Five-fold cross validation was used (see Section 8.2 of Chapter 8 for a discussion of cross validation), based on a set of 200 metamorphic viruses. For each fold, the resulting HMM was used to score 40 viruses and 40 representative benign samples. In all experiments, the scores were normalized by dividing the overall score by the number of opcodes, giving us a log likelihood per opcode (LLPO) score. By normalizing the HMM result in this way, all scores are directly comparable, regardless of the length of the opcode sequence.

A typical scatterplot for this type of experiment appears in Figure 9.1. In every case, a threshold could easily be set that would provide ideal separation, that is, no false positives or false negatives would occur, and hence the corresponding ROC curve would have an AUC of 1.0 (see Section 8.4 of Chapter 8 for a discussion of ROC analysis). From the malware writer's perspective, this is bad news, while from the good guys' perspective, this is as good as it gets.

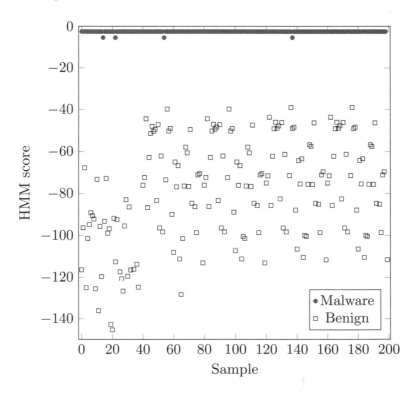

Figure 9.1: NGVCK vs benign

The work summarized in this section illustrates the strength of machine learning in the realm of malware detection. Although the viruses analyzed were not detectable using signature-scanning, they were easily distinguished by HMMs.

This work raises the question of whether a practical metamorphic generator can defeat both signature detection and detection based on machine learning. The paper [39] provides a first attempt to settle this question, while [88] shows conclusively that a metamorphic generator can evade both signature detection and the HMM-based approach considered here. However, it is not yet entirely clear where, in a practical sense, the ultimate balance of power lies between metamorphic viruses and malware detection.

9.4 Classic Cryptanalysis

Since HMM training is based on a hill climb, in general, we only obtain a local maximum. Also, the specific local maximum that we actually reach depends on the starting point, i.e., the initial values selected for the matrices that define the model $\lambda = (A, B, \pi)$. Therefore, by training multiple models on the same data, each with different initial conditions, we would generally be able to find a better solution. We'll see that this approach is particularly valuable in cases where the amount of training data is limited.

In this section, we illustrate the benefits of multiple random restarts through the prism of attacks on classic ciphers. Specifically, we focus on a simple substitution cipher, and a generalization known as a homophonic substitution. The work presented here follows Vobbilisetty [158], which is presented in a condensed form in the paper [159].

A simple substitution cipher is based on a fixed permutation of the plaintext characters. For example, in the well-known Caesar's cipher,[4] a message is encrypted by substituting the letter that is 3 positions ahead in the alphabet. In general, any permutation of the alphabet can serve as a simple substitution key [137].

Before discussing our HMM-based attack, we present Jakobsen's algorithm, which is a powerful technique for breaking simple substitution ciphers. We'll compare HMM-based attacks to this algorithm.

9.4.1 Jakobsen's Algorithm

Throughout this section, we assume that the plaintext message is English text consisting only of the upper-case letters A through Z. We'll denote a

---

[4]Historians generally agree that the Caesar's cipher was named after the Roman dictator Julius Caesar, not the salad [137].

simple substitution key as a permutation of the form

$$K = (k_1, k_2, k_3, \ldots, k_{26}).\tag{9.1}$$

For example, the key

$$K = (\texttt{DEFGHIJKLMNOPQRSTUVWXYZABC})$$

maps each plaintext letter to the letter three positions ahead in the alphabet. As mentioned above, this special case of the simple substitution is known as the Caesar's cipher. In general, the key need not be a shift—any permutation of the alphabet will work.

It's a textbook exercise to show that a simple substitution can be broken using frequency analysis. Since the distribution of plaintext letters in English is far from uniform, and the mapping from plaintext to ciphertext is fixed, we can determine useful information about the key directly from the ciphertext. For example, the letter E is the most common letter in English, accounting for more than 12% of the characters in typical English text.[5] It follows that the most common letter in a simple substitution ciphertext message will likely correspond to E in plaintext.

For any automated hill climb attack on a simple substitution, the following issues must be addressed.

1. How should we select an initial putative key?

2. Given a putative key, how do we compute a score?

3. How should we systematically modify the putative key?

For the initial key, we'll use information derived from the monograph statistics. Specifically, we map the most frequent letter of the ciphertext to E, we map the second most frequent letter of the ciphertext to the second most frequent letter in English, and so on. This putative key might only have a few of the letters correctly mapped, and the shorter the message, the more uncertain is this initial key.

There are many ways to systematically modify the putative key. Swapping elements of a permutation will always result in another permutation. It follows that swapping any two elements of a simple substitution key will yield another valid key. Furthermore, any permutation can be obtained via a series of swaps. Therefore, Jakobsen's algorithm uses only swaps to modify the putative key. Specifically, Jakobsen's algorithm modifies the key as follows: Given a putative key K as in (9.1), the algorithm swaps pairs of elements

---

[5]This explains why you have to pay extra for a vowel in *Wheel of Fortune* [164].

according to the "key schedule"

$$
\begin{array}{lllllllll}
\text{row 1:} & k_1|k_2 & k_2|k_3 & k_3|k_4 & \ldots & k_{23}|k_{24} & k_{24}|k_{25} & k_{25}|k_{26} \\
\text{row 2:} & k_1|k_3 & k_2|k_4 & k_3|k_5 & \ldots & k_{23}|k_{25} & k_{24}|k_{26} \\
\text{row 3:} & k_1|k_4 & k_2|k_5 & k_3|k_6 & \ldots & k_{23}|k_{26} \\
& \vdots & \vdots & & \ddots \\
\text{row 23:} & k_1|k_{24} & k_2|k_{25} & k_3|k_{26} \\
\text{row 24:} & k_1|k_{25} & k_2|k_{26} \\
\text{row 25:} & k_1|k_{26},
\end{array}
\tag{9.2}
$$

where "|" indicates a swap. That is, we first swap adjacent elements, then elements at distance two, then elements at distance three, and so on.

After each swap, we compute a score, based on the putative plaintext obtained from the modified key. If the current swap improves the score, we update the putative key to include the swap; otherwise the putative key remains unchanged. Also, whenever the score improves, we restart swapping from the beginning of the key schedule given in (9.2). If we reach the final swap in row 25 and the score does not improve, the algorithm terminates, as we have reached a local maximum and the scoring algorithm cannot climb further from that point.

Finally, we must specify a scoring function. Let $E = \{e_{ij}\}$ be a 26×26 matrix containing expected digraph frequencies of English text. Then, for example, $e_{1,1}$ contains the expected frequency of the digraph AA, while $e_{20,8}$ is the expected frequency of the pair TH, and so on. Figure 9.2 provides a heatmap of the expected digraph frequencies in English, where the darker shades correspond to less frequent digraphs. From this heatmap, we see that the digraph distribution of English is highly non-uniform.

Suppose that we are given a simple substitution ciphertext message, and we want to attempt to break it by applying Jakobsen's algorithm. We first select the initial putative key by matching the monograph statistics of the ciphertext with that of English. Then we conduct a hill climb based on digraph distribution of English, following the swapping pattern in (9.2). Let $D = \{d_{ij}\}$ be a 26×26 matrix containing the digraph statistics of the putative plaintext at any point in this process. That is, the matrix D contains the digraph statistics of the putative plaintext obtained by decrypting the ciphertext using the corresponding putative key K. In Jakobsen's algorithm, the score for the putative key K is computed as

$$
\texttt{score}(D, E) = \sum_{i,j} |d_{ij} - e_{ij}|.
\tag{9.3}
$$

Note that $\texttt{score}(D, E) \geq 0$, and the lower the score, the better the match.

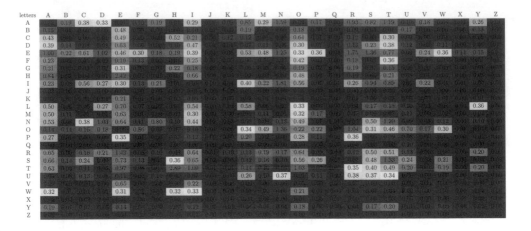

Figure 9.2: English digraph relative frequencies (as percentages)

The efficiency of Jakobsen's algorithm derives from the fact that swapping elements of the putative key K corresponds to swapping the corresponding rows and columns of the digraph distribution matrix D. Consequently, we only need to decrypt the message once—each time we swap elements of the key, the score computation only requires elementary manipulations of the rows and columns of D. Next, we give a small example that illustrates the steps of Jakobsen's algorithm.

To simplify the presentation, suppose that we have an alphabet consisting of only the eight letters

$$\texttt{E H I K L R S T}$$

and we are given the ciphertext

$$\texttt{HTHEIHEILIRKSHEIRLHKTISRRKSIIKLIEHTTRLHKTIS.} \qquad (9.4)$$

The frequency counts for the ciphertext in (9.4) are

E	H	I	K	L	R	S	T
4	7	9	5	4	5	4	5

We suspect this ciphertext was generated using a simple substitution.

Assuming that the letters in our reduced alphabet appear in plaintext at the same relative frequencies as in ordinary English, listing the letters from most frequent to least frequent gives us

$$\texttt{E T I S H R L K.}$$

Matching the expected frequencies of the plaintext to the observed frequencies of the ciphertext, we obtain the initial putative key

Plaintext	H T E I K S L R
Ciphertext	E H I K L R S T

(9.5)

Using this putative key, we decrypt the ciphertext in (9.4) to obtain the initial putative plaintext

TRTHETHEKESILTHESKTIRELSSILEEIKEHTRRSKTIREL.

From this plaintext, we have the digraph frequency matrix

	E	H	I	K	L	R	S	T
E	1	1	1	1	2	0	2	1
H	3	0	0	0	0	0	0	1
I	0	0	0	1	2	2	0	0
K	2	0	0	0	0	0	0	2
L	1	0	0	0	0	0	1	1
R	2	0	0	0	0	1	1	1
S	0	0	2	2	0	0	1	0
T	0	3	2	0	0	2	0	0

$$(9.6)$$

which is denoted as D.

The next step in Jakobsen's algorithm swaps elements of the putative key. For the first swap, we interchange the roles of E and H in the row labeled "plaintext" in (9.5), giving us the putative key

Plaintext	E T H I K S L R
Ciphertext	E H I K L R S T

Using this key, the ciphertext decrypts to

TRTEHTEHKHSILTEHSKTIRHLSSILHHIKHETRRSKTIRHL

and this putative plaintext yields the digraph frequency matrix

	E	H	I	K	L	R	S	T
E	0	3	0	0	0	0	0	1
H	1	1	1	1	2	0	2	1
I	0	0	0	1	2	2	0	0
K	0	2	0	0	0	0	0	2
L	0	1	0	0	0	0	1	1
R	0	2	0	0	0	1	1	1
S	0	0	2	2	0	0	1	0
T	3	0	2	0	0	2	0	0

$$(9.7)$$

which we denote as D'. Note that the updated matrix D' in (9.7) can be obtained from the matrix D in (9.6) by simply swapping the first two rows and the first two columns. Therefore, it's not necessary to decrypt the message to determine the updated matrix D', since it can be obtained directly from D.

In general, if we swap elements i and j of the putative key, we swap rows i and j, and columns i and j of the D matrix to obtain the digraph distribution matrix for this new putative decryption. Thus, Jakobsen's algorithm is extremely efficient, since we only need to decrypt once—after the initial decryption, Jakobsen's algorithm consists entirely of matrix manipulations and score computations.

A more precise description of Jakobsen's algorithm is given here in the form of Algorithm 9.1. The notation $\text{swap}_K(k_i, k_j)$ is used to denote the putative key obtained by swapping elements in the ith and j^{th} positions of the key K, and $\text{swap}_D(i, j)$ denotes the matrix obtained by swapping the ith and j^{th} rows and columns of the matrix D.

Algorithm 9.1 Jakobsen's algorithm

1: **Given:**
     Digraph statistic matrix E and ciphertext C
2: **Initialize:**
     $N = 26$ // number of ciphertext symbols
     $K = (k_1, k_2, \ldots, k_N)$ // initial key
     decrypt C with K and compute digraph matrix D
     $s = \text{score}(D, E)$ // score as defined in (9.3)
     $a = 1, b = 1$
3: **while** $b < N$ **do**
4:      $i = a, j = a + b$
5:      $K' = \text{swap}_K(k_i, k_j)$, $D' = \text{swap}_D(i, j)$, $s' = \text{score}(D', E)$
6:      **if** $s' < s$ **then** // score improved
7:          $s = s', K = K', D = D'$ // update
8:          $a = 1, b = 1$ // reset swapping
9:      **else** // get next key swap
10:          $a = a + 1$
11:          **if** $a + b > N$ **then**
12:              $a = 1, b = b + 1$ // next row of (9.2)
13:          **end if**
14:      **end if**
15: **end while**
16: **return** K

Experimental results obtained using Jakobsen's algorithm are given in Figure 9.3. Each of the results in this figure is based on an average of 1000 test cases, with plaintext selected from the Brown Corpus [21] and with keys generated at random. In Figure 9.3, "key" refers to the elements of the key that are recovered correctly, while "data" refers to the letters of the decrypted message that are correct. It is not surprising that the "data" results exceed the "key" results on average, since infrequent letters are unlikely to be determined correctly, and such letters account for a small percentage of the data, but a relatively large proportion of the key.

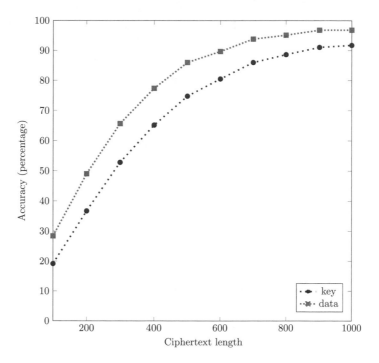

Figure 9.3: Jakobsen's algorithm

Whenever about 80% of the characters are recovered correctly, the remaining 20% are easily determined from context [43]. Therefore, we consider an accuracy of 80% or more as a complete success. From Figure 9.3, we see that for this level of accuracy, Jakobsen's algorithm requires about 400 characters of ciphertext.

9.4.2   HMM with Random Restarts

In this section, we consider the effectiveness of HMMs with multiple random restarts, within the context of solving simple substitution ciphers. But, it's important to realize that these results are generally applicable when HMMs are used.

Recall the HMM English text example considered in Section 9.2. Instead of English text, suppose that the observation sequence consists of ciphertext from a simple substitution. Given a sufficiently long ciphertext message, an HMM with $N = 2$ hidden states would yield a B matrix that tells us which ciphertext letters correspond to consonants and which correspond to vowels. This would certainly be an aid to solving a simple substitution, but we can actually do much better by increasing the number of hidden states.

Instead of using $N = 2$ hidden states in our HMM, we might try $N = 26$ hidden states. Since there are 26 distinct plaintext symbols, it seems plausible that the underlying Markov process would then correspond to the transitions between individual letters in the (hidden) plaintext. If so, the resulting B matrix would, in a probabilistic sense, reveal the correspondence between plaintext symbols and ciphertext symbols. That is, the B matrix of such a trained HMM would reveal the simple substitution key. Furthermore, in this scenario, the A matrix would correspond to the expected plaintext digraph statistics. Therefore, we could initialize the A matrix based on the digraph statistics of English, and there would be no need to re-estimate A during the training process.

As in the discussion of Jakobsen's algorithm above, we first consider an example using a restricted alphabet. From the Brown Corpus, we extract words that have all of their letters among the 8-letter alphabet

$$\texttt{E T I S H R L K.} \qquad (9.8)$$

We append all of these words to obtain a sequence of about 370,000 letters. To avoid 0 (or nearly so) probabilities, we initialize each digraph count to five. Then we tabulate digraph frequencies from our sequence of 370,000 letters. Finally, we normalize each element by its corresponding row sum to obtain the row stochastic matrix A. In this case, we obtain (to three decimal places of accuracy) the A matrix

	E	H	I	K	L	R	S	T
E	0.020	0.123	0.161	0.002	0.027	0.062	0.061	0.544
H	0.878	0.000	0.115	0.000	0.000	0.006	0.000	0.001
I	0.007	0.014	0.036	0.030	0.028	0.064	0.519	0.301
K	0.758	0.015	0.136	0.006	0.005	0.004	0.014	0.062
L	0.276	0.032	0.341	0.004	0.194	0.001	0.041	0.110
R	0.378	0.095	0.109	0.003	0.015	0.004	0.082	0.314
S	0.096	0.204	0.146	0.005	0.018	0.002	0.040	0.489
T	0.011	0.851	0.038	0.000	0.012	0.005	0.025	0.059

$$(9.9)$$

For example, based on the digraphs in this 8-letter "language," we see that HE is the most common of the digraphs that begin with H, while HI is the next most common, and the other digraphs beginning with H are all relatively uncommon. Note also that this A matrix is essentially the same as the E matrix in Jakobsen's algorithm, except that A is normalized to be row stochastic, which is a necessary condition for an HMM.

We conducted an experiment using a plaintext message consisting entirely of words that only use the 8-letter alphabet in (9.8). For this experiment, we used a plaintext of length 1000, and we have $M = 8$, since the 8 letters in the restricted alphabet are the only possible observations. We choose $N = 8$

hidden states, and we assume that the hidden states will correspond to the plaintext letters. Therefore, we can initialize A using the matrix in (9.9), and this A matrix is not re-estimated during training.

We initialize each element of B to approximately $1/8$, subject to the row-stochastic condition. For this example, we initialized B^T as

Plaintext (hidden)

		E	H	I	K	L	R	S	T
	E	0.126	0.135	0.118	0.119	0.133	0.120	0.122	0.115
	H	0.131	0.117	0.135	0.124	0.131	0.128	0.125	0.128
	I	0.119	0.117	0.115	0.138	0.130	0.118	0.128	0.131
Ciphertext	K	0.123	0.119	0.120	0.125	0.122	0.132	0.131	0.126
	L	0.131	0.136	0.124	0.117	0.113	0.131	0.120	0.126
	R	0.122	0.127	0.131	0.140	0.124	0.121	0.122	0.123
	S	0.131	0.127	0.126	0.119	0.124	0.134	0.123	0.125
	T	0.119	0.122	0.131	0.119	0.125	0.116	0.131	0.126

After about 200 iterations of the Baum-Welch re-estimation algorithm (see Section 2.8 of Chapter 2), we find that B^T converges to

Plaintext (hidden)

		E	H	I	K	L	R	S	T	
	E	0.03	0.00	0.00	0.00	0.00	0.48	0.00	0.00	
	H	0.00	0.00	0.00	0.00	0.05	0.23	0.78	0.00	
	I	0.00	0.00	0.00	0.00	0.00	0.00	0.22	1.00	
Ciphertext	K	0.97	0.00	0.00	0.00	0.05	0.29	0.00	0.00	(9.10)
	L	0.00	0.99	0.00	0.00	0.00	0.00	0.00	0.00	
	R	0.00	0.00	1.00	0.00	0.00	0.00	0.00	0.00	
	S	0.00	0.00	0.00	0.80	0.00	0.00	0.00	0.00	
	T	0.00	0.01	0.00	0.20	0.90	0.00	0.00	0.00	

Recall that for an HMM, we denote the element in row i and column j of B as $b_i(j)$, where $b_i(j)$ gives the probability of observation j when the model is in the hidden state i. In this example, we assume that the hidden states of A correspond to the plaintext letters E, H, I, K, L, R, S, T. It follows that the probabilities in B relate the observations (i.e., ciphertext symbols) to the plaintext. From the definition of $b_i(j)$, we see that $\operatorname{argmax}_j b_i(j)$ gives us the most likely mapping of ciphertext i to plaintext. That is, the largest probability in row i of B (equivalently, column i in B^T) gives us the mapping of the plaintext symbol corresponding to the ith symbol, with respect to encryption. Hence, we deduce that in this example, the most likely key is given by the underlined entries in (9.10), that is,

Plaintext	E H I K L R S T
Ciphertext	K L R S T E H I

In this case, we have determined the correct key, since a Caesar's cipher was indeed used to generate the ciphertext.

In general, HMM success depends on the initial values selected for the matrices A, B, and π, and hence we may get better results by training multiple times, using different initial values each time, and selecting the model with the best final score. Next, we summarize extensive HMM experiments using multiple random restarts for simple substitution cryptanalysis. These experiments were motivated by the work presented in [16], where a similar method is used to analyze the unsolved Zodiac 340 cipher.

All experiments discussed below were performed on English text selected from the Brown Corpus, using only the 26 lower-case letters. The encryption permutations were selected at random. And for all experiments reported here, we used 200 iterations when training the HMM. Also, the A matrix was initialized based on English digraph statistics, and it remains fixed throughout. The elements of the B matrix are initialized at random, subject to the row stochastic condition.

In Figure 9.4, we have plotted accuracy versus the length of the ciphertext, where the number of random restarts varies from 1 (i.e., a single iteration) to 10^5. From this graph, it's easy to see that there is a rapid improvement in the results up to about 1000 restarts, beyond which there is only a relatively small improvement. Nevertheless, for very short messages, it might be well worth using a large number of random restarts—perhaps as many as 10^5, or more.

As mentioned above, an accuracy of 80% is sufficient to recover the entire message. According to Figure 9.4, this level of accuracy is exceeded with 1000 restarts for a message of length 300. And a message of length 200 can almost be solved with 10^5 random restarts. In contrast, Jakobsen's algorithm only achieves 80% accuracy for a ciphertext of length greater than 400. The comparison between Jakobsen's algorithm and an HMM with 10^5 random restarts is given in Figure 9.5.

Both Jakobsen's algorithm and the HMM are based on digraph statistics, yet the HMM is able to extract considerably more statistical information from the data than Jakobsen's algorithm. Of course, this doesn't come for free, as we need to do a large number of random restarts for the HMM to achieve such a level of accuracy.

In Figure 9.6, we give a 3-d plot of accuracy as a function of the ciphertext length and number of restarts. This same data is presented from another angle in Figure 9.7. Several additional related experiments and results are discussed in the report [158].

Our results indicate that a simple substitution ciphertext with fewer than 400 characters can't be solved using Jakobsen's algorithm. However, an HMM with a large number of random restarts can solve a simple substitution with about 200 characters, although the work factor is high. In fact,

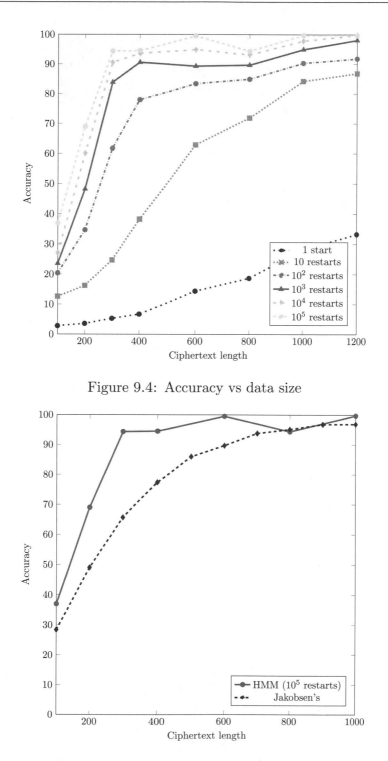

Figure 9.4: Accuracy vs data size

Figure 9.5: Jakobsen's algorithm vs HMM

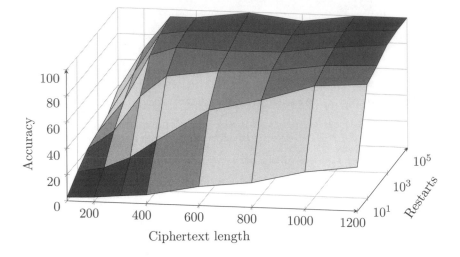

Figure 9.6: Accuracy vs data size vs restarts (200 iterations)

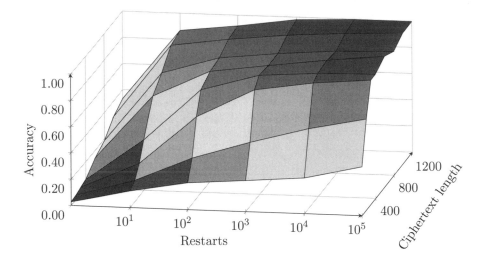

Figure 9.7: Accuracy vs restarts vs data size (200 iterations)

for a simple substitution, each instance of the HMM is comparable in cost to an entire run of Jakobsen's algorithm. Therefore, using an HMM with large numbers of random restarts is only sensible in the most challenging cases.

For Jakobsen's algorithm, the E matrix contains digraph statistics for the plaintext language. In comparison, for the HMM-based attack we use these same statistics to specify the A matrix, which can remain fixed throughout the training. However, typically when training an HMM, the A matrix is re-estimated as part of the hill climb. Consequently, if we do not know the plaintext language, an HMM can still work (see the English text example in Section 9.2) while Jakobsen's algorithm is not applicable. Of course, it is likely that more data (or more random restarts) will be required when we re-estimate A, since there are many more parameters to determine.

Even when the plaintext language is known, a particular message might not follow the language statistics closely. In such cases, we could initialize the A matrix based on language statistics, and then re-estimate A as part of the hill climb. This would likely give us a reasonable starting point for A, and it would also enable the A matrix to adapt so that it could better match the actual statistics of the message, as opposed to forcing the message to fit a generic language model. This approach is likely to be most valuable for short messages, which are precisely the cases where the HMM with multiple random restarts strategy is most beneficial.

We conclude this section with a brief discussion of a generalization of the simple substitution cipher. A *homophonic substitution* cipher is like a simple substitution, except that multiple ciphertext symbols can map to a single plaintext letter. For example, if several ciphertext symbols map to the letter E, then English language statistics would be "flattened" (i.e., more uniform) in the ciphertext, making statistical attacks more difficult.

In the paper [43], Jakobsen's algorithm is generalized to the homophonic substitution case, using a nested hill climb—an outer hill climb on the distribution of plaintext letters within the ciphertext, and an inner hill climb consisting of Jakobsen's algorithm with multiple restarts for various mappings to plaintext letter.

In general, the difficulty of breaking a homophonic substitution depends on both the ciphertext length and the number of ciphertext symbols. For the Jakobsen-like approach in [43], good results are obtained for a ciphertext alphabet of size 28, when the ciphertext is of length 500, but messages with a ciphertext alphabet of size 45 require a length in excess of 1000 characters for any reasonable chance of success.

As mentioned above, in [16], a technique that is essentially the same as an HMM with random restarts (and fixed A matrix) is applied to the unsolved Zodiac 340 cipher.[6] The solved Zodiac 408 cipher was a homophonic substitution cipher with more than 60 symbols, and the unsolved Zodiac 340 looks similar. However, the work presented in [16] provides good evidence that the Zodiac 340 is not a homophonic substitution—which is not too surprising given that it has remained unsolved for more than 40 years. In contrast, the Zodiac 408 cipher was broken within a few days of its release.

Using an HMM to break a homophonic substitution is similar to the simple substitution case. In fact, the A matrix remains the same, that is, the A

---

[6]See Problems 15 and 16 at the end of Chapter 2 for illustrations of the Zodiac 408 and Zodiac 340 cipher, respectively. Problem 15 also includes a brief discussion of the Zodiac Killer, the murderer who created these ciphers.

matrix is 26×26 and contains English language digraph statistics. The B matrix is $26 \times M$, where M is the number of distinct ciphertext symbols. As in the simple substitution, the trained B matrix contains a probabilistic representation of the key. However, deducing the key from the B matrix is somewhat more challenging for a homophonic substitution.

An example of the final B^T for a homophonic substitution is given in Table 9.4, where all elements greater than 0.10 are underlined. As with previous examples, the English plaintext consists of the 26 uppercase letters. In this example, there are 29 distinct ciphertext symbols, which we denote as 0 through 28. From the results in Table 9.4, most of the key is obvious—the letter A maps to 3, and B maps to 4, and so on. We could use the fact that uncommon letters are more likely to give ambiguous results when selecting the most likely key. For example, the numbers in the E column in Table 9.4 are likely to be far more reliable than the numbers in the J, Q, or Z columns.

For the example in Table 9.4, the actual key is

Plaintext	A	B	C	D	E	F	G	H	I	J	K	L	M	N	O	P	Q	R	S	T	U	V	W	X	Y	Z
	3	4	5	6	7	8	9	10	11	12	13	14	15	16	17	18	19	20	21	22	23	24	25	0	1	2
Ciphertext					26															27						
					28																					

Note that if we simply take the element with the largest probability in each row of Table 9.4, we obtain the correct key. In this case, the key corresponds to a Caesar's cipher, except when encrypting E, in which case we choose from ciphertext symbols 7, 26, and 28, and when encrypting T, where we select either 22 or 27.

Table 9.4: Example B^T for homophonic substitution

	A	B	C	D	E	F	G	H	I	J	K	L	M	N	O	P	Q	R	S	T	U	V	W	X	Y	Z
0	0.00	0.00	0.00	0.00	0.00	0.00	0.00	0.00	0.00	0.00	0.00	0.00	0.00	0.00	0.00	0.00	0.00	0.00	0.00	0.00	0.00	0.00	0.00	0.82	0.00	0.00
1	0.00	0.00	0.00	0.00	0.00	0.00	0.00	0.00	0.00	0.00	0.00	0.00	0.00	0.00	0.00	0.00	0.00	0.00	0.00	0.00	0.00	0.00	0.00	0.00	0.98	0.00
2	0.00	0.00	0.00	0.00	0.00	0.00	0.00	0.00	0.00	0.00	0.00	0.00	0.00	0.00	0.00	0.00	0.00	0.00	0.00	0.00	0.00	0.00	0.00	0.00	0.00	0.00
3	0.97	0.00	0.00	0.00	0.00	0.00	0.00	0.00	0.00	0.00	0.00	0.00	0.00	0.00	0.00	0.00	0.00	0.00	0.00	0.00	0.00	0.00	0.00	0.00	0.00	0.32
4	0.00	0.00	0.00	0.00	0.00	0.00	0.00	0.01	0.00	0.00	0.00	0.00	0.00	0.01	0.00	0.00	0.00	0.00	0.00	0.00	0.00	0.03	0.00	0.00	0.00	0.00
5	0.00	0.87	0.98	0.00	0.00	0.00	0.00	0.00	0.00	0.00	0.00	0.00	0.00	0.00	0.00	0.00	0.00	0.00	0.00	0.00	0.00	0.00	0.00	0.00	0.00	0.17
6	0.00	0.00	0.00	1.00	0.25	0.00	0.08	0.00	0.00	0.00	0.00	0.00	0.00	0.00	0.00	0.00	0.00	0.00	0.00	0.00	0.00	0.00	0.01	0.00	0.00	0.00
7	0.01	0.00	0.00	0.00	0.00	0.25	0.00	0.00	0.00	0.00	0.00	0.01	0.00	0.00	0.00	0.00	0.00	0.00	0.00	0.00	0.00	0.00	0.00	0.00	0.00	0.00
8	0.00	0.00	0.01	0.00	0.00	0.90	0.00	0.00	0.00	0.37	0.00	0.00	0.00	0.00	0.00	0.00	0.28	0.00	0.00	0.00	0.00	0.00	0.00	0.00	0.00	0.08
9	0.00	0.00	0.00	0.00	0.00	0.00	0.00	0.00	0.00	0.00	0.00	0.00	0.00	0.00	0.00	0.00	0.00	0.00	0.00	0.00	0.00	0.00	0.00	0.00	0.00	0.00
10	0.00	0.00	0.00	0.00	0.00	0.00	0.78	0.89	0.00	0.00	0.00	0.00	0.00	0.00	0.00	0.00	0.00	0.00	0.00	0.00	0.00	0.11	0.01	0.00	0.00	0.00
11	0.00	0.00	0.00	0.00	0.00	0.00	0.00	0.02	1.00	0.00	0.00	0.00	0.00	0.00	0.00	0.00	0.00	0.00	0.00	0.00	0.00	0.00	0.00	0.00	0.00	0.00
12	0.00	0.00	0.00	0.00	0.00	0.00	0.00	0.00	0.00	0.63	0.00	0.00	0.00	0.00	0.00	0.00	0.00	0.00	0.00	0.00	0.00	0.00	0.00	0.00	0.00	0.00
13	0.00	0.00	0.00	0.00	0.00	0.00	0.01	0.00	0.00	0.00	0.43	0.00	0.00	0.00	0.00	0.00	0.41	0.00	0.00	0.00	0.00	0.09	0.00	0.00	0.00	0.00
14	0.00	0.00	0.00	0.00	0.00	0.00	0.00	0.01	0.00	0.00	0.00	0.99	0.84	0.02	0.00	0.00	0.00	0.00	0.00	0.00	0.00	0.00	0.00	0.00	0.00	0.00
15	0.00	0.00	0.00	0.00	0.00	0.00	0.00	0.03	0.00	0.00	0.00	0.00	0.00	0.00	0.00	0.00	0.00	0.00	0.00	0.00	0.00	0.00	0.06	0.01	0.00	0.00
16	0.00	0.00	0.00	0.00	0.00	0.00	0.00	0.00	0.00	0.00	0.00	0.00	0.00	0.90	1.00	0.00	0.00	0.00	0.00	0.00	0.00	0.00	0.00	0.06	0.00	0.00
17	0.00	0.00	0.00	0.00	0.00	0.00	0.00	0.00	0.00	0.00	0.00	0.00	0.06	0.00	1.00	1.00	0.00	0.00	0.00	0.00	0.00	0.00	0.00	0.00	0.00	0.00
18	0.00	0.02	0.00	0.00	0.00	0.00	0.00	0.02	0.00	0.00	0.00	0.00	0.00	0.00	0.00	1.00	0.02	0.00	0.00	0.00	0.00	0.00	0.00	0.00	0.00	0.00
19	0.00	0.00	0.00	0.00	0.00	0.00	0.00	0.00	0.00	0.00	0.00	0.00	0.05	0.00	0.00	0.00	0.29	1.00	0.00	0.00	0.00	0.00	0.00	0.00	0.00	0.00
20	0.00	0.09	0.00	0.00	0.00	0.00	0.04	0.00	0.00	0.00	0.00	0.00	0.00	0.05	0.00	0.00	0.00	1.00	0.00	0.00	0.00	0.00	0.00	0.11	0.00	0.00
21	0.00	0.03	0.00	0.00	0.00	0.00	0.00	0.00	0.00	0.00	0.26	0.00	0.00	0.00	0.00	0.00	0.00	0.00	1.00	0.52	0.00	0.05	0.00	0.00	0.00	0.27
22	0.00	0.00	0.00	0.00	0.00	0.00	0.00	0.00	0.00	0.00	0.00	0.00	0.00	0.02	0.00	0.00	0.00	0.00	1.00	0.00	1.00	0.00	0.02	0.00	0.00	0.16
23	0.00	0.00	0.00	0.00	0.00	0.01	0.00	0.00	0.00	0.00	0.00	0.00	0.00	0.00	0.00	0.00	0.00	0.00	0.00	0.00	0.00	0.00	0.00	0.00	0.00	0.00
24	0.00	0.00	0.00	0.00	0.00	0.00	0.01	0.00	0.00	0.00	0.00	0.00	0.04	0.00	0.00	0.00	0.00	0.00	0.00	0.00	0.00	0.72	0.90	0.00	0.00	0.00
25	0.00	0.00	0.00	0.00	0.52	0.00	0.00	0.00	0.00	0.00	0.00	0.00	0.00	0.00	0.00	0.00	0.00	0.00	0.00	0.00	0.00	0.00	0.00	0.00	0.00	0.00
26	0.00	0.00	0.00	0.00	0.00	0.00	0.00	0.00	0.00	0.00	0.00	0.00	0.00	0.00	0.00	0.00	0.00	0.00	0.00	0.00	0.00	0.00	0.00	0.00	0.02	0.00
27	0.00	0.00	0.01	0.00	0.00	0.08	0.08	0.00	0.00	0.00	0.32	0.00	0.00	0.00	0.00	0.00	0.00	0.00	0.00	0.48	0.00	0.00	0.00	0.00	0.00	0.00
28	0.02	0.00	0.00	0.00	0.23	0.00	0.00	0.01	0.00	0.00	0.00	0.00	0.00	0.00	0.00	0.00	0.00	0.00	0.00	0.00	0.00	0.00	0.00	0.00	0.00	0.00

Chapter 10

PHMM Applications

Models are to be used, not believed.
— Henri Theil

10.1 Introduction

In this chapter, we'll discuss two applications of profile hidden Markov models (PHMM) to problems in information security. First, we consider the topic of masquerade detection, which is a special case of intrusion detection. Then we show that PHMMs can be effective for malware detection, at least in certain cases.

10.2 Masquerade Detection

A masquerader is someone who makes unauthorized use of another user's computer account [121]. In the report [61] and the paper [62], we consider masquerade detection, which can be viewed as a type of anomaly-based intrusion detection system (IDS). We assume a UNIX environment, and detection is based on UNIX command sequences.

The goal of the paper [61] is to analyze a novel method for masquerade detection based on PHMMs. We compare results to an HMM-based detection scheme and to a popular technique based on n-gram analysis.

All of the experiments discussed in this section are based on the Schonlau data set [120], which has been widely used in masquerade detection research. Although this dataset is old and leaves much to be desired (especially with respect to PHMM analysis), it does enable researchers to easily compare different proposed techniques.

Next, we briefly discuss the Schonlau data set. Then we'll present our experimental results.

The Schonlau data consists of 50 data files, one file for each of 50 users. In each file, there are 15,000 commands, collected using the UNIX audit tool `acct` [57]. The first 5000 commands in each file are from a specific user, and these commands are intended to serve as training data. The remaining 10,000 commands include both user and masquerader command blocks, and these blocks are intended to serve as test data. The test data can be viewed as 100 distinct blocks, with 100 commands per block.

The Schonlau dataset includes a map file that specifies the locations of the masquerader blocks within the test set. The entries of the map file are either zero or one, where a zero indicates the commands in the corresponding block are not a masquerader, and a one indicates masquerader data.

10.2.1   Experiments with Schonlau Dataset

We tested both an HMM technique and a weighted n-gram score. For more details on the n-gram technique, see the report [61]. For all HMM results reported here, we use $N = 2$ hidden states—experiments have been conducted with larger numbers of hidden states, but the effect on the results is insignificant [61]. Figure 10.1 gives ROC curves for HMMs and various n-gram models. From these results, it appears that the HMM performance is similar to that of the n-gram models.

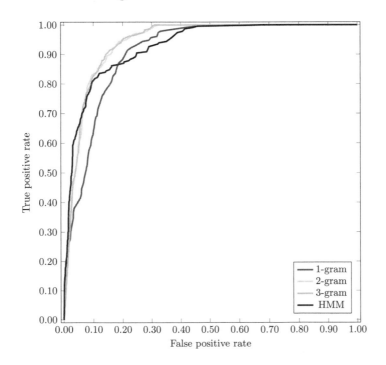

Figure 10.1: Comparison of HMM and weighted n-grams

For the ROC curves in Figure 10.1, the corresponding area under the curve (AUC) and partial area under the curve (AUC_p) values are listed in Table 10.1. From these results, we see that with respect to the AUC statistic, the HMM is comparable to the n-gram techniques, and slightly outperforms these scores in terms of the AUC_p statistic. Here, we are using a "useful region" where FPR ≤ 0.1 for the AUC_p calculations which, as in Section 8.4 of Chapter 8, we shorthand as $AUC_{0.1}$.

Table 10.1: AUC and $AUC_{0.1}$ for ROC curves in Figure 10.1

Score	AUC	$AUC_{0.1}$
1-gram	0.9098	0.4048
2-gram	0.9406	0.5314
3-gram	0.9410	0.5441
HMM	0.9275	0.5845

As we know from the discussion in Chapter 3, PHMM training data must be in the form of multiple sequences. However, the Schonlau training data only provides a single list of 5000 training commands per user. To generate an MSA for a given user from such data, we first need to derive multiple sequences. Ideally, we would divide the list into distinct sessions, with meaningful start and end criteria. Unfortunately, session information is not available for the Schonlau dataset.

For any PHMM, there is an inherent tradeoff between sequence length and the number of sequences. On the one hand, more sequences will tend to result in more gaps in the MSA, thereby weakening the resulting PHMM. On the other hand, if there are too few sequences, then each state in the constructed PHMM has an insufficient number of symbols to generate reliable emission probabilities. Table 10.2 lists the different combinations of sequences and lengths that we used in our PHMM experiments involving the Schonlau data.

Table 10.2: Sequence parameters

Number	Length
4	1250
5	1000
10	500
20	250
50	100

Figure 10.2 summarizes some of our experimental results, in the form of multiple ROC curves. While the PHMM generated using five sequences yields the lowest false negative rates, the overall detection results do not differ significantly for any of these cases.

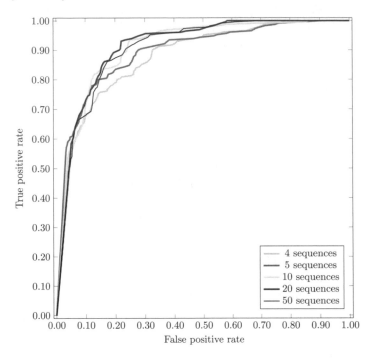

Figure 10.2: Detection results for PHMM

Table 10.3: AUC and $AUC_{0.1}$ for PHMM scores in Figure 10.2

Sequences	AUC	$AUC_{0.1}$
4	0.8766	0.4387
5	0.8943	0.5208
10	0.9098	0.4694
20	0.9139	0.4658
50	0.9076	0.4590

Figure 10.3 compares the detection results for a PHMM (using 20 sequences) with those obtained using an HMM and a 3-gram model. The results of the PHMM models are comparable to these other models. The corresponding AUC and $AUC_{0.1}$ values can be found in Tables 10.1 and 10.3.

A PHMM relies on positional information, particularly in the training phase where we must align sequences. In contrast, an HMM depends on the

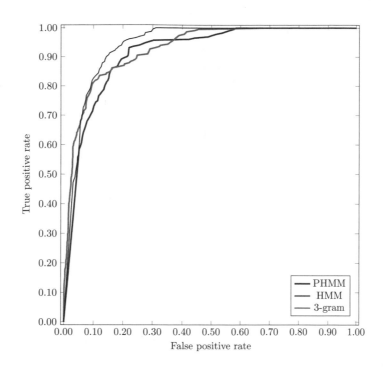

Figure 10.3: Comparison of PHMM, HMM, and 3-gram scores

overall observation sequence, without regard to specific positions within the sequence. Therefore, it is perhaps surprising that the PHMM is competitive with the HMM on this particular data set, since reliable positional information is not available. It seems likely that if accurate positional information was known, a PHMM would perform better, and likely outperform the HMM. To test this hypothesis, we have generated simulated datasets that include relevant session information. Next, we'll compare HMMs and PHMMs on this simulated data.

10.2.2   Simulated Data with Positional Information

To simulate user command sequences that include session beginning and ending information, we designed and implemented a user command sequence generator. For each user in the Schonlau data set, we determine a Markov chain and we use the resulting Markov process to generate training command sequences.

To construct such a Markov chain, we determine an initial state distribution matrix π, and a state transition probability matrix A. To calculate these matrices, we first count the number of distinct commands in the user training command sequence. Let n be the number of distinct commands issued by a given user. Then π is an array of size $n \times 1$ containing the relative frequencies of each command. For the matrix A, we create an $n \times n$ row-stochastic matrix with the probabilities determined by the relative frequencies of command pairs. We use these matrices to generate user command sequences, which we can then use as training data. For more details on this sequence generation process as it applies to the Schonlau data, see [61].

Since this simulated training data is actually generated using a Markov process, we expect that an HMM-based detector will perform extremely well on this data. Perhaps a PHMM might also do well, but there is no obvious reason to expect a PHMM to outperform an HMM. In other words, this synthesized training data does not offer any artificial advantage to the PHMM, relative to the HMM; instead it is more likely that this approach puts any PHMM at a disadvantage.

Finally, we need to generate test data. The "normal" user test data is generated in the same way as the training data, while the attack data is taken from the Schonlau dataset. To generate the attack data, we randomly select blocks from the Schonlau data, as in [120].

Recall that the Schonlau training data consists of 5000 commands and that the test data consists of 10,000 commands divided into 100 blocks. We have generated simulated training and test data sets of the same size using the method outlined above. We then use these datasets to construct HMM and PHMM masquerade detectors as discussed previously.

The detection results for our experiments on this simulated dataset are given in Figure 10.4. We can see that the detection rates for the HMM and PHMM that use the simulated data are much better than those for an HMM based on the Schonlau data set. The improvement for the HMM-based detection is expected, given the method used to construct the simulated data. However, the strength of the PHMM results are somewhat surprising.

Table 10.4 gives AUC results for the ROC curves in Figure 10.4. From the AUC statistic, we see that the HMM and PHMM perform similarly well on the synthetic data set, with the HMM having a slight edge terms of $\text{AUC}_{0.1}$.

Table 10.4: AUC and $\text{AUC}_{0.1}$ for synthetic data

Score	AUC	$\text{AUC}_{0.1}$
HMM	0.9637	0.8690
PHMM	0.9621	0.8424

Finally, we consider the case where the amount of training data is more limited. In Figure 10.5, we give ROC curves for HMMs and PHMMs, where the training data was reduced from 5000 commands to 800, 400, and just 200 commands. These results are based on the simulated dataset.

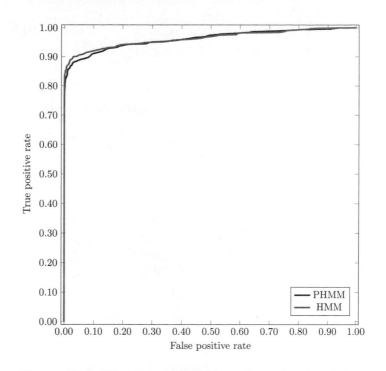

Figure 10.4: HMM vs PHMM based on simulated data

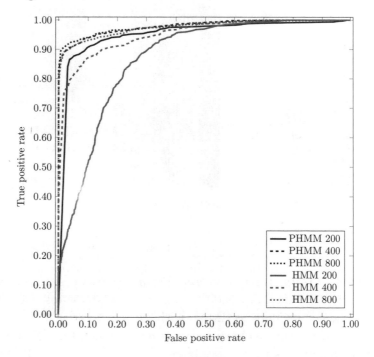

Figure 10.5: HMM vs PHMM with limited training data

The AUC and $AUC_{0.1}$ values for the experiments in Figure 10.5 are given in Table 10.5. These same results are also given in the form of a bar graph in Figure 10.6.

Table 10.5: AUC and $AUC_{0.1}$ with limited synthetic data

Score	Commands	AUC	$AUC_{0.1}$
	200	0.8715	0.3374
HMM	400	0.9516	0.7726
	800	0.9762	0.8958
	200	0.9512	0.7206
PHMM	400	0.9786	0.9007
	800	0.9793	0.8658

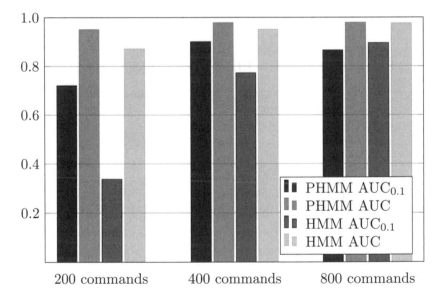

Figure 10.6: Results based on limited synthetic data

From the results in Table 10.5 and Figure 10.6, we see that when the training data is reduced from 5000 to 400 commands or less, a PHMM far outperforms the corresponding HMM, with respect to $AUC_{0.1}$.

It could be very useful to have a strong model when limited data is available. Perhaps an ideal strategy would be to initially use a PHMM, since it can be effective with much less training data than an HMM. Later, after sufficient training data has been accumulated, an HMM could then be trained, and we could switch over to using the HMM for detection.

It is also worth noting that a PHMM could have a significant advantage over an HMM in the case where an attacker hijacks an existing session—as opposed to an attacker who begins a new session masquerading as a user. If an attacker hijacks a session, a logical approach to evade detection would be to mimic previous commands in the session, making only small deviations. If an HMM (or weighted n-gram model) is used, such an attack would likely succeed for a significant number of commands. In contrast, a PHMM is more likely to quickly detect such a hijacked session, due to the fact that commands are more likely to be "out of place" relative to the training data. That is, the reliance on sequential information provides a significant advantage for a PHMM in such a scenario.

10.3 Malware Detection

In this section, we focus on a malware detection technique that is based on a PHMM. The work presented here is given in more detail in the report [155]; see also the paper [156].

The report [155] uses the terminology of *software birthmark*, where a "birthmark" is an inherent characteristics that can be used to identify specific software [99, 145]. This is in contrast to a *watermark*, which is data that is added to make identification easier.

If the birthmarks extracted from samples are sufficiently similar, then we might assume that the samples are closely related to each other. A similar similarity-based strategy has been used to detect metamorphic malware based on various statistical properties of the code [53, 73, 99, 115, 145, 146, 162, 169].

Software birthmarks can be either static or dynamic [53]. Static birthmarks are characteristics that can be extracted from a program without executing it [169]. For example, a static birthmark could be based on an opcode sequence. In contrast, dynamic birthmarks are obtained from a program when it is executed or emulated [73, 145, 169]. An example of a dynamic birthmark is the sequence of API calls that occur when a program actually executes [146].

Here, we focus on dynamic birthmarks, with PHMMs used as the basis for our detection technique. For the sake of comparison, we also present results based on HMM analysis. Both HMMs and PHMMs have been previously applied to the malware detection problem.

We note in passing that PHMMs and HMMs have also been applied to static birthmarks, such as opcode sequences extracted via disassembly. While HMMs can achieve considerable success on static data (at least in some cases), previous results for malware detection using PHMMs have generally been less than impressive [9].

10.3.1   Background

In this section, we assume that the reader is familiar with the standard terminology related to malware. A brief discussion of the relevant terminology can be found in Section 9.3 of Chapter 9.

As in previous research involving static HMM analysis [166], we use opcodes as our static birthmarks. To extract opcodes, we first disassemble malware samples and extract the mnemonic opcodes from the resulting files. We train HMMs on the extracted opcode sequences and these models are then used for testing. Following the approach taken in [166], we use $N = 2$ hidden states for all HMMs. When training the HMM, we use 800 iterations of the Baum-Welch re-estimation algorithm. Finally, we employ five-fold cross-validation, and results are compared based on ROC analysis—for more details on these data analysis topics, see Chapter 8.

For our dynamic birthmark, we extract API calls at runtime. Dynamic API calls would seem to be more robust than static opcodes, since such API calls focus on the actual functionality of the program. In comparison, opcodes can be easily obfuscated.

To collect API calls, we use the Buster sandbox analyzer [22] (BSA), which logs information about file system changes, windows registry changes, ports, etc. As the name implies, BSA executes in a protected sandbox, which reduces the risk of malware causing damage during the data extraction phase.

Once the API call sequences have been collected, they can be used for training and testing. However, extracting dynamic features is not as straightforward as extracting static features. The API call sequence depends on the actual execution path, which can, in turn, depend on input parameters, for example; see [155] for more discussion of these issues.

We use the same extracted API call sequences for both HMM and PHMM analysis. For the PHMM we must generate a multiple sequence alignment (MSA) before we can generate the model, while for the HMM, we simply append the sequences and train a model.

In our data, the top 36 API calls constitute more than 99.8% of all API calls. Consequently, we only consider the top 36 API calls, with all remaining API calls classified as "other." In [155], it is shown that this preprocessing step strengthens the resulting models.

For our PHMM experiments, we define a substitution matrix and a gap penalty function. As in Section 3.3 of Chapter 9, we use the Feng-Doolittle algorithm [51] to generate the MSA. After constructing the MSA, we build the PHMM. Once we have constructed the PHMM, we use the forward algorithm to score sequences against the PHMM. See Chapter 9 for general information on the PHMM training and scoring process, and see [155] for more specifics on the application of PHMMs to this malware problem.

10.3.2 Datasets and Results

For the experiments in this section, we use the following seven Windows malware families.

Cridex is a worm that multiplies and spreads through removable drives. It downloads malicious programs onto systems that it infects [149].

Harebot is a backdoor that enables hackers to gain access to a compromised system and steal information. Harebot is a rootkit [59].

Security Shield is fake antivirus software that claims it will protect a system from malware. Security Shield tries to convince the user to pay money to remove nonexistent threats [122].

Smart HDD reports various non-existent problems with the hard drive and tries to convince the user to purchase a product to fix the "errors." The name Smart HDD is intended to be confused with S.M.A.R.T., which is a legitimate tool for monitoring hard disk drives; thus the "HDD" in Smart HDD [72, 132].

Winwebsec is a Windows Trojan that pretends to be antivirus software. Winwebsec displays messages claiming that the user's system has been infected, and it tries to convince the user to pay for a fake antivirus product [165].

Zbot is a Trojan horse that compromises a system by downloading configuration files or updates. Also known as Zeus, the Zbot malware steals confidential information, such as online credentials [150].

Zeroaccess is a Trojan horse that makes use of an advanced rootkit to hide itself. ZeroAccess generates a hidden file system, creates a backdoor on a compromised system, and it is capable of downloading additional malware [151].

All of our malware samples were obtained from the Malicia Project [89, 100] website. Table 10.6 lists the number of samples from each family used in our experiments.

A set of 20 Windows executables serves as our representative benign data. All of these executables are available in Windows 7 or as freeware. For a complete list of the benign applications, see [155].

We'll first perform our analysis on each malware family using both static and dynamic analysis with HMMs. In each case, we plot the ROC curve for each family and calculate the AUC, which we use to compare the effectiveness of the techniques under consideration.

Table 10.6: Malware samples

Malware family	Number of samples
Cridex	50
Harebot	50
Security Shield	50
Smart HDD	50
Winwebsec	100
Zbot	100
Zeroaccess	100

For the Security Shield family, Figure 10.7 (a) shows the scatterplot for an HMM that was trained on opcode sequences, where the opcode sequences were extracted using static means. The corresponding ROC curve appears in Figure 10.7 (c). Note that the ROC curve in Figure 10.7 (c) gives us an AUC of 0.676.

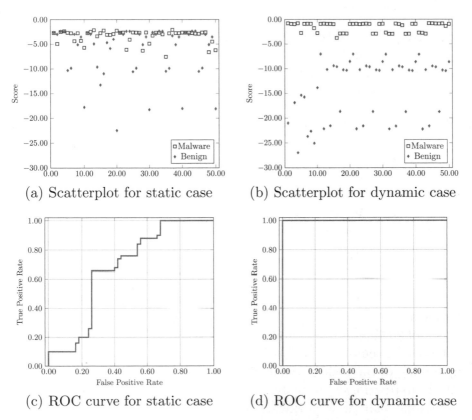

(a) Scatterplot for static case   (b) Scatterplot for dynamic case

(c) ROC curve for static case   (d) ROC curve for dynamic case

Figure 10.7: Security Shield HMM results

For comparison, the results of an HMM based on dynamically extracted API call sequences is given in Figure 10.7 (b). Again, these results are for the Security Shield family. In this case, the corresponding ROC curve is in Figure 10.7 (d) and yields an AUC of 1.0.

HMMs based on static opcode sequences have performed well when tested on some malware families [3, 166]. However, the AUC of 0.676 for the static HMM indicates that Security Shield likely represents a challenging detection problem. Yet, for an HMM trained on dynamic API calls, we obtain an AUC of 1.0 for this same family.

We have performed the same experiments on each of the seven malware families discussed above. That is, for each family, we tested HMMs based on static and dynamic opcodes. The results for all of these HMM-based detection experiments are summarized in Table 10.7.

Table 10.7: AUC curve results for static and dynamic HMMs

Malware family	AUC	
	Dynamic	Static
Cridex	0.964	0.596
Harebot	0.974	0.622
Security Shield	1.000	0.676
Smart HDD	0.980	0.996
Winwebsec	0.985	0.835
Zbot	0.990	0.847
Zeroaccess	0.979	0.923

From the results in Table 10.7, we see that the dynamic HMM outperforms the static HMM in every case, with the exception of the Smart HDD family. Furthermore, for Smart HDD, we see that the difference between the static and dynamic cases is small, with both HMMs performing very well. The average AUC for the dynamic HMM cases is 0.976, whereas the average AUC for the static HMM cases is only 0.785. This clearly shows the advantage of dynamic birthmarks, at least with respect to these particular malware families.

Next, we consider PHMMs trained on the same dynamic birthmarks that we used for the dynamic HMMs. For a PHMM, the number of sequences used to train is a critical parameter. Table 10.8 contains results for our PHMM experiments, where "group n" means that we trained the corresponding PHMM using n sequences. In each case, we were able to achieve an AUC of 1.0, and once we have attained such a result, there is no point to any further experiments involving the parameter n.

Table 10.8: PHMM results

Malware family	AUC results				
	Group 5	Group 10	Group 15	Group 20	Group 30
Cridex	0.958	1.000	—	—	—
Harebot	0.875	0.952	1.000	—	—
Security Shield	0.988	0.964	1.000	—	—
Smart HDD	0.812	0.905	0.963	1.000	—
Winwebsec	0.997	0.995	1.000	—	—
Zbot	0.915	0.970	1.000	—	—
Zeroaccess	0.905	0.988	0.968	0.975	1.000

The PHMM results in Table 10.8 are somewhat surprising when compared to results obtained in previous research [9]. The poor showing in previous work appears to be due to obfuscations that cause the location of opcode sequences to shift within the code, weakening the resulting PHMM. In comparison, it's far more difficult to obfuscate the dynamic API calls considered here. That is, positional information in API call sequences is highly informative, whereas positional information in opcode sequences is much less so.

Finally, in Figure 10.8 we compare the results for static and dynamic HMMs, and a dynamic PHMM, in the form of a bar graph. While the dynamic HMM results are indeed strong, the PHMM results are the best possible.

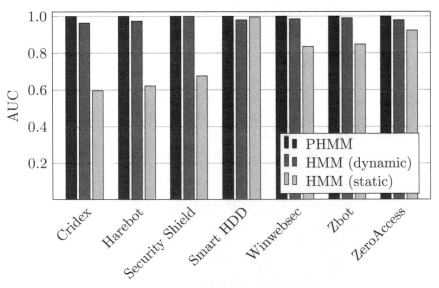

Figure 10.8: PHMM vs HMMs

Malware has become increasingly difficult to detect with standard approaches, such as signature scanning. Consequently, new techniques are needed, and machine learning is a promising line of research. HMMs have been used effectively for malware detection in previous work [3, 11, 71, 166]. In contrast, PHMMs seem to have been rarely studied in this context, with previous results being mixed, at best [9]. However, the research summarized here makes it clear that PHMMs can be effective for malware detection.

Chapter 11

PCA Applications

...it is for want of application, rather than of means, that men fail to succeed.
— François de La Rochefoucauld

11.1 Introduction

This chapter includes three closely related applications of principal component analysis (PCA). First, we briefly discuss a technique known as eigenfaces, which is a PCA-based approach to facial recognition. Then we turn our attention to the problem of malware detection and show that essentially the same approach is effective in this problem domain. Finally, we consider the use of PCA for the challenging problem of image spam detection.

11.2 Eigenfaces

Facial recognition is an interesting problem in artificial intelligence, and a topic of considerable interest in security. In the security domain, facial recognition can be viewed as a type of biometric, and has been proposed, for example, as a means of detecting terrorists in airports. Facial recognition has long been used by casinos in Las Vegas to detect cheaters. However, it's doubtful that the current state of the art is sufficiently robust for security applications such as these. Nevertheless, facial recognition might act as a deterrent in some applications, even if the effectiveness of the technique is somewhat questionable.

In [152], eigenvector analysis is applied to the facial recognition problem, where it's given the clever name of eigenfaces. An analogous eigenviruses technique is applied to the malware detection problem in [119], and the same technique is further analyzed in [41]. In Section 11.3, we'll discuss some of the analysis and results in [41].

Essentially the same strategy that is used in eigenfaces and eigenviruses has been applied to the challenging problem of image spam detection. Predictably, the application of PCA to image spam detection goes by the name of *eigenspam*. We discuss the eigenspam process is some detail in Section 11.4, where we also provide extensive experimental results.

For the facial recognition problem, we assume that we are given a training set consisting of n facial images. These images could be of n different people, or the training images could be different views of one person, or any combination thereof. The training process then consists of the following steps. First, a covariance matrix is determined based on the pixel values in the set of training images. Then the eigenvalues and eigenvectors of this covariance matrix are computed, typically using a singular value decomposition (SVD). The eigenvectors corresponding to the m largest eigenvalues define the *face space*. Each of the n images in the training set is projected onto the face space to obtain n sets of weights. These weights are collected into a scoring matrix to be used in the scoring, as discussed below. The optimal choice of $m \leq n$ could be determined experimentally, or based on the relative sizes of the eigenvalues. In any case, once we have determined a scoring matrix, the training phase is complete.

The scoring process is straightforward. After completing the training phase, suppose we are given an image F that we want to score. As in the training phase, F is projected onto the face space to obtain its weight vector. The distance between this weight vector and each of the n weight vectors from the training phase (i.e., the columns of the scoring matrix) is computed, and the minimum of these distances is the score. Since the score is a distance, it will be non-negative. Furthermore, if F is actually an element of the training set, the score will be 0. The larger the score, the greater the distance from F to the training set, where distance is measured relative to the projections onto the face space.

To illustrate the training process in eigenfaces, suppose that the images in Figure 11.1 are the training set. The corresponding eigenfaces for these images are given in Figure 11.2. That is, the eigenfaces are the images obtained by projecting the training images onto the face space corresponding to the most significant eigenvalues. In general, for a training set of n facial images, only the $m < n$ most significant eigenvectors (as determined by the magnitude of the corresponding eigenvalues) are used to define the face space. That is, by using the eigenvectors that correspond to the dominant eigenvalues, we obtain n sets of weights—one for each image in the training set—where each weight vector is of length m.

Next, we consider the effectiveness of PCA when applied to the malware detection problem. Then in Section 11.4, we'll analyze the strength of PCA when used for image spam detection. This latter application is very similar to the eigenfaces technique discussed in this section.

Figure 11.1: Training images

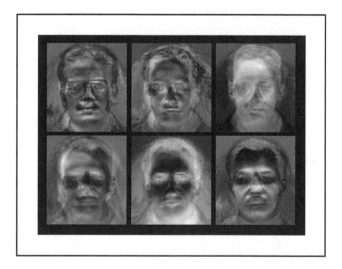

Figure 11.2: Eigenfaces of images in Figure 11.1

11.3 Eigenviruses

For the virus detection problem discussed in this section, we'll use raw byte values extracted from malware samples. We have also considered the case where the "experiment" consists of opcode sequences extracted from executable files. Regardless of the source of the data, we determine the principal components from the training set, using SVD. We can then score any given samples to determine how well they match the members of the malware family that were used for training.

We also apply SVD to the problem of determining the compiler used to generate a given executable file. Previous research has shown that HMMs and other statistical techniques can be used to easily distinguish between compilers, based on extracted opcode sequences [11].

While viruses and compilers might seem to have little in common, in fact, metamorphic malware generators have some similar characteristics to compilers. We'll make this connection more explicit below.

The work presented in this section is a variation on the eigenviruses technique in [119], which was further analyzed in [41]. Eigenviruses is essentially the same as eigenfaces, which is summarized in Section 11.2, above. For additional relevant experimental results, see [41, 42, 67, 68].

Of course, our PCA-based malware detection technique includes a training phase and a scoring phase. In the training phase, we form a matrix with columns consisting of bytes extracted from metamorphic viruses, where each virus in the training set belongs to the same malware family. We then apply the SVD algorithm and use the resulting dominant eigenvectors to determine a set of weights. These weights will be used to score samples during the scoring phase.

For malware detection, the training and scoring phases follow the approach outlined in Section 4.5 of Chapter 4. Here, each "experiment" consists of a sequence of bytes extracted from the .text (i.e., code) section of a malware executable file. All of the samples used for training belong to the same metamorphic family. Note that each "measurement" consist of the specific byte values in the corresponding positions in the extracted byte sequences. We simply pad shorter sequences with 0 bytes as needed.

Although training is somewhat complex and involved, the scoring process is extremely efficient, since each score only requires a small number of dot products. In particular, no SVD computation or other expensive linear algebra operation is needed when scoring. Next, we briefly summarize our malware detection results, as well as results for compiler analysis.

11.3.1   Malware Detection Results

MWOR is an experimental, highly metamorphic worm that carries its own generator [135]. The worm was loosely modeled on MetaPHOR [93]. However, unlike MetaPHOR, the MWOR worm employs a stealth technique that can defeat many types of statistical analysis. Specifically, MWOR inserts dead code extracted from benign programs, which has the effect of making the statistics of the malware more closely match those of benign samples. The amount of dead code is specified as a padding ratio, where, for example, a ratio of 2.0 means that twice as much dead code is inserted as actual worm code. As in [135], here we experiment with MWOR using padding ratios of 1.0, 1.5, 2.0, 2.5, 3.0, and 4.0.

ROC curves for selected padding ratios of these PCA-based experiments on the MWOR family can be found in [135]. The AUC statistics for these experiments are given here in Table 11.1. In each case, the AUC that we provide is averaged over the five experiments conducted in a five-fold cross validation. The same results as in Table 11.1 are presented in the form of a line graph in Figure 11.3. For more details on ROC analysis, see Section 8.4 of Chapter 8, or the paper [19].

Table 11.1: Area under the ROC curve for MWOR

Padding ratio	AUC
1.0	0.99998
1.5	0.99998
2.0	0.99746
2.5	0.99660
3.0	0.99350
4.0	0.98336

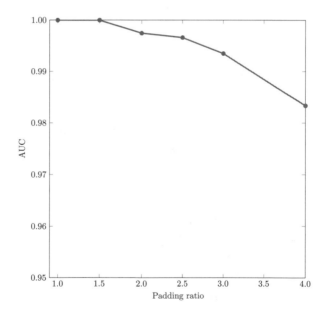

Figure 11.3: Graph of AUC for MWOR

For the results summarized in Table 11.1, we used only one singular value. Perhaps surprisingly, using additional singular values does not yield improved results in any of these cases. Overall, these results do offer a marginal improvement over the comparable experiments in [41].

The next generation virus construction kit (NGVCK) [103] is a highly metamorphic Windows virus generator. When scoring NGVCK viruses, using only one singular value and its corresponding eigenvector yielded an average AUC of 0.9142, and when using two singular vectors, the AUC deteriorated slightly to 0.9028. These results are comparable to those obtained using the eigenvalue technique in [41], where an AUC of 0.9473 was attained on a similar NGVCK dataset.

In Table 11.2, we compare our PCA results to the results in [41], a score based on HMM analysis [135], and a simple substitution distance (SSD) score, which is based on simple substitution cryptanalysis [126]. Note that the results in the PCA column of Table 11.2 are reproduced from those in Table 11.1. These same results are presented here in the form of line graphs in Figure 11.4.

Table 11.2: AUC comparison for MWOR

Padding ratio	Area under ROC curve		
	PCA	HMM	SSD
1.0	0.9999	0.9900	1.0000
1.5	0.9999	0.9625	0.9980
2.0	0.9975	0.9725	0.9985
2.5	0.9966	0.8325	0.9859
3.0	0.9935	0.8575	0.9725
4.0	0.9834	0.8225	0.9565

At higher padding ratios, the PCA score offers a significant improvement over both the HMM and simple substitution scores. In fact, the PCA score is almost unaffected by additional padding.

The HMM and simple substitution scores are based on statistical properties of opcode sequences, while the PCA score reflects structural properties of the samples. The MWOR worm was specifically designed to defeat statistical detection, without any effort made towards defeating such structural scores. From this perspective, the PCA results for MWOR are not too surprising.

11.3.2   Compiler Experiments

In [11], experiments were performed using HMMs to distinguish code generated from each of the following compilers: TurboC, Clang, MinGW, and GCC. For each compiler, an HMM was trained on opcode sequences, and these models were then used to score other samples from these same compilers. The results showed that HMMs can be used to distinguish the compiler with very good accuracy.

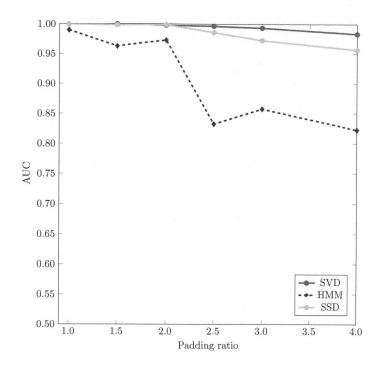

Figure 11.4: AUC comparison for MWOR

Here, we consider analogous experiments using a score based on PCA. This PCA scoring approach was tested to see how well it could distinguish the compiler that was used to generate a given sample. For these experiments, we used the same data sets as were used in the HMM-based research reported in [11].

The results of our compiler experiments are summarized in Table 11.3, where "compiler a vs compiler b" means that we used the PCA model trained on compiler a to score samples from compilers a and b. None of the test cases in Table 11.3 produce useful results, and in many cases, the PCA-based classifier yields results that are essentially no better than flipping a coin.

Why does a PCA score perform so poorly in this compiler experiment? The PCA score is based on geometric structure. In these compiler experiments, the score relies on the geometry derived from the program samples in the training set. Clearly, the structure of compiled code depends heavily on the structure of the source code.

In contrast, the success of HMM-based detection tell us that there is much statistical similarity within code generated by a given compiler (and considerable difference between different compilers). In this context, it might be interesting to compare the PCA score considered here to other structural-based scores, such as those based on entropy [14, 133] and compression ratios [38, 85, 168], for example.

Table 11.3: AUC for compiler experiments

Experiment	Singular vectors		
	1	2	3
TurboC vs Clang	0.7034	0.6743	0.6440
TurboC vs MinGW	0.6061	0.5970	0.5756
TurboC vs GCC	0.7183	0.6916	0.6618
Clang vs TurboC	0.6079	0.6987	0.7302
Clang vs MinGW	0.6520	0.7268	0.7432
Clang vs GCC	0.5074	0.5038	0.4983
MinGW vs Clang	0.6569	0.5494	0.5596
MinGW vs TurboC	0.5291	0.5102	0.5078
MinGW vs GCC	0.6716	0.5761	0.5905
GCC vs Clang	0.5254	0.5236	0.5222
GCC vs TurboC	0.7049	0.7351	0.7438
GCC vs MinGW	0.6982	0.7498	0.7179

11.4   Eigenspam

Unsolicited bulk email is known as *spam*. During 2015, it is estimated that spam accounted for an astonishing 60% of all inbound email [142]. Consequently, spam filtering is essential for the viability of email communications.

Image spam consists of spam text embedded within an image, and is used by spammers as a means to evade filters. Some typical examples of spam images are given in Figure 11.5.

Figure 11.5: Image spam

To distinguish between non-spam images and spam, we'll refer to the former as *ham*. Thus, the problem of detecting image spam boils down to distinguishing between ham and spam.[1]

---

[1] Discussing meat products and cooking methods makes your carnivorous author hungry.

11.4.1 PCA for Image Spam Detection

In this section, we consider a PCA-based image spam detection strategy in some detail. The work presented here was inspired by the eigenfaces technique [152], which is outlined in Section 11.2, above. Perhaps not surprisingly, we refer to this image spam detection technique as eigenspam.

The training phase in eigenspam is similar to the training phase in eigenfaces, except, of course, we use a collection of spam images in place of the facial images. For more details on the PCA training and scoring process, see Section 4.5 of Chapter 4.

There are few image spam datasets available to the public. For the research discussed here, we use the following two datasets, which we refer to as the standard dataset and the improved dataset.

Standard dataset This dataset was created by the authors of [55] and is available at [54]. The data includes 928 spam images and 810 ham images, all of which are in the JPEG format. We excluded eight images from the spam data, as they were corrupted.

Improved dataset This is a new set of spam images that we generated. Our goal here is to develop a challenging dataset that can be used when comparing proposed image spam detection techniques. This dataset contains more than 1000 images. Note that this dataset is improved from the perspective of the spammer, and it is also designed to lead to improved detection techniques. This dataset can be downloaded at [5].

We measure success based on accuracy, false positive rate, and (primarily) the area under the ROC curve (AUC); see Chapter 8 for more information on these topics.

For the standard dataset, we constructed a training set with 500 spam images. Figure 11.6 shows sample spam images from this training set and Figure 11.7 shows the corresponding projections onto the eigenspace.

11.4.2 Detection Results

After training on 500 images from the standard dataset, we tested the resulting score using 414 image spam samples and 414 benign samples. We use the $m = 5$ dominant eigenvectors in this experiment. We constructed an ROC curve based on the results of this experiment, and for this ROC curve, we obtained an AUC of 0.99. This experiment also achieves an accuracy of 97%.

We have conducted analogous experiments using the m dominant eigenvectors, for each of the cases $m = 1, 2, \ldots, 500$. Furthermore, for each of these 500 experiments, we constructed ROC curves and determined the AUC. The resulting AUC values are graphed in Figure 11.8. From this graph, we

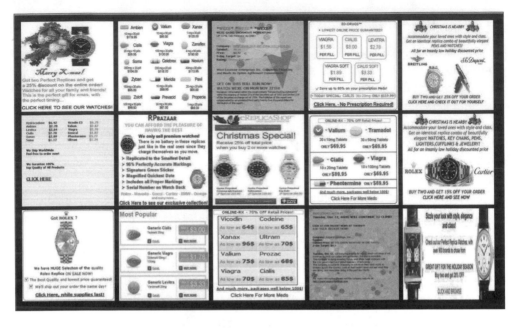

Figure 11.6: Spam images from standard dataset

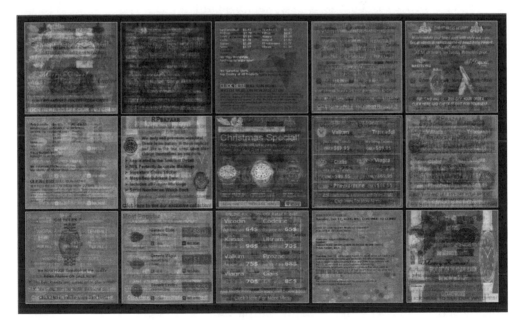

Figure 11.7: Projections onto eigenspace for images in Figure 11.6

see that the maximum success is achieved when the number of eigenvectors is between three and 10, and we see that the AUC decreases significantly for $m > 10$. Scoring efficiency is higher for smaller values of m, so about $m = 5$ eigenvectors is optimal.

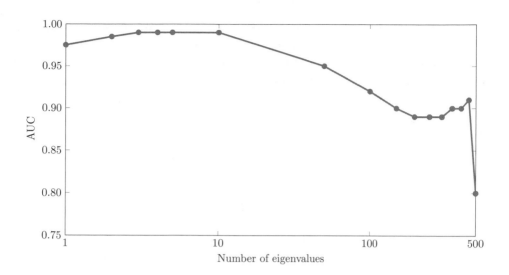

Figure 11.8: AUC for different numbers of eigenvalues (standard dataset)

In Section 12.3 of Chapter 12 we revisit the image spam detection problem using support vector machines (SVM) instead of PCA. From that work, we find that the most significant distinguishing features of image spam are the compression ratio, the variance of the color histogram, signal to noise ratio, and the local binary pattern. We have used this knowledge to create a more challenging spam image dataset—the aforementioned "improved" dataset. These improved spam images have texture similar to ham images and the color elements have been modified so that the resulting color histogram is virtually indistinguishable from that of ham images. We also introduce noise to the spam images and we modified the spam image metadata, both of which serve to make the spam images more similar to ham images. Following this approach, we've created 1000 improved spam images—Figure 11.9 contains two examples from this improved dataset.

Figure 11.9: Examples of improved spam images

We have analyzed the effectiveness of PCA-based detection on our improved image spam. For this experiment, we again use the $m = 5$ dominant eigenvectors. In this case, the AUC is 0.38, which indicates that the spam images in our improved dataset cannot be reliably detected using the eigenspam technique discussed in this section. The results of these eigenspam experiments are summarized in Table 11.4.

Table 11.4: Eigenspam results

Dataset	AUC
Standard	0.99
Improved	0.38

For more details on the image spam experiments reported here, see the full report [4]. The paper [6] provides a more condensed version of these same results.

As mentioned above, we'll reconsider the image spam detection problem using support vector machines in Section 12.3 of Chapter 12. That analysis will provide more insight into the strengths of our improved dataset as compared to typical spam images that are used today—as represented by the standard dataset.

Chapter 12

SVM Applications

[T]omfoolery, having passed through a ... machine,
is somehow ennobled and no-one dares criticize it.
— Pierre Gallois

12.1 Introduction

Two very different security-related applications of support vector machines (SVM) are covered in this chapter. First, we apply SVMs to the problem of malware detection, where we use an SVM to generate a classification based on three distinct malware scores. We show that the SVM generally outperforms each of the three individual scores, and the improvement is largest in the most challenging cases. We then turn our attention to the use of SVMs for image spam detection.

12.2 Malware Detection

In this section, we consider the use of an SVM as a "meta-score" for malware, that is, we use the SVM to generate a classification based on a set of scores. We show that the SVM results exceed those obtained using the individual scores, and the improvement provided by the SVM is greatest in cases where the malware is highly obfuscated. The results presented here are discussed in more detail in the report [129] and the paper [130].

Beyond elementary signature detection, most malware scoring techniques fit into one of the following three broad (not necessarily mutually exclusive) categories.

Statistical-based scoring techniques rely on statistical properties that can be used to distinguish elements of a malware family from other code.

Structural-based scores analyze various structural properties.

Graph-based scores use graph structure derived from code. Such scores are
natural to consider since there exist a wide variety of graphs that can
be extracted from software.

Examples of statistical-based scores include those that rely on HMMs [148]
and simple substitution distance (SSD) [126]. Examples of graph-based scores
include the opcode graph similarity (OGS) score considered in [118] and the
function call graph score in [40]. Examples of structure-based scores include
the entropy analysis found in [14], and related work involving compression
rates [85], as well as PCA-based analysis [42, 68].

In this section, we'll focus on HMM, SSD, and OGS scores. We've implemented each of these scoring techniques, and we have also implemented
morphing strategies that are designed to defeat these scores. For each score,
we analyze the degree of modification needed to defeat the individual score,
where the area under the ROC curve (AUC) serves as our measure of success.

Then we apply an SVM to these scores, which serves to combine the scores,
and we measure the success of this SVM-based meta-score in comparison to
the individual scores. We show that the SVM significantly improves on the
detection capability of each individual score. But first, we provide a brief
review of some related research.

12.2.1   Background

In this section, we focus on the SSD and OGS scores, which are used in the
research presented in this chapter. We also employ an HMM score, which
is essentially equivalent to that discussed in Section 9.3 of Chapter 9, so we
omit the details of the HMM score. Note that all three of these scores are
based on extracted opcode sequences.

The OGS score [118] relies on a weighted directed graph, where each
distinct opcode is a node in the directed graph. There is a directed edge from
a node to each possible successor node, based on the opcode labelings. Edge
weights are determined by successor node probabilities.

Figure 12.1 illustrates the opcode graph corresponding to the opcode sequence in Table 12.1. Note that the edge weights are normalized so that for
any given node, the weights from all outgoing edges sum to one.

To generate OGS scores for malware detection, we first construct an opcode graph corresponding to a collection of family viruses. Then, given a
sample that we want to score, we construct its opcode graph. The distance
between the family graph and the sample graph is computed as the absolute
sum of the differences between the corresponding edge weights, normalized by
the number of edge weights. The smaller this distance, the better the sample

Table 12.1: Opcode sequence

Number	Opcode	Number	Opcode
1	CALL	11	JMP
2	JMP	12	ADD
3	ADD	13	NOP
4	SUB	14	JMP
5	NOP	15	CALL
6	CALL	16	CALL
7	ADD	17	CALL
8	JMP	18	ADD
9	JMP	19	JMP
10	SUB	20	SUB

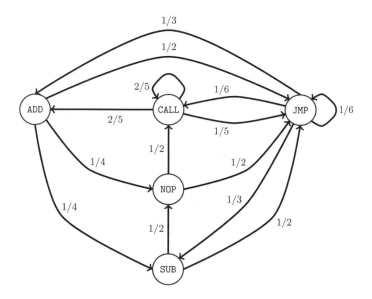

Figure 12.1: Opcode graph

matches the malware family that was used to construct the family graph, and hence the more likely the sample belongs to that same family.

Due to the normalization used, the OGS score weights each opcode the same. This is in contrast to the HMM score, where opcodes are, in effect, weighted according to their relative frequencies. Consequently, the OGS and HMM scores can yield significantly different results.

The simple substitution distance (SSD) malware score in [126] is based on a fast and effective hill climb technique known as Jakobsen's algorithm [66], which was developed for simple substitution cipher cryptanalysis. Although the malware families considered in this paper are not encrypted, they are obfuscated, and simple substitution cryptanlaysis can, in effect, undo some types of obfuscations. See Section 9.4.1 of Chapter 9 for a detailed discussion of Jakobsen's algorithm.

The SSD score nicely complements the HMM and OGS scores. Whereas HMM and OGS scores rely on opcodes that are extracted from malware samples, the SSD score, in effect, modifies opcodes during its scoring (i.e., "decryption") process, allowing us to deal effectively with certain elementary types of obfuscation.

In addition to analyzing each of the individual scores, we combine these three scores using an SVM. This is a reasonable approach, since an SVM generates a classification based on its training data. In this usage, we can view the resulting SVM as operating on a "higher plane" than the HMM, OGS, and SSD scores.

Our malware samples are drawn from the following seven malware families: Harebot, Security Shield, NGVCK, Smart HDD, Winwebsec, Zbot, and Zeroaccess. With the exception of NGVCK, all of these malware families were obtained from the Malicia Project [89]; see also [100]. For a description of each of these Malicia families, see Section 10.3 of Chapter 10. The NGVCK family is briefly discussed in Section 9.3 of Chapter 9.

Table 12.2 lists the number of samples from each malware family and the benign set. As in the paper [166] (and elsewhere), we use Cygwin utilities [34] as our representative examples of benign applications.

Table 12.2: Datasets

Family	Number of samples
Harebot	50
NGVCK	200
Security Shield	50
Smart HDD	50
Winwebsec	200
Zbot	200
Zeroaccess	200
benign	40

In all of the experiments discussed here, we use 5-fold cross validation, and for the HMM experiments, we use $N = 2$ hidden states. Finally, for the SVM, we experimented with various kernel functions, as discussed below.

12.2.2   Experimental Results

We first consider the NGVCK malware family. To test the robustness of our scores, we further morph the NGVCK malware. Below, we conduct similar experiments with the other malware families in our dataset.

For the NGVCK malware, the individual scores (HMM, OGS, and SSD) each provide ideal separation. That is, there exists a threshold for which no false positives or false negatives occur. Consequently, the ROC curve in each case yields an AUC of 1.0. These results for the NGVCK metamorphic family are not surprising, since similar results were obtained in previous research, including [118, 126]. Of course, an SVM also provides ideal separation.

Scatterplots for each of the three individual scores—as well as the SVM classifier—are given in Figure 12.2 (a) through (d). In each case, the AUC is clearly 1.0, so we omit the corresponding ROC curves.

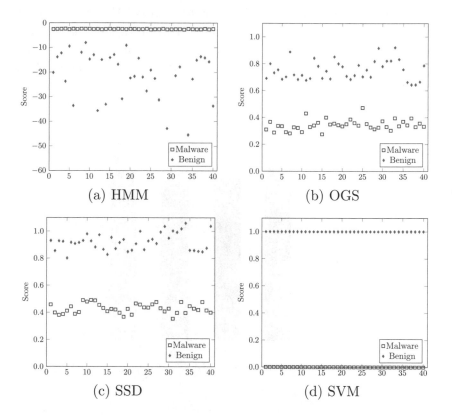

Figure 12.2: NGVCK score scatterplots

As mentioned above, to generate more challenging test cases, we apply additional morphing to the NGVCK opcode sequences. Specifically, we insert opcode subsequences extracted from benign samples into the NGVCK malware opcode sequences. This process serves to simulate the effect of a higher degree of code morphing—this same approach has been used in several previous studies, including [85, 88]. By selecting the morphing code from the benign samples, the statistical profile of the malware will tend to merge with that of the benign set, making detection more difficult, particularly with respect to scores that rely on statistical information.

We experimented with various ways of inserting the benign subsequences and we found that "block morphing" has the largest effect on the scores. Consequently, we insert a benign opcode subsequence directly into each NGVCK opcode sequence in the form of a consecutive block. The amount of code inserted is measured as a percentage of the number of opcodes in the original NGVCK sample. For example, if an NGVCK sample contains 1000 opcodes, then 40% morphing means that we randomly select a block of 400 consecutive opcodes from a benign sample and insert this block directly into the NGVCK opcode sequence.

Before giving our results for the morphed NGVCK experiments as described in the previous paragraph, we need to determine a kernel function for the SVM. When experimenting with several standard kernel functions, we obtained the results in Figure 12.3. For these experiments, the radial basis function (RBF) kernel yielded the best results. Consequently, for all subsequent SVM experiments in this section, we use the RBF kernel.

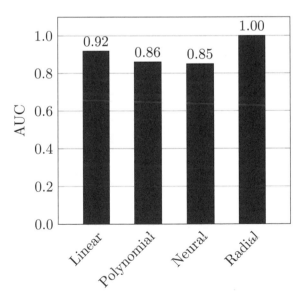

Figure 12.3: Comparison of SVM kernels (NGVCK at 80% morphing)

Figure 12.4 gives our experimental results for the morphed NGVCK family, where the additional morphing ranges from 0% to 120%. We see that the HMM score deteriorates significantly at just 10% morphing. In contrast, the OGS score only begins to fail at about 50% morphing, while the decline in the

SSD score begins at about 60%. On the other hand, the SVM achieves ideal separation until the morphing rate reaches 100%. Furthermore, in all cases with less than perfect separation, the SVM is superior to the result attained by any of the individual scores. This experiment clearly demonstrates the strength of SVM as a method for combining malware scores into a unified meta-score.

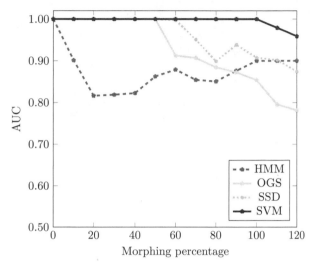

Figure 12.4: AUC at various morphing percentages (NGVCK)

Next, we consider analogous experiments involving the malware families Harebot, Security Shield, Smart HDD, Winwebsec, Zbot, and Zeroaccess. Since all of these were obtained from the Malicia Project [89], we collectively refer to these as the Malicia families.

Figure 12.5 presents our experimental results for the Malicia families. Of the individual scores, we see that the HMM consistently performs well, the SSD score does well in some cases, and the OGS score is the weakest. Also, the SVM achieves ideal separation for all families, even in cases where one (or more) of the individual scores performs poorly.

We now present experimental results where additional morphing is applied to each of the Malicia families. These experiments correspond to the NGVCK experiments that are summarized in Figure 12.4. The results for all of our morphed Malicia family experiments are given in Figure 12.6. For these experiments, the additional morphing varies from from 0% to 150%.

As in the NGVCK experiments, the HMM score tends to decline significantly at low morphing rates, suggesting that this score is the least robust, at least with respect to the specific morphing technique under consideration. In contrast to the NGVCK experiments, the OGS score generally gives the poorest results on the Malicia families. The SSD score is somewhat erratic, and in some cases this score actually improves at low morphing rates. And,

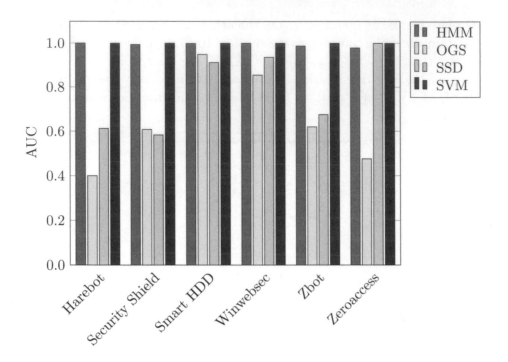

Figure 12.5: AUC comparisons for Malicia families

not surprisingly, an SVM generally yields the best results, although there are a few cases where the SSD score does do slightly better than the SVM near the midrange of the morphing rates.

As noted in Section 8.4 of Chapter 8, an AUC value of $x < 0.5$ is equivalent to an AUC of $1 - x > 0.5$. That is, by simply reversing the sense of the binary classifier, we can change an AUC of x into an AUC of $1 - x$. Consequently, some of the low AUC results in Figure 12.6 actually represent relatively strong scores. Interestingly, it is apparent that the SVM is able to properly interpret such "inverse" scores. For example, in Figure 12.6 (b), the HMM score is extremely low, which implies that by inverting the sense of the classifier, it is actually a relatively strong score. And in this particular case, we see that the SVM results are indeed strong. Of course, this strength of SVMs is to be expected, based on the geometric intuition behind the technique. In any case, the results in Figure 12.6 provide additional evidence of the usefulness of SVMs when used to combine scores.

12.3   Image Spam Revisited

In Section 11.4 of Chapter 11, we discussed image spam detection using principal component analysis (PCA). In this section, we again consider the problem of image spam detection, but using SVM analysis instead of PCA. We'll

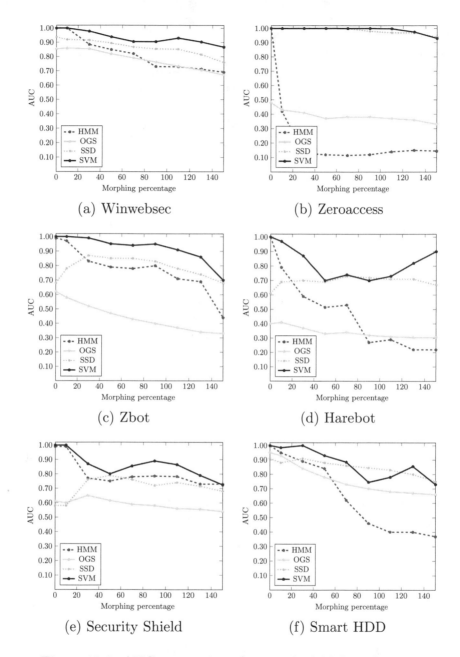

Figure 12.6: AUC comparison for morphed Malicia families

see that the SVM approach performs slightly better than PCA in the most challenging cases. In this section, we also use SVM to determine the relative importance of the various features under consideration. We'll then compare and contrast two approaches to reducing the dimensionality of the input data via feature selection. The exposition given in this section largely follows the report [4]; see also the paper [6].

For a brief introduction to image spam, see Section 11.4. We won't repeat that introductory material here, but we do want to recall that non-spam images are known as ham images. Examples of typical image spam can be found in Figure 11.5 in Chapter 11.

In this section, we use the same datasets as in the PCA analysis given in Section 11.4. And, as in the PCA analysis, the data from [54, 55] is referred to as the standard dataset. Recall that this standard dataset includes more than 900 spam images collected from the wild, and in excess of 800 ham images. We have also generated an "improved" dataset, consisting of 1000 spam-like images. As discussed in Section 11.4, these improved images offer a greater challenge with respect to detection.

12.3.1   SVM for Image Spam Detection

The SVM training and scoring phases are similar to the generic description given in Chapter 5. For completeness, we describe these phases in the specific context of the image spam detection problem.

In the training phase, we use a labeled set containing both spam and ham images. First, we resize all images so they are of the same dimension. Then we extract the relevant features from all of these samples. The following broad set of 21 features are considered in this section.

Color To obtain the entropy of the color histogram, we first build a color histogram of size 10^3 in the RGB space by quantizing each color band [46]. The entropy is then computed based on this color histogram.

Mean, variance, skew, kurtosis For these features, we construct a 100-dimensional histogram for each of the three color channels. Then the mean, variance, skewness, and kurtosis for each of the three histograms is calculated, each of which is considered a separate feature.

LBP The entropy of the local binary pattern (LBP) histogram is a texture feature. We extract a 59-dimensional texture histogram and compute its entropy.

HOG We construct a $40 \cdot 8 = 320$ gradient-based histogram, the histogram of oriented gradients (HOG). The entropy of this histogram is a shape feature.

Edges, edgelen The total number of edges and the average length of the edges are computed using the Canny edge detector [23].

Comp The compression ratio is computed as

$$\text{Compression ratio} = \frac{\text{height} \times \text{width} \times \text{bit depth}}{\text{file size}}.$$

Aspect The aspect ratio is computed as the ratio between the width and height of the image.

SNR The signal to noise ratio (SNR) is computed as the proportional relationship between mean and variance.

Noise The noise of an image is based on the deviation at each pixel.

We illustrate selected features in Figure 12.7. The original image appears in Figure 12.7 (a), and it is given in grayscale in Figure 12.7 (b). The Canny edge detector is illustrated in Figure 12.7 (c), while the HOG feature is displayed in Figure 12.7 (d). In Figure 12.8, an analogous example is given for a spam image.

(a) Ham image   (b) Grayscale

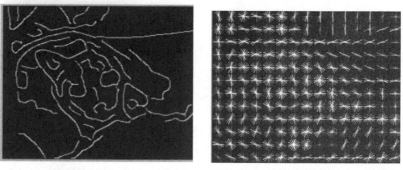

(c) Canny edges   (d) HOG

Figure 12.7: Features of a ham image

The extracted features, along with the class label, are given as input to a linear SVM classifier. We also generate models based on subsets of the features, as discussed below. To test each of our models, a set of spam and ham images are classified. Of course, these ham and spam images are not part of the training set that was used to construct the SVM classifier. Next, we present some results from these experiments; for more details, see [4].

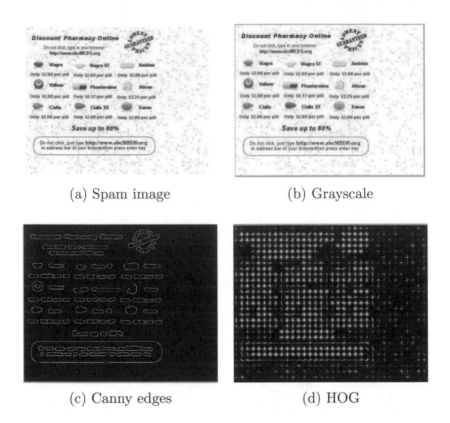

(a) Spam image   (b) Grayscale

(c) Canny edges   (d) HOG

Figure 12.8: Spam image feature extraction

12.3.2   SVM Experiments

We first want to determine the potential discriminating power of each feature, independent of the other features. We have plotted the ham and spam distributions for each of the 21 features, based on the standard dataset. From these distributions, the most distinguishing features are presented in Figure 12.9.

For each of the features in Figure 12.9, we see that there is good separation between the ham and spam distributions. Therefore, we expect scores based on these features to easily distinguish between ham and spam. To determine whether this is the case, we trained SVMs for each feature.

The distributions and ROC graphs for each of the 21 features are given in the report [4]. The bar graph in Figure 12.10 shows the AUC for SVMs trained on each of the individual features, using the standard dataset.

Training an SVM using all 21 features yields an AUC of 0.99. This level of success appears to equal or exceed any results from previous research.

Since there is work involved in collecting each feature, we would like to eliminate redundancy in the features to the maximum extent possible. Some of the less distinguishing features may be worse than nothing, that is, they

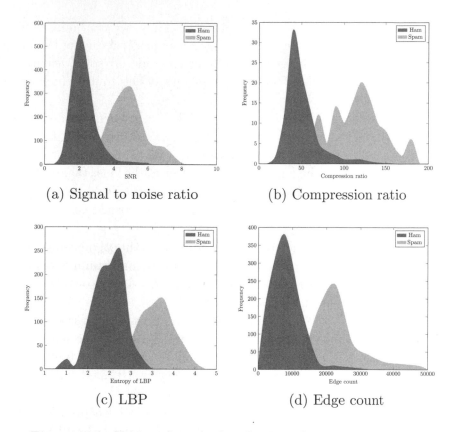

(a) Signal to noise ratio (b) Compression ratio

(c) LBP (d) Edge count

Figure 12.9: Ham and spam distributions for standard dataset

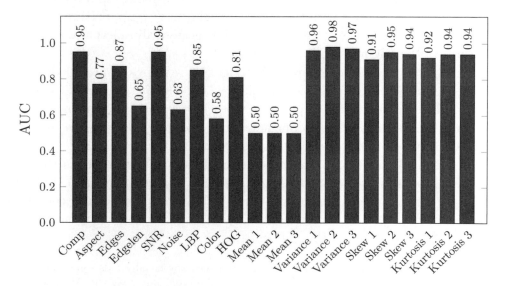

Figure 12.10: AUC for individual features

might essentially act as noise in the process. Thus, we can gain efficiency, and possibly even improve the accuracy, by strategically reducing the number of features. And, we might even be willing to trade off some accuracy for improved efficiency. But, how can we systematically determine which features to remove?

To eliminate features, we can simply rank the features based on linear SVM weights, selecting those features that are ranked highest. Alternatively, we can employ recursive feature elimination (RFE) as described in [58]. The RFE algorithm discards the feature that contributes the least (again, based on the linear SVM weights). Then we recompute a linear SVM on the reduced feature set, and discard the least significant feature based on this reduced feature set, and so on.

Again, our goal is to find an optimal subset of the 21 features so as to reduce the computational complexity and provide maximum classification accuracy. Note that these experimental results are based on the standard dataset, and the analysis uses linear SVMs.

Figure 12.11 shows the number of selected features used for training, along with the corresponding AUC values and accuracy. Here, the features were selected using the RFE algorithm. We can obtain an AUC of 0.99 with just three features, although the maximum accuracy is attained with an SVM based on 13 features.[1]

In Figure 12.12, we graph the weights for the full 21-feature SVM. When we reduce to three features using RFE, we obtain Comp, LBP, and Variance 3. This is in contrast to the straightforward feature rankings in Figure 12.12, where the three features with the highest weights are Comp, SNR, and HOG. Consequently, we can see that RFE does not necessarily select the strongest features in the original SVM.

In Figure 12.13, we compare RFE to feature rankings as provided by the full 21-feature linear SVM. We see that when selecting features via RFE, the resulting models tend to perform much better when a small number of features are used. This is significant, since the fewer features we need to extract, generally the more efficient the scoring.

Tables 12.3 and 12.4 give a more detailed view of the results in the case where 13 features are selected using the RFE algorithm. In Table 12.3, we compare different kernel functions, while Table 12.4 provides the confusion matrix for the linear SVM case. From Figure 12.11, we see that using a linear SVM, we can obtain an AUC of 0.99.

---

[1]As an aside, we note that in this example, the accuracy usually falls somewhat below the AUC. This is often the case, which leads some to conclude that the AUC tends to "overstate" the success rate. However, the AUC has some significant advantages that make it useful for comparing experimental results. And, if the AUC is interpreted correctly, this "overstating" concern can be seen to be itself overstated—see Chapter 8 for additional details on ROC analysis.

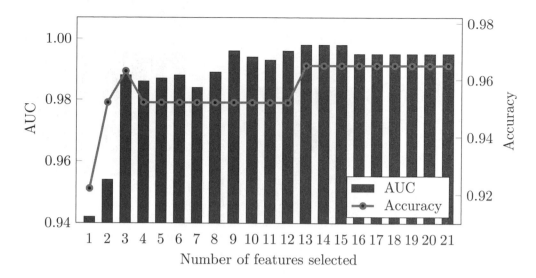

Figure 12.11: RFE results for standard dataset

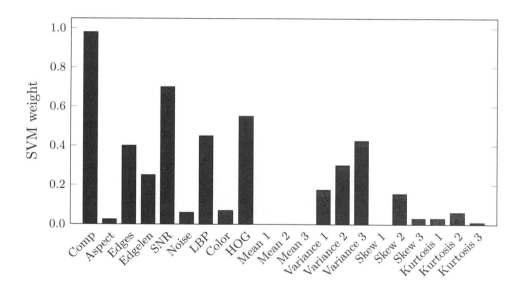

Figure 12.12: Linear SVM weights for standard dataset

Without any use of feature selection, we obtained an accuracy of 96%. Yet by selecting 13 of the 21 features using RFE, the accuracy actually improves to 97.25%, which shows that using more features is not necessarily better. Also, when only three features are used, we can achieve an accuracy that is essentially the same as that for the much costlier 21-feature model. This example nicely illustrates the potential benefit of using feature reduction in general, and RFE in particular.

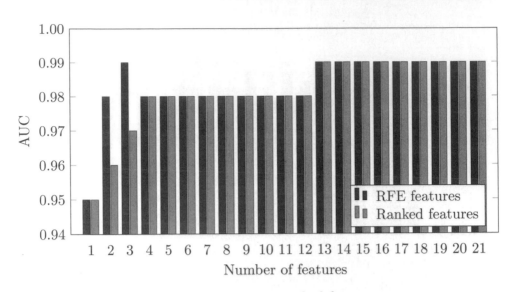

Figure 12.13: RFE vs ranked features

Table 12.3: Accuracy and FPR for 13 features

Kernel	Accuracy	FPR
Linear	0.97	0.04
RBF	0.97	0.05
Polynomial	0.96	0.03

Table 12.4: Linear SVM classification with 13 features

Class	Classification		Total
	Spam	Ham	
Spam	811	9	820
Ham	33	677	710

12.3.3 Improved Dataset

Finally, we discuss the application of SVM analysis to our improved dataset. From Figure 12.14, we see that there is no clear separation between the spam and the ham distributions for this data. The feature distributions are further analyzed by computing the AUC (based on SVMs) and comparing the results to the AUC values obtained for the standard dataset—these results are given in Figure 12.15. We see that the classification capability of the individual features have been dramatically reduced in the improved dataset.

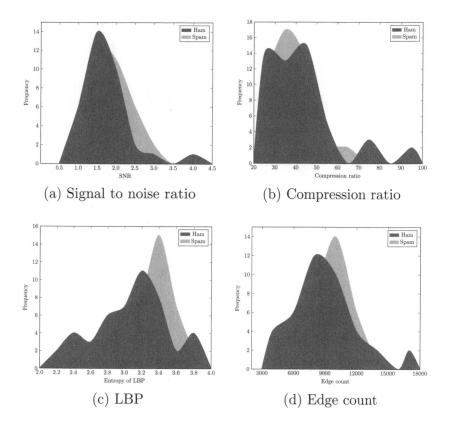

(a) Signal to noise ratio   (b) Compression ratio

(c) LBP   (d) Edge count

Figure 12.14: Ham and spam distributions for improved dataset

It's interesting to note that according to the results in Figure 12.15, the Edges feature is the most distinguishing for the improved dataset. This makes sense, since embedded spam messages increase the number of edges, as can be seen from the Canny edges examples in Figures 12.7 and 12.8.

In Table 12.5, we compare SVM kernel functions, based on our improved dataset. For the linear SVM, the AUC value is only 0.67, and regardless of the kernel, we see that the improved dataset presents a much greater challenge, as compared to the standard dataset. Thus the improved dataset can serve to test the strength of proposed image spam detection methods.

Table 12.5: Comparing kernel functions on improved dataset

Kernel	Accuracy	FPR
Linear	0.70	0.25
RBF	0.63	0.30
Polynomial	0.50	0.85

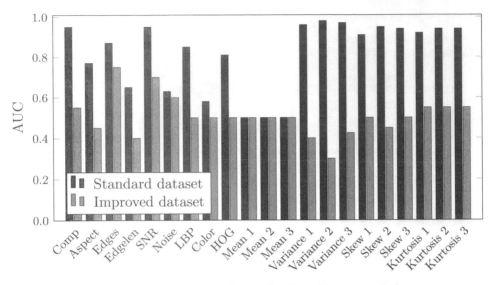

Figure 12.15: Comparison of standard and improved datasets

Table 12.6 provides a comparison of the SVM experiments in this section to the PCA experiments that we presented in Section 11.4 of Chapter 11. Both SVM and PCA perform very well on the standard dataset, but both perform poorly on the improved dataset.

Table 12.6: Cumulative results

Dataset	Eigenspam AUC	SVM		
		AUC	Accuracy	FPR
Standard dataset	0.99	0.99	0.97	0.04
Improved dataset	0.38	0.67	0.70	0.25

Our results show that image spam can be detected using standard machine learning techniques. However, the results make it equally clear that with relatively minor modification, image spam becomes undetectable when using these same techniques. This suggests that much improvement will be needed if we hope to detect advanced forms of image spam.

Chapter 13

Clustering Applications

> *The Milky Way is nothing else but a mass of innumerable stars planted together in clusters.*
> — Galileo

13.1 Introduction

You should not be surprised to learn that clustering applications are the focus of this chapter. First, we apply clustering to the problem of malware classification. Automatically classifying malware is a challenging task, and we show that reasonably good results can be obtained based on clustering. Then we attempt to take these results a step further by applying clustering to one of the most challenging problems in information security, namely, the automatic detection of new malware. While not conclusive, our results indicate that clustering might be useful in this difficult problem domain.

13.2 K-Means for Malware Classification

HMMs have been successfully applied to selected malware detection problems [11, 166]. In this section, we apply clustering, based on HMM scores, to the related problem of classifying malware. The results outlined here are discussed in considerably more detail in the report [2]; see also the paper [3].

Recall that metamorphic malware changes its internal structure with each infection. Such morphing can be used to evade signature-based detection [18] and can also be an effective defense against advanced statistical-based detection techniques [88].

Here, we train HMMs for each of several metamorphic malware generators, and we also train models for several different compilers. The rationale is that, roughly speaking, we can view a metamorphic generator as a type of compiler [11]. We then use these HMMs to score more than 8000 malware samples. Based on the resulting scores, the malware samples are clustered using the K-means algorithm. We analyze the resulting clusters and show that they correspond to certain identifiable characteristics of the malware.

Note that in this research, none of the specific malware families in our test set were used to generate the HMMs. This is intentional, as we want to ultimately consider the problem of automatically classifying new malware strains—a topic that we expand on in Section 13.3.

Next, we provide a brief discussion of relevant related work in malware analysis. Then we turn our attention to malware clustering experiments.

13.2.1 Background

Malware analysis can be based on static or dynamic features. Static features are extracted directly from samples, without code execution, while dynamic analysis relies on features that are extracted via code execution (or emulation). Static-based approaches are generally more efficient, but also more limited in their ability to determine behavior-based information. Static features can include low-level information, such as calls to external libraries, strings, or byte sequences [79]. Other static approaches extract higher-level information from binaries, such as API call sequences [26] or opcode information [166].

Although variants in a malware family may have very different static signatures, they almost certainly share many characteristic behaviors. In [24], for example, an automatic classification system is analyzed. This system can be trained to accurately identify new variants within a given malware family, based on observed similarities in behavioral features. Examples of such features include resource usage and the frequency of calls to specific kernel functions. The results presented in [24] indicate that a behavioral classifier can accurately identify new variants, at least within selected malware families.

In [79], the authors extract byte sequences from executables and analyze the resulting n-grams [70]. Several types of classifiers are considered, including instance-based learning, naïve Bayes, decision trees, SVMs, and boosting. The best results in [79] are obtained using boosted decision trees.

Control flow information is often analyzed in the form of a graph. In [26], a malware classification system based on approximate matching of control flow graphs is analyzed. This system is shown to be fairly robust when applied to metamorphic malware.

In the malware context, a binary classification problem consists of classifying a sample as either malicious or benign. In contrast, for a familial classification scheme, a sample is classified as belonging to one of several families. An example of familial malware classification can be found in [83], where a system known as VILO is analyzed. The VILO system applies the

k-NN algorithm to weighted opcode features, in the form of overlapping op-codes subsequences of length n. These n-gram features are shown to be somewhat robust against certain elementary code obfuscations [166]. The results presented in [83] indicate that VILO is fast and reasonably effective.

13.2.2 Experiments and Results

As in [11], for the experiments described in this section, HMMs were trained for each of four different compilers, namely, GCC, MinGW, TurboC, and Clang. Another HMM was trained to detect hand-written assembly code, which we refer to as the TASM model. In addition, we generated models for two metamorphic malware families, namely, NGVCK [160] and the experimental metamorphic worm in [135], which we refer to as MWOR.

For each HMM, we used 800 iterations of the Baum-Welch re-estimation algorithm. We experimented with various numbers of hidden states N, but this parameter had little effect on the results, so for all experiments discussed here, we use $N = 2$. The number of samples used for training each model is given in Table 13.1, where a sample consists of one executable that has been disassembled and its opcodes extracted.

Table 13.1: Number of samples used to train HMMs

Case	Samples
GCC	75
Clang	72
TurboC	64
MinGW	72
MWOR	100
NGVCK	50
TASM	56

For this research, we used the malware in the Malicia Project dataset [100]. This dataset contains more than 11,000 malware samples collected from more than 500 drive-by download servers over a period of 11 months [100]. Each malware sample is available in the form of a binary executable. A database is also provided, which contains metadata on each sample, including when the malware was collected, where it was collected, and the malware family type. However, the malware type was unspecified or listed as "unknown" for a significant percentage of the samples. Type information is necessary for the analysis of our experiments, and therefore only samples with a specified type were used. We found that 8119 of the malware samples had a specified family type, and these were all used in our experiments.

Since our classification scheme is based on opcode sequences, each of the 8119 executables (i.e., **exe** or **dll** file type) was disassembled using the tool *objdump*. Then each mnemonic opcode sequence was extracted and scored against each of the seven HMMs in Table 13.1, giving us a 7-tuple of scores for each sample.

After successful training, an HMM should assign scores to samples based on their similarity to the training set—the more similar, the higher the score. An HMM score is computed in the form of a log likelihood and the resulting score depends on the length of the observation sequence. We normalize each score by dividing by the length of its observation sequence (i.e., number of opcodes) to obtain a log likelihood per opcode (LLPO) score. Using this score, we can directly compare samples, regardless of the relative lengths of their observation sequences.

Again, each malware sample was scored against each of the seven trained HMMs and the resulting 7-tuple of scores was used for clustering. We experimented with the K-means algorithm with the number of clusters varying from $k = 2$ to $k = 15$. For each k, we selected the initial centroids to be "uniformly" spaced throughout the data, as discussed beginning on page 140 in Section 6.3.

Given a clustering, the process of recomputing the centroids is straightforward. Suppose that cluster ℓ contains the malware samples $V_1, V_2, \ldots, V_n$. Then, given the scores in Table 13.2, we calculate the mean in each dimension. For example, the mean of MinGW scores is

$$\mu_2 = \frac{(a_{12} + a_{22} + \cdots + a_{n2})}{n}.$$

The resulting 7-tuple of means is the new centroid, that is

$$c_\ell = \left(\mu_1, \mu_2, \mu_3, \mu_4, \mu_5, \mu_6, \mu_7\right).$$

Each of the k centroids is updated in this same manner.

Table 13.2: Malware scores

Sample	Hidden Markov Models						
	GCC	MinGW	TurboC	Clang	TASM	MWOR	NGVCK
V_1	a_{11}	a_{12}	a_{13}	a_{14}	a_{15}	a_{16}	a_{17}
V_2	a_{21}	a_{22}	a_{23}	a_{24}	a_{25}	a_{26}	a_{27}
$\vdots$	$\vdots$	$\vdots$	$\vdots$	$\vdots$	$\vdots$	$\vdots$	$\vdots$
V_n	a_{n1}	a_{n2}	a_{n3}	a_{n4}	a_{n5}	a_{n6}	a_{n7}

Once the updated centroids have been computed, the malware samples are regrouped by placing each sample in the cluster corresponding to the nearest of the k centroids. This process of recomputing centroids and regrouping the data points continues until the Euclidean distance between the previous centroids and the new centroids is negligible, or until the regrouping has no effect. As previously mentioned, we have tested each k from $k = 2$ to $k = 15$, but here we only present selected cases; for additional results, see [2].

As can be seen from Table 13.3, among the samples in our dataset, there are three dominant families, namely, Winwebsec, Zbot, and Zeroaccess. In this section, we focus on these three families. A description of each of the significant families in the Malicia dataset can be found in in Section 10.3.

Table 13.3: Malware samples

Family	Samples
Cleaman	32
Cridex	74
Cutwail	2
Dprn	1
Fakeav-rena	2
Fakeav-webprotection	3
Harebot	53
Ramnit	4
RansomNoaouy	5
Russkill	1
Securityshield	58
Smart HDD	68
Spyeye-ep	5
Ufasoft-bitcoin	3
Winrescue	5
Winwebsec	4361
Zbot	2136
Zeroaccess	1306
Total	8119

Our goal is to cluster Winwebsec, Zbot, and Zeroaccess malware samples, based on HMM scores generated using the seven models in Table 13.1. Again, we emphasize that Winwebsec, Zbot, and Zeroaccess are not among these seven HMM models, since our goal is to consider the feasibility of clustering new malware, based on existing models. This simulates the case of *zero-day malware*, that is, malware that has not previously been seen.

We performed experiments testing every possible score combination from the seven HMMs in Table 13.1. This was done to determine which subsets of these scores yield the best results. In addition, this experiment was conducted for each of $k = 2, 3, \ldots, 15$ clusters. Thus, each individual clustering experiment consists of selecting a value of $k \in \{2, 3, \ldots, 15\}$, and a subset of the scores from Table 13.1, and then performing K-means clustering. This gives us a total of

$$14 \cdot \left(2^7 - 1\right) = 1778$$

distinct clustering experiments. For each of these experiments, we use the purity of the resulting clusters (see Section 6.4.2 of Chapter 6 for a discussion of the purity measure) as our measure of the quality of the resulting clustering.

Suppose that $C_1, C_2, \ldots, C_k$ are the clusters we obtain from K-means. Let

$$x_i = \text{number of Winwebsec samples in cluster } C_i$$
$$y_i = \text{number of Zbot samples in cluster } C_i$$
$$z_i = \text{number of Zeroaccess samples in cluster } C_i$$

and let $M_i = \max\{x_i, y_i, z_i\}$. Then we define the score for this particular set of clusters as

$$\texttt{score} = \frac{M_1 + M_2 + \cdots + M_k}{T}$$

where T is the total number of all Winwebsec, Zbot, and Zeroaccess samples. In the ideal case, each cluster would be of a single type and we would have $\texttt{score} = 1$. In general, we have $0 \leq \texttt{score} \leq 1$, and the smaller the score, the further we are from the ideal case.

Our scoring results are given in Figure 13.1 in the form of a heatmap. On the top of this figure, score combinations are represented as binary vectors (listed in Gray code order), where the bit order corresponds to

GCC, MinGW, TurboC, Clang, TASM, MWOR, NGVCK.

For example, 1111111 indicated that the clustering score is based on all seven HMM scores, while 0111111 implies that all scores other than the model for GCC were used, 1111100 indicates that all scores except MWOR and NGVCK were used, and so on. For each of these experiments, we used $N = 2$ hidden states for all HMMs, and uniform initial placement of centroids, as discussed above. A larger (and colorful, and more legible) version of the heatmap in Figure 13.1 can be found online [138].

From Figure 13.1, we see that six or more clusters are needed to obtain reasonably good results. We also see that many different score combinations yield near-optimal results, and the best result exceeds 0.82. This implies that we could expect to correctly classify malware from these three families

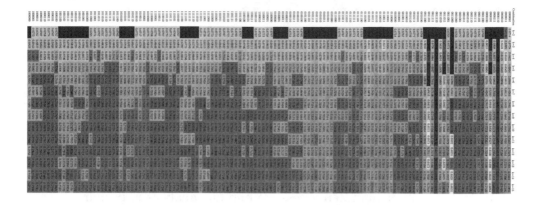

Figure 13.1: Heatmap of HMM scores (Gray code order)

at a rate of 0.82 by simply choosing the dominant family in the cluster to which a sample is assigned. In comparison, a strategy of simply guessing the category based on relative frequencies would, according to Table 13.3, have a probability of success of only

$$\left(\frac{4361}{7803}\right)^2 + \left(\frac{2136}{7803}\right)^2 + \left(\frac{1306}{7803}\right)^2 \approx 0.4150.$$

Consequently, the HMM-based clustering technique considered here provides a major improvement over this random case.

13.2.3 Discussion

The HMMs we used in these experiments were not specific to the malware families under consideration. Therefore, the results here suggest that it may be possible to automatically classify previously unseen malware with reasonable accuracy via clustering. We consider this problem further in the next section.

There are several other potential benefits to clustering malware. For example, rapid clustering of malware might enable a quick response to a new threat. If a new malware sample fits into an existing cluster, it is likely that the sample is similar to the previously known samples that predominate in that cluster. Then this new malware could be analyzed more quickly, and possibly even dealt with using known detection or removal strategies.

Clustering could also serve as a useful tool for categorizing malware. In spite of previous attempts to develop malware classification and naming schemes [95, 131, 141], each anti-virus vendor has its own classification system, and these appear to have little or no logical connection to malware structure or function. A rapid and automated clustering-based method could serve to bring some order to this classification chaos.

13.3   EM vs K-Means for Malware Analysis

As in the previous section, we consider the problem of clustering malware. However, our focus here is on a comparison of K-means and EM clustering, in the context of classifying new malware. The work presented in this section is discussed in more detail in the report [106]; see also the paper [107]. Closely related work can be found in the report [101] and the paper [102].

As in Section 13.2, most of the malware datasets used for this research were obtained from the Malicia Project website [100]. We focus on the 7,800 samples that are distributed among three dominant families, which consist of Winwebsec, Zbot, and Zeroaccess. While our analysis is primarily based on these three families, we do consider four additional datasets in some of our experiments. A brief description of each of these malware families can be found in Section 12.2 of Chapter 12.

13.3.1   Experiments and Results

We'll consider a set of experiments where we perform EM and K-means clustering based on HMM scores. The classification is then based on the purity of the resulting clusters.

After training the HMMs, we score each sample in the test set using each of the HMM models. Specifically, we train one HMM for each of the Zbot, Zeroaccess, Winwebsec, SmartHDD, and NGVCK malware families. Then a malware sample is represented by the resulting 5-tuple of scores, where each dimension corresponds to the score with respect to one of these families. The 5-tuples of scores—or a subset thereof—serve as the input to the K-means and EM clustering algorithms.

We performed experiments varying the number of clusters and the number of dimensions (i.e., models). We vary the number of dimensions from two to five, and the number of clusters varies from two to 10. The specific malware family models used for each of the "dimensions" are listed Table 13.4. In each case, the analysis of the resulting clusters is based on the three dominant families in the dataset, as discussed in more detail below.

Table 13.4: Models used for scoring

Dimensions	Scores
2	Winwebsec and Zbot
3	Winwebsec, Zbot, and Zeroaccess
4	Winwebsec, Zbot, Zeroaccess, and NCGVK
5	Winwebsec, Zbot, Zeroaccess, NCGVK, and SmartHDD

Based on the clustering results for each case in Table 13.4, we compute scores, and these scores are used to plot ROC curves, from which we determine the AUC. This AUC statistic serves as our measure of success.

The scores we use to generate ROC curves from clusters are computed as follows. Suppose that we have a set of clusters $C_1, C_2, \ldots, C_k$ and a given data point x that belongs to cluster C_j. Then we compute $p_{ij} = m_{ij}/m_j$, where m_{ij} is the number of elements of family i in cluster C_j, and m_j is the number of elements in cluster C_j. We define the scoring functions

$$\texttt{score}_i(x) = p_{ij}.$$

That is, $\texttt{score}_i(x)$ is the proportion of the data in cluster C_j that is of type i, where $x \in C_j$. Note that this score is based on the purity of the clusters.

We want to focus on the three major families in the dataset, namely, Zbot, Zeroaccess, and Winwebsec. Consequently, we define the scores

$$\texttt{score}_0(x) = \text{Zbot score of sample } x,$$
$$\texttt{score}_1(x) = \text{Zeroaccess score of sample } x, \text{ and}$$
$$\texttt{score}_2(x) = \text{Winwebsec score of sample } x.$$

From Table 13.4 we see that in the 2-dimensional experiments, we use scores from the Winwebsec and Zbot families to generate clusters, where the number of clusters ranges from two to 10. In each case, we use $\texttt{score}_0(x)$ to generate an ROC curve relative to the Zbot family, and, similarly, we use $\texttt{score}_1(x)$ and $\texttt{score}_2(x)$ to plot ROC curves for the Zeroaccess and Winwebsec families, respectively. That is, we apply $\texttt{score}_0(x)$ to all data points in all clusters, with the Zbot samples serving as the positive cases (for which we expect higher scores), and all other malware and benign samples serving as negative cases (for which we expect lower scores). We plot the ROC curve and compute the AUC based on the resulting scatterplot of scores. We repeat this process using $\texttt{score}_1(x)$ with Zeroaccess samples serving as the positive cases, and, finally, using $\texttt{score}_2(x)$ and the Winwebsec samples.

In the extreme, we could cluster each point into its own cluster, in which case the purity is maximized. Consequently, we expect that as we add more clusters, our purity-based scores will tend to improve. Also, as we add more dimensions, we increase the available "space," making it more likely that we can better separate data of different types. However, the actual separation will depend on the strength of the scores used.

The results of these purity-based scoring experiments are summarized in Figure 13.2. Each sub-figure in Figure 13.2 includes both K-means and EM line graphs.

In Figure 13.3 (a) and (b), respectively, we give stem plots corresponding to the results for K-means and EM clustering in Figure 13.2. These stem plots provide a useful visual representation of all of our clustering experiments.

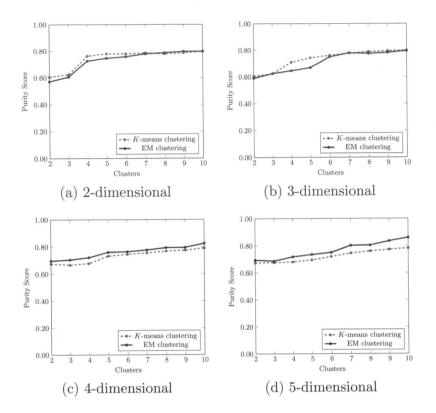

(a) 2-dimensional

(b) 3-dimensional

(c) 4-dimensional

(d) 5-dimensional

Figure 13.2: Purity scores for EM and K-means clustering

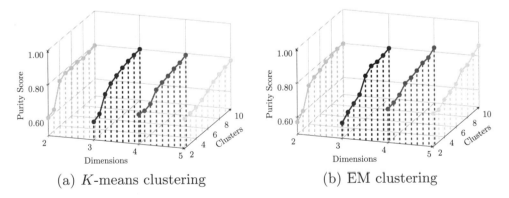

(a) K-means clustering

(b) EM clustering

Figure 13.3: Clustering stem plots

From Figure 13.3 (a), we see that for K-means, the number of clusters is a critical parameter, but the number of dimensions has little effect. This suggests that we can expect only limited improvement from including additional models. In contrast, Figure 13.3 (b) shows that the EM clustering results improve as the number of clusters increase, and as the number of dimensions increase. Furthermore, in most cases the overall accuracy is better using EM.

This illustrates the advantage of EM clustering for this particular problem. Most significantly, the EM clusters suggest that with a sufficient number of models, we may be able to automatically cluster new malware samples with reasonably high accuracy.

13.3.2 Discussion

Detecting zero-day malware is one of the greatest challenges in anti-virus research. Typically, no reliable signature or statistical model is available for such malware. Hence, signature detection is not a realistic option, and straightforward statistical or machine learning techniques are unlikely to be successful, either. The clustering results in this section, together with the work in Section 13.2, indicate that clustering can be useful for classifying malware. And in some cases, we successfully clustered without using any model specific to the malware family under consideration. These type of results strongly suggest that clustering could have a useful role to play in detecting zero-day malware.

Annotated Bibliography

[1] Y. Altun, I. Tsochantaridis, and T. Hofmann, Hidden Markov support
vector machines, *Proceedings of the Twentieth International
Conference on Machine Learning* (ICML-2003), Washington DC,
2003, http://cs.brown.edu/~th/papers/AltTsoHof-ICML2003.pdf
Cited on page 125

[2] C. Annachhatre, Hidden Markov models for malware classification,
Master's Report, Department of Computer Science, San Jose State
University, 2013,
http://scholarworks.sjsu.edu/etd_projects/328/
Cited on pages 307 and 311

[3] C. Annachhatre, T. H. Austin, and M. Stamp, Hidden Markov models
for malware classification, *Journal of Computer Virology and Hacking
Techniques*, 11(2):59–73, 2015,
http://link.springer.com/article/10.1007/s11416-014-0215-x
Cited on pages 141, 273, 275, and 307

[4] A. S. Annadatha, Image spam analysis, Master's Report, Department
of Computer Science, San Jose State University, 2016,
http://scholarworks.sjsu.edu/etd_projects/486/
Cited on pages 288, 298, 299, and 300

[5] A. S. Annadatha, Improved spam image dataset, https:
//www.dropbox.com/s/7zh7r9dopuh554e/New_Spam.zip?dl=0
Cited on page 285

[6] A. S. Annadatha and M. Stamp, Image spam analysis and detection,
to appear in *Journal of Computer Virology and Hacking Techniques*
Cited on pages 288 and 298

[7] G. Arfken, Diagonalization of matrices, in *Mathematical Methods for
Physicists*, 3rd edition, Academic Press, pp. 217–229, 1985
Cited on page 78

[8] P. Asokarathinam, 2D shear, `http://cs.fit.edu/~wds/classes/cse5255/thesis/shear/shear.html`
Cited on page 79

[9] S. Attaluri, S. McGhee, and M. Stamp, Profile hidden Markov models and metamorphic virus detection, *Journal in Computer Virology* 5(2):151–169, 2009,
`http://www.springerlink.com/content/3153113q2667q36w/`
Cited on pages 45, 49, 269, 274, and 275

[10] D. Austin, We recommend a singular value decomposition,
`http://www.ams.org/samplings/feature-column/fcarc-svd`
Cited on page 79

[11] T. H. Austin, E. Filiol, S. Josse, and M. Stamp, Exploring hidden Markov models for virus analysis: A semantic approach, *Proceedings of 46th Hawaii International Conference on System Sciences* (HICSS 46), January 7–10, 2013
Cited on pages 275, 280, 282, 283, 307, 308, and 309

[12] J. Aycock, *Computer Viruses and Malware*, Advances in Information Security, Vol. 22, Springer-Verlag, 2006
Cited on pages 4 and 240

  • A very well-written, humorous, and easily accessible introduction to malware—highly recommended.

[13] S. Balakrishnama and A. Ganapathiraju, Linear discriminant analysis — A brief tutorial, 2007, `http://www.music.mcgill.ca/~ich/classes/mumt611_07/classifiers/lda_theory.pdf`
Cited on page 201

[14] D. Baysa, R. M. Low, and M. Stamp, Structural entropy and metamorphic malware, *Journal of Computer Virology and Hacking Techniques*, 9(4):179–192, 2013,
`http://link.springer.com/article/10.1007/s11416-013-0185-4`
Cited on pages 283 and 290

[15] K. P. Bennett and C. Campbell, Support vector machines: Hype or hallelujah?, *SIGKDD Explorations*, 2(2):1–13, December 2000
Cited on page 97

[16] T. Berg-Kirkpatrick and D. Klein, Decipherment with a million random restarts,
`http://www.cs.berkeley.edu/~tberg/papers/emnlp2013.pdf`
Cited on pages 33, 156, 254, and 257

[17] R. Berwick, An idiot's guide to support vector machines (SVMs), 2003, http://www.svms.org/tutorials/Berwick2003.pdf
Cited on page 125

   • A good resource with a memorable title.

[18] J. Borello and L. Me, Code obfuscation techniques for metamorphic viruses, *Journal in Computer Virology* 4(3): 211–220, 2008, http://www.springerlink.com/content/233883w3r2652537
Cited on pages 240, 241, 242, and 307

[19] A. P. Bradley, The use of the area under the ROC curve in the evaluation of machine learning algorithms, *Pattern Recognition*, 30:1145–1159, 1997
Cited on pages 226 and 281

[20] L. Breiman and A. Cutler, Random forests™, https://www.stat.berkeley.edu/~breiman/RandomForests/cc_home.htm
Cited on page 192

   • A brief and very readable introduction to random forests by the inventors of the technique. It suffers a bit from a "this-is-the-greatest-thing-since-sliced-bread" attitude. Also, the authors trademarked the term "random forest" (and its variants), and it really bothers me that I can't decide whether this is ingenious or just annoying.

[21] The Brown corpus of standard American English, available for download at http://www.cs.toronto.edu/~gpenn/csc401/a1res.html
Cited on pages 238 and 250

[22] Buster sandbox analyzer, http://bsa.isoftware.nl/
Cited on page 270

[23] J. Canny, A computational approach to edge detection, *IEEE Transactions on Pattern Analysis and Machine Intelligence*, (6):679–698, 1986
Cited on page 298

[24] R. Canzanese, M. Kam, and S. Mancoridis, Toward an automatic, online behavioral malware classification system, https://www.cs.drexel.edu/~spiros/papers/saso2013.pdf
Cited on page 308

[25] R. L. Cave and L. P. Neuwirth, Hidden Markov models for English, in J. D. Ferguson, editor, *Hidden Markov Models for Speech*, IDA-CRD,

Princeton, NJ, October 1980,
http://cs.sjsu.edu/~stamp/RUA/CaveNeuwirth/
Cited on pages 237 and 240

- An oldie but a goodie, where the English text HMM example is
first presented.

[26] S. Cesare and Y. Xiang, Classification of malware using structured
control flow, 8th Australasian Symposium on Parallel and Distributed
Computing, pp. 61–70, 2010
Cited on page 308

[27] E. Chen, How does randomization in a random forest work?, Quora,
https://www.quora.com/How-does-randomization-in-a-random-forest-work
Cited on page 192

- A readable and intuitive discussion of random forests.

[28] E. Chen, Introduction to conditional random fields,
http://blog.echen.me/2012/01/03/introduction-to-conditional-random-fields/
Cited on page 213

- A good introduction to CRFs.

[29] E. Chen, What are the advantages of different classification
algorithms?,
Quora, https://www.quora.com/What-are-the-advantages-of-different-classification-algorithms/answer/Edwin-Chen-1
Cited on page 212

[30] C. Collberg, C. Thomborson, and D. Low, Manufacturing cheap,
resilient, and stealthy opaque constructs, Principles of Programming
Languages, POPL98, San Diego, California, January 1998
Cited on page 243

[31] R. Collobert and S. Bengio, Links between perceptrons, MLPs and
SVMs, Proceedings of the 21st International Conference on Machine
Learning, Banff, Canada, 2004,
http://ronan.collobert.com/pub/matos/2004_links_icml.pdf
Cited on page 181

[32] N. Cristianini and J. Shawe-Taylor, An Introduction to Support Vector
Machines and Other Kernel-Based Learning Methods, Cambridge
University Press, 2000
Cited on page 125

[33] *The Curse of Frankenstein*, IMDb,
http://www.imdb.com/title/tt0050280/
Cited on page 97

[34] Cygwin, Cygwin utility files, 2015, http://www.cygwin.com/
Cited on page 292

[35] J. Davis and M. Goadrich, The relationship between precision-recall
and ROC curves,
http://www.autonlab.org/icml_documents/camera-
ready/030_The_Relationship_Bet.pdf
Cited on page 230

[36] R. DeCook, The bivariate normal, http://homepage.stat.uiowa.
edu/~rdecook/stat2020/notes/ch5_pt3_2013.pdf
Cited on page 164

[37] J. De Doná, Lagrangian duality, 2004, http://www.eng.newcastle.
edu.au/eecs/cdsc/books/cce/Slides/Duality.pdf
Cited on page 108

[38] W. Deng, Q. Liu, H. Cheng, and Z. Qin, A malware detection
framework based on Kolmogorov complexity, *Journal of
Computational Information Systems* 7(8):2687–2694, 2011,
http://citeseerx.ist.psu.edu/viewdoc/download?doi=10.1.1.
469.1934&rep=rep1&type=pdf
Cited on page 283

[39] P. Desai, Towards an undetectable computer virus, Master's Report,
Department of Computer Science, San Jose State University, 2008,
http://scholarworks.sjsu.edu/etd_projects/90/
Cited on page 245

[40] P. Deshpande, Metamorphic detection using function call graph
analysis. Master's Report, San Jose State University, Department of
Computer Science, 2013,
http://scholarworks.sjsu.edu/etd_projects/336
Cited on page 290

[41] S. Deshpande, Eigenvalue analysis for metamorphic detection,
Master's Report, San Jose State University, Department of Computer
Science, 2012, http://scholarworks.sjsu.edu/etd_projects/279/
Cited on pages 277, 280, 281, and 282

[42] S. Deshpande, Y. Park, and M. Stamp, Eigenvalue analysis for
metamorphic detection, *Journal of Computer Virology and Hacking*

Techniques, 10(1):53–65, 2014,
`http://link.springer.com/article/10.1007/s11416-013-0193-4`
Cited on pages 280 and 290

[43] A. Dhavare, R. M. Low and M. Stamp, Efficient cryptanalysis of homophonic substitution ciphers, *Cryptologia*, 37(3):250–281, 2013, `http://www.tandfonline.com/doi/abs/10.1080/01611194.2013.797041`
Cited on pages 251 and 257

[44] T. G. Dietterich, Machine learning for sequential data: A review, in T. Caelli (ed.), *Structural, Syntactic, and Statistical Pattern Recognition*, Lecture Notes in Computer Science 2396, pp. 15–30, Springer, `http://web.engr.oregonstate.edu/~tgd/publications/mlsd-ssspr.pdf`
Cited on page 213

   • An interesting, high-level perspective.

[45] C. B. Do and S. Batzoglou, What is the expectation maximization algorithm?, *Nature Biotechnology*, 26(8):897–899, August 2008, `http://ai.stanford.edu/~chuongdo/papers/em_tutorial.pdf`
Cited on page 155

   • A very readable introduction to EM.

[46] M. Dredze, R. Gevaryahu, and A. Elias-Bachrach, Learning fast classifiers for image spam, CEAS 2007
Cited on page 298

[47] R. Durbin, S. Eddy, A. Krogh, and G. Mitchison, *Biological Sequence Analysis: Probabilistic Models of Proteins and Nucleic Acids*, Cambridge University Press, 1988
Cited on pages 41, 51, 56, and 62

   • The standard reference on PHMMs.

[48] C. Elkan, Log-linear models and conditional random fields, 2012, `http://cseweb.ucsd.edu/~elkan/250Bwinter2012/loglinearCRFs.pdf`
Cited on page 213

   • Includes a discussion of the algorithms for CRFs.

[49] Expectation-maximization algorithm, Wikipedia, `http://en.wikipedia.org/wiki/Expectationmaximization_algorithm`
Cited on page 170

[50] A. A. Farag and S. Y. Elhabian, A tutorial on data reduction: linear discriminant analysis (LDA), `http://www.di.univr.it/documenti/OccorrenzaIns/matdid/matdid437773.pdf`
Cited on pages 193 and 201

- An excellent introduction to LDA.

[51] D. Feng and R. F. Doolittle, Progressive sequence alignment as a prerequisite to correct phylogenetic trees, *Journal of Molecular Evolution*, 25(4):351–360, 1987
Cited on pages 46 and 270

[52] E. Filiol, Metamorphism, formal grammars and undecidable code mutation, *International Journal of Computer Science*, 2:70–75, 2007
Cited on page 240

[53] K. Fukuda and H. Tamada, A dynamic birthmark from analyzing operand stack runtime behavior to detect copied software, in *Proceedings of SNPD '13*, pp. 505–510, July 2013, Honolulu, Hawaii
Cited on page 269

[54] Y. Gao, Image spam hunter dataset, 2008, `http://www.cs.northwestern.edu/~yga751/ML/ISH.htm`
Cited on pages 285 and 298

[55] Y. Gao, M. Yang, X. Zhao, B. Pardo, Y. Wu, T. N. Pappas, and A. Choudhary, Image spam hunter, Acoustics, speech and signal processing (ICASSP 2008), pp. 1765–1768
Cited on pages 285 and 298

[56] A. Gersho and R. M. Gray, *Vector Quantization and Signal Compression*, Springer, 1992
Cited on page 203

[57] GNU accounting utilities, `http://www.gnu.org/software/acct/`
Cited on page 262

[58] I. Guyon, J. Weston, S. Barnhill, and V. Vapnik, Gene selection for cancer classification using support vector machines, *Machine Learning*, 46(1-3):389–422, 2002
Cited on pages 128 and 302

[59] Harebot.M, Panda Security, `http://www.pandasecurity.com/usa/homeusers/security-info/220319/Harebot.M/`
Cited on page 271

[60] N. Harris, Visualizing DBSCAN clustering,
     https://www.naftaliharris.com/blog/visualizing-dbscan-
     clustering/
     Cited on page 170

[61] L. Huang, A study on masquerade detection, Master's Report,
     Department of Computer Science, San Jose State University, 2010,
     http://scholarworks.sjsu.edu/etd_projects/9/
     Cited on pages 43, 44, 261, 262, and 266

[62] L. Huang and M. Stamp, Masquerade detection using profile hidden
     Markov models, Computers & Security, 30(8):732–747,
     November 2011, http://www.sciencedirect.com/science/
     article/pii/S0167404811001003
     Cited on page 261

[63] IDA Pro, http://www.hex-rays.com/idapro/
     Cited on page 243

[64] Introduction to support vector machines, OpenCV Tutorials, 2014,
     http://docs.opencv.org/doc/tutorials/ml/introduction_to_
     svm/introduction_to_svm.html
     Cited on page 125

[65] A. K. Jain and R. C. Dubes, Algorithms for Clustering Data,
     Prentice-Hall, 1988,
     http://www.cse.msu.edu/~jain/Clustering_Jain_Dubes.pdf
     Cited on pages 152 and 170

[66] T. Jakobsen, A fast method for the cryptanalysis of substitution
     ciphers, Cryptologia, 19(3):265–274, 1995
     Cited on page 291

[67] R. K. Jidigam, Metamorphic detection using singular value
     decomposition, Master's Report, Department of Computer Science,
     San Jose State University, 2013,
     http://scholarworks.sjsu.edu/etd_projects/330/
     Cited on page 280

[68] R. K. Jidigam, T. H. Austin, and M. Stamp, Singular value
     decomposition and metamorphic detection, Journal of Computer
     Virology and Hacking Techniques, 11(4):203–216, 2015,
     http://link.springer.com/article/10.1007/s11416-014-0220-0
     Cited on pages 280 and 290

[69] R. Jin, Cluster validation, 2008,
http://www.cs.kent.edu/~jin/DM08/ClusterValidation.pdf
Cited on page 141

[70] K. Jones, A statistical interpretation of term specificity and its
application in retrieval, *Journal of Documentation*, 28(1):11–21, 1972
Cited on page 308

[71] A. Kalbhor, T. H. Austin, E. Filiol, S. Josse, and M. Stamp, Dueling
hidden Markov models for virus analysis, *Journal of Computer
Virology and Hacking Techniques*, 11(2):103–118, May 2015,
http://link.springer.com/article/10.1007/s11416-014-0232-9
Cited on page 275

[72] Kaspersky Lab,
http://support.kaspersky.com/viruses/rogue?qid=208286454
Cited on page 271

[73] S. Kazi and M. Stamp, Hidden Markov models for software piracy
detection, *Information Security Journal: A Global Perspective*,
22(3):140–149, 2013, http:
//www.tandfonline.com/doi/abs/10.1080/19393555.2013.787474
Cited on page 269

[74] E. Kim, Everything you wanted to know about the kernel trick (but
were too afraid to ask), http://www.eric-kim.net/eric-kim-
net/posts/1/kernel_trick.html
Cited on page 101

[75] D. Klein, Lagrange multipliers without permanent scarring, http:
//nlp.cs.berkeley.edu/tutorials/lagrange-multipliers.pdf
Cited on page 124

  • Well written, and one of the all-time great titles.

[76] D. Knowles, Lagrangian duality for dummies, http://cs.stanford.
edu/people/davidknowles//lagrangian_duality.pdf
Cited on page 102

[77] D. Knuth, *Art of Computer Programming*, volume 3
Cited on page 179

[78] Y. Ko, Maximum entropy Markov models and CRFs,
http://web.donga.ac.kr/yjko/usefulthings/MEMM&CRF.pdf
Cited on page 213

  • Includes a nice example of the label bias problem.

[79] S. Kolter and M. Maloof, Learning to detect and classify malicious
executables in the wild, *Journal of Machine Learning Research*,
7:2721–2744, 2006
Cited on page 308

[80] D. Kriesel, A brief introduction to neural networks,
`http://www.dkriesel.com/_media/science/neuronalenetze-en-`
`zeta2-2col-dkrieselcom.pdf`
Cited on page 182

[81] A. Lad, EM algorithm for estimating a Gaussian mixture model,
`http://www.cs.cmu.edu/~alad/em/`
Cited on page 170

[82] J. Lafferty, A. McCallum, and F. Pereira, Conditional random fields:
Probabilistic models for segmenting and labeling sequence data,
`http://repository.upenn.edu/cgi/viewcontent.cgi?article=`
`1162&context=cis_papers`
Cited on page 213

  • Discusses the relationship between CRFs, HMMs, and MEMMs,
    with especially good information on the label bias problem.

[83] A. Lakhotia, A. Walenstein, C. Miles, and A. Singh, VILO: A rapid
learning nearest-neighbor classifier for malware triage, *Journal in
Computer Virology*, 9(3):109–123, 2013
Cited on pages 308 and 309

[84] M. Law, A simple introduction to support vector machines, 2011,
`http://www.cise.ufl.edu/class/cis4930sp11dtm/notes/intro_`
`svm_new.pdf`
Cited on page 125

[85] J. Lee, T. H. Austin, and M. Stamp, Compression-based analysis of
metamorphic malware, *International Journal of Security and
Networks*, 10(2):124–136, 2015, `http://www.inderscienceonline.`
`com/doi/abs/10.1504/IJSN.2015.070426`
Cited on pages 283, 290, and 294

[86] A. Liaw and M. Wiener, Classification and regression by
randomForest, *R News*, 2/3:18–22, December 2002
`http://www.bios.unc.edu/~dzeng/BIOS740/randomforest.pdf`
Cited on page 192

[87] Y. Lin and Y. Jeon, Random forests and adaptive nearest neighbors,
Technical Report 1055, Department of Statistics, University of

Wisconsin, 2002,
https://www.stat.wisc.edu/sites/default/files/tr1055.pdf
Cited on page 192

[88] D. Lin and M. Stamp, Hunting for undetectable metamorphic viruses,
Journal in Computer Virology, 7(3):201–214, August 2011,
http://www.springerlink.com/content/3231224064522083/
Cited on pages 241, 243, 245, 294, and 307

[89] Malicia Project, 2015, http://malicia-project.com/
Cited on pages 271, 292, and 295

[90] *Marvin the Martian*, IMDb,
http://www.imdb.com/character/ch0030547/
Cited on page 237

[91] S. McKenzie, CNN, Who was the real fifth Beatle?, March 2016,
http://www.cnn.com/2016/03/09/entertainment/who-was-real-
fifth-beatle/
Cited on page 166

[92] Mean vector and covariance matrix, NIST, http:
//www.itl.nist.gov/div898/handbook/pmc/section5/pmc541.htm
Cited on page 81

[93] The Mental Driller, Metamorphism in practice or "How I made
MetaPHOR and what I've learnt," 2002, http://download.adamas.
ai/dlbase/Stuff/VX%20Heavens%20Library/vmd01.html
Cited on page 280

[94] B. Mirkin, Choosing the number of clusters,
http://www.hse.ru/data/2011/06/23/1215441450/noc.pdf
Cited on page 170

[95] MITRE, Malware attribute enumeration and characterization, 2013,
http://maec.mitre.org
Cited on page 313

[96] E. Mooi and M. Sarstedt, Cluster analysis, Chapter 9 in *A Concise
Guide to Market Research: The Process, Data, and Methods Using
IBM SPSS Statistics*, Springer 2011
Cited on page 170

[97] A. W. Moore, *K*-means and hierarchical clustering, 2001,
http://www.autonlab.org/tutorials/kmeans11.pdf
Cited on page 139

[98] J. Morrow, Linear least squares problems, `https://www.math.washington.edu/~morrow/498_13/demmelsvd.pdf`
Cited on page 205

[99] G. Myles and C. S. Collberg, k-gram based software birthmarks, *Proceedings of ACM Symposium on Applied Computing*, pp. 314–318, March 2005, Santa Fe, New Mexico
Cited on page 269

[100] A. Nappa, M. Zubair Rafique, and J. Caballero, Driving in the cloud: An analysis of drive-by download operations and abuse reporting, *Proceedings of the 10th Conference on Detection of Intrusions and Malware & Vulnerability Assessment*, Berlin, Germany, July 2013
Cited on pages 271, 292, 309, and 314

[101] U. Narra, Clustering versus SVM for malware detection, Master's Report, Department of Computer Science, San Jose State University, 2015, `http://scholarworks.sjsu.edu/etd_projects/405/` Cited on page 314

[102] U. Narra, F. Di Troia, V. A. Corrado, T. H. Austin, and M. Stamp, Clustering versus SVM for malware detection, *Journal of Computer Virology and Hacking Techniques*, 2(4):213–224, November 2016, `http://link.springer.com/article/10.1007/s11416-015-0253-z`
Cited on page 314

[103] Next Generation Virus Construction Kit (NGVCK), `http://vxheaven.org/vx.php?id=tn02`
Cited on page 282

[104] A. Ng and J. Duchi, The simplified SMO algorithm, `http://cs229.stanford.edu/materials/smo.pdf`
Cited on page 121

[105] M. Nielson, How the backpropagation algorithm works, `http://neuralnetworksanddeeplearning.com/chap2.html`
Cited on page 182

[106] S. Pai, A comparison of malware clustering techniques, Master's Report, Department of Computer Science, San Jose State University, 2015, `http://scholarworks.sjsu.edu/etd_projects/404/`
Cited on pages 151 and 314

[107] S. Pai, F. Di Troia, V. A. Corrado, T. H. Austin, and M. Stamp, Clustering for malware classification, *Journal of Computer Virology*

and Hacking Techniques, 2016, `http://link.springer.com/article/10.1007%2Fs11416-016-0265-3` Cited on page 314

[108] J. C. Platt, Sequential minimal optimization: A fast algorithm for training support vector machines, Microsoft Research, 1998, `https://www.microsoft.com/en-us/research/wp-content/uploads/2016/02/tr-98-14.pdf` Cited on page 121

[109] P. Ponnambalam, Measuring malware evolution, Master's Report, Department of Computer Science, San Jose State University, 2015, `http://scholarworks.sjsu.edu/etd_projects/449/` Cited on page 241

[110] N. Ponomareva, P. Rosso, F. Pla, and A. Molina, Conditional random fields vs. hidden Markov models in a biomedical named entity recognition task, `http://users.dsic.upv.es/~prosso/resources/PonomarevaEtAl_RANLP07.pdf` Cited on pages 209 and 213

   • Comparison of HMMs and CRFs for a specific problem.

[111] R. C. Prim, Shortest connection networks and some generalizations, *Bell System Technical Journal*, 36(6):1389–1401, November 1957 Cited on page 47

[112] A. Quattoni, Tutorial on conditional random fields for sequence prediction, `http://www.cs.upc.edu/~aquattoni/AllMyPapers/crf_tutorial_talk.pdf` Cited on page 213

   • The focus is on HCRFs, that is, hidden conditional random fields.

[113] L. R. Rabiner, A tutorial on hidden Markov models and selected applications in speech recognition, *Proceedings of the IEEE*, 77(2):257–286, February 1989, `http://www.cs.ubc.ca/~murphyk/Bayes/rabiner.pdf` Cited on page 11

   • A solid introduction to HMMs, even for those who have no interest in speech recognition.

[114] M. Ramek, Mathematics tutorial: The Jacobi method, `http://fptchlx02.tu-graz.ac.at/cgi-bin/access.com?c1=0000&c2=0000&c3=0000&file=0638` Cited on page 93

[115] H. Rana and M. Stamp, Hunting for pirated software using metamorphic analysis, *Information Security Journal: A Global Perspective*, 23(3):68–85, 2014, http://www.tandfonline.com/doi/abs/10.1080/19393555.2014.975557 Cited on page 269

[116] S. Raschka, Linear discriminant analysis — bit by bit, 2014, http://sebastianraschka.com/Articles/2014_python_lda.html Cited on page 201

[117] R. Rojas, AdaBoost and the Super Bowl of classifiers: A tutorial introduction to adaptive boosting, http://www.inf.fu-berlin.de/inst/ag-ki/adaboost4.pdf Cited on page 182

  • An excellent and highly readable introduction to boosting.

[118] N. Runwal, R. M. Low, and M. Stamp, Opcode graph similarity and metamorphic detection, *Journal in Computer Virology*, 8(1-2): 37–52, 2012, http://www.springerlink.com/content/h0g1768766071046/ Cited on pages 127, 290, and 293

[119] M. Saleh, A. Mohamed, and A. Nabi, Eigenviruses for metamorphic virus recognition, *IET Information Security*, 5(4):191–198, 2011 Cited on pages 277 and 280

[120] M. Schonlau, Masquerading user data, http://www.schonlau.net/intrusion.html Cited on pages 261 and 266

[121] M. Schonlau, et al., Computer intrusion: Detecting masquerades, *Statistical Science*, 15(1):1–17, 2001 Cited on page 261

[122] Security Shield, Microsoft Malware Protection Center, http://www.microsoft.com/security/portal/threat/encyclopedia/Entry.aspx?Name=SecurityShield Cited on page 271

[123] A. A. Shabalin, *K*-means clustering, http://shabal.in/visuals/kmeans/1.html Cited on page 170

[124] C. Shalizi, Logistic regression, Chapter 12 in *Advanced Data Analysis from an Elementary Point of View*, http://www.stat.cmu.edu/~cshalizi/ADAfaEPoV/ADAfaEPoV.pdf Cited on page 207

[125] C. Shalizi, Principal component analysis, `https://www.stat.cmu.edu/~cshalizi/uADA/12/lectures/ch18.pdf`
Cited on pages 87 and 130

[126] G. Shanmugam, R. M. Low, and M. Stamp, Simple substitution distance and metamorphic detection, *Journal of Computer Virology and Hacking Techniques*, 9(3):159–170, 2013, `http://link.springer.com/article/10.1007/s11416-013-0184-5`
Cited on pages 127, 135, 282, 290, 291, and 293

[127] J. Shlens, A tutorial on principal component analysis, `http://www.cs.cmu.edu/~elaw/papers/pca.pdf`
Cited on pages 73, 76, 78, and 87

   • A very nice and well-written introduction to PCA and SVD.

[128] Singular value decomposition, Wolfram MathWorld, `http://mathworld.wolfram.com/SingularValueDecomposition.html`
Cited on page 79

[129] T. Singh, Support vector machines and metamorphic malware detection, Master's Report, San Jose State University, 2015, `http://scholarworks.sjsu.edu/etd_projects/409/`
Cited on page 289

[130] T. Singh, F. Di Troia, V. A. Corrado, T. H. Austin, and M. Stamp Support vector machines and malware detection, *Journal of Computer Virology and Hacking Techniques*, 12(4):203–212, November 2016, `http://link.springer.com/article/10.1007/s11416-015-0252-0`
Cited on page 289

[131] F. Skulason, A. Solomon, and V. Bontchev, CARO naming scheme, 1991, `http://www.caro.org/naming/scheme.html`
Cited on page 313

[132] Smart HDD, 2015, `http://support.kaspersky.com/viruses/rogue?qid=208286454`
Cited on page 271

[133] I. Sorokin, Comparing files using structural entropy, *Journal in Computer Virology*, 7(4):259–265, 2011
Cited on page 283

[134] D. Spinellis, Reliable identification of bounded-length viruses is NP-complete, *IEEE Transactions on Information Theory*, 49(1):280–284, January 2003
Cited on page 240

[135] S. Sridhara and M. Stamp, Metamorphic worm that carries its own
      morphing engine, *Journal of Computer Virology and Hacking
      Techniques*, 9(2): 49–58, 2013,
      `http://link.springer.com/article/10.1007/s11416-012-0174-z`
      Cited on pages 241, 280, 281, 282, and 309

[136] Stack Exchange, Making sense of principal component analysis,
      eigenvectors & eigenvalues, `http:`
      `//stats.stackexchange.com/questions/2691/making-sense-of-`
      `principal-component-analysis-eigenvectors-eigenvalues`
      Cited on page 87

      - A very brief and intuitive introduction to PCA.

[137] M. Stamp, *Information Security: Principles and Practice*, second
      edition, Wiley, 2011
      Cited on pages 4, 202, and 245

[138] M. Stamp, Heatmaps for the paper [3], 2014,
      `http://cs.sjsu.edu/~stamp/heatmap/heatmapsBig.pdf`
      Cited on page 312

[139] Support vector machines (SVMs), The Karush-Kuhn-Tucker (KKT)
      conditions, `http://www.svms.org/kkt/`
      Cited on page 124

[140] C. Sutton and A. McCallum, An introduction to conditional random
      fields, *Foundations and Trends in Machine Learning*, 4(4):267–373,
      2011, `http://homepages.inf.ed.ac.uk/csutton/publications/`
      `crftut-fnt.pdf`
      Cited on pages 211 and 213

      - Book-length treatment of CRFs. Not for the faint of heart.

[141] M. Swimmer, Response to the proposal for a "C virus" database,
      1990, *ACM SIGSAC Review*, 8:1–5,
      `http://www.odysci.com/article/1010112993890087`
      Cited on page 313

[142] Symantec Trend Report, 2016,
      `https://www.symantec.com/security_response/publications/`
      `monthlythreatreport.jsp#Spam`
      Cited on page 284

[143] P. Szor and P. Ferrie, Hunting for metamorphic, Symantec Security
      Response, `http://www.symantec.com/avcenter/reference/`
      `hunting.for.metamorphic.pdf`
      Cited on page 240

[144] Talking Heads, Once in a lifetime, http://www.azlyrics.com/lyrics/talkingheads/onceinalifetime.html

[145] H. Tamada, K. Okamoto, M. Nakamura, A. Monden, and K. Matsumoto, Design and evaluation of dynamic software birthmarks based on API calls, Nara Institute of Science and Technology, Technical Report, 2007
Cited on page 269

[146] H. Tamada, K. Okamoto, M. Nakamura, A. Monden, and K. Matsumoto, Dynamic software birthmarks to detect the theft of Windows applications, International Symposium on Future Software Technology 2004 (ISFST 2004), October 2004, Xian, China
Cited on page 269

[147] P.-N. Tan, M. Steinbach, and V. Kumar, Cluster analysis: Basic concepts and algorithms, in *Introduction to Data Mining*, Addison-Wesley, 2005, http://www-users.cs.umn.edu/~kumar/dmbook/ch8.pdf
Cited on page 170

[148] A. H. Toderici and M. Stamp, Chi-squared distance and metamorphic virus detection, *Journal of Computer Virology and Hacking Techniques*, 9(1):1–14, 2013, http://link.springer.com/article/10.1007/s11416-012-0171-2
Cited on page 290

[149] Trojan.Cridex, Symantec, 2012, http://www.symantec.com/security_response/writeup.jsp?docid=2012-012103-0840-99
Cited on page 271

[150] Trojan.Zbot,, Symantec, 2010, http://www.symantec.com/security_response/writeup.jsp?docid=2010-011016-3514-99
Cited on page 271

[151] Trojan.ZeroAccess, Symantec, 2013, http://www.symantec.com/security_response/writeup.jsp?docid=2011-071314-0410-99
Cited on page 271

[152] M. A. Turk and A. P. Pentland, Eigenfaces for recognition, *Journal of Cognitive Neuroscience*, 3(1):71–86, 1991
Cited on pages 277 and 285

[153] R. Unterberger, *AllMusic*, Creedence Clearwater Revival biography, http://www.allmusic.com/artist/creedence-clearwater-revival-mn0000131627/biography
Cited on page 18

[154] Vector quantization, http://www.data-compression.com/vq.shtml
Cited on page 203

[155] S. Vemparala, Malware detection using dynamic analysis, Master's
Report, Department of Computer Science, San Jose State University,
2010, http://scholarworks.sjsu.edu/etd_projects/403/
Cited on pages 269, 270, and 271

[156] S. Vemparala, F. Di Troia, V. A. Corrado, T. H. Austin, and
M. Stamp. Malware detection using dynamic birthmarks, 2nd
International Workshop on Security & Privacy Analytics (IWSPA
2016), co-located with ACM CODASPY 2016, March 9–11, 2016
Cited on page 269

[157] S. Venkatachalam, Detecting undetectable computer viruses, Master's
Report, Department of Computer Science, San Jose State University,
2010, http://scholarworks.sjsu.edu/etd_projects/156/
Cited on pages 240, 242, and 243

[158] R. Vobbilisetty, Classic cryptanalysis using hidden Markov models,
Master's Report, Department of Computer Science, San Jose State
University, 2015,
http://scholarworks.sjsu.edu/etd_projects/407/
Cited on pages 33, 245, and 254

[159] R. Vobbilisetty, F. Di Troia, R. M. Low, V. A. Corrado, and
M. Stamp, Classic cryptanalysis using hidden Markov models, to
appear in *Cryptologia*, http://www.tandfonline.com/doi/abs/10.
1080/01611194.2015.1126660?journalCode=ucry20
Cited on page 245

[160] VX Heavens, http://vxheaven.org/
Cited on pages 242 and 309

[161] H. M. Wallach, Conditional random fields: An introduction, 2004,
www.inference.phy.cam.ac.uk/hmw26/papers/crf_intro.pdf
Cited on page 213

[162] X. Wang, Y. Jhi, S. Zhu, and P. Liu, Detecting software theft via
system call based birthmarks, in *Proceedings of 25th Annual Computer
Security Applications Conference*, December 2009, Honolulu, Hawaii
Cited on page 269

[163] M. Welling, Fisher linear discriminant analysis, http://www.ics.
uci.edu/~welling/classnotes/papers_class/Fisher-LDA.pdf
Cited on pages 193 and 201

[164] *Wheel of Fortune*, http://www.wheeloffortune.com
Cited on page 246

[165] Winwebsec, Microsoft, Malware Protection Center,
http://www.microsoft.com/security/portal/threat/
encyclopedia/Entry.aspx?Name=Rogue:Win32/Winwebsec
Cited on page 271

[166] W. Wong and M. Stamp, Hunting for metamorphic engines, *Journal in Computer Virology*, 2(3):211–229, 2006,
http://www.springerlink.com/content/448852234n14u112/
Cited on pages 241, 242, 243, 270, 273, 275, 292, 307, 308, and 309

[167] P. Zbitskiy, Code mutation techniques by means of formal grammars and automatons, *Journal in Computer Virology*, 5(3):199–207, 2009,
http://link.springer.com/article/10.1007/s11416-009-0121-9
Cited on page 240

[168] Y. Zhou and M. Inge, Malware detection using adaptive data compression, *AISec '08 Proceedings of the 1st ACM Workshop on AISec*, pp. 53–60, 2008
Cited on page 283

[169] X. Zhou, X. Sun, G. Sun, and Y. Yang, A combined static and dynamic software birthmark based on component dependence graph, *Proceedings of International Conference on Intelligent Information Hiding and Multimedia Signal Processing*, pp. 1416–1421, August 2008, Harbin, China
Cited on page 269

Index